The Moral Philosophy of Maria Montessori

Also available from Bloomsbury

Children, Religion and the Ethics of Influence, by John Tillson
Intellectual Agency and Virtue Epistemology, by Patrick R. Frierson
Philosophy and the Metaphysical Achievements of Education, by Ryan McInerney
Socially Just Pedagogies, edited by Rosi Braidotti, Vivienne Bozalek, Tamara Shefer, and Michalinos Zembylas

The Moral Philosophy of Maria Montessori

Agency and Ethical Life

Patrick R. Frierson

BLOOMSBURY ACADEMIC
LONDON • NEW YORK • OXFORD • NEW DELHI • SYDNEY

BLOOMSBURY ACADEMIC
Bloomsbury Publishing Plc
50 Bedford Square, London, WC1B 3DP, UK
1385 Broadway, New York, NY 10018, USA
29 Earlsfort Terrace, Dublin 2, Ireland

BLOOMSBURY, BLOOMSBURY ACADEMIC and the Diana logo
are trademarks of Bloomsbury Publishing Plc

First published in Great Britain 2023
This paperback edition published 2024

Copyright © Patrick R. Frierson, 2023

Patrick R. Frierson has asserted his right under the Copyright,
Designs and Patents Act, 1988, to be identified as Author of this work.

For legal purposes the Acknowledgments on pp. viii–ix constitute
an extension of this copyright page.

Cover credits: *Madonna della seggiola*, 1513–1514, Raphael / Wikipedia, public domain.

All rights reserved. No part of this publication may be reproduced or transmitted
in any form or by any means, electronic or mechanical, including photocopying,
recording, or any information storage or retrieval system, without prior
permission in writing from the publishers.

Bloomsbury Publishing Plc does not have any control over, or responsibility for,
any third-party websites referred to or in this book. All internet addresses given in this
book were correct at the time of going to press. The author and publisher regret any
inconvenience caused if addresses have changed or sites have ceased to exist,
but can accept no responsibility for any such changes.

A catalogue record for this book is available from the British Library.

A catalog record for this book is available from the Library of Congress.

ISBN:	HB:	978-1-3501-7637-9
	PB:	978-1-3503-4580-5
	ePDF:	978-1-3501-7638-6
	eBook:	978-1-3501-7639-3

Typeset by Integra Software Services Pvt. Ltd.

To find out more about our authors and books visit www.bloomsbury.com
and sign up for our newsletters.

For Zechariah, Phoebe, and Cyrus

Contents

Acknowledgments		viii
1	Introduction	1
2	The Moral Sense	15
3	Character and Agency	33
4	Respect for Others	69
5	Solidarity and Obedience	93
6	Adulthood, Abstraction, and Reflective Deliberation	115
7	Paternalism	145
8	Embodied Agency, Embodied Ethics	175
9	Love	201
Notes		218
Bibliography		240
Index of Names		252
Subject Index		255

Acknowledgments

Ethical life consists of character-driven activity in communities of mutual respect and solidarity in shared activity. Work on this book has been a labor of love for me, one that would not have been possible without the support of the communities and relationships in which I am situated. I have been privileged to be a member of the Whitman College community, a community of inquisitive, creative, and respectful students, faculty, and staff. I owe special thanks to students in my "Education and Autonomy" courses, who enriched me with their own understandings of education and ethical life and pushed me to better understand and explain Montessori. I particularly thank two student research assistants, Siri Danielson and Gavin Victor. Siri helped me develop many of the ideas in Chapters 4 and 6, and Gavin worked over drafts of the entire manuscript helping me refine and better defend my ideas. Work with Siri and Gavin was partly funded through the Louis B. Perry Summer Research Endowment and the Parents Fund Student-Faculty Research Fund.

Most of this book was written during an eight-month furlough from Whitman College in 2021. I am grateful to the National Endowment for the Humanities for the Research Fellowship (FEL-273130-21) that funded my work during that time. This project shows the importance of organized structures of national solidarity, of which the NEH is an example.

Many ideas in this book developed in conversation with other scholars. Lucy Allais, Don Rutherford, and other participants in the UCSD History of Philosophy Roundtable provided excellent discussion of an early version of this book. Colin Marshall engaged with early drafts and referred me to several important sources that made their way into the book. Tamar Schapiro's published work was pivotal for my own thinking about the issues in this book, and she generously read portions of the final manuscript to offer helpful corrections and clarifications. Erica Moretti helped me track down crucial Italian primary and secondary sources. Joke Verheul reviewed the penultimate draft of the book; it would have many more errors and infelicities without her careful attention. I especially thank my dear friends, Chris and Renée, not only for important conversations that clarified and deepened points I make in this book, but for consistent and meaningful friendship during the tumultuous times in which it was written.

Throughout the writing of this book, anonymous reviewers have played important roles in refining my arguments. These reviewers include those commissioned by Bloomsbury, but also reviewers for several journals to which I submitted early drafts of material that eventually made its way into the book. I continue to find diligent and conscientious anonymous reviewers to be exemplars of scholarly solidarity.

Colleen Coalter at Bloomsbury believed in the possibility of this project, helped me turn it into something she could back, and then stood by at every stage of the process. Suzie Nash saw the process through to its completion. I owe both of them my sincere thanks.

I can't write about Montessori without thanking the community of guides and children at Three Tree Montessori School, where my children formed their characters, learned respect for others, experienced true solidarity, and developed into the individuals they are today. Three Tree set the tone for my engagement with Montessori and continues to inform not only how I think and write about Montessori, but how I live and engage with the world.

Finally, and most importantly, I thank my family, especially my children Zechariah, Phoebe, and Cyrus. I started working on Montessori with and for my children, and they have provided not only an essential touchstone for my philosophizing but, more importantly, a constant source of love and joy in my life. I dedicate this book to them.

1

Introduction

"The method cannot be seen, one sees the child. *One sees the child's soul, freed from obstacles, acting in accordance with its true nature."*

(Secret 22: 123, emphasis original)

1 Maria Montessori, Philosopher of the Child

By her own account, Montessori discovered "the fundamental fact which led me to define my method" (9: 51) through attention to the actions of a particular three-year-old girl:

> I was making my first essays in applying the principles and part of the material I had used for many years previously in the education of deficient children, to the normal children of the San Lorenzo quarter in Rome, when I happened to notice a little girl of about three years old deeply absorbed in a set of solid insets, removing the wooden cylinders from their respective holes and replacing them. The expression on the child's face was one of such concentrated attention that it seemed to me an extraordinary manifestation; up to this time none of the children had ever shown such fixity of interest in an object; and my belief in the characteristic instability of attention in young children, who flit incessantly from one thing to another, made me peculiarly alive to the phenomenon.
>
> I watched the child intently without disturbing her at first, and began to count how many times she repeated the exercise; then, seeing that she was continuing for a long time, I picked up the little armchair in which she was seated, and placed chair and child upon the table; the little creature hastily caught up her case of insets, laid it across the arms of her chair, and gathering the cylinders into her lap, set to work again. Then I called upon all the children to sing; they sang, but the little girl continued undisturbed, repeating her exercise even after the short song had come to an end. I counted forty-four repetitions; when at last she ceased, it was quite independently of any surrounding stimuli which might have distracted her, and she looked round with a satisfied air, almost as if awaking from a refreshing nap.
>
> (9: 51; see too 22: 106–7)[1]

This three-year-old child—who for ease of reference I call Sofia—became a paradigm of agency and even of ethical life within Montessori's pedagogy, the key to "discovery of the treatment required by the soul of the child" (9: 51). From this initial recognition of a new form of agency in the life of the child, this "apparition" which "spr[a]ng forth and struck the mind," Montessori turned to a "second phase, the study of the conditions in which the new phenomenon shows itself" (22: 100–1). Montessori developed her teaching materials to allow for and sustain the sort of "concentrated attention" found in this small girl, and gradually this sort of active engagement "became common among the children … in connection with certain external conditions" (9: 52). Sofia exemplifies many features Montessori came to observe and identify as fundamental to excellent human lives, and her expressions of agency, self-governance, and persistence define the agency that lies at the heart of Montessori's moral theory.

Continued attention to children by Montessori and the teacher-scientists she trained also led to "finding new things … [and] further genuine discoveries" (22: 100–1). A four-year-old child in another class, whom Montessori designates "O" (and I will call Onorado), went beyond Sofia's "work" to a further degree of agency, one his teacher called "work and kindness" (9: 89):

> Before the daily hot meal was instituted, the children used to bring their own luncheons, which varied very much; two or three of the children were very generously provided, and had meat, fruit, etc. O[norado] was seated next to one of these. The table was set, and O[norado] had nothing to put upon his plate but the piece of bread he had so strenuously acquired[2]; he glanced at his neighbor as if to regulate himself by the time the latter would take over his meal … [W]ith great dignity he tried to eat his piece of bread very slowly, in order that he might not finish before the other, and thus make it evident that he had nothing more to eat while the other was still busy. He nibbled his bread slowly and seriously.
>
> What a sense of his own dignity—subduing the desires of an appetite exposed to temptation—existed in this child, together with his sense of the fundamental needs of his own life, by which he was impelled to struggle and to conquer what was "necessary." And there was further that exquisite sensibility, which manifested itself in the affectionate expression of his … face, and in the effusion of a general tenderness which looked for no return.
>
> (9: 89)

Not only is Onorado's self-governance more explicit than Sofia's, he also demonstrates a strong sense both of his own dignity and of others' worth. The sense of dignity in oneself and others, so pronounced in Onorado's case, is something Montessori found to follow naturally from the kind of agency expressed by Sofia: "after these manifestations [of agency in attentive work], a true discipline is established, the most obvious results of which are closely related to what we will call 'respect for the work of others and consideration for the rights of others'" (9: 70). More generally, children in conditions conducive to freedom manifest a range of features of ethical life that Montessori comes to identify as human ideals.

Shortly after Montessori's death, another important twentieth-century philosopher, Elizabeth Anscombe, published *Modern Moral Philosophy,* in which she argued that "it is not profitable for us at present to do moral philosophy; that should be laid aside ... until we have an adequate philosophy of psychology" (Anscombe 1958: 1). Over the last sixty years, moral philosophy has come to take psychology and the philosophy of psychology more seriously, even if not as seriously as Anscombe would like. More than twenty years earlier, however, Maria Montessori had insisted, "Today [1936] it is impossible to study any branch of ... philosophy ... without taking into account the contributions gained from the study of child life" (22: 7). Unfortunately, Montessori's exhortation has not been taken as seriously as Anscombe's. With very few exceptions, children's lives have played little role in any branch of professional philosophy at any point in its history. Even when philosophers think about children,[3] adult life is taken as paradigmatic of human excellence, with children at best developing *toward* genuine agency, respect, or ethical life. It is time for a revolution in moral philosophy, one that takes seriously the moral life of the child and the possibility that children can teach adults what human flourishing looks like.

As the stories of Sofia and Onorado illustrate and her own explicit statement makes clear, Montessori's philosophy takes its start from attentive, respectful, and loving observation of the lives of children. Often, in fact, she rejects the notion that her philosophy is in any way *hers*.

> Other methods are the result of the efforts of people—people of genius—people endowed with a great love of humanity. Although this method bears my name, it is not the result of the efforts of a great thinker who has developed his own ideas. My method is founded on the child himself. Our study has its origins in the child. The method has been achieved by following the child ... It is always based on our ability to interpret the observations of those phenomena which originate in the child himself.
>
> (17: 7)

In fact, while the publisher of the first English translation of her work (in 1912) gave it the title *The Montessori Method*, Montessori's Italian title makes no reference to herself, and she entitled her later English editions *The Discovery of the Child*.[4] Montessori's role was to create contexts within which to learn from children and to distill children's implicit moral insights into a coherent moral philosophy:

> Directly these children found themselves under conditions of real life, with serious implements for their own use, of a size proportionate to theirs, unexpected activities seemed to awaken within them. These were as unmistakable as they were surprising and it was our effort to follow them and interpret their meaning, helping others like them to appear also, that brought this method of education into being. No educational method, in the accepted sense, had caused these happenings. On the contrary, it was they—as they progressively unfolded—that became our guide and taught us how to treat the children. All began with our efforts to give satisfactory conditions of life, wherein the children should find no

obstacles to their development, and in leaving them free to choose the various means of activity that we had provided.

(1: 153, cf. 173–4)

Children in conditions of freedom revealed a nature quite unlike both "so-called bad qualities" and so-called "good and superior" ones (1: 181). Montessori describes this process as "normalization," "a psychological recovery, a return to *normal conditions*" (22: 134) whereby "a unique type of child appears, a 'new child'; but really ... the child's true 'personality' allowed to construct itself normally" (1: 183):

> Observing the features that disappear with normalization, we find to our surprise that these embrace nearly the whole of what are considered characteristics of childhood ... Even the features that have been scientifically studied as proper to childhood, such as imitation, curiosity, inconstancy, instability of attention, disappear. And this means that the nature of the child, as hitherto known, is a mere semblance masking an original and normal nature.
>
> (22: 134–5)

Montessori bases her philosophy on these "revelations" from children (9: 52). In the moral realm in particular, they lead her to "consider morality as a fact of life, which can be studied in the developing child" (Montessori [1938] 2012: 83). In "an environment ... conducive to the most perfect conditions of life, and the freedom which allows that life to develop," children "reveal to us the phases through which social [and intellectual] life must pass in the course of its natural unfolding" (18: 54; 1: 212; cf. 17: 81–2).[5] In that sense, the proper title for this book should really be something like "The Ethical Life of the Child."

Nonetheless, while recognizing her own role as a spokeswoman for children, it is time to publish a book devoted to *Maria Montessori*'s moral philosophy.[6] Montessori rendered observations of children into an overall approach to pedagogy, developmental psychology, and also philosophy; and philosophers, educators, and the general public can and should see Montessori as an important early twentieth-century philosophical voice. The editors of her *Educazione e Pace* (*Education and Peace*) rightly note that "once a firm basis for her theories had been established through practical experience, [Montessori's] thoughts as an educator *and a philosopher* ranged further and unveiled new perspectives that seem broader and broader as time goes by" (10: vii, emphasis added). Montessori herself describes her work as contributing to various "branches ... of philosophy," and she reports that at the outset of her pedagogical career, when she "decided to study the education of normal children and the principles upon which it is based[, she] therefore enrolled as a student of philosophy at the university" (22: 1; 2: 23).

At age thirty-one, after having completed her medical degree, established a private medical practice, served as a university lecturer, and been appointed co-director of an orthophrenic research institute, Montessori (re)enrolled in the University of Rome, now as a doctoral student in philosophy.[7] There she studied Italian humanism and the history of philosophy with philosophers such as Giacomo Barzellotti (scholar of Kant, Schopenhauer, and Herbert Spencer), Luigi Credaro (a specialist in and translator of the educational philosophy of G. F. Herbart), and the Hegelian Marxist Antonio Labriola.[8] She was further influenced by a general surge of interest amongst Italian students in American pragmatism, particularly that of William James and by the "evolutionary positivism" she would have been exposed to in Paris during her visit to the Bicêtre Hospital to study Edouard Séguin's work.[9] Her early recognition of the value of philosophy for pedagogy did not disappear when she observed Sofia working with cylinder blocks. It extended throughout her life in writings exemplary not only for pedagogical insights, but for her philosophical vision. Her corpus explicitly engages with James, Nietzsche, Bergson, and others, and implicitly draws from philosophers such as Aristotle, Kant, Schopenhauer, and Hegel.

Unfortunately, despite her background and insights, Montessori has not been taken seriously as a philosopher. Some have studied her philosophy of education (Colgan 2016), her feminism (Babini 2013; Babini and Lama 2000), her pacifism (Moretti 2013; 2021), or her place in the history of psychology (Babini 2013; Foschi 2012; Kramer 1976; Trabalzini 2011). But Montessori also makes valuable contributions across a wide range of philosophical issues. Elsewhere, I have discussed some features of her metaphysics (Frierson 2019) and epistemology (Frierson 2014b, 2016a, 2020). There is room for further exploration of her philosophy of mind (see Frierson 2020: 35–59), political philosophy, environmental philosophy, and philosophy of technology (see especially Montessori volume 10). This book focuses on Montessori's contributions to moral philosophy, particularly her accounts of agency and of the various dimensions of humans' ethical life.

The turn to Montessori is particularly apt at a time when academic philosophy, especially in the United States, is reckoning with its history of marginalizing certain voices from its canon. Given her philosophical background at the University of Rome, Montessori speaks from and to the European philosophical tradition, even if, like many other marginalized voices in philosophy, she was a woman who did not hold an academic position in philosophy and whose extensive writing on philosophical themes took place in genres not traditionally philosophical.[10] Unlike philosophers like Hannah Arendt or Margaret Cavendish, Montessori's writings are not directly related to those of widely accepted, canonical (male) philosophers like Heidegger or Descartes,[11] which makes integrating Montessori into the history of philosophy both more challenging and more conducive to taking women philosophers seriously in their own right. Beyond her sex, Montessori was further marginalized by virtue of her being Italian and thereby outside of mainstream philosophical developments in Europe in her time. Moreover, like Sigmund Freud, she developed her philosophy primarily for advancing her views of how to transform humanity for the better. She elucidated her philosophy in writings and teachings oriented toward laying out her philosophical vision for those who would go on to teach in accordance with it. Finally, and most importantly, as an advocate for children and particularly for taking seriously children's perspectives in philosophical theorizing, Montessori suffers both the marginalization typical for women and the even more profound marginalization of children's voices in philosophy.[12] Her self-conception as an astute observer of children provides an occasion for thinking about how children and their perspectives have been marginalized from philosophical discourse.

As I show in this book, Montessori develops a coherent and insightful approach to agency and ethics through reflecting on insights gleaned from careful attention to the lived reality of children in conditions of freedom. Children's "extraordinary manifestations" (9: 51) and consequent "technique ... to live together harmoniously" (Montessori 1938: 82) provide the basis for her moral theory, which focuses on agency, character, mutual respect, and solidarity. In contrast to traditional educational paradigms within which schools typically taught that "'good conduct' means inertia and 'bad conduct' means activity," in Montessori's prepared environments children found peace and joy in activity rather than passivity, and they manifested an "overpowering instinct to ... raise and perfect [themselves]" (9: 227, 224). They "show inner [moral] sensibility by expressing sentiments by positive acts, and not by passive obedience," but we adults often mistake their moral wisdom for obstinance (18: 263). Montessori's writings are filled with vignettes describing adult misinterpretations of the moral sense of children, such as when an older brother, rather than strictly following the rules of the game he was supposed to be playing, "did not want to desert" his younger brother and so "placed his smaller brother in front of him and ... whilst walking round and round ... looked with tender care at the little brother so that he should not fall," but "the teacher thought the child obstinate because he had not done exactly what she told him" (18: 264). In other cases, children show remarkable sensitivity to the proper sort of help to offer to one another, revealing what sort of help is good, and when: "the children go to the aid of others only when there is a real need for help, for instance, when something has fallen down and is broken, or where there are too many objects to put away and only a little time to do it" (24: 49). As we will see in later chapters, adults tend to give both too much help—interrupting the children's effortful activity—and too little—failing to give the support children actually need. Children in conditions conducive to freedom have a fine-grained sensitivity to the moral value of activity and also to the value of help when actually needed.

These few examples highlight the important role of children's uncorrupted moral sense in Montessori classrooms. Philosophers (and others) can be tempted to take adult experiences as paradigmatic and thereby discount the unique insights of children. Even amongst Montessori teachers, it is tempting to impose adult values on the lives of young children, showing them the right and wrong ways to manage conflict, and so on.[13] Montessori's central insight is that adults should "follow the child" (22: 166) even in the realm of moral formation. The case here is similar to the case of Montessori's materials for teaching reading, writing, math, and other academic subjects. She did not develop materials for teaching those things and then find a way to get children interested in them. Rather, she looked for the sorts of materials that children found interesting, and put those in her classrooms. Similarly, the goal of moral education in a Montessori classroom is not to find a way to get children to share our adult values or our adult ways of solving social problems. Rather, the goal is to create an environment within which children must live and work together, and then observe how *they* solve problems, what *they* find to be good and right and just. Teachers can then help crystallize these lessons for them through giving the relevant language or highlighting and isolating particular moral insights. Philosophers attuned to children can further articulate and systematize these lessons. But the focus should be on allowing children to be "normal" and then learning from them.

The central value of Montessori's moral philosophy is that of agency expressed through attentive work, a value evident in Sofia's engagement with her cylinders, a value worthy of both cultivation and direct respect (cf. Adams 2006). As I showed in *Intellectual Agency and Virtue Epistemology* (Frierson 2020), Montessori's conception of "intelligence" is "the sum of *activities* which enable the mind to *construct itself*" (9: 147, emphasis original), and intellectual agency is the central pillar of her approach to cultivating intellectual virtues. Within her moral theory, agency is even more important. *Character*, the primary value and central virtue within her moral theory, manifests freedom through pursuit of excellence in activities one chooses, and it is oriented toward ever-increasing capacities for agency. *Respect* recognizes the value of others' agency and thereby of their equal rights to pursue freely chosen work. *Solidarity* expresses a social dimension of freedom, wherein *we* freely pursue common tasks together. And the movement from embodiment to abstraction tracks the development of free human agency from early childhood through adolescence. Even Montessori's moral epistemology is rooted in natural responses of individuals in conditions of freedom. In those senses, moral virtue consists in the perfection of human agency.

As I show especially in Chapters 3 and 6, Montessori defends a conception of respect-worthy agency that applies to children as well as to adults, and the core principle of her pedagogy calls on teachers and those seeking to understand human nature to "Follow the child," where this requires granting children complete freedom while providing the resources they need in order to use that freedom well. This freedom is not the fickle following of every whim, but a form of self-governance that even young children are capable of if provided with an environment conducive to sustained attention to self-chosen work. Educators must first provide carefully prepared environments with sufficient resources for children to freely choose work that sustains attention and fosters development, and then they should allow children to develop themselves in those environments.

Mere agency-in-attentive-work is not the sum total of ethical life, however; ethical life includes respect, solidarity, and forms of abstraction and reflection that further refine agency. Ethical life as a whole is built on a foundation of agency in attentive work, the sort of agency illustrated by Sofia, but adds to that Onorado's concern for others and eventually, in adults, reflective and rational capacities such as those embodied by Maria (Montessori).

2 Varieties of "Agency"

As I have just noted, the concept of agency is central to Montessori's moral philosophy. Unlike many adults both in her day and our own, Montessori sees children first and foremost as agents, striving to express their characters through free choices. In later chapters of this book, I defend Montessori's ascription of agency to children, and also the centrality of agency within ethical life. In focusing on "agency," I rely on important terminology from contemporary philosophy. Montessori herself occasionally uses the term "agent" to refer to "the ego" (22: 83) or "humanity" (6: 15), though her more common term to describe what I call agency is the "will" (*volontà*, e.g. 9: 127ff.), and when discussing agency as a moral ideal, she typically emphasizes the notion of "character" (e.g. 1: 173). Nonetheless, I make use of the term "agency" throughout when discussing the moral characteristic present in Sofia as she works and central to Montessori's moral philosophy. In this section, I thus pause to offer some introduction to the concept of agency.

The notion of "agency" plays important roles in contemporary moral philosophy, moral psychology, philosophy of mind, discussions of free will, and even epistemology. On the most general (traditional) conception of agency, an agent is whatever brings about a change, while a patient is that in which a change is brought about, such that when I boil eggs, my stove is the agent of the change in state of the eggs. While agency in this sense does play *some* role in Montessori's theory (see Chapter 3, §5), the agency to which I refer in the subtitle of my book is much narrower. One narrower concept of agency, made particularly important in the mid-twentieth century, is the notion of "agency" as "intentional action" (see Schlosser 2019; Anscombe 1957; Davidson 1963). According to this narrower account, when I boil eggs, *I* am an agent because I *intend* to cook the eggs, but my stove is not an agent because its causal efficacy is not mediated by any intentions. Precisely what is required by "intention" here, and also whether intentionality is necessary or sufficient for agency, are hotly contested issues (see Schlosser 2019). Partly the debates are metaphysical—about whether the relevant sort of intentionality requires some metaphysically loaded (libertarian) sort of "free will"—and partly they are practical or moral, about whether the relevant agency requires rational deliberation, for example, or wholehearted authenticity.

For the sake of this book, and more generally within moral philosophy, it is important to note that philosophers often connect agency with the concept of "autonomy," which implies not merely intentionality but some level of self-governance, responsibility, and/or authority over one's choices and actions. A common strategy within contemporary moral philosophy takes the quintessential agent to be a human being in the midst of deliberation, reflecting on various desires or inclinations and considering whether or not to act on this or that desire, generally via some form of practical reasoning. Agents on this picture are free, at least from a practical point of view, where this freedom implies a capacity to decide for or against each of one's desires, and agency takes place primarily within deliberation and decision-making, so that even prisoners bound in chains are agents in that they decide for themselves how to act given their situation.

On this standard approach, agency figures into moral philosophy in at least three ways. First, human beings are accountable to moral norms by virtue of our agency. Agency as such is at least a necessary (and for many philosophers a sufficient) condition of being held morally responsible. Second, agency is a—and perhaps even *the*—proper focus of moral obligations. That is, we have a moral obligation to respect others' agency (and perhaps also one's own). Particularly within Kantian approaches to moral philosophy, but even within utilitarian (Mill 1863) and other approaches (e.g. Nussbaum 2000: 79), moral vices such as deception or theft or even violence are wrong by virtue of violating others' agency. Third, many philosophers see the preservation, promotion, or cultivation of agency as constitutive of the moral life, or conversely, see morality as the ultimate fulfillment of what it is to be an agent. Thus Christine Korsgaard, for example, argues for the moral law as a "constitutive standard" of agency as such (Korsgaard 2009: 28).

This short discussion highlights the range of uses for the concept of agency, particularly the agency-as-autonomy that plays such a significant role in contemporary moral philosophy. The philosopher Nomy Arpaly offers a helpful catalog of at least six different senses in which the concept of autonomy is used in contemporary moral philosophy.[14]

1. Reflective "agent-autonomy": "a relationship between an agent and her motivational states that can be roughly characterized as the agent's ability to decide which of them to follow" (Arpaly 2002: 118; see Frankfurt 1971). This sense of agency focuses on a second-order reflective capacity paradigmatic of adult agency and conflates this sense of "autonomy" with agency as such.
2. Autonomy as "acting for reasons we endorse" (Arpaly 2002: 125), a notion of agency that itself combines two important features, acting *for reasons*, which is also often taken to be constitutive of intentionality (see Mele and Moser 1994; Mele 2003; Clark 2010), and the notion that genuine autonomy requires some personal *endorsement* of the reasons on which we act (see Chapter 3, §4).
3. "The notion of normative, moral autonomy—the one invoked when people ask to be allowed to make their own decisions and to be free from paternalistic intervention" (Arpaly 2002: 120). This is the sense of agency as that which moral obligations require us to respect.
4. Autonomy as "that on which moral responsibility depends, whatever it happens to be" (Arpaly 2002: 126).
5. Autonomy as "authenticity," or "being true to oneself" (Arpaly 2002: 121; see Chapter 3, especially §9.3; Frankfurt 1988: 184; and cf. Velleman 2001).
6. "Heroic" or "Ideal" autonomy, such as the autonomy of "Aristotle's life of contemplation, Freud's or Jung's ideals of the liberation that their methods were to aim at bringing, [or] Nietzsche's ideal of the free spirit" (Arpaly 2002: 124).[15]

Many moral philosophers conflate one or more of these senses of agency, either explicitly through argument or merely implicitly by assumption. In particular, one or both of the first two senses of agency (1, 2) are often invoked as necessary or sufficient for one or both of the next two senses (3, 4), and the final two senses of agency (5, 6) are often seen as culminations or fulfillments of values implicit in one or more of the others. As we will see in detail in Chapter 3, many contemporary moral philosophers (e.g., Bratman, Frankfurt 1971, Korsgaard, and Schapiro) see reflective agency (1) as necessary for the full identification with one's reasons for action (2), where this full identification is in turn a necessary condition for the possibility of both moral autonomy (3) and responsibility (4). Among those, many (e.g., Korsgaard and Schapiro) see ideal agency (6) as a satisfaction of norms that are partly constitutive of reflective agency, such that being an ideal agent (6) is a matter of fully being an agent as such (1–4).

Within Montessori's moral philosophy, agency refers pre-eminently to what Arpaly calls moral autonomy (3), that is, the agency that makes people worthy of moral consideration and respect. When we seek freedom from paternalistic interference, it is our agency in this sense that we seek to protect. Montessori also endorses the general definition of agency as reasons-responsiveness (2), and—as we will see in Chapter 3—supports a robust concept of agency as requiring internality, activity as opposed to passivity, normative self-governance, and persistence. However, she rejects the widespread[16] contemporary view that these forms of agency require deliberation, reflection, or rationality (agency in sense 1). Her paradigmatic cases of agency are present in very young children like Sofia, who choose work they are interested in and attentively engage in that work for sustained periods. Nonetheless, she argues that this non-reflective agency, present in childhood, is morally significant in senses 3–6 above. We can and should respect children's choice of work and their efforts to focus on their particular tasks (sense 3), even if investment in those tasks does not involve or follow from deliberation. In the context of effortful work, children rightly hold themselves responsible in ways that are at least continuous with moral responsibility (sense 4)[17]. Such effortful work is engaged in with a wholeheartedness that constitutes authenticity (5), and this sort of authentic engagement is an ideal toward which all agents should aspire (6).

The heart of this book is a sustained articulation and defense of a form of agency that can be present in very young children like Sofia and Onorado, that does not require reflective deliberation, and that satisfies the requirements for agency in senses 2–6 above. After laying out this definition of agency in Chapter 3, I show in Chapter 4 that it is worthy of respect, and in Chapter 7 I apply this conclusion to the issue of paternalism toward children. Even while rejecting the idea that reflection is necessary for (other forms of) agency, however, Montessori does not deny the important role that reflective agency (1) has in adults' lives, so in Chapter 6, I detail how she incorporates reflection into her conception of agency.

Throughout this book, the primary sense in which I use the term "agent" is in terms of moral agency, or moral autonomy. That is, to be an agent is to have a relationship to one's choices and actions such that others ought to let one choose and act for oneself. Substantively, I argue that to be an agent in this sense, one must govern oneself in accordance with reasons one endorses, and I show how the cultivation and perfection of agency in this sense is the proper focus for moral aspirations. Throughout, I attend to the ways that such agency is present in children, which helps highlight important features of that agency, such as its essential embodiment (Chapter 8) and manifestation as love (Chapter 9).

3 Ethical Life

In his *Philosophy of Right* (Hegel [1820] 1991),[18] G.W.F. Hegel distinguishes between "morality" [*Moralität*] and "ethical life" [*Sittlichkeit*], where the former refers to excessively abstract principles and the latter includes socially situated and embedded norms for living well. Bernard Williams, too, distinguishes the "ethical" as a general category of thinking about how one should live one's life, from the "moral" as a "narrower conception" of the ethical, concerned among other things with the concept of "obligation" and with "strict boundaries" between moral and non-moral considerations (Williams 1985: 6–7). While I refer throughout this book to Montessori's moral philosophy, my allusion to ethical life in part highlights that the aim of her philosophizing is not to delimit an abstract or formal system of obligations but rather to present a rich set of factors that contribute to living human life well. In that way, her philosophical reflection fits more in line with theorists from Aristotle through Hegel, Nietzsche, and Williams than with moral philosophers like Kant or Mill (at least as each of the last has traditionally been construed).

Beyond its function in broadening the normative scope of this investigation, the concept of ethical life has particular importance for Montessori. As we will see in more detail in Chapter 2, Montessori sees her moral philosophy as essentially "a *positive philosophy of life* ... because ... we are *immoral* when we disobey the laws of life" (Montessori [1910] 1913: 27) and "we should consider as *good* that which helps life and as *bad* that which hinders it" (Montessori 1903: 263) such that "absolute" moral values are those "bound up with life itself" (9: 251). Montessori began her career as a medical doctor and then a psychiatrist. A pivotal moment for her was when she came to see problems with so-called "deficient" children "not as medical, but as pedagogical" and, by extension, philosophical. The problem with, or rather for, such children was that they were denied the opportunity to participate in ethical life, that is, in a community oriented toward the promotion of life. Montessori identifies "life" as "the primary cause of *progress* and the *perfectionment* of living creatures" (Montessori [1910] 1913: 46–7) and even describes the "this force which is life" as that "which reconstructs the world and at the same time perfects its functioning" (Montessori [1936] 2008: 56). The primary function of teachers and caregivers is thus to "allow the maximum of all activities—in other words, the development of life" (18: 106).

I return briefly to the role of life in Montessori's metaphysics of morals in Chapter 2, and elsewhere I have discussed life in more detail. In this introduction, I highlight the role of life only to emphasize that for Montessori, moral philosophy consists of reflection on the conditions that promote excellent human lives, lives rich with activity, expansion of personality, social interaction, cooperation, and ultimately love. Life essentially involves work, and in human beings, such work manifests a form of agency that is worthy of respect and capable of refinement and cultivation. Ultimately, for Montessori, to live an excellent life is first and foremost to be an excellent agent, which is really just fully to *be* an agent. Sofia's cylinder blocks work is a paradigmatic manifestation of life in this sense. And ethical life is always also life in community with others (cf. Wallace 2019), where this shared ethical life is built on a foundation of mutual respect and realizes heightened agency in shared projects that involve social cohesion and solidarity (Chapters 4 and 5). Ethical life is always also embodied (Chapter 8), and Montessori is particularly attuned to the complex bodily capabilities involved in various dimensions of living well (together). And as agents mature, ethical life comes to be increasingly shaped by rational deliberation and abstract ideas of the good (Chapter 6).

Montessori's vision for ethical life amongst human beings is an ideal theory. Drawing from her experiences with young children, she sees how human beings can be intrinsically motivated to pursue projects that give life meaning, can naturally and attentively respect one another, and can feel so deeply united with others that they come to share a single life and shared agency. Through reflecting on older children, she sees how abstraction and reflection can give rise to new levels of character, respect, and solidarity, without compromising whole-hearted authenticity or generating inner strife and conflict. Nonetheless, Montessori is not blind to the challenges of the world in which we live, with environments often unconducive to ideal forms of life and within which adults who fail to live fully human lives oppress and repress children, who then grow into the next generation of flawed adults. She presents concrete suggestions for improving our world, exhortations to live more fully into ethical life, and—as we will see in Chapters 4 and 7—allowances for the imperfect forms of interaction required by our non-ideal world. But Montessori's focus throughout her moral theory is hopeful without being naïve; she articulates a vision of an ethical life that is possible for human beings, even from the very youngest ages, and that is realized— albeit often with limited scope—in well-constructed (Montessorian) environments.

4 Conclusion

In attending to Montessori's notion of ethical life, this book aims to capture the range of features she identifies as important for fulfilling ideal human lives. As we will see, all of these features revolve in one way or another around agency. My goal in this book is to provide a broad overview of her ethics as a whole while highlighting the important role(s) of agency in that ethics.

In Chapter 2, I start with a discussion of Montessori's moral epistemology. As I have already emphasized in this chapter, Montessori sees every aspect of her philosophy as arising from careful attention to the lives of children. As I show in Chapter 2, this attention to children fits into an overall moral-sense-based moral epistemology. Moral distinctions are first directly perceived through the moral sense, but free children in healthy environments exhibit less corrupted moral perceptions than adults, most of whom have suffered various repressions and all of whom have internalized culturally specific moral rules.

Chapter 3 is the heart of the book. Here I develop a Montessorian account of agency and the character that agency expresses. I show how the agency expressed by Sofia in her work with cylinder blocks exhibits the internality, activity, normative self-governance, and persistence required for agency, all without higher-order reflection or deliberation. I further introduce the core concept of character as a tendency to express agency with an orientation towards perfection.

Chapter 4 turns from individual character and agency to the obligation that each has to respect the agency of others. Ethical life always takes place in community with others, and mutual respect for one another's character provides the harmony of activity each needs to pursue her or his work well. This life of mutual respect also manifests one form of social solidarity, but Chapter 5 explains how social solidarity goes beyond mere respect to enact forms of shared agency and shared character.

Chapters 3 through 5 develop conceptions of agency, character, respect, and solidarity that can be present even in children younger than three years old, but Montessori recognizes that as children mature into adults, ethical life changes. Chapter 6 discusses the nature and importance of two key developments as children mature from infancy through adulthood: abstraction and rational reflection. While emphasizing that neither is necessary in order to have an agency worthy of direct respect, I show how they expand the scope and change the nature of ethical life.

Chapter 7 provides something of an interlude, as I draw together the implications of preceding chapters for how adults should treat children. In particular, I argue against a double-standard by which paternalistic treatment is prima facie acceptable toward children but not toward adults. Instead, I argue that for both adults and children, we should avoid paternalism whenever possible and, when we behave paternalistically, we should do so only as part of non-ideal theory and always with an eye to eliminating the conditions that make paternalism necessary.

Chapter 8 emphasizes and discusses some ways in which Montessori's conception of agency in general and ethical life in particular are essentially embodied, and in Chapter 9, I conclude with an elucidation of how Montessori's moral philosophy as a whole can be seen as a philosophy of love.

2

The Moral Sense

This book lays out the substantive features of Maria Montessori's moral theory. Some might question, however, whether any such moral theory is or could be justified, and if so, what sort of justifications are available for substantive moral claims. Strong moral claims might seem particularly out of bounds for a philosopher who emphasizes "the human individual taken from actual life" instead of "general principles or abstract philosophical ideas" (Montessori [1910] 1913: 14). Moral values might seem to belong in the realm of mere opinion, or at best culturally local standards, rather than anything universally applicable for all peoples in all places. Montessori herself emphasizes that "Man does not have a precise heredity to do one special thing ... [and] is not obliged to do just one thing" (17: 91) and that "We ... are almost decided against [the concept of an absolute good] because we see that in society the idea of good changes ... [and] we rely on society's judgment on moral issues" (18: 271).

This chapter lays out the basic structure of Montessori's moral epistemology, and in the process shows how she can develop a robust moral theory given her empiricism[1] and acknowledgment of moral diversity. In general, moral epistemology refers to the theory of how one comes to know moral truths. Some philosophers eschew the possibility of an universal moral theory, arguing for some form of nihilism, subjectivism, or cultural relativism.[2] Most philosophical accounts of moral knowledge, however, appeal to moral "intuitions" (Moore 1903; Audi 1998; 2004), a priori rational arguments (Kant 1996; Korsgaard 2009), or calculations aimed to optimize good consequences such as overall happiness (Mill 1863; Singer 2015). Some argue in terms of a social contract to which all would or could assent (Rawls 1971; Rousseau 1762; Scanlon 1998) or in terms of virtues as excellences of organisms like us (Foot 2001; Hursthouse 1999). Yet others appeal to moral sentiments, moral feeling, or moral perceptions (Audi 2013; Hume [1751] 1975; Hutcheson [1728] 2002; Prinz 2007; Wallace 1996).

Maria Montessori falls into that last group of moral epistemologists, though her empiricist and pedagogically oriented approach to moral sense incorporates her insight that all senses—including the moral sense—are grounded in basic human capacities but are dependent upon both specific interest in the objects of sensory attention and the cultivation of those senses through directed practice in a well-ordered environment.

1 Empiricism and the Moral Sense

In *Intellectual Agency and Virtue Epistemology: A Montessori Perspective*, I lay out the basic structure of Montessori's "interested empiricist" epistemology, according to which all knowledge begins from sense experience, but that experience requires taking an *interest* in the world (see Frierson 2020). Moreover, both interest and the sensory acuity by which one experiences the world can be cultivated. "For this reason," Montessori explains, "children's education begins with the education of the senses" (18: 260). Immediately after explaining the centrality of sensory education in general, Montessori goes on, "I take the same view of moral education" and emphasizes a "great analogy between ... moral education ... and intellectual education" (18: 260).

> Education of the senses is the foundation of the entire intellectual organism and might be called the intellectual raw material ... [In] the moral realm, another form of sensitivity exists which I argue is fundamental, in an absolute sense, to moral education, just as the education of the [outer] senses is fundamental to the education of the intellect: we have a special inner sensitivity to something which we judge to be good, or bad. And this judgment, which is later made by reasoning,[3] we have already made through an inner sensation or something which can be compared to sensation ... The word *conscienza*[4] is today used by psychologists in a broad manner when they speak of the mind. Moralists and theologians instead limit it to this sort of inner sensory organ, if we may call it thus, *sine materia*, which gives us these ... sensations of good and bad.
>
> (18: 260–1)

Moral distinctions primarily arise neither from reasoning nor even from moral "intuitions" but from *sensation*. Montessori reiterates this by analogy with color.

> You will say, "How can this sensibility be given and refined?" That is impossible, it cannot be done, if it does not [already] exist. It would be like setting ourselves the problem, "what shall we do so that children should see the red [and] the green if children do not see it?" If children do not see it, you cannot make them see it. Children see—that is why they are capable of education ... And how to educate it? Make them see the red and the white. But do you create the red and the white? No, these colors are everywhere. There we call attention to the red and the white and we say, "This is the red and this is the white" ... [M]oral life should be presented in the same way.
>
> (18: 266, cf. 17: 236–7)

Whereas we perceive colors by means of visual acuity, we perceive moral distinctions through an "inner" sensitivity. Some recent advocates of moral perception see the primary object of that perception as some instance of virtue, vice, justice, or injustice in the world, where we perceive moral properties either directly akin to so-called "secondary qualities" like color (McDowell 1998: 131) or as "a kind of impression of [e.g., injustice] ... as phenomenally integrated with a suitable ordinary perception of the properties on which injustice is consequential" (Audi 2013: 38–9). On these accounts, we quite literally *see* (or hear, or touch) moral properties. For Montessori, by contrast, we perceive the wrongness of injustice, for example, not through vision or hearing or even memory or imagination, but through an inner sensation, a *feeling* of good and bad.[5] She describes various cases of sensible injustice in the lives of children, such as the child who fails a quiz because, the night before, "some quarrel in his home, or insufficient food, ... caused him to lie in bed sleepless" (9: 228). While "light and darkness" and even "a harmonious note and strident sound affect" are, for Montessori, "evident to our *external* organs of sense," such "facts and reactions which affect conscience" affect an "*inner* sensibility" (28: 261, emphases added).

Consistent with British moral sense theorists such as Francis Hutcheson, for whom "Actions have to Men an immediate Goodness" when "by a superior Sense, which I call a Moral one, we perceive pleasure in the Contemplation of such Actions" (Hutcheson [1726] 2004: 87), Montessori describes our inner moral sensibility in terms of "sensations of pleasure and pain, which are sensations of good and bad" (18: 261). In another context, echoing sentimentalists such as Hume and Smith for whom "sympathy" is the basis of the moral sense, she even adds that "the 'moral sense' ... is to a great extent the sense of sympathy with our fellows" (9: 242[6]; cf. Montessori 1902: 19; Hume [1740] 1975; Smith [1759] 1982). Unlike Hume or Smith, however, Montessori does not ascribe the whole foundation of the moral sense to sympathy, listing it as one of three aspects of moral sense, alongside "comprehension of [others'] sorrows" and "the sentiment of justice" (9: 242). Moreover, she often explains the "inner sensation" of good or bad in terms of joy, peace, or remorse, rather than sympathy: "We experienced a feeling of joy, of peace and tranquility, in certain moments, and at other times we felt remorse and realized the lack of peace and inner joy" (18: 261). Elsewhere, she refers to the same three features, though with different terminology:

> We always speak of a "voice of conscience" which teaches us from within to distinguish the two things: good confers serenity [that is, peace], which is order; enthusiasm [joy], which is strength; evil is signalized as an anguish which is at times unbearable: remorse, which is not only darkness and disorder, but fever, a malady of the soul.
>
> (9: 251)

The emphasis on peace, joy, and remorse allows Montessori to distinguish qualitatively and immediately between the kind of pleasure or pain that constitutes appraisal of something as good or evil and other pleasures and pains. Individuals directly distinguish the pain of a stubbed toe from the pain of remorse in having sent an email unjustly accusing a colleague. We distinguish the joy of helping someone overcome a challenge from the pleasure of a good cup of coffee, and the "peace" of sleeping in from the peace that comes when we have fulfilled a responsibility well. Likewise, in our love for or sympathy with others, a well-tuned moral sense does not merely feel empathy with the pleasures and pains of others, but "loves" them, with a fine-tuned attentiveness to what is really good for them, where the good is indicated by peace, joy, and the absence of remorse (9: 93f.).[7] For Montessori, then, people make moral distinctions by means of a moral sense, an *inner* sense that consists of affective responses to situations. To see something as good is to feel peace or joy in or toward it. To see it as bad is to feel distressed by or remorseful about it.

Consistent with empiricism, these feelings respond to specific experiences. Montessori's own brand of empiricism, however, sees all senses—including the moral sense—as *active* in that they depend upon a particular interest in and thereby sensitivity to features of one's situation. No harmony in music can be perceived without *attending* to the music, and even differences between light and dark depend upon interest in those features of one's visual world (see Frierson 2020: 17–22). Montessori extends this point to the moral sense; without an interest in the morally salient features of one's situation, one will not immediately "sense" good or bad.

Moreover, all senses are open to *cultivation*, particularly during special *sensitive periods*, and to degradation or loss, if not properly cultivated. Like other senses, the moral sense must be exercised in the right context in order to cultivate, refine, and preserve it. "To know how to keep this inner sensibility alight and to refine it, this is our principal task" (18: 263; cf. 18: 260–1; 12: 5–6, 12–3; 17: 204). Consistent with her emphasis on sensory experience, when Montessori asks, "How can we educate this sense?," she rejects as an "illusion" the view that "we can make people moral by talking of morality" (18: 262): "it is not by philosophizing or discussing metaphysical conceptions that the morals of mankind can be developed: it is by activity, by experience, and by action" (12: 83; cf. 1: 188; Montessori 1938: 83–7). Moral education requires an "auto-education" (18: 262), albeit one within which (as in the case of sensory education) the teacher should carefully prepare an environment for activity in a social context and may appropriately teach the vocabulary associated with the child's (inner) perceptions. Just as one cultivates children's visual acuity by providing them with examples of different colors and words to associate with those colors—"This is blue; this is yellow"—so too one cultivates *moral* acuity with carefully chosen examples of moral realities and appropriately simple terms to describe these examples:

> A teacher who says ... "this is good" and "this is bad" safeguards them in the most delicate way possible from evil, permitting them to develop freely in what is good without in any way placing obstacles. This teacher, if not giving moral education, at least begins to educate "moral sensory organs" and classify the facts of moral conscience.
>
> (18: 263)

Crucially, the teachers' statement that "this is good" is not instruction in *what things are good*, any more than her statement that "this is blue" is an instruction in what things are blue. In both cases, the child must be presented with cases that stimulate his interest in the quality to be perceived—the moral goodness of the deed, or the color of the material—and then *he* must recognize these traits himself. The teacher merely provides a *word* for what the child has already recognized.

When teachers *do* prescribe how to use the words "good" and "evil," they often apply these terms improperly, based on prejudice or non-moral interests, and they thereby introduce deviations, repressions, and disorders into the moral sense. These disorders are most acute when "prizes and punishments ... misle[a]d [children] into an unconscious acceptance of injustice" (9: 232–8) or when "esteem" is used to teach that "the good are those who are quiet and motionless; the naughty those who talk and move" (9: 227). Even in cases where teachers use moral distinctions properly, whenever moral words are used in the absence of a child's moral-sense-based recognition of the relevant moral realities, the result is a set of memorized formula rather than real understanding of moral distinctions. We "need to be acutely aware to respect all the inner acts of children's sentiment" (18: 264), not seeking to project our concepts of good and bad but only to provide occasions for the exercise of their moral sense.

This exercise does not happen merely passively. Montessori's moral pedagogy emphasizes provision of well-ordered occasions for moral reflection, particularly through social interactions: "the growing sentiment of the conscience of the individual [...] develops through and by means of social experiences" (12: 84). Even when one helps children formulate moral principles, one should always only "giv[e] moral principles *together with social experiences*" (Montessori 1938: 87, emphasis added). Montessori classrooms are social spaces with opportunities for self-cultivation but also for conflict and cooperation, solidarity and social friction.

> There is only one specimen of each object, and if a piece is in use when another child wants it, the latter—if he is normalized[8]—will wait for it to be released. Important social qualities derive from this. The child comes to see that he must respect the work of others, not because someone has said that he must, but because this is a reality that he meets in his daily experience. There is only one between many children, so there is nothing for it but to wait ... We cannot teach this kind of morality to children of three, but experience can.
>
> (1: 202–3)

Just as Montessori teachers focus children's attention on particular qualities of external senses, and their classrooms are filled with materials that cultivate the outer senses in deliberate, graded, and ordered ways; so too they focus on creating conditions for moral perception. Thus, there are a limited number of materials of each type and a large number of students, so that students are faced with competing desires for materials and must learn to recognize appropriate and inappropriate ways of handling scarce resources in a carefully delimited context. They regularly face opportunities for cooperative work but also for potential conflict, both of which prompt moral consciousness. "The stimuli of the environment are not only the objects, but also the persons" (9: 242). Throughout daily life, children's abilities to recognize morally salient features of situations and to appropriately sense good and bad responses to those situations depend upon capacities for moral perception, and these capacities increase—like all senses—through "exercise" (17: 237).

Crucially, for Montessori, the teacher's ability to set up an environment that allows children to cultivate *their own* moral sense is essential if morally good actions are to also be autonomous expressions of agency. As we will see in Chapter 3, many moral philosophers connect agency and moral self-governance by appealing to the structure of reflection, deliberation, or rational self-legislation (cf. e.g., Korsgaard 1996a, 2009; Reath 2006). But for Montessori, one reconciles freedom with morality when—and only when—one acts in the light of moral ideals that one *sees* for oneself. As in all cultivation of the senses, this depends upon having the right sorts of experiences during specific developmental "sensitive" periods:

> Powerful among [children's] instincts is the social drive. It has been our experience that if the child and the adolescent do not have a chance to engage in a true social life, they do not develop a sense of discipline and morality. These gifts in their case become end products of coercion rather than manifestations of freedom. The human personality is shaped by continuous experiences; it is up to us to create for children, for adolescents, for young people an environment, a world that will readily permit such formative experiences ... Thus from early childhood on, human beings must have practical experience of what association is.
>
> (10: 29)

Children's natural tendency to socialize, combined with their innate moral sense, facilitates self-governance in terms of socially important norms that they form for themselves.

Adults who lacked opportunities for refinement and exercise of moral sense in childhood usually fail to directly perceive moral distinctions for themselves. They can be brought to self-discipline and "morality" in the sense of respect for others through "coercion" of some sort, whether literal force and threat of force (in the case of civil laws or divine commands) or appeals to honor and vanity (as with social pressures and the allocation of esteem) or even by means of compromises made for the sake of self-interest (anticipating reciprocation or operating within various implicit or explicit social contracts). Even in the ideal Kantian case of recognizing, on reflection in the light of reason, that one's basic impulses are inconsistent with universal standards of rightness, the endorsement of those standards by one who does not "see" their truth at the level of direct, felt experience of the world will feel coercive (see Chapter 6, §2.1.3–4; and Frierson 2021). As opposed to those who "are always feeling tempted ..., need moral support to protect them from temptation ..., [and so] impose rules upon themselves to save them from falling" (1: 189), those with well-cultivated moral sense are "stronger types" for whom "Perfection attracts them because it is in their nature. Their search for it is not sacrificial, but is pursued as if it satisfied their deepest longings" (1: 189–90).[9] The most autonomous expressions of agency come from that wholehearted commitment to the good that arises when one *sees* what is good about self-discipline and mutual respect and reflectively endorses (and even expands) that insight in the light of reason. Such people are fully moral and truly free.

2 Challenges to Moral Sense Theory: Subjectivism, Relativism, and Error

Moral sense theories face various important challenges. This section will focus on three: relativism, subjectivism, and error. The first two problems arise from the fact of ethical pluralism, namely that people's perceptions of moral situations seem to differ. Subjectivism emphasizes individual differences in ethical assessment, while relativism highlights *cultural* differences. The problem of error in one's moral sense generates what has been called the *calibration challenge* (see Kauppinen 2014), namely that just as other senses can be mistaken, so too moral sense can be mistaken, but then we require some independent ground for establishing a standard by which to measure the accuracy of one's moral sense. As Hutcheson put it, describing the views of his adversaries, "Must we not know therefore antecedently what is morally good or evil by our reason, before we can know that our moral sense is right?" (Hutcheson [1728] 2002: 177, cited in Kauppinen 2014).[10]

Montessori's response to these problems starts with an account of why there is divergence in moral perceptions. This divergence arises partly from the fact that there are real differences in what is morally good for one person (or in one culture) and what is morally good for another, partly from the fact that all senses are selective and so people can be sensitive to different moral goods, and partly from the occurrence of repressions and deviations in the formation of moral sense. Particularly by showing that deviations occur through oppressive lack of freedom while variations emerge from freedom itself, she helps distinguish erroneous perceptions from moral or epistemic diversity. Montessori supports a moral-sense-based realism about moral distinctions both through her error theory about how we get moral distinctions wrong and through a metaphysics of morals that identifies what moral sense perceives in the world when it perceives "good" and "evil." Finally, while admitting that moral sense can err in particular cases, she vindicates moral sense theory by showing that the moral sense's susceptibility to error is shared by all senses, and that senses—including the moral sense—are no *more* susceptible to error or mistakes than reason. Just as all senses require cultivation and refinement through sense-directed action, so too one improves and corrects moral sense as one governs oneself in accordance with it. I start in this section by addressing the issues of pluralism (subjectivism and relativism) and then turn—at the end of this section and in the following sections—to the problem of error.

The challenge of ethical pluralism for moral sense theories is sufficiently serious that Adam Smith—one of the most important historical defenders of moral sentimentalism—devotes much of his *Theory of Moral Sentiments* ([1759] 1982) to addressing it, including a whole section (V) focused on the cultural relativist version of the problem. For ethical theories grounded on rational arguments of one sort or another, pluralism might seem easier to address (though see below), but if one bases ethical prescriptions on moral sense, and if people's moral senses *differ*, then morality—at least of any universal kind—is seemingly undermined at its root. The problem might seem *particularly* severe for Montessori, who argues that moral sense can and should be cultivated through education. If different educations give rise to different moral senses, there seems no legitimate standard by which to define an "ideal" for moral pedagogy.

With respect to subjectivism, Montessori's substantive moral theory—as we will see in Chapter 3[11]—provides considerable, legitimate room for individual variation in moral demands. The responsibilities of an Arctic explorer are not the same as those of a working-class mother or an independently wealthy artist. Nonetheless, general ethical norms such as the value of character, respect for oneself and others, and social solidarity ought to govern the lives of every individual. Montessori is aware, however, that not every individual *does* govern their lives by these general norms, and many do not even perceive them as moral goods. Some "abnormal personalities ... have a different intelligence and a different morality" and a "deficient moral sense on which [they] build up systematic delusions" (9: 209), and even those "who are on a high intellectual plane and speak of morals" can "yet have a lack of moral sensitiveness" (18: 261). While subjective variation in application of moral norms to individuals plays a central role in Montessori's ethics, she still needs to explain divergences of moral sensibility in a way that does not make her whole moral theory merely subjective.

Fortunately, Montessori's emphasis on the active, interest-driven, and cultivatable nature of the senses provides an excellent framework for seeing how individual differences emerge in humans' moral perceptions, which in turn sets the stage for seeing to what extent such differences are (or are not) a problem for Montessori's moral epistemology. As with all senses, moral sense requires exercise for its preservation and cultivation. "The sensibility of the conscience may be perfected like the aesthetic sense, till it can recognize and at last enjoy 'good' up to the very limits of the absolute, and also until it becomes sensitive to the very slightest deviations towards evil" (9: 253). Montessori repeatedly emphasizes the importance of sensory exercises, equipping her classrooms with color tablets to develop more refined visual acuity and smelling bottles to foster olfactory sense. While it may seem that people all have basic sensory capacities, Montessori rightly points out that even with respect to brute senses, humans vary, not only due to physical-biological endowments but also due to the experiences by which those are cultivated during sensitive periods of development, experiences that require the possibility of *action* in the light of sensory perceptions (see discussion in Frierson 2020: 135–58). One raised in environments where it *matters* to cultivate this or that form of sensory acuity (say, perfect pitch, distinguishing subtle differences in shapes of letters, or a capacity for dead reckoning) will cultivate those forms of acuity. The same is true for the moral sense. Those who lack opportunities to exercise this moral sense during sensitive periods of early childhood and adolescence develop a "conscience [that] will become like water which has been made turbid and ... poisonous" (9: 250). If children are given an environment where the primary possible motivators are rewards and punishments, for instance, rather than their own moral perceptions, they will become adept at discerning sources of reward and punishment rather than at making fine moral distinctions. Even in the absence of other influences, children raised in contexts where they are not free to act in the light of their recognitions of this or that as good or evil will not cultivate moral sense. In contexts where they need not solve morally important social problems, they will not cultivate moral-sensory acuity with respect to those problems. Similar lack of experience in other areas will similarly deprive them of various capacities for discernment. When those with power over children stifle children's capacities to act on their own moral perceptions, they cause the moral sense to atrophy and be replaced by other action-guiding motives. The results are various deviations and deviances in "moral" perception, deviations that, given the nature of much education in the world of Montessori's—and our—day, are widespread.[12]

Moral sense is corrupted through the failure to provide contexts within which moral distinctions are relevant. Moral sense develops normally, however, with sensitivity to culturally specific norms of behavior. Humans' moral sensibilities are modified to considerable degrees by our cultural contexts: "things are established by social groups. For example, habits and customs which finally become imbued with the force of morals ... [M]orals are a superstructure of social life, which fixes them in determinate form" (1: 167–8). Thus, Montessori takes seriously the problem of an ethical relativism that considers "morality ... as something that varies according to the epochs of time and the conditions of life" (1938: 81). Moral pluralism—as a descriptive claim about humans' sensibilities—is a fact about the world, one grounded in a psychological trait at the core of Montessori's pedagogical method: the "absorbent mind."

> Nothing has more importance for us than this absorbent form of mind, which shapes the adult and adapts him to any kind of social order ... On this, the whole of our study is based ... We can therefore understand how the child, thanks to his particular psyche, absorbs the customs and habits of the land in which he lives until he has formed the typical individual of his place and time ... Thus the respect for life in India is so great that animals also are included in a veneration firmly rooted in the hearts of the people. So deep a sentiment can never be acquired by people already grown up. Just to say: "Life is worthy of respect," does not make this feeling ours. I might think the Indians were right; that I also should respect animals. But in me this would only be a piece of reasoning; it would not stir my emotions. That kind of veneration which Indians have for the cow, for example, we Europeans can never experience. Nor can the native Indian, reason as he may, ever rid himself of it. [...] Every personal trait absorbed by the child becomes fixed forever, and even if reason later disclaims it, something of it remains in the subconscious mind.
>
> (1: 56–7)

Moral pluralism is *deep*, affecting the cores of people's personalities. And pluralism is *wide*, affecting *all* people at all times; being human depends upon absorbing culture deeply. And absorbed cultural values are *ineradicable*, at least at the level of moral perception. The adult Indian will always *feel* that killing a cow is wrong, even if she comes to reflectively reject that moral belief.

In conjunction with her moral sense theory, this pluralism might seem to require relativism. If people "sense" good and bad in different and incommensurable ways—

seeing the same act as "horrid" or "sacred" —then it seems impossible to talk about *the* good or *the* right at all:

> We ask ourselves if absolute good exists. And we are almost decided against it, because we see that in society the idea of good changes ... And ... many times we rely on society's judgment on moral issues. If society says something is moral, then [we think that] certainly it must be ... [I]f the good of society is not the absolute good, it is not stable.
>
> (18: 271)

If there is no universal standard of "good" and "right," then any attempt to articulate a substantive moral theory will be at best only the local description of a particular point of view, a "prejudice baptized as truth" (Nietzsche 1966: 13). For a moral sense theory, moral pluralism (incommensurable diversity of moral feelings) seems to imply moral relativism (incommensurable diversity of moral goods) or even moral nihilism (absence of any "absolute good").

Montessori responds that, despite all the apparent diversity and sociocultural relativity of ethics, there is a universal normative core: "There is a greater good and absolute, as the truth which has assured life. Life is one, and its laws are established and humankind tends with mysterious and supreme aspirations to obey them" (18: 271). This universal core is evident even in those areas where human beings seem most divergent. Thus, leaving dead bodies to be eaten by birds of prey, which some find "horrid" and others "sacred," is an expression of a "fundamental moral instinct common to all," a *universal* human recognition that it is important to "do something special" for those who have died (18: 97). "[O]bserving the ... expression [of these universal moral instincts] in different groups, one can see how deeply the adaptation of ... these sentiments goes" (18: 97), but one can also see *shared* moral values. In this potential variability, moral sense is like other senses. We can cultivate hearing to the point that human beings are capable of literally hearing different things based on languages they are exposed to when young (cf. Bornstein 1989; Deutsch et. al. 2004), and we can also have different moral values. But the basic capabilities that develop in culturally specific ways are constrained by the biology of the ear and the sounds available to be heard in the world. Similarly, we form different moral sensitivities and varying moral principles based on cultural upbringing, but only in the context of biological and world-imposed constraints on what we can consider good and evil.

Moreover, Montessori's moral sense theory is realist in a way that vindicates universal values over their particular manifestations.[13] The capacity for culturally specific moral values to run into barriers of moral reality is particularly evident in cases of social change:

> All social revolutions come from people's aspirations to draw as close as possible to this absolute good. Just as children rebel when we do not want them to follow the road of their own salvation and judge them as naughty, so people at certain

times rebel against a social condition because they have felt a higher plan and wish to make a further step towards the good. Such people must have a sensitivity to feel *absolute* good and evil and not only that transitory perception of good and evil in society.

(18: 271)

The central moral-epistemological claim of this passage is that humans' moral sensitivity, while it can be coopted, inhibited, refined, and/or corrupted by the societies in which people find themselves, is prior to those cultural modifications in something like the way that the basic structure of our outer senses is prior to the culturally specific ways that our attention gets directed. Just as the view that one gets epistemic access to objects' shapes through senses of sight and touch does not preclude (and is in fact conducive to) realism about shape, so too a moral sense theory does not preclude (and can be conducive to) realism about moral values. And just as we can remain "blind" to what is present to the outer senses but can also—eventually and in the right conditions—come to see clearly, so too we can transcend transitory social concepts of good and evil in the light of innate moral sensibilities.

Montessori's responses to subjectivism and cultural relativism depend upon being able to distinguish corrupted moral sense from well-cultivated moral sense, and the "transitory perception of good and evil in society" (18: 271) from the perfected "sensibility of conscience" (9: 253). The need to compare the operations of moral sense in a particular context with an ideal of how the moral sense *should* operate raises the calibration challenge (Kauppinen 2014), namely what to calibrate moral sense with in order to ensure that it is right, or healthy, or attentive to absolute rather than culturally specific goods. Hutcheson articulated this problem as part of defending his own moral sense theory, and he and Montessori both reject the notion that "we [must] know therefore antecedently what is morally good or evil by our reason, before we can know that our moral sense is right" (Hutcheson [1728] 2002: 176–7). Reason can play some *role* in correcting moral sense in particular contexts. Hutcheson notes that in cases where one's moral sense in a given instance diverges from previous moral perceptions or those of other people, reason might "suggest ... to its Remembrance its *former Approbations*, and represent ... the *general Sense* of Mankind" (Hutcheson [1728] 2002: 178). Montessori goes so far as to argue for a "positive science" that "concentrates on the 'inner life' of man" and could "produce a [mental] hygiene which will give to all men practical guidance in moral life" (9: 217). For neither, however, can reason precede or replace moral sense, and both analogize the role of reason here with its role in correcting (other) sensory perceptions. As Hutcheson explains, "this does not prove Ideas of *Virtue* and *Vice* to be previous to a *Sense*, more than a like *Correction* of the Ideas of *Color* in a Person under the *Jaundice*, proves that *Colors* are perceived by *Reason*, previously to *Sense*" (Hutcheson [1728] 2002: 178).

Montessori goes even further in rejecting reason as "the" solution to the calibration problem. In the context of her concern with relativism, Montessori points out that bad moral concepts rather than defects in the moral sense itself are primary causes of variations in moral judgment:

[Insofar as i]t is possible that good and evil may be distinguished by means of an "internal sense," *apart from cognitions of morality* ..., the good and evil in question would be absolute; that is to say, they would be bound up with life itself and not with acquired social habits.

(9: 250–1, emphasis added)

Moral *cognitions* (principles), rather than diversity of moral feelings, provide the primary impetus toward relativistic moral conflicts. Thus the primary role of education is less to *shape* the moral sense than to *refrain from corrupting* it: "To keep alive and to perfect psychical sensibility is the essence of moral education ... [T]he distinction between right and wrong is perceived. No one can *teach* this distinction in all its details to one who cannot see it" (9: 249–50).

Both Montessori and Hutcheson argue that the moral sense can and should be calibrated like other senses, with reference to its operation under "normal" or "healthy" circumstances. This is a version of what Kauppinen calls an "ideal dispositionalist" account, where something is good if one would perceive it as good under ideal conditions (Kauppinen 2014; cf. Lewis 1989: 117). Such an approach fits well with Montessori's medical background, where diagnoses in terms of health were a normal part of her training and practice. In the moral context, however, any ideal dispositionalist account requires a description of what the relevant "ideal conditions" are; in Montessori's case, it requires some way of making sense of what counts as the normal or healthy functioning of the moral sense. In the next two sections, I discuss two ways in which Montessori addresses this task, first with a teleological-normative metaphysics within which human capacities exist for certain ends and can and should be cultivated toward those ends (see §3), and then through optimism about "the child" as "a great assistance in understanding this question of morality" (1938: 81; see §4).

3 Metaphysics of Morals

Montessori enriches her moral sense theory with a moral metaphysics wherein virtues are excellences of human beings as living, teleologically ordered beings. Her arguments for diagnosing social change in terms of responsiveness to absolute good or protecting children from corrupting moral concepts depend upon being able to distinguish social reforms that are fundamentally parochial and destructive from those that are aspirations toward absolute good. Partly this task is epistemic, about how we can *know* absolute goodness, but partly it is also metaphysical, about what it *is* that one senses when one senses that something is "good."

Montessorian moral values are not platonic forms or other "very strange" metaphysical entities "utterly different from anything else in the universe" (Mackie 1977: 38); rather, they are grounded in humans' form of "life." Montessori's ethics orients toward an "ideal of 'life'" (9: 212; cf. 9: 257). As she puts it in some of her earliest reflections, "we may rise [...] toward a *positive philosophy of life*; [...] [W]e are *immoral* when we disobey the laws of life; for the triumphant rule of life throughout the universe is what constitutes our conception of beauty and goodness and truth (Montessori [1910] 1913: 27, cf. Montessori [1910] 1913: 473, 475).

> [W]e should consider as *good* that which helps life and as *bad* that which hinders it. In this case we should have an absolute good and evil, namely, the good which causes life and the evil which leads to the road of death, the good which causes a maximum degree of development and the evil which—even in the smallest degree—hinders development.
>
> (18: 263)

As a medical doctor influenced by early evolutionary positivism,[14] Montessori saw "life" as an active and creative biological force, and she explains and defends "theories of evolution"[15] that "attribute the variability of species to *internal* rather than external causes—namely, to a spontaneous activity, implanted in life itself" (Montessori [1910] 1913: 46).

As she uses the term, "life" is not merely the perpetuation of organic form, but a vivacity akin to what Nietzsche has in mind when he asks, about the value of values, "Are they a sign of distress, of impoverishment, of the degeneration of life? Or is there revealed in them, on the contrary, the plenitude, force, and will of life, its courage, certainty, future?" (Nietzsche 1967: 17). Life in this sense is about fullness, plenitude, progress, and exuberance, rather than mere "survival." As Montessori explains, "The internal factor, namely life, is the primary cause of *progress* and the *perfectionment* of living creatures" (Montessori [1910] 1913: 46–7). Later, she draws attention to various "guiding instincts" conducive to the preservation and increasing perfection of "the individual and the species" (22: 178) that, she says, are "bound up the very existence of life," tied to "life in its great cosmic function," and consisting of "delicate inner sensibilities, *intrinsic to life*, just as pure thought is an entirely intrinsic quality of the mind" (22: 178).[16] "Life" is an active force in the universe, teleologically oriented toward increasing complexity and perfection, and manifested in the child's striving for excellence.

This emphasis on life ascribes normative importance to impulses that proceed from one's "guiding instincts" or "vital force," the striving for self-perfection implicit in our natures as living beings. The notion of finding moral value in biological teleology is an old one, going back at least to the *ergon* argument in Aristotle's *Nicomachean Ethics* (Aristotle 2002: 101–2). And while this approach might seem contrary to mechanistic, post-Darwinian conceptions of biology, we can understand Montessori's philosophy of life in terms of the thickly value-laden concept of life articulated by Michael Thompson (2008), the implications of which have been developed by Philippa Foot in a particularly Montessorian way, with a clear sense of medical analogy:

> [E]valuations of human will and action share a conceptual structure with evaluations of characteristics and operations of other living things, and can only be understood in these terms ... *Life* will be at the center of my discussion, and the fact that a human action or disposition is good of its kind will be taken to be simply a fact about a given feature of a certain kind of living thing.
>
> (Foot 2001: 5)[17]

What it is to be excellent or perfect is tied to one's kind of life. And just as human bodies can be excellent (healthy) or not, so too human actions and dispositions (souls) can be excellent or not.

Here Montessori's emphasis on the moral sense adds an important element to life-based virtue ethical theories. While Montessori and Foot may both be correct to put life at the center of moral theory, Montessori rightly points out that the fundamental means of access to moral truth is not by scientific study of life but by immediate perceptions of moral goods and ills through feelings of peace or joy in socially rich environments. The metaphysics of life, even if metaphysically fundamental, is epistemically secondary to concrete perceptions of good and evil in particular cases. Like other senses, of course, the moral sense is reliable only insofar as it is healthy; and as in the cases of other senses, its health in a particular instance can be assessed only on the basis of judgments rooted in other(s'), healthy, uses of moral sense. And the ultimate *standard* of health is (partly) constitutive of the kinds of living beings that we—human beings—are.[18]

A moral sense theory and a life-based metaphysics of morals fit together into an integrated and coherent whole in two ways. First, Montessori's metaphysics of life makes clear what the moral sense perceives when it perceives good and evil. Just as a theory of vision might explain that what colors pick out are actually reflective properties of objects,[19] so too Montessori's metaphysics identifies the object of moral sense as those characteristics or conditions that either express life or foster life. Second, the metaphysics of life serves as a reminder that concepts like "health" can only be defined in relation to what Michael Thompson calls "natural historical judgments," judgments that ascribe qualities to life-forms—such as that "the horse is a four-legged animal"—through "a logically special form of predicative expression" irreducible to other sorts of judgment (Thompson 2008: 74, 76). The notion of "health" involved in describing a moral sense as healthy is similarly—and relatedly—an irreducible, basic notion. As with other senses, and indeed other features of living things, moral sense provides a basis for its own assessment and correction; one determines that a given exercise of the moral sense is unhealthy by comparing it with the operation of an obviously healthy moral sense. There is no further court of appeal, and the *moral* sense is even *less* susceptible to alternative sources of correction than other senses because other senses can be assessed based on how conducive they are to a healthy "life," but what counts as a healthy life can only be recognized by the moral sense.

4 Children in Conditions of Freedom

When discussing the relation between absolute good and evil and culturally local expressions of it, I quoted Montessori's claim that

> just as children rebel when we do not want them to follow the road of their own salvation and judge them as naughty, so people at certain times rebel against a social condition because they have felt a higher plan and wish to make a further

step towards the good. Such people must have a sensitivity to feel *absolute* good and evil and not only that transitory perception of good and evil in society.

(18: 271)

In my earlier discussion, I passed over the first sentence of this quotation, where Montessori compares the rebellion of children in defense of what they perceive as good with revolutions against social injustice. For understanding the overall structure and sources of her moral theory, however, this sentence is crucial. Children, for Montessori, provide the best means for diagnosing corruptions in (adults') moral perception.

Human beings recognize moral truths by means of a moral sense, and these truths are normative facts about human life. Life is teleologically oriented in its unfolding, such that living things, when given freedom in a healthy environment, tend toward their good. But human adults have already absorbed culturally specific influences on both natural tendencies and the natural exercise of moral sense. Moreover, because most human adults were raised in conditions that did *not* grant them freedom in a healthy environment, the "cultural influences" on their actions and sensibilities are more likely to corrupt than cultivate their natural tendencies (see Montessori 2007–, volumes 3 and 9). One who wants to develop a moral theory from reflection on *natural* human moral possibilities should study children, and particularly children left in freedom in an environment conducive to the exercise of freedom and the practice of moral sense. That is, the children must "reveal to us the phases through which social life must pass in the course of its natural unfolding" (1: 212; cf. 1938: 81–2).

Crucially, children reveal their true nature—including their moral sensibility—only in healthy conditions conducive to free activity: "the conditions of observation are made up of two elements: an environment which is conducive to the most perfect conditions of life, and the freedom which allows that life to develop" (18: 54; cf. Frierson 2015; 2016b). Children's worlds tend to be constructed in ways that both limit their freedom directly—through discipline and coercive control—and deny them the environment they need. Studying the "good" of children under such conditions, like studying adults with ill-formed characters, is like trying to study what is "healthy" for one who has (and has had) access only to fast food and sedentary occupation or studying octopuses raised entirely in fish tanks. In conditions conducive to liberty, however, children reveal their "normal" nature.

As noted in the introduction, Montessori's moral philosophy takes its start from the moral perceptions of free children in environments prepared for their thriving. This methodology of moral philosophizing through emphasis on the child involves a kind of circularity, since Montessori creates "normal" conditions and then looks to children for their natural responses in those conditions. One might object that different moral prejudices will lead teachers to create different environments and thereby elicit different "natural" moral responses. In the context of her metaphysics of morals, this value-loaded empirical methodology is just what one would expect, and it is neither trivial nor viciously circular (cf. Thompson 2008). The method could even be seen as akin to "reflective equilibrium," where we construct moral principles theoretically and "see if the principles ... match our considered convictions of justice or extend them in an acceptable way" and then "go ... back and forth" until we get "principles which match our considered judgments duly pruned and adjusted" (Rawls 1971: 19–20). Whereas Rawlsian reflective equilibrium takes place through armchair speculation based on intuitions about imagined cases, however, Montessorian equilibrium arises as a practicing educator or caregiver begins with a particular conception of what a normal or healthy psyche would be, but modifies and develops this in the context of actual observations of and work with children.

The model for this sort of empirically informed value theory can be found in Montessori's early and persisting interest in medicine. Doctors and medical researchers begin their work with a conception of what constitutes a "healthy" human being. Much of what doctors do is promote pre-existing conceptions of health, and medical researchers seek better methods and materials for promoting good health. But in the course of this work, concepts of health can change. For example, what counts as "health" for human beings might be modified or transformed through observing how changes associated with youth or aging contribute to the emergence of new forms of life that are recognizably "healthy" or through respectful attention to how those with various "disabilities" thrive when given appropriate conditions for flourishing.

Admittedly, it can be difficult for moral insights to cut through ingrained expectations and prejudices. In her obliquely autobiographical report of her own process of discovery, Montessori writes,

> It is impossible to observe something that is not known, and it is not possible for anyone all at once, by a vague intuition, to imagine that a child may have two natures and to say, "Now I will try to prove it by experiment." Anything new must emerge, so to speak, by its own energies; it must spring forth and strike the mind, evoked by what we call chance. Often there is no one more incredulous than the person to whom this happens; he rejects the new fact just like everyone else. The novelty must present itself again and again before it is finally seen, recognized, and eagerly received.
>
> (22: 100)

Moral phenomena are no easier—and no harder—to receive than other phenomena. One steeped in various prejudices will tend to reject the perception of new moral goods or new forms of flourishing or excellence, but the moral sense, like all the senses, can eventually push through such resistances in one suitably attentive.

Montessori herself changed her concepts of moral excellence through observing children. The core of her moral philosophy—character as self-directed work toward perfection—emerged from observations of children at work, not from prior conviction that such personal striving for excellence is a fundamental moral ideal. Her conception of virtue as holistic and internal, as opposed to "dutiful" (in Kant's sense) or derived fundamentally from external sources (e.g., God, society), was based on her observations of children's agency rather than cultural norms of her Italian Catholic background (but see Babini and Lama 2000). Even while constructing environments with some prior conceptions of what counts as good, children revealed moral ideals she would not have constructed for herself.

Finally, even her metaphysics of life and observations of the child depend, epistemically, on a moral sense that is precisely a *sense*, a capacity to *recognize* what is good or ill. Like all senses, one can recognize only what one comes to see. Moral theory does not emerge a priori from abstract reflection; rather, it comes from observation of living and developing human beings and sensitivity to what is good and what is ill in their forms of life. And children provide a particularly fertile field for such observation. A morally attuned teacher engaged in constructing a life together with children will find her prejudices about good and evil constantly challenged by her moral perceptions of the good and ill in children's exercises of agency. The teacher who once assumed that children's self-directed activity is a bad lack of discipline will see, in their concentrated attention to work, an excellence of human agency that requires rather than precludes movement. An attuned teacher who assumed that children are distracted and flighty will recognize, perhaps for the first time, the evil involved in interrupting children's persistent work for the sake of new activities. So, too, countless other revisions of moral prejudices are possible, but all of these observations depend upon a certain kind of environment/classroom and a teacher-philosopher with a sensitive and attuned moral sense that sees not only what is but what nature is teleologically oriented toward.

5 Conclusion

As noted in the Introduction, Montessori sees her own moral theory as merely an articulation of moral insights discovered and revealed by children with whom she had the privilege to work. By preparing environments that allowed children to engage in active social life together and by carefully and open-heartedly both attending to her own moral perceptions and sympathizing with the moral perceptions of the children she observed, Montessori discovered new moral values and corresponding forms of ethical life. Over the rest of this book, I lay out some of the key insights Montessori gleaned from her observations of children. I start in Chapter 3 with her discovery of a new sort of agency that is present in children, worthy of respect, and fundamental to the core virtue of her moral philosophy: character. I then show how, in the children with whom Montessori worked, the free expression and thereby development of character gave rise to norms of mutual respect (discussed in Chapter 4) and higher forms of agency expressed through what Montessori calls "social solidarity" or "social cohesion" (Chapter 5). In Chapter 6, I show how these primitive forms of character, respect, and solidarity are transformed through abstraction and higher order deliberation as children mature. Chapter 7 takes up some consequences of this account for our treatment of children, and Chapter 8 highlights how Montessori's concern with the cultivation of virtue in young children helped her attend to the essentially embodied nature of ethical life. I conclude in Chapter 9 by showing how every aspect of her philosophy, from the moral sense through the embodiment of virtue, manifests the central guiding light of her moral philosophy: love.

3

Character and Agency

When the child chooses from among a considerable number of objects the one he prefers, when he moves to go and take it from the sideboard, and then replaces it, or consents to give it up to a companion; when he waits until one of the pieces of the apparatus he wishes to use is laid aside by the child who has it in his hand at the moment; when he persists for a long time and with earnest attention in the same exercise, correcting the mistakes which the didactic material reveals to him; when, in the silence-exercise, he retains all his impulses, all his movements, and then, rising when his name is called, controls these movements carefully to avoid making a noise with his feet or knocking against the furniture, he performs so many acts of the "will." It may be said that in him the exercise of the will is continuous; nay, that the factor which really acts and persists among his aptitudes is the will, which is built up on the internal fundamental fact of a prolonged attention. Let us analyze some of the coefficients of will.

(Maria Montessori, Spontaneous Activity in Education, 9: 127)

For Montessori, we recognize moral values through feelings such as peace, joy, and remorse. At an individual level, these emotions are means by which we morally perceive what is good for oneself. Through love, sympathy, and direct appreciation, we also recognize others' goods as good. Moral perceptions guide ethical inquiry. However, because such perceptions can be shaped by culture and individual circumstances and are often corrupted by poor conditions of socialization present in many families and schools, ethical inquiry is most effective by teacher-scientist-philosophers who attend to actions, reactions, and interactions amongst children in conditions conducive to their healthy development. Too many theorists "start with grown-ups" and "overlook the little child" (1: 174). When Montessori attended to children in these contexts, she identified multiple dimensions of ethical life that brought children peace and joy and inspired their emulation and love. These include the value of mutual respect, appropriately given help, and various forms of shared agency and social solidarity. Her most important realization, however, was that children have a substantial form of agency that they express and value. Such agency is worthy of others' respect and a proper focus of individual self-cultivation. Montessori calls the tendency to express this agency "character," wherein "lies the source of those moral and intellectual values which could bring the whole world on to a higher plane" (1: 217). Character, along with the agency through which it is expressed, is the central value of her moral theory.

1 Character

Within her pedagogy, Montessori rightly notes both the importance of character and the fact that the concept of "character" is often poorly defined.

> Old time pedagogy has always given a prominent place to character training, though it failed to say what was meant by character or to indicate how it should be trained ... [T]his showed ... insight because it meant that educators were trying to bring out the important elements of human personality. Certain virtues have always been highly valued: courage, perseverance, the sense of duty, good moral relationships with others, and a high place has always been given to moral education. But this notwithstanding, ideas remain vague in all parts of the world as to what character really is.
>
> (1: 173)

In her moral philosophy, Montessori seeks to clarify the nature of character, that sum and source of moral virtues. For her, to have character is to have a "strong will" of one's own as opposed to a mere "mechanical will," to be unified into a coherent agent, to be "persistent ..., faithful to his own word, his own convictions, his own affections" (9: 142, 132–3).

Character is both a moral ideal and a "normality" to "preserve" rather than a non-existent state to bring about (1: 217). Adults with character are "those who—despite ... wrong treatment—have succeeded in *keeping* some ... character," and in that sense character is normal, but "All too often the majority have none" (1: 187, emphasis added). "It is not that character is lacking in the [human] race; it is that school distorts ... and weakens the spirit" through "abnormal conditions" that prevent people from "giv[ing] expression to the creative energies that naturally belonged to them" (9: 141, 2: 41). Agency develops over time, as children engage in the "conquest of independence" whereby they become capable of choosing and pursuing a wider range of activities in more complex ways, but character even in its ideal—which we will see consists of the tendency fully to choose for oneself (§4), actively engage in work (§5), govern oneself (§6), and persist (§8)—is already present in young children. Character must simply have opportunities to be exercised, without those "abnormal conditions" that have prevented people from "giv[ing] expression to the creative energies that naturally belonged to them" (2: 41). Such abnormal conditions generate various "psychic deviations" or "repressions" that suppress and stunt character (22: 136–7). The "establishment" of character often requires a process of "normalization," "a psychological recovery, a return to *normal conditions*" in which an already existent character expresses itself and thereby further develops (22: 133–4, 185).

Character consists of a capacity and tendency[1] toward fully expressing agency, which, as this chapter will show, consists of choosing for oneself active work that involves normative standards and persistently engaging in that work. Because character is defined in terms of agency, this chapter starts with a discussion of agency, showing how Montessori develops a concept of agency-in-work that applies even to very young children and that forces a reconsideration of some characteristics thought essential to human agency by many contemporary philosophers. As noted in the introduction, discussions of agency can often be bogged down by terminological differences; in the present chapter, the predominant senses of agency on which I focus are respect-worthy agency and ideal agency. These senses of agency are connected, within Montessori's moral philosophy, because character as such is open-ended in that agents with character always strive for greater and greater perfection, including increased scope, precision, and refinement of their own agency (see discussion in §9). Because character is both expressed in and cultivated through specific expressions of agency, and because strength of character comes in ever-increasing degrees, even forms of agency that fall short of ideal agency are often worthy of respect (see Chapter 4). At the same time, every act of agency is governed by what Christine Korsgaard has called a "constitutive standard applying to [the] activity" (Korsgaard 2009: 28). One can build a house, albeit badly, even if one fails to properly seal the corners, but in building a house, one commits oneself, whether implicitly or explicitly, to doing what is required (including sealing the corners) to build it well. So too, in exercising respect-worthy agency, one commits oneself, whether implicitly or explicitly, to ideal agency, and thereby to character.

§2–8 focus on respect-worthy agency. I show how children can have a form of agency that we ought to directly respect by "allow[ing the agent] to make their own decisions and to be free from paternalistic intervention" (Arpaly 2002: 120), and I thereby develop a new conception of what respect-worthy agency is and requires. §9 turns to character itself with its correlative emphasis on perfection, and §10 briefly addresses the connections (or not) between this respect-worthy agency and the agency required for moral accountability. This chapter focuses only on laying out a Montessorian account of agency as a prima facie plausible candidate for respect. In Chapter 4, I show that this agency *is* worthy of direct respect; and in Chapter 6, I show how reflection, deliberation, and reason differentiate adults' agency from children's. Only in Chapter 7 do I apply this overall account to the issue of paternalism toward children. Still, throughout this discussion, an anti-paternalistic background distinguishes my Montessorian approach from contemporary treatments of agency that take paternalism toward children as obviously legitimate.

2 Paternalism, Childhood, and the Characteristics of Agency

As noted in Chapter 1, Maria Montessori's conception of agency takes its start from an observation of what "became the fundamental fact which led me to define my method," the "extraordinary manifestation" of Sofia's "concentrated attention" as she was "deeply absorbed in a set of solid insets, removing the wooden cylinders from their respective holes and replacing them" (9: 51). Attention to the conditions for fostering this "polarization of attention" (9: 55) provided the basis for "a [pedagogical] method exemplifying spiritual liberty" (9: 52). And Montessori's focus on these moments helped her attend to a sort of agency more basic than the reflective or deliberative agency on which many contemporary philosophers focus. While not highly reflective or deliberative, Sofia shows a concentration of her whole self on a norm-governed task of her own choosing that requires sustained attention. Through her investment in this activity, she organizes herself into a coherent agent, even if only temporarily.

Before laying out Montessori's positive account of agency rooted in children's liberty, I pause in this section to present an alternative approach to thinking about agency through thinking about children, one that starts not with deference toward children in healthy conditions but from "uncontroversial" "everyday attitudes" according to which children are "not their parents' [or other adult care-givers'] equals when it comes to having a say in how their own lives are to be lived" (Schapiro 1999: 717; 2003: 577). Tamar Schapiro describes explicitly what is implicit in many contemporary discussions of respect-worthy agency:

> The philosophical task is to … explain more clearly the sense in which children are undeveloped and the reason why their lack of development is significant from a moral point of view [and in particular,] … why children are proper objects of paternalistic treatment.
>
> (Schapiro 1999: 717, 724; see too Schapiro 2003: 584)

Schapiro develops an account of agency according to which "a child [is] incapable of making her own choices, whether good or bad" (Schapiro 2003: 579) because she "does not really 'have' a will yet [and] is still internally dependent upon alien forces to determine what she does and says" (Schapiro 1999: 730). From this early article on childhood, Schapiro's more recent work focuses on agency as such, but she continues to make use of the legitimacy of paternalism toward children and the sort of agency they instantiate as a central component of her view. Thus in her discussion of how to justify the "distribution of authority" within a well-constituted soul, she uses an "analogy … between adult authority over children and the authority of the higher motives over the lower" to show how reason and second-order reflection can legitimately govern lower-order desires in a way that would be a form of "being paternalistic towards oneself" were those higher-order motives to "second-guess" themselves (Schapiro 2014: 334–5). The legitimacy of paternalism toward children, and the *way* that paternalism is justified toward children, provides a basis for thinking that genuine agency involves second-order reflective or deliberative rational governance over one's impulses and desires. While sharing Montessori's interest in reflecting on children as a way of conceptualizing agency in general, Schapiro rejects what she calls "romantic" views of agency, which recognize non-rational components of the self as "determinative of our 'true selves'" (Schapiro 2021: 13–4),[2] and she does so for reasons widely shared amongst contemporary philosophers.[3]

Schapiro recognizes, of course, that even very young children *seem* to have wills and make choices. (Many two-year-olds might even seem to have a bit too *much* will!) She distinguishes children's expressions of preference from genuine agency on several grounds, drawn from Kant and widely shared amongst contemporary philosophical accounts of agency. First, she emphasizes the difference between motivations where one is "internally dependent upon alien forces" from actions with one fully identifies, that is, that truly "express her will" (Schapiro 1999: 732n).[4] Second, Schapiro rightly connects internal identification with the motives for one's actions with a second feature, namely that agents are active rather than passive: a genuinely agential choice must be "action rather than mere reaction" (Schapiro 1999: 728; 2021).[5] Third, if one is to be truly active with respect to one's actions, one's motivational structure "cannot appear to her a mere clash of unintelligible pushes and pulls [but] ... must appear to the agent as a conflict between rival claims" for which she "demand[s] justification" (Schapiro 1999: 728, 2003: 587). At the most basic level, there is some requisite self-control involved in being an agent: "in order to act, an agent must resolve conflicts among her various motivational impulses" (Schapiro 1999: 728). More substantively, such self-control requires a normative conception of what *warrants* action; that is, one acts on *reasons* rather than mere impulse: "a person [unlike an animal] must act on a reason" (Korsgaard 1996a: 99n). Fourth, Schapiro highlights the important role of *persistence* in constituting agency. Agents must have an "established deliberative perspective" that provides a "plan of life" and "determinate ordering of [various] impulses" (1999: 733, 730; cf. 2003: 589). Like Michael Bratman and Christine Korsgaard, Schapiro argues that in order to "determine which claims really do conform to the law of her will," the agent requires a "law of her will [that] is already in effect ..., a unified, regulative perspective which counts as the expression of her will" (Schapiro 1999: 729).[6]

These four features—internality, activity, normative self-governance, and persistence—are widely regarded by contemporary philosophers as essential to agency. Strikingly, as I show in §§2–5, they are also present in Sofia's work with her cylinder blocks. Most contemporary philosophers, however, including Schapiro, look to adults in their most reflective moments for paradigms of agency. Such philosophers thus elucidate all four features above in terms of capacities for reflection or deliberation in the light of Reason. (Here I capitalize Reason to refer to a higher-order capacity that categorizes the world in abstract terms, as opposed to various capacities whereby people respond to reasons concretely and pre-reflectively.) For example, when Schapiro says that the agent's actions must "express her will" (internality), she immediately equates that will with "her capacity for reflective choice," and when she says that one must be active rather than passive, the only alternative to "mere reaction" is activity that is "the outcome of her own deliberative activity" (Schapiro 1999: 728, see too Schapiro 2021). Similarly, R. Jay Wallace states as basic philosophical common sense that "it is important to our conception of persons as rational agents that ... the motivations and actions of rational agents are guided by and responsive to their deliberative reflection about what they have reason to do" (Wallace 2006: 44).

Given these requirements, Schapiro justifies paternalism because children lack genuine agency. Because "our capacity to reflect ... develops gradually ... childhood has to be conceived as a condition of as-yet-incomplete liberation from nature's rule" (Schapiro 2003: 589). Infants are "almost wholly reactive" and even older children are "only partially free from the governance of instinct" (Schapiro 2003: 589, 590). Children lack the "reflective[ness] about ... motivation" (Bratman 2007: 21; cf. Frankfurt 1971, 2006: 6) or "rational understanding" (Herman 2007: 15, cf. 9–10, 138–43) requisite for seeing their "actions" as governed by *reasons* as opposed to mere desires. Moreover, they lack sufficiently persistent character, at most doing "play-action" with "the status of a rehearsal or experiment" (Schapiro 1999: 733). "Liberating children from adult authority would not be a way of respecting their humanity" but only a way of relinquishing them to enslavement to instinct (Schapiro 2003: 590).

Schapiro starts from the commonplace belief that behavior that would be unjustly paternalistic if directed toward adults can rightly be enacted toward children. Her conception of agency vindicates this commonplace belief by showing that, in the case of children, "Paternalism is ... justified ... [because] by interfering with a child's action, we do not thereby violate *her*" (Schapiro 2003: 587; cf. 1999: 730–1). Because children lack reflection on desires, deliberation in the light of Reason, and persistent principles of action, they lack agency.

In the rest of this chapter, I adopt a different approach. By examining the sorts of agency that children do have, I elucidate a sense of agency that involves internality, activity rather than passivity, normative self-governance, and persistence, all without extensive capacities for second-order reflection, Reason-guided deliberation, or long-term persistence of principles.[7] The next chapter shows why this agency is worthy of direct respect. Chapter 6 then shows what deliberation and Reason add to agency, and Chapter 7 draws the implications for paternalism.

3 Agency and Work

Montessori developed her account of agency by observing cases like Sofia's, where children evinced concentrated attention in work followed by peace and joy upon completion of a cycle of activity. As the description of Sofia quoted in Chapter 1 shows, Montessori's own moral-perceptual capacities recognized in this concentrated work an agency that both manifested virtue and constituted positive good for Sofia. Attention to such moments of heightened agency in children also highlighted similar moments in which adults feel most themselves:

> Take the case of a writer under the influence of poetic inspiration ... Or that of the mathematician who perceives the solution of a great problem, from which will issue new principles beneficial to all humanity. Or again, that of an artist, whose mind has just conceived the ideal image which it is necessary to fix upon the canvas lest a masterpiece be lost to the world.
>
> (9: 16–7; cf. 17: 36–7)

Psychologist Mihaly Csiksentmihalyi describes such phenomena as involving "flow," which occurs when intensely engaged in challenging activities that absorb our attention. In such states, we "feel in control of our actions, masters of our own fate, ... *in control of [our] lives*" (Csikszentmihalyi 1996: 111–2, emphasis original):[8]

> This ... is what the sailor holding a tight course feels when the wind whips through her hair ... It is what the painter feels when the colors on the canvas begin to set up a magnetic tension with each other ... For a violinist, it [occurs when she] master[s] an intricate musical passage.
>
> (Csikszentmihalyi 1990: 3)

As with reflective agency, such exercises of agency involve internality and identification with one's motives, they are *active* rather than passive (e.g., Csikszentmihalyi 1990: 3), and they involve holding oneself to various normative standards.[9] As with Montessori's concept of agency, "the best moments usually occur when a person's body or mind is stretched to its limits in a voluntary effort to accomplish something difficult and worthwhile" (1990: 3). Unsurprisingly, among Csikszentmihalyi's examples of agential self-control is the "child ... placing with trembling fingers the last block on a tower she has built" (1990: 3).

Consistent with Arpaly's notion of "moral autonomy," Montessori identifies these moments of flow as ones the interruption of which provokes a moral response:

> Imagine these men at such psychological moments, broken in upon by some brutal person shouting to them to follow him at once, taking them by the hand, or pushing them out by the shoulders. And for what? The chess-board is set out for a game. Ah! such men would say, You could not have done anything more atrocious! Our inspiration is lost; humanity will be deprived of a poem, an artistic masterpiece, a useful discovery, by your folly.[10]
>
> (9: 17)

Montessori's point is not that it is "atrocious" ever to interrupt someone or frustrate their desires. Neither she nor Csikszentmihalyi sees impulse-driven activity *in general* as involving the sort of agency characteristic of flow, worthy of respect, or partly constitutive of a good human life. Instead, within the category of impulses, desires, or inclinations, Montessori distinguishes between genuinely agential "guiding instincts" (22: 178) that direct attention toward norm-governed and sustained activities by which one constitutes oneself as the sort of agent one is, and those transient or passive desires that can be merely reactive or oriented toward non-activity, and that, even when directed at various goods, treat those goods as merely *for* oneself rather than good *activities* to be done as part of self-constitution. Montessorian "education of the will" allows children "to learn to save themselves from the vanities that destroy man, and concentrate on work which causes the inner life to expand" (9: 143).[11]

Rather than focusing on what distinguishes adults from children or on conditions of deliberation, Montessori turns to observations of when we most clearly observe agency taking place in children, when they seem most satisfied with themselves, and to where being interfered with generates a sense that *selves* have been interfered with, where children most experience frustration and throw tantrums. Her attention to these moments of heightened agency in children reoriented Montessori's awareness toward similar moments in which adults, too, feel most alive and most themselves, and when interference most prompts moral reaction. For both children and adults, agency is most vivid when one engages in concentrated, attentive, work one selects for oneself.

4 Internality

In describing the call to character, to a life of genuine agency, Montessori gives the example of Vittorio Alfieri:

> Alfieri felt that he was ruining himself by remaining the slave of his passion; an internal impulse urged him to raise himself; he felt the great man latent within him, full of powers not yet developed, but potential and expansive; he would fain have turned them to account, responded to their inner call, and dedicated himself to them.
>
> (9: 142)

Alfieri's passionate love for a "capricious society lady" interfered with his pursuit of his "inner call"; both his passionate love and his inner call are impulses, but one is an *internal* impulse, which he sees as his own, as expressive of him*self*, while the other he ascribes to the woman's "scented note[s] …, [which] overcame his will" (9: 142).

Like Montessori in her description of Alfieri, Schapiro rightly notes that there is a certain sort of internality requisite for genuine agency. Agents act for themselves; they are not "dependent upon alien forces" (Schapiro 1999: 732n). This emphasis on internality is widespread, though what precisely internality requires remains contested (see, e.g., Frankfurt 1988: 58–68, Jaworska 2007). We can identify at least three different accounts of the "internality" required for agency.

First, Schapiro, Frankfurt, and others often define the internality of agency in opposition to externality; to be internally related to my choices is for them *not* to derive from something external to me. In the case of Montessori's Alfieri, the external force was conceived of by Alfieri as literally external—scented notes—and Montessori often emphasizes the connection between "children … form[ing] their own decisions" and their being "independent of the suggestion of others" (9: 137). Unfortunately, merely saying that an internal motivation is "not external" leaves undefined what "I" those motives would be external to; Schapiro and Frankfurt argue, for example, that at least some of our feelings and desires are themselves "external" in that they don't reflect who "I" am, while Frankfurt and Velleman describe cases where even outcomes of reflective deliberation don't reflect my "real self" (Frankfurt 1988, 1999; Schapiro 1999, 2021; Velleman 2006: 330–60). Being wholly determined by *seemingly* "internal" forces, such as my own desires, is not sufficient for genuine internality. At the same time, since most expressions of agency are dependent on alien forces to some degree, as when I decide to attend a nearby concert after seeing an advertisement for it, internality in a strong sense cannot be strictly necessary. Without further explanation, defining "internality" in contrast to "external" influences is question-begging.

Second, both (early) Frankfurt and Schapiro emphasize reflection as a necessary criterion for internality. For them (and many others), the "I" that must not be determined by alien forces is my deliberative or second-order self, one that reflects *on* my first-order desires and incorporates some but not all of these as motivations for action. On this account, Alfieri's internal impulse only becomes internal subsequent to being taken up and endorsed in reflection. In the context of the present account, however, to simply *stipulate* that internality requires reflection is question-begging. The examples of both children at work and adults (and children) in states of flow provide examples of internality without reflection. In these cases, as Csikszentmihalyi explains, one has considerable agential "control of psychic energy" and "a very active role for self" even with "loss of consciousness *of* the self" and "no room for self-scrutiny" (Csikszentmihalyi 1990 63–4). Moreover, as David Shoemaker points out, at least on Frankfurt's model,

> [what] makes a certain motivationally efficacious first-order desire mine (i.e., one with which I identify) is that I form a higher-order volition to have it be my will. And what renders a desire external to me is that I have a contrary higher-order volition about it. But of course higher-order volitions are just desires themselves, so what could it be about their higher-order status that lends them any special authority whatsoever with respect to self-determination and externality?
> (Shoemaker 2003: 89)

Unless there is some independent reason for seeing reflection, Reason, or second-order desires as internal in ways that other desires are not, endorsement by reflection cannot be sufficient for internality. And if there is some independent reason that reflection is internal, then that independent reason might also give grounds for seeing first-order desires as internal. Finally, as Frankfurt himself has come to see, there can be "volitional necessities" that "belong to the essential nature of [one's] will" and that can legitimately conflict with outcomes of rational deliberation (Frankfurt 1999: 135).

Third, some philosophers have developed a "wholeheartedness" standard to flesh out the requirements for internality.[12] Frankfurt suggests the notion of wholeheartedness in the context of a theory wherein second-order reflection is essential to agency; on that theory, a person's volitional life may fall short of complete internality when "there is a lack of coherence ... between the person's higher-order volition ... concerning which of his desires he wants to be most effective and the first-order desire that actually is most effective" (Frankfurt 1988: 164). One who wants to smoke a cigarette (first-order desire) but also wants not to act on that desire (second-order) and who smokes the cigarette anyway suffers a failure of agency in that he is not internally related to the desire on which he acts; he doesn't really identify with it because he doesn't endorse it. But Frankfurt realizes that "another sort of inner division occurs when there is a lack of coherence within the realm of a person's higher-order volitions themselves," and Frankfurt initially defines "*wholehearted*" with reference to those higher-order volitions, in contrast to the case where "there is no unequivocal answer to the question of what the person really wants" (Frankfurt

1988: 165). Someone who lacks wholeheartedness wants to stop smoking for the sake of their health, but doesn't want to become a person who obsesses about health, and so smokes sometimes while worrying about health and refrains other times while worrying about worrying. This agent suffers a failure of agency, and she is not internally related to either of her second-order desires because she finds herself in conflict with herself about what she is really committed to. In such cases, "Our hearts are at best divided, and they may even not be in what we are doing at all" (Frankfurt 1988: 163). By contrast with both cases, the wholehearted person can make a "decision ... without reservation, [such that] the commitment it entails is decisive. Then the person no longer holds himself apart from the desire to which he has committed himself" (Frankfurt 1988: 170). In this case, one is internally related to the desire(s) on which one acts by virtue of being *wholeheartedly committed* to that desire.

Even while insisting that reflection is not *sufficient* for internality without some degree of wholeheartedness, Frankfurt still reaffirms its *necessity*: those "incapable of ... volitional reflexivity necessarily lack the capacity to make up their minds" (Frankfurt 1988: 176). His argument, however, suggests ways that first-orders desires themselves might be genuinely internal.

> What leads people to form desires of higher orders is similar to what leads them to go over their arithmetic ... A person may be led to reflect on his own desires either because they conflict with each other or because a more general lack of confidence moves him to consider whether to be satisfied with the motives as they are. Both in the case of desire and in the case of arithmetic a person can without arbitrariness terminate a potentially endless sequence of evaluations when he finds that there is no disturbing conflict, either between results already obtained or between a result already obtained and one he might reasonably expect to obtain if the sequence were to continue. Terminating the sequence at that point—the point at which there is no conflict or doubt—is not arbitrary. For the only reason to continue the sequence would be to cope with an actual conflict or with the possibility that a conflict might occur. Given that a person does not have this reason to continue, it is hardly arbitrary for him to stop.
>
> (Frankfurt 1988: 169)

Frankfurt has in mind a case here where someone has a particular first-order desire (say, to smoke a cigarette), finds a reason to reflect on that desire (say, by noticing the health warning on the pack), and then reflects on whether to affirm the first-order desire. On deciding that negative health effects give her a reason to disown her desire to smoke, she then continues reflecting on whether she wants to be someone who obsesses about health effects and concludes that this sort of basic concern about lung cancer need not be obsessive, so she continues to disown her desire to smoke. And then she *doesn't* deliberate about whether she should be concerned about being unconcerned in this case about obsessing over health. She reaches a point in deliberation where every desire she identifies with points in the same direction. She has a wholehearted desire to stop smoking, so that desire is internal to her.

Frankfurt's description of wholeheartedness is illuminating, but there is no reason the process he describes has to occur only after reflection has begun. When Sofia sees the cylinder blocks and is attracted to them, and especially once she begins to work with them, she has a first-order desire to engage in a particular activity. She is wholeheartedly invested in that activity. She treats this desire as something that expresses who she is. There is no disturbing conflict within her motivational structure, and she has no reasonable expectation that a conflict will or would occur. Just as the decision to *cease* the sequence of deliberation is non-arbitrary when one wholeheartedly accepts evaluations that have emerged from deliberation thus far, so too *refraining from deliberation entirely* is non-arbitrary when one wholeheartedly identifies with one's first-order desire. Given the possibility of wholehearted identification with first-order desires, those desires can be internal to oneself even without an (unused) capacity for deliberation.

For Montessori, some first-order desires—even without reflection—have the requisite internality to express agency, but others are merely reactive impulses to which one is not internally related. The smoker who never reflects on her habit or the child who compulsively eats Doritos are not internally related to these desires, while a fiancée who finds betrayal of his beloved "unthinkable" (Frankfurt 1988: 184), an artist in a state of flow, or a child invested in finishing her puzzle are all internally related to the volitional necessities that govern them at that time. Distinguishing desires that are "in the most authentic way his own forces ... [and] integral to his nature" (Frankfurt 1988: 184) from those that are *mere* desires requires careful and morally sensitive perception. As Frankfurt says about ending deliberation, "no criterion or standard can guarantee that it will be wielded accurately and without arbitrariness" (Frankfurt 1988: 169). One of the primary goals of Montessori classrooms, in fact, is to cultivate in children the ability to identify and follow through on their "guiding instincts" (22: 178), those desires that are truly agential because truly their own, "internal" as opposed to mere "flit[ting] incessantly from one thing to another" as "the effect of external factors" (9: 51–2, 120). Likewise, caregivers and moral perceivers need to "recognize the difference between pure impulse and the spontaneous energies ... [of] a tranquil spirit, ... two kinds of activities, each of which has the appearance of spontaneity ... but which are in fact directly opposed" (1: 240).

> It is not ... free choice when all kinds of external stimuli attract a child at the same time and, having no will power, he responds to every call, passing restlessly from one thing to another ... The child who cannot yet obey an interior guide is not that free being who sets out to follow the long and narrow path toward perfection. He is still a slave to superficial sensations which leave him at the mercy of his environment. His spirit bounces back and forth like a ball.[13]
>
> (1: 246)

Consistent with her overall moral epistemology, Montessori acknowledges that this distinction between true agency and governance by external stimuli "is one of the most important distinctions the teacher must be able to make" (1: 246), and she compares this "power to know good from bad" to the refined judgment of "the doctor, who must learn ... how to distinguish the physiologically normal state from the ... diseased one" (1: 240).[14] "The teacher should have an acute intuition which enables her to understand inner manifestations as distinct from ones that are not manifestations of the spontaneous inner life of the child" (18: 106). No list of criteria can substitute for good judgment and caring attention, and Montessori often distinguishes true attentive work from undisciplined or passive stances toward objects as much from an "expression on the child's face ... of such concentrated attention that it seem[s] ... extraordinary" (9: 51) as from any specific and articulable criteria. The discernment of respect-worthy agency depends upon moral perception.

Nonetheless, without giving specific necessary and sufficient conditions for internality, Montessori presents characteristics of the right kind of internality, distinguishing genuinely agential interests from mere whims (say, for watching TV) or merely physical-biological desires (such as hunger). These characteristics include emphasis on activity rather than passivity, normative self-governance, and persistence. Such features are independently important features of agency, and also reasons that certain interests are *internal* rather than external motives.

5 Activity vs. Passivity

Beyond internality, and as partly constitutive of it, non-passivity is another common way to distinguish agency from mere behavior. Schapiro distinguishes genuine agency from mere inclination in part on the grounds that "being inclined ... is ... a condition in which you are distinctively passive in relation to [your] activity" (2021: 127–8; see too Frankfurt 1988: 163). Etymologically, an "agent" is literally one who acts, rather than one who is merely acted upon. Explaining the precise sense in which an agent is active rather than passive, however, enters philosophically contested space. Schapiro brings out some of this tension. On the one hand, she notes that when inclined, "you are aware of your experiences as constituting a form of your own activity," but on the other hand, she insists that reflection and deliberation are essential in order to relate to one's activity actively rather than passively (Schapiro 2021: 127). By contrast, while allowing that reflection and deliberation can express agency, Montessori rejects the claim that they are essential in order to avoid passivity. Instead of reflection as source of agential control, she focuses more straightforwardly on ways genuinely agential desires—as opposed to mere inclinations or whims—are impulses toward literal activity: "The life of volition is the life of action" (9: 128).

When Sofia works with the cylinder blocks, her orientation toward action helps explain why her impulses are genuinely agential. She does not merely want something given to her or done for her. Rather, her impulse is specifically a desire to act in the world, to express *herself* in her *work*. She does not merely wish; she wills.

Although not involving higher-order reflection, Sofia's action-oriented desire differs from many other "desires" or "inclinations." The child glued to a television is typically passive rather than active, and so Montessori would not see most TV-watching as expressing "agency." Likewise, philosophical "paradigm cases" of mere desire are often desires merely to receive some good, as with "hunger [and] thirst" or even "cravings for chocolate or tobacco ... [or] to see a Cary Grant movie" (Schueler 1995: 9–11; cf. Nagel 1970: 29–30; Scanlon 1998: 37–9). Even if satisfying hunger involves some sort of action on the part of an agent, hunger paradigmatically understood is oriented not toward the activity of eating but toward the satisfaction of need. By contrast, Sofia desires to engage in an activity; she doesn't just want the blocks returned to their proper spots.[15] Even with respect to eating, Montessori warns adults to respect desires for activity rather than for mere physical sustenance: "The adult hems in [the child] ever more closely: he does everything for the child, dresses him, even feeds him. But the child's desire is not to be dressed and materially nourished: his deep desire is to 'do,' to exercise his own powers intelligently" (9: 225). Onorado's hunger is taken up into his agency by becoming incorporated into active work rather than mere passive enjoyment.

We might also put this point about activity and passivity in terms of effort or ease. In her account of inclination, Schapiro describes inclination as having "asymmetric pressure" such that "when you are inclined ... to [do something], it is ... *easier* for you to go along with your inclination ... than not to," such as "when you are inclined to scratch an itch, or to fight back, or to stay up late reading an engrossing book" (Schapiro 2021: 44). Strikingly, however, the "guiding instincts" that Montessori identifies as pre-reflectively agential in the lives of children do not have this characteristic. What sustains the attention of Onorado and especially Sofia is precisely the effort required in order for them to engage in their tasks. Sofia may be engrossed, but she is engrossed by her cylinder blocks in the same sort of intensely effortful and active way that one might be engrossed in working through a challenging passage of Hegel. Her interest in these blocks is not the passive and easy interest of losing oneself in an engaging novel. Rather than the path of least resistance, the agency of these children expresses itself in the desire to work at something difficult. In the case of *these* sorts of desires, it is true that "when you are motivated by your desire, you are not being pushed around by a brute, external force" (Schapiro 2021: 57).

Montessori's emphasis on *intelligent* do-ing further distinguishes Sofia's work with cylinder blocks from examples of "action" such as "To drum one's fingers on the table, altogether idly and inattentively," which, as Frankfurt says, "is surely [neither] a case of passivity ... [nor] a case of action ... but only of being active" (Frankfurt 1988: 58). Because "the will is not a simple impulse towards movement, but the intelligent direction of movements" (9: 127), mere drumming of fingers does not count as the expression of agency. Relatedly, Sofia's work does not fit Schapiro's description of the "emergency situation" like "when you sense yourself falling," where "your action is wholly reactive" and we are in "something like an animal condition ... that allows us to act instinctively" (Schapiro 2021: 125). Though non-reflective, Sofia's attention to where to place her cylinder is intensely *active* and not at all merely reactive. Likewise, proficiently playing a challenging violin piece involves pro-active attunement rather than mere reactivity, and even seemingly reactive flow-activities—say, returning a tennis serve—are expressions of an overall engagement with the world that flows from one's interests toward one's situation rather than sidestepping agency to deal with an extraordinary situation.[16]

Even so, many might argue that desires as such, even desires to engage in work by which we intelligently direct our own movements, are essentially passive because we do not have sufficient control over the desires themselves. As Schapiro explains,

> What I mean by saying they are "passive" forms of motivation is they are not under our direct volitional control. For example, you can't will yourself to want to eat a nutritious salad, even if you are convinced that eating a nutritious salad is the best thing to do. Nor can you rid yourself of a craving for ice cream just by deciding you ought not to crave ice cream. In both cases, you have to work on your appetites indirectly, by developing new habits and using your imagination to forge new associative links. The same is true with motives that are not physiological appetites. You know you ought to grade those papers, but you do not feel like grading them. And you cannot make yourself feel like grading them just by deciding you ought to grade them, or by deciding you ought to feel like grading them.
> (Schapiro 2012: 335[17])

Desires seem like states we merely find ourselves with, or that we just wait for, or—at most—that we cultivate indirectly. We do not seem to be able to directly control what our desires are, so we are passive with respect to them.

Schapiro offers this argument from within the perspective of deliberation, assuming that "volitional control" would have to mean something like control by means of rational deliberation. In that context, the claim that conclusions of deliberation are under volitional control is tautologically true, while desires seem largely out of control. However, by *assuming* that "control" is exercised through deliberation, the argument begs the question against Montessori. If what it means for something to be under my "control" is, say, for it to be dictated by my "volitional necessities" (Frankfurt 1999: 135), then many desires are under my control and at least some deliberation is not. More generally, as Nancy Sherman has rightly pointed out, with respect to the "standard objection to holding persons responsible for their emotions ... [, namely] that emotional experiences, unlike actions, cannot be started or stopped immediately, at will,"

> [T]he requirement for immediate control, even in the case of actions, is suspect. Some basic actions may flow from the will in an instant, but even the simple act of snapping a finger can be, for the novice, a painstaking project that builds upon incremental willings ... More complex actions like playing the piano, doing philosophy, baking bread, building cabinets, painting the interior of a house, weaving a carpet, leading in battle, all cannot be done, as full-fledged activities, in an instant. They are skill-based, involve complex sequencings, and build on previous efforts. They have developmental histories. Being able to engage in them depends upon an accumulation of past efforts, as well as some humility, in the face of a world that we cannot fully control. Put differently, our will, even in the case of simple physical action, is not a wish that magically works wonders ... [T]hat we cannot start a specific sort of emotion, on a dime, so to speak, does not make it so terribly different from being able to perform certain complex actions.
> (Sherman 1999: 300–1)

To return to Schapiro's example, just as "you cannot make yourself feel like grading [papers] just by deciding you ought to grade them," so too you cannot make yourself actually grade the papers just by deciding that you ought to grade them. Performing the action, like having the inclination, requires the development of patterns of movement and thought constitutive of grading papers. Moreover, for Montessori, "There can be no manifestation of the will without completed action; he who thinks of performing a good action but leaves it undone … does not accomplish an exercise of the will" (9: 127). Someone without the *ability* to grade papers cannot even properly *decide* to grade them, so even decisions are not wholly under one's control.

Deliberation itself is not under direct volitional control except in the tautological sense described above. Philosophers Nomy Arpaly and Timothy Schroeder rightly point out that "beginning deliberation is itself something [one] does not deliberate upon" (Arpaly and Schroeder 2014: 48). As noted above with respect to wholeheartedness and internality, deliberation arises in cases where our desires or habits are not sufficient to motivate, when we face conflict or novel situations, or when we find ourselves in environments not conducive to working from guiding instincts. What Schapiro elsewhere calls "the moment of drama," where one is "having an inclination … but not yet acting on it," is something we cannot generate through choice (Schapiro 2021: 10). We simply find ourselves in such moments, find ourselves reflecting or deliberating. If to be "under volitional control" is to be an *effect* of deliberation, then the beginnings of deliberation are not under one's volitional control. Even *within* deliberation, we do not exercise direct control over what considerations occur to us.

> [E]xtended deliberative actions are made up, not just of … basic exercises of agency over thought, but also of the occurrence in consciousness of thoughts and feelings that serve as inputs to deliberation but which are not brought to consciousness through exercises of [deliberative[18]] agency.
>
> (Arpaly and Schroeder 2014: 25)

Neither the start of deliberation nor the process of deliberation is under our "control," if we interpret "control" to mean that we can simply decide to bring something about based on deliberation.[19]

Moreover, actions motivated by desires of certain kinds, what Montessori calls guiding instincts, are more "under my control" than Schapiro suggests. When I act on a desire, I identify with and act in the light of the desire, just as, when I deliberate, I (ideally) identify with and act in the light of my deliberations. For many desires, my identification is quite strong, such that the force of desire is "in the most authentic sense [my] own" (Frankfurt 1988: 184), and often this identification is wholehearted, whether grounded in the overall structure of my cares and interests or simply representative of what I am most committed to at a given time. Sofia would rightly have seen a provocation to reflection or deliberation as an interruption, and guided by a desire with which she fully identified and that prompted her to concentrate on her work, she would have resisted being forced to deliberate. This resistance might have had to rise to the level of *deliberate* resistance—if her caregivers violently insisted on a justification for her continued activity—but it might also, in a more respectful community, never rise to reflection. She might simply not be at all tempted by alternative courses of action (including the action of reflecting) and she might unreflectively but authentically follow through on her desire to work with cylinders. The fact that she does not allow herself to be swept into deliberation does not imply that she relates "passively" to her desire.

6 Normative Self-Governance

The desires that express agency within Montessori's moral philosophy are those "guiding instincts" with which one fully identifies and that are oriented toward one's own activity in the world. Many philosophers of agency add a further feature, that of "normativity." As R. Jay Wallace puts it, genuine action "is an inherently intelligent phenomenon" such that "if there is room for a substantial conception of the will in contemporary theorizing about human agency, it is mostly likely to be found in the vicinity of the phenomenon of normativity" (Wallace 2006: 62, 71). Agents do not merely do things in response to impulses; when we set ourselves to do something in the light of identification with one or another impulse, we control ourselves in the light of *reasons* that *justify* decisions; our "activity [is] controlled by ... normative reflection" (Wallace 2006: 62). While an impulse might directly prompt an animal to run at the sight of fire, an agent must take fire to be a good *reason* for running (and/or must take survival to be a good reason for running away from fire). The decision to do this or that "cannot appear to her a mere clash of unintelligible pushes and pulls [but] ... must appear to the agent as a conflict between rival claims" for which one "demand[s] justification" (Schapiro 1999: 728, 2003: 587). As Korsgaard puts it, "a person [unlike an animal] must act on a reason" (Korsgaard 1996a: 99n). In place of Montessori's "guiding instincts," Schapiro proposes what she calls a "guiding conception," a

> description of an activity under which the participant chooses it and finds it worth engaging in ... Its role is to specify the aims and methods in which the activity consists, as well as to identify what is at stake in doing it successfully. It thereby sets a standard ... with reference to which the participant can judge whether she is engaging in it properly, and whether she is thereby achieving what she is striving to achieve by engaging in it.
>
> (Schapiro 2021: 21)

Agency, in other words, requires self-governance in the light of normative standards.

For Schapiro, Korsgaard, Wallace, and others, the necessity to govern oneself by normative standards implies that one must engage in processes of reflective deliberation in the light of Reason, but Montessori consistently emphasizes the extent to which normative self-governance is present within the attentive work of children following their guiding instincts: "The child who is involved in some task inhibits all movements which do not conduce to the accomplishment of this work; he makes a selection among the muscular coordinations of which he is capable" (9: 129). Sofia, working with cylinder blocks, undertakes a set of fine motor movements that are, for her, quite difficult and not directly instinctual. In contrast to animals, for whom "each species is characterized by its own special movements... [that are] hereditary,... [human] movements are not hereditary. Man constructs his movements for himself" (17: 158). Sofia lifts blocks by a small knob and coordinates visual and proprioceptive awareness with muscle movements to maneuver each block over its corresponding hole, which she must discriminate visually. For those who have mastered these tasks or gained generalized proficiency in manual manipulation, visual discrimination, and hand-eye coordination, such activities are trite exercises barely involving self-control. But *she* must force her hands to move in unfamiliar ways and visually attend to hard-to-discriminate details. She almost certainly errs in her efforts, so she must correct mistakes and refine self-control, only gradually taking control over her own movements, shifting from a body that "first moves in a funny, strange way" to one that "now [s]he can move correctly" (15: 219). None of these activities are possible without inhibition of impulses toward routine patterns of movement. "Attention" here involves concentrated effort to shift activities from one (familiar and easy) set of patterns to another (new and challenging) set. Every movement of block to corresponding hole involves "complex internal activities of comparison and judgment" (9: 137) wherein Sofia refrains from placing the block in the hole that immediately strikes her fancy and instead attends carefully to relevant (sensory) data to select the *right* hole: "The *constant work*... is all set in motion by *decisions*, and this takes the place of the primitive state... in which... actions were the outcome of [mere] *impulses*" (9: 137, emphasis original).

In these respects, the concentrated activity of working on cylinder blocks is a paradigm of controlling natural impulses and tendencies. But Sofia lacks second-order reflection on her desire to work on those blocks, and she lacks the felt conflict implicit in many Kantian accounts of self-control (Schapiro 1999: 729; Wood 2014: 37).[20] Despite some sense in which her body "wants" to continue moving in its customary way, she has no psychological *desire* to do so. She desires, wholeheartedly, to work with blocks properly. There is no part of her *will* against which she must struggle,[21] and her case beautifully shows what is wrong with demanding any such struggle. In the context of various internal-physical resistances (tension in muscles, difficulty in carrying out tasks), Sofia knows what she wants. She wholeheartedly, albeit pre-reflectively, controls herself.

This self-control is normatively governed. Not only does Sofia's work requires that she complete her task properly, but Sofia herself "take[s] great pleasure in doing things *well*" and "rejoice[s] in *the perfection of [her] achievements*" (15: 219; 22: 111, emphasis added). Each motion of her hands, placement of cylinders, and decision about which cylinder to take up next is measured by a standard of excellence internal to the cylinder block work. Lack of fit provides reason to try a different hole; a leftover cylinder gives reason to double-check her work. Precisely these standards inherent in the work engage children's attention: "the child not only needs something interesting to do but also likes to be shown exactly how to do it. Precision is found to attract him deeply;" "he has naturally the tendency of interesting himself in exact things in an exact way;" and he has an "eagerness to have laws to obey[, a]n eagerness perfectly natural, because without these laws, he would not be able to orient himself" (1: 161; 24: 68; 14: 79). Whether moving blocks or playing sports or composing poetry, agents engage in activities with internal normative standards that allow them to do the activities *well*.

For this reason, Montessori highlights the importance of error and the awareness of error as central to agency: "it is well to cultivate a friendly feeling towards error, to treat it as a companion inseparable from our lives, as something having a purpose, which it truly has ... If we seek perfection, we must pay attention to our own defects,[22] for it is only by correcting these that we can improve ourselves" (1: 223). Sofia has an inclination *specifically for* doing work well, and her work with the material—trying and failing to get the blocks right, and then succeeding—"develops an ever clearer sensibility towards error and therefore, we might say, a primordial distinction between right and wrong" (Montessori in De Giorgi 2019: 62).

Given the importance of norm-directed work, Montessori insists that environments and materials include a "control of error" (1: 224–6) that allows students to recognize manageable goals and correct errors even without articulated principles of excellence. Thus, furniture is light enough to be moved, but also to be knocked over accidentally, and children learn to "tak[e] care not to knock into things" (22: 111). Cylinder blocks vary in size from large to small, each fitting in its own cylindrical hole, so that children try to replace them in their proper places, getting increasingly good at recognizing the size of each block, and "correct[ing] ... [their own] mistakes" (9: 127). This sort of norm-governed, focused interest anticipates Alasdair MacIntyre's concept of a "practice," a "coherent and complex form of ... activity" with "goods internal to that form of activity" that involve "standards of excellence which are ... partially definitive of that form of activity" (MacIntyre 1981: 187).[23] Likewise, Csikszentmihalyi shows how flow activities aim at doing well, in accordance with determinate even if unarticulated standards of excellence (Csikszentmihalyi 1990: 49–53). As in practices and flow experiences, children aim not only to do each particular activity well but also to improve: "Every exercise in movement that is susceptible of control by error ... helps the children to perfect their powers" (22: 111).

In these activities, we might describe agents as "reflective [*reflessivo*]" or "governed by reason" (22: 80), but the relevant reflection is about how best to perform a particular activity rather than about the status of their desires, and the relevant reasons are internal to the practices in which they are engaged. This local and practice-internal conception of normativity provides sufficient normative constraint to distinguish the agency involved in attentive work from the passive whimsy involved in mere impulses. Like Schapiro's—and Kant's—insistence that one transform immediate desires into value-conferring reasons, Montessori insists on reasons-responsive and normatively directed control over one's impulses. But she rejects Kant/Schapiro's contention that justificatory norms arise from or must be endorsed by Rational reflection. Instead, the pursuit of challenging work can be self-governing because it involves intrinsic normative standards.

7 Reflection, Deliberation, and Reason

In her observations of young children, Montessori emphasizes the value of agency expressed in attentive work. This agency deserves respect and grounds her ideal of character, but it need not involve self-conscious reflection or abstract principles of practical reason. Adult ethical life, however, is often reflective, involving abstract principles or values and perspectives one weighs in deliberation. While contemporary philosophers are wrong to see reflective deliberation in the light of Reason as essential to agency as such, often exaggerating the extent to which even adult agency at its best relies on such deliberation, they are not wrong to see various forms of reflective deliberation as distinguishing features of adult agency. In Chapter 6, I discuss Montessori's developmental account of moral maturation, pointing out how reflective deliberation in the light of abstract concepts and principles enhances human agency. Here, I highlight several reasons not to see deliberation as essential to agency as such.

First and most basically, human beings—both children and adults—engage in forms of agency that do not involve reflective deliberation, and we can directly perceive such agency as worthy of cultivation and respect. When Sofia works on cylinder blocks, or the artist paints his masterpiece, or the scientist solves the puzzle that has been occupying her all afternoon, these agents are engaged in attentive, norm-governed, active work flowing from interests with which they wholeheartedly identify. Interrupting such attentive work is prima facie disrespectful, a violation of the *wills* of these agents. The moral difference between such expressions of agency and aimless flitting about or mere whimsy is evident to any well-cultivated moral sense.

Second and relatedly, when an adult agent reflectively endorses a given desire, the structure of that endorsement can often include reference to the fact that the desire is one she *already* identifies as her own, as expressive of her agency. Say I feel like investing more time in a meaningful but difficult friendship, and I deliberate about whether to follow my inclination. Whatever other reasons I consider, it may be that my decisive reason for recommitting to the relationship is simply that I find my feelings toward my friend to be ones that already define who I am, such that my inclination to invest in this friendship is one with which I (already) wholeheartedly identify. In some cases, we might even specifically endorse in reflection a tendency to follow certain impulses *without* reflection, or reflectively *reject* a tendency to excessively reflect. I might find that my deliberations about whether to invest in my friendship actually take away from my capacity to fully invest. Schapiro has discussed cases like these as ones where "You have found that your gut tends to lead you in the right direction, and your head tends to lead you astray" (Schapiro 2012: 341), but this treats the value of the gut merely instrumentally, along the lines of what Schapiro elsewhere calls a "proficiency argument" (Schapiro 2003). In some cases, going with the gut is preferred because it gets better results, but in other cases, the value of the gut is specifically that it flows from who I really am more truly than the head does. I might find myself to be overly deliberative in initiating relationships, for instance, not in such a way that I find my gut to be more reliable in picking good friends, but in that I end up looking back and thinking, "It wasn't really *me* that decided to befriend her; it was an argument that I found convincing at the time." In such cases, I might decide to go with my gut not because it leads me in the *right* direction, but because when my gut leads, *I* lead *myself*, whereas deliberation takes me places that *I* don't really want to go.

That reflective deliberation is not *necessary* for agency is shown by our direct moral perception of the value of non-deliberative agency and our reflective endorsement of certain desires as already-expressive of our agency. Deliberation is also not *sufficient* for agency. Frankfurt rightly points out that even if "Someone does what he *really wants* to do only when he acts in accordance with a pertinent higher-order volition," "this condition not be sufficient unless the higher-order volition were *itself* one by which the person *really wanted* to be determined" (Frankfurt 1988: 166[24]). Similarly, people can and do often feel alienated from their own processes of deliberation. Frankfurt gives the example of Lord Fawn (from Trollope's *The Eustace Diamonds*), who decided to inquire into his fiancée's possible improprieties and then "could not bring himself" to do it because "every feeling of his nature revolted" (Frankfurt 1988: 183). In some cases, our immediate attractions or repulsions are more truly our own than our deliberations, and they rightly guide us even against commitments "we" make in reflective deliberation.

Relatedly, deliberation only counts as agential for me if such deliberation is *my own*. In the most extreme case, my deliberation might literally be guided by someone else. I might be happily enjoying a game of tennis when someone asks me whether I should really be spending my time that way and then offers up a series of reasons for and against what I'm doing, until by the end of the process I don't see a way out of the conclusion that I should probably clean the garage rather than play tennis. But I still might not see this as a conclusion that *I've* drawn. Even if another person isn't literally present, I might feel like spending the morning playing tennis and run through a series of considerations that I "know" provide "good" reasons for and against spending my time this way, but where this whole train of deliberation involves merely running through a script I don't identify with. Relatedly, I might do what is "rational," where "rational" just refers to legal or social standards, and where it doesn't seem like it's really *my* reason governing me. I might even engage in practical reasoning governed by my own Reason, but do so as a chore, something I don't really want to do, don't think is necessary, and don't care about.

Finally, deliberation itself requires a capacity to identify with choices that are not themselves results of deliberation. As noted in §4 above, deliberation involves several steps—starting deliberation, considering this or that reason, and ending deliberation—that cannot ultimately be results of deliberation, on pain of infinite regress. In order to settle on a particular outcome of deliberation, agents must be free of the "mania of doubt" that involves an "impossibility of taking a decision, and which produces a serious state of distress, though it ... may even arise from a moral scruple" (9: 138). As I show in more detail in Chapter 6, the capacity for deliberation is an important special case of a more general capacity to choose norm-governed activities that we invest active effort into doing well; without that general capacity, we cannot engage in deliberation for ourselves. And unless that general capacity expresses our agency, deliberation itself cannot express that agency. The general and pre-reflective capacity for active, normative self-governance in the light of interests with which we identify is thus more fundamental than deliberation, and is sufficient (with one further proviso) for having a will of one's own.

8 Persistence

As I noted in §2, one important feature in many contemporary approaches to agency is *persistence*. Schapiro emphasizes the importance of a "plan of life" or "law of her will ... already in effect" (Schapiro 1999: 733, 729). Michael Bratman, arguably the most important contemporary philosopher for understanding the importance of persistence for agency, defends the importance of persistence in the context of a "puzzle" about "the capacity to take a stand as an agent—to determine where *I* stand with respect to a given first-order desire." In particular, for any given set of attitudes, however reflective they might be, "How could we get from the fact that certain *attitudes* favor a form of motivation to the fact that the *agent* endorses the motivation?" (Bratman 2007: 24). Bratman argues that establishing one's identity as a self-governing agent requires that one be "a planner who projects her agency over time" (Bratman 2007: 28; cf. Korsgaard 2009: 75–6). He starts by considering broadly Lockean approaches to the continuity of the self over time, according to which one remains the same person over time by virtue of linked psychological features such as "memory, forward-looking connections like those between a prior intention and its later execution, and continuities in desires and the like" (2007: 29). An agent, on this Lockean account, is not a mere "time-slice agent."

> She is, rather, and understands herself to be, a temporally persisting agent, one whose agency is temporally extended. This makes it natural to suppose that for her to endorse a desire is, roughly, for that desire to be endorsed by attitudes whose role it is to support the temporal organization of her agency by way of constituted and supporting Lockean ties characteristic of her temporal persistence.
> (Bratman 2007: 31)

In other words, for *me* to govern *myself*, the desires on which I act must be ones endorsed by attitudes "whose primary roles support connections ... which help constitute the identity of the agent over time" (Bratman 2007: 31).

For Montessori, as for Bratman, Schapiro, and others, persistence is essential for agency. She contrasts children exercising agency from those who "flit incessantly from one thing to another" (9: 51) and even claims that "persistence [is] the true foundation of the will" (9: 134). She contrasts one who "responds to every call, passing restlessly from one thing to another" with a genuinely "free being" who "sets himself a task [and] finds his way" (1: 246).

> I would like you to think about a child who does this exercise so minutely, continuing up to the end. Does it not seem to you that he is obedient to someone? Certainly, he is obeying his own will! In doing so he shows two virtues: constancy and patience.
> (24: 119)

Montessori's argument for the importance of persistence even anticipates Schapiro's and Bratman's:

> This quality ["constancy, or persistence"] is really the exponent of the uninterrupted concord of the inner personality. Without it, a life would be a series of episodes, a chaos; it would be like a body disintegrated into its cells, rather than an organism which persists throughout the mutations of its own material. This fundamental quality, when it embraces the sentiment of the individual and the direction of his

ideation, that is to say, his whole personality, is what we have called *character*. The man of character is the persistent man, the man who is faithful to his own word, his own convictions, his own affections.

(9: 133; cf. 15: 148–9)

Acting in the light of consistent attitudes is necessary for a coherent self to avoid being merely a "series of episodes." But while Schapiro's notion of consistency as an "established constitution" involves a rational-principle-based juridical model (Schapiro 1999: 729), Montessori allows character to be located in habits, consistent values and ideals, well-cultivated sensibilities, or affections. The artisan's constancy of *techne*, for example, may be fundamental to his agency while remaining inarticulable in terms of principles or practical maxims. Montessori emphasizes such things as handwriting and basic muscle memory as forms of constancy in activity, without requiring "principles" governing the way one writes the letter "s" or shoots a basketball.

Here our previous discussion of wholeheartedness is helpful. In discussing wholehearted commitments, Frankfurt suggests that they "resound endlessly" because they are made "without reservation" (Frankfurt 1998: 168). Frankfurt conceives of these wholehearted commitments reflectively or deliberatively, but we have already seen in §3 that Sofia can be wholeheartedly committed to her interest in the cylinder blocks through committing to that interest without reservation, even if also without deliberation. What we need to add here is that such an interest can serve as an attitude that "support[s] connections … which help constitute the identity of the agent over time" (Bratman 2007: 31). Bratman himself acknowledges that "one might be a nonreflective but planning agent" (Bratman 2007: 28), though he nonetheless sees reflectiveness as essential for self-governance.[25] What Montessori highlights is that one can identify an agent distinct from fleeting desires whenever an attitude persists that organizes other impulses over time.

In discussing Sofia, after highlighting her intense concentration, Montessori emphasizes this *persistence*:

> I watched the child intently without disturbing her at first, and began to count how many times she repeated the exercise; then, seeing that she was continuing for a long time, I picked up the little armchair in which she was seated, and placed chair and child upon the table; the little creature hastily caught up her case of insets, laid it across the arms of her chair, and gathering the cylinders into her lap, set to work again. Then I called upon all the children to sing; they sang, but the little girl continued undisturbed, repeating her exercise even after the short song had come to an end. I counted forty-four repetitions; when at last she ceased, it was quite independently of any surrounding stimuli which might have distracted her, and she looked round with a satisfied air, almost as if awaking from a refreshing nap.

(9: 51)

In §5, I noted the extent to which the interest in this particular work requires Sofia's synchronic organization of bodily movements and fleeting impulses, whereby she moves her body (especially her hands) in ways required to satisfy the requirements of this particular work. In this new passage, Montessori emphasizes the diachronic organization of Sofia's impulses by her interest in this particular activity; she must ignore the singing around her, gather up her materials and restart her work, and remain focused not only from start to finish of each completion of the activity but also over the course of dozens of repetitions of it. As Montessori explains elsewhere, "The child who is involved in some task [not only] inhibits all movements which do not conduce to the accomplishment of this work [and] makes a selection amongst the muscular coordinations of which he is capable [but also] *persists in them*" (9: 129; emphasis added; cf. 15: 219–20; 17: 156–64).

While Montessori shares with many contemporary accounts a focus on persistence, however, she resists a tendency present in some theorists—especially Schapiro and Korsgaard—to require commitments that are at least provisionally lifelong. In that respect, we might helpfully compare Sofia's persistence with one of Bratman's examples of agency extended over time.

> I see my activity of, say, writing a paper as something I do over an extended period of time. I see myself as beginning the project, developing it over time, and (finally!) completing it. I see the agent of these various activities as one and the same agent—namely, me. In the middle of the project I see myself as the agent who began the project and (I hope) the agent who will complete it. Upon completion, I take pride in the fact that *I* began, worked on, and completed this essay. Of course, there is a sense in which when I act, I act at a particular time; but in acting I do not see myself, the agent of the act, as simply a time-slice agent. I see my action at that time as the action of the same agent as he who has acted in the past and (it is to be hoped) will act in the future. In this respect I differ importantly from those nonhuman agents who do not have the resources to understand their own agency as temporally extended.
>
> (Bratman 2007: 28–9)

There are several important differences between Bratman's exercises of planning agency in writing a paper and Sofia's persistent agency in working on her cylinder blocks,[26] but I want here to focus on an important similarity, namely, how both examples contrast with approaches that emphasize a "fixed constitution" (Schapiro 1999: 732) or Frankfurt's appeal to commitments that "resound endlessly" (Frankfurt 1998: 168) or even Korsgaard's suggestion that agency requires at least *"provisional"* lifelong application (Korsgaard 2009: 74).[27] Both Sofia and Bratman—and Montessori's examples of artists or scientists with a "will to work" or the "humblest artisan who 'works'" (9: 133)—have persistence sufficient for agency without even provisionally lifelong commitments. Such persistence provides sufficient stability to distinguish oneself from passing impulses and to supply a basis for normative self-governance. The child who flits from toy to toy insisting on playing with each for a moment before moving on to the next, or who covets his friend's toy until he gets hold of it and then discards it, shows a sort of "willfulness" that lacks an enduring self to stand apart from and govern the impulses of successive moments. But the child who "persists for a long time and with earnest attention in the same exercise, correcting the mistakes which the didactic material reveals to him" (9: 127), avoiding distractions and being genuinely offended by interruptions, exhibits agency worthy of respect.

Bratman rightly sees his own account of agency as a "middle ground" between "a broadly Humean theory that sees action as the output of the causal functioning of desires" and "a broadly Kantian theory that sees agency and will as essentially involving, and as embedded in, a system of universal principles" according to which "it is only when the role of one's desire has been 'incorporated' into a system of universal principles that there is an agent and a will, and not merely a system of pushes and pulls" (Bratman 2007: 86). Kantians often describe human volition such that one has either consistent commitments fitting into a coherent life-plan or mere passing desires (Korsgaard 2009: 62; Schapiro 1999: 729–31), but on a Bratman-Montessorian middle-ground view, the persistence involved in focused projects provides a stable background against which one is distinguished from passing impulses. Human life is full of commitments with relatively narrowly specified temporal horizons. When teaching a course or writing a paper or playing a game of tennis or practicing a musical instrument, I have an agency that persists within the limits of my activity and that distinguishes *me* from passing impulses. Just as Sofia's fingers might not naturally grip the block in the right way or her teacher might present her the distraction of a lively song, so I might want to stop writing my paper, or get tired of playing tennis, or feel my hand's resistance to violin practice. When I resist those inclinations and remain "persistent in work," I express agency. Relatedly, it is precisely *persistence* in work that I feel to be violated when someone interrupts my "flow." While the overall importance of these commitments may depend upon how they fit into a bigger picture, I need not appeal to any role in life as a whole to distinguish commitment to the present activity from passing whims.

Montessori's focus on the kind of persistence involved in focused work goes further than merely rejecting those Kantian models that depend upon character as a commitment that lasts (or aims to last) for an entire life. Her focus on the persistence involved in even relatively short-term tasks highlights an implicit assumption of many contemporary discussions of agency, one best described in term of a prioritizing of "extensive" stability over "intensive" stability. A commitment is *intensively* stable if it *strongly* resists being changed in the light of passing impulses and changing conditions; it is *extensively* stable if it resists change *over a long period of time*. Not only Schapiro, for whom one's constitution must be "established" over one's entire life, but even those who set narrower time horizons, often articulate conceptions of persistence that focus on how long commitments persist (Sayre-McCord and Smith 2014: 134; Schapiro 1999: 729). Intensive stability requires *some* degree of extensive stability in order to distinguish it from mere strength of impulse, but the two concepts are not identical. Sofia had great intensive stability but relatively little extensive stability. While focused on her work, almost nothing could deflect her. But she focused for only a short period of time. One might watch TV for hours while spending only thirty minutes climbing a rock's face or making a pie, but the rock-climbing and pie-making could have greater intensive stability than the TV-watching. Similarly, "the student who goes off to college and then comes home every couple of months with a completely new set of enthusiasms and ideals" (Sayre-McCord and Smith 2014: 140) might be only loosely committed to each ideal, such that her ideals would lack both intensive and extensive persistence. Or she might be intensely committed, but then change her ideals. In this second case, it would be right to say that the reason her ideals change is that *she* changes. One might even deliberately assume an identity—say a particular occupation or foster-parenting responsibility—with a modest time horizon. Someone committed to their two-year stint with Teach-For-America could well have more intensive persistence than someone who simply remains in their job for life from a passive lack of pursuing alternatives.

Admittedly, something would be lacking were one *merely* to pass from particular project to particular project without any consistent background into which these projects fit as a coherent whole. For adults, conscious endorsement of this whole may even be an agential ideal. In that sense, Kantians are correct to advocate a persistence that is at least provisionally universal. Again, Bratman's "middle view" approach is helpful:

> [A]gency and will can involve various kinds of higher-order commitments embedded in a system of intentions and plans. Such commitments can be singular and yet still bring to bear characteristic normative demands. But there are also substantial pressures—grounded in the temporal extension of our agency and captured in the idea of the temporally persistent agent's identification with a desire—in the direction of higher-order policies.
>
> (Bratman 2007: 86–7)

Even if not mere "chaos," one who always only persists within the confines of a particular project would perhaps live a life that approaches what Montessori calls a mere "series of episodes" (9: 133). Still, within each episode, there would be a self—a will—to respect. Moreover, even any life that has lifelong consistency in some respects will largely consist in activities with narrower horizons of persistence. Montessori thus articulates and illustrates a concept of persistence that satisfies necessary conditions of agency but, because not dependent upon a sense of life as a whole (or relevantly similar sort of robustness), can apply to children.

9 Character and Perfection

9.1 Character as Moral Ideal

Thus far, this chapter has focused on a concept of respect-worthy agency that does not rely upon reflective deliberation. At the end of §8, however, I distinguished the persistence intrinsic to respect-worthy agency from more complex sorts of persistence worth promoting. More generally, we can and should distinguish minimal agency that warrants non-paternalistic respect from agency as a moral ideal (cf. Arpaly 2002: 124–5; Bratman 2018: 210). One exercises agency and deserves respect even when one exercises that agency partially or badly, but agency is also something toward which individuals can and should aspire. While "caution must be exercised when mixing intuitions about [agency] as an ideal condition and intuitions about [agency] as a property that a great majority of humans have ... most of the time" (Arpaly 2002: 124–5), Montessori argues that to be a better agent is also to be *more* of an agent. Particularly when she discusses agency aspirationally as a good to be developed, Montessori employs the terminology of "character," which not only shifts focus from individual agential acts to a *disposition or tendency*, but also describes an *ideal* tendency toward choosing active work with normative standards and persistently engaging in that work.

Christine Korsgaard's notion of "constitutive standards" is helpful for understanding the relationship between agency as such and the ideal agency expressed by one with character (see Korsgaard 2009: 28f.). Drawing from "the ancient [Greek] metaphysical thesis of the identification of the real with the good," Korsgaard explains how "it is ... the form of the object that supports normative judgments about it," such that, for instance, to be a good house is to be an especially house-y house, that is, to be fully and completely what a house really *is*. In §6, I showed how each individual exercise of agency is governed by normative standards internal to a particular activity, but agency itself also has constitutive standards, and these can be satisfied more or less completely. Someone may express agency of a sort even when they choose an activity they are not really that interested in and sloppily aim at conforming to its internal standards with some degree of persistence, but they are far from an agent in the fullest sense. Just as a child might work with cylinder blocks even while barely getting any cylinders in their correct holes, so too someone may express respect-worthy agency even while only partially having the characteristics described in §§3–8. But such an "agent," like a house with a leaky roof or a cylinder-block-worker who can't place cylinders correctly, fails to *fully* be what it is. When Montessori employs her concept of character, she emphasizes agency that satisfies its own constitutive standards.[28]

Particularly when discussing character, Montessori frequently introduces the concept of "perfection." Agents persistently engage with norm-governed and active work that they choose for themselves. Agency thus requires some basis for choosing to engage in some particular work. The central value that governs paradigmatic exercises of agency, for Montessori, is perfection: "the soul of a normal human being is an immense journey toward perfection" (Montessori 1903: 351). Those with character have "a natural attraction ... toward perfection," "a tendency, however vague and unconscious, to raise themselves up," such that "the great task of education must be to secure and to preserve a normality which, of its own nature, gravitates towards the center of perfection" (1: 189, 188, 217). Even if one does not consciously attend to perfection in one's choices and activity, the interests that motivate and express agency are oriented toward perfection. "In this path to perfection, children find their joy ... This is also true of the adult" (24: 77).

9.2 Three Kinds of Perfection

Agents govern themselves by ideals of perfection at three different levels, each of which provides both constitutive norms for activity and motives to engage in it. First, standards of perfection are internal to each activity. When agents "work," they have "a tendency to organize a set of movements around an idea, which constitutes a definite aim," a tendency "to become interested in an action, to carry it out, and to accomplish it to perfection" (24: 42, 53). A child interested in a puzzle seeks to complete the puzzle properly, in accordance with the standard of perfection internal to puzzle-work. And children (and other agents) *become* interested in activities because those activities have internal standards of perfection; "it is necessary to arouse his interest with something exact" (24: 76). Normative self-governance, in other words, is governance in accordance with standards of perfection for the activities in which one engages.

Second, those with character orient themselves toward activities that involve *self*-perfection, that is, that can enhance their own overall excellence. Consistent with standard accounts of perfectionism that identify human excellence with "the development and exercise of one's natural or essential capacities" (Dorsey 2010: 59), Montessori claims that "enhancing our abilities is the real source of our delight," for both children engaged with work such as cylinder blocks and "ourselves," such as "in sport" (1: 161). Self-perfection takes place at varying degrees of specificity. Thus, "for example, if I want to play the piano, … I must train my hands, my movements of my fingers in order to acquire agility of movement, which is necessary to play the piano efficiently" (24: 21). Beyond intrinsic norms governing playing any particular piece, one seeks self-perfection in that one cultivates muscular capacities for playing piano well in general. One becomes more perfect by gaining a new skill.

More broadly, self-perfection involves cultivating "our abilities." Particularly when discussing children, Montessori emphasizes the overarching drive for "independence." One with character is "independent in his powers and character, able to work and assert his mastery over all that depends on him" (1: 151). "Normal" childhood is fundamentally a "conquest of independence" where the child seeks "to co-ordinate his movements and to bring them under his control" (1: 161, see 1: 75–86).[29] Those with character pursue activities that cultivate capacities that enable them to perform more exercises of agency in general. J. F. Herbart, whose account of character likely influenced Montessori,[30] elucidates "the idea of perfection" in terms of "the *activity* of the growing man—the totality of his inward unconditioned vitality and susceptibility. The greater this totality—*the fuller, more expanded, and harmonious*—the greater is the perfection, and the greater the promise of the realization of our good will" (Herbart 1908: 110). In §5, I pointed out that agency involves being literally active rather than passive. Here there is a further point. Agents pursue activities that promote capacities for fuller, more expanded, and more harmonious activity.

Self-perfection also inspires agents to push the limits of their capabilities. To some degree, this pushing of limits is intrinsic to normative self-governance; once one has fully mastered an activity, that activity can no longer be effortful work. While in some sense it can still reflect who one is (and one might even be held responsible for it), it no longer engages one as an agent. To some degree, too, pushing limits is necessary in order to enhance one's abilities. For Montessori, however, the effort to go further, and even to develop new but recognizable standards of perfection is simply part of self-perfection. Alasdair MacIntyre makes similar points about practices, building into his definition of a practice that through engaging in practices "human powers to achieve excellence, and human conceptions of the ends and goods involved, are systematically extended" (MacIntyre 1981: 187). Nietzsche comes closer to Montessori's conception of self-extension with claims such as that "your true nature lies, not hidden deep within you, but immeasurably high above you" (Nietzsche [1873] 1997: 129). Agents seek self-perfection in part by seeking to go beyond wherever they find themselves to be.

Third and finally, beyond self-perfection and the perfections internal to their activity, agents seek the perfection of their species, community, and even "cosmos." Montessori regularly refers to a "cosmic purpose" (17: 166) or to one's "cosmic task, his collaboration with others in work for his environment, for the whole universe ... towards creative fulfillment" (6: 25). Young children pursue this cosmic task unconsciously through their efforts at self-perfection and absorption of culture. Even adults often primarily promote perfection of the whole only implicitly. Those with character, however, increasingly strive explicitly for perfection of wholes greater than each individual:

> By character we mean the behavior of men driven (though often unconsciously) to make progress. This is the general tendency. Humanity and society have to progress in evolution ... [L]et us consider a purely human center of perfection, the progress of mankind. Someone makes a discovery and society progresses along that line ... If we consider what is known of geography and history, we see this constant progress, because in every age some man has added a point to the circle of perfection which fascinated him and drove him to action.
>
> (1: 191)

Even if not fully consciously, those with character are attracted to activities that facilitate reaching new heights individually and also pushing humanity to new heights. Children's interest in absorbing culture develops independence that enables them to contribute in their own ways to the advancement of culture. The artist and scientist whose work Montessori describes as being interrupted cry out not only "Our inspiration is lost" but also, equally importantly, "humanity will be deprived of a poem, an artistic masterpiece, a useful discovery" (9: 17). We need "an education that will give ... readiness to shed prejudices in the interests of common work for the cosmic plan" (6: 47).

When those with character have "a natural attraction towards ... perfection" (1: 189), it is this threefold perfection to which they are attracted. Such agents seek activities that they can do well, and they seek to do those activities well, and in doing so they seek self-perfection and they seek to contribute to the increased perfection of their species and their world. None of these intentions need be wholly conscious (1: 191). Neither the child working on cylinder blocks nor the athlete heading toward the goal is consciously attentive to the ways that they are building up their own capacities, for example, but their ability to remain interested in the work they are doing in part depends upon the role of that work in self-perfection.[31]

9.3 Open-ended Perfectionism

For Montessori, both self-perfection and species-perfection are open-ended in two crucial ways. First, unlike the perfectionisms of Aristotle or Aquinas—or even Marx or T.H. Green—Montessori's perfectionism is open-ended in that it leaves open what work or kinds of self-governance to perfect: "Man does not have a precise heredity to do one special thing ... he is not obliged to do just one thing ... Every man must prepare in himself an adaptation that is not hereditary. He must prepare his own adaptation" (17: 91). While other animals have specific, determinate "perfections" of their natures, *human* nature has no specific perfections built in; perfecting one's character involves setting for oneself a determinate "task" (17: 91) that is not itself determined by one's nature: "the urge for perfection can be seen ... in many forms" (24: 53). In that sense, Montessori's perfectionism is open in a way similar to that of some readings of Nietzsche's perfectionism, where there is no single sort of life toward which every noble soul should aspire, but the diversity of lives that noble souls will aim toward are all, say, life-affirming rather than life-denying, or all ways of "being oneself" or living a life of "genius" (Conant 2010: 207; Rutherford 2018a).[32] As Donald Rutherford has put it, for Nietzsche "there is one *kind* of ideal appropriate to every human being—that of an autonomous existence in which one 'becomes who one is'—but that ideal will take different forms" (Rutherford 2018b: 226). Likewise, for Montessori, the ideal form of human life is a life of character, wherein one expresses agency in self-chosen, persistent work and strives for perfection,[33] but what work one engages in, and what specific forms of perfection one aims to realize, varies from person to person: "It is certain that all the individuals are different from each other; there are ... individual differences, very great ones" (24: 62).[34]

Importantly, openness in Montessori is not mere situation-dependence. In Aristotle's ethics, what is fitting for a given situation depends upon specific features of that situation. A virtuous person must have phronesis (practical wisdom) to discern, based on those features, what to do in that situation; indeterminacy regarding what constitutes excellent activity arises from *situation-dependence*. For Montessori, by contrast, character is *open-ended* in that even in a fully specified situation, there is no specific course of action that the person with character (and practical wisdom) would do. Admiral Byrd, one of Montessori's exemplars of character, first set foot on the South Pole because he "felt ... the attraction of doing something never before done, and so he planted his banner among the others in the zone of perfection" (1: 191–2). There were, however, many things that had never been done before, many things that could have contributed to his own self-perfection and the perfection of the species. Adventuring to the South Pole, excelling in portraiture, seeking new principles of chemistry (or even refining current principles), or investigating moral philosophy can all manifest character. One who engages in any of these tasks well has character; in that sense, character underdetermines the course of one's life.

There is a second sense in which perfection is open-ended, namely that the pursuit of perfection is always on-going, something humanity as a whole never completes: "human evolution is continuous" (17: 145). As individuals pursue individual perfections and the improvement of human culture, standards of perfection develop in new directions: "man's needs become more and more refined as his progress goes on" (Montessori [1936] 2009: 37). The artistic masterpiece of today opens up new visions for what art can be, which prompt new efforts of new generations of artists toward new perfections, which in turn modify future possibilities.

Those with character raise society to new levels from which it reaches even higher: "now man is in a phase in which he must decide for himself how far he can proceed in the culture that belongs to the whole of humanity ... no matter what he chooses, he must realize that culture never finishes" (14: 37). In this context, part of children's power and promise is precisely their capacity to absorb as commonplaces what were magnificent accomplishments in the past. Children who speak and write and engage in mathematical operations and mix colors and paint and learn geography all absorb in a few years cultural inheritances that required generations to develop. From those inheritances, children grow to create new cultural products and possibilities that will be absorbed by future generations. Throughout, cultural progress develops without a fixed end-point, constantly creating new opportunities to push new limits of human perfection.

Because the concept of perfection is open-ended, it provides a context for the development and expression of individuality. Montessori repeatedly emphasizes that as people "form their character ... [t]hey become individuals" (17: 156). Because "man ... must construct ... his [own] movements" and human "potential is immense," "each individual can develop some of this potential [and] construct his own unique type ... that distinguishes him from the others" (17: 167). At the level of individual self-perfection, "every individual has different powers to bring to fruition" and "they are not ... all destined to 'do the same thing,'" so each "produces his own perfection" (1: 65–6). In terms of species-perfection, we might emphasize that each person who "added a point to the circle of perfection" did so because of what specifically "fascinated *him* and drove *him* to action" (1: 191, emphasis added).

There are at least two ways to think about the relationship between individualism and open-endedness. On the one hand, we might see each person as having a set individual destiny, such that while perfection *as such* is open-ended, my individuality dictates what counts as perfection *for me*.[35] Thus, for instance, while other ways of doing something never before done might have been possible in general, for *Admiral Byrd*, only something like going to the South Pole could satisfy *his* striving for perfection. At times, Montessori suggests this approach to individuality. When she points out, for instance, that "In order to bring out individuality, we must have identical objects upon which each individual works" (24: 67), she seems to have in mind that children have innate individualizing features that educators can observe in how each chooses to work with different materials in a common classroom. On the other hand, however, we might see individuality as a *consequence* of open-endedness. In a rich environment, individuals can pursue different activities to different degrees, thereby cultivating different agential capacities and interests, and thereby becoming different individuals. On this account, Admiral Byrd became the unique individual that he was through, in part, choosing to enact ideals of perfection by going to the South Pole rather than by refining principles of chemistry. Montessori suggests this understanding of individualism, at least as it applies to children, when she emphasizes with Wordsworth that "the child is father of the man" (22: 169; cf. Wordsworth 1802):

> Man ... brings no abilities with him into the world, yet his gifts are unsurpassed in ... learning ... [For example,] of skilled movements he can acquire the most varied imaginable: those of the craftsman, the acrobat, the dancer, the musician and champions in the many fields of sport. But none of these come from a mere ripening of the organs ... It is always a matter of experience in action; of

practice; ... of education. Every person is the author of his own skills, yet the physical constitution with which he starts is the same. It is the man himself who produces his own perfection.

(1: 65)

While we start with similar basic capacities, we shape those capacities through exercises of agency in which we select specific work, cultivating specific individual perfections, equipping ourselves to contribute to species-perfection in unique ways.

Ultimately, it is neither necessary nor possible to arbitrate between these two ways of understanding individuality. Individuals manifest subtle differences in the way they attend to the world around them. An "inner force" "draws the attention of each individual especially to certain things in preference to certain others ..., forming creative constructions of varying types" (18: 197). Even in early life, when guiding instincts are relatively uniform in prompting development in generic ways, "individuals choose their own different roads; for example, ... in attaining perfect coordination of movement some children unconsciously analyze these motions in one way, others in another. Each one seeks their own way of reaching the same end" (18: 80). Who a child becomes is due in part to these subtle variations in how they develop their capacities, but this development—and thus the individuality of each person—is also dictated by what opportunities for action there are in the world around them. Each child learns the language(s) with which they grow up, with accents at least in part unique to them. Each absorbs skills, interests, and concepts of perfection from cultures in which they live, though with their own individual variations. As we grow, these variations shape different individuals: "the individuality which unfolds is of the child's own making" (Montessori [1936] 2009: 34). By the time Admiral Byrd reached adulthood, making advances in chemistry was no longer a sort of advancement that *he* could make, partly due to lack of skills, and partly due to lack of interest. My unique individuality, which helps concretize an otherwise open-ended concept of perfection, arises due to my own agency, which agency is in turn shaped by how my individuality interacts with my environment.

This open-ended and individualizing conception of character, which requires striving for and shaping one's distinctive perfection, provides a valuable focus for contemporary moral sensibilities. We arguably live in an era of "the ethics of authenticity," within which being "true to oneself" is one of, if not *the*, highest ethical ideal (Taylor 1992). Montessori's concept of perfection likewise emphasizes authenticity. The "good" person pursues *his own* passions to "add a point to the circle which fascinate[s] *him*" (1: 191). This moral ideal of an agency-promoting and authentic but deeply indeterminate pursuit of perfection consists in "multiplying the forces of the free spirit, making it almost divine" in a way that "Frederick Nietzsche has embodied ... in ... Zarathustra" (Montessori 1912: 69; 2: 361; cf. Conant 2010). Like Nietzsche, Montessori emphasizes how the perfection one pursues need be neither "universal" human perfection nor even perfections pursued by others:

> the child ... selects his own tendencies, which were at first confused and disordered in his unreflected acts. Every child reveals himself, and it is remarkable how clearly individual differences stand out if we follow this procedure.
>
> (2: 55–6; cf. Nietzsche 1967: 217; Rutherford 2018b: 215–6)

However, Montessori's notion of character corrects the contemporary focus on individuality and authenticity in several important respects. Most fundamentally, character is *normative*; it depends upon ideals of perfection toward which one strives. These ideals need not be universal or external to particular activities of self-perfection, but truly to express oneself is to strive for perfection in accordance with norms one prescribes to oneself through activities one engages in and capacities one cultivates. Relatedly, *effortful work* is the proper locus of self-expression. In contemporary culture, people too often express themselves through consumption, but Montessori rightly notes that consumptive activity cannot ultimately be a form of self-perfection because consumption, however self-directed, is fundamentally about passive enjoyment rather than active work. Moreover, not only is character oriented toward work, but it takes work to *develop* character. Too often, authenticity is seen as being true to some "self" that one just happens to find oneself to be, and more and more people find themselves at a loss both to discern who they are and to be "true" to that self. But Montessori recognizes that the "self" worth being true to is a self that emerges through what Nietzsche calls "obedience over a long period of time and in a single direction" (Nietzsche 1966: 101), that is, a consistent and sustained effort toward tasks that one takes to be worth pursuing. Choice of and endurance in work are perfections that require practice and attention. This is particularly true because, like Nietzsche, Montessori sees authenticity and self-*overcoming* as intrinsically linked. While one might think that *overcoming* oneself and being *true to* oneself would be opposed, both Montessori and Nietzsche recognize (albeit in different ways) that the human "self" aims for perfections whereby it transcends itself (Nietzsche 1997: 129; cf. Rutherford 2018b: 226–7). And Montessori recognizes that this process of authentic self-overcoming depends upon a strength of character that can only (or primarily) be cultivated in childhood, because authentic self-overcoming—like the moral sense itself (see Chapter 2)—manifests a capacity that depends upon *early exercise* for healthy development. In a culture that increasingly—and rightly—values authenticity, the recognition that authenticity depends upon normative orientation toward the work of self-perfection invaluably clarifies this moral ideal. Given widespread malaise caused when people find themselves unable to realize this ideal, attention to processes by which children's capacities for character can be cultivated marks an essential contribution to solving some of the most important moral crises of our contemporary, post-Nietzschean world.

10 Agency and Responsibility

In §2, I discussed the commonplace view that "children are proper objects of paternalistic treatment" (Schapiro 1999: 717), such that one need not defer to their wills even in matters of concern to them, and much of this chapter has laid out an approach to agency that supports anti-paternalism even regarding children. For Schapiro and others, however, paternalism is linked with another "uncontroversial" intuition in our treatment of children, namely that "we tend not to hold children responsible for what they do in the same way that we hold adults responsible for their actions" (Schapiro 1999: 717):

> [C]hildren are objects but not full subjects of duties. The very youngest of children have no moral or legal duties to adults or to anyone else ... Even older children, who are regarded as subjects of at least a range of duties, are not held strictly accountable for them. This is so insofar as their infractions are regarded by adults as occasions for discipline and instruction, rather than resentment and blame. Resentment and blame issue from the standpoint of an equal; they are the responses of an aggrieved party who stands to the offender as an equal party to a mutually binding social contract. Discipline and instruction, by contrast, issue from the perspective of a moral supervisor, one whose role it is to see to it that others comply or are made fit to comply with certain standards of conduct. It is a feature of children's less-than-full status that their violations of the moral, legal, and institutional duties to which they are subject are dealt with from a supervisory, rather than a participatory perspective.
>
> (Schapiro 2003: 576–7)

Alongside respect-worthy agency, then, we should add a conception of responsibility-agency, on the basis of which individuals are held responsible for their actions. The denial of respect-worthy agency and of responsibility-agency is often linked, and many theorists see the agential conditions for moral responsibility as equivalent to those for moral respect (e.g., Schapiro 1999, 2003). Matthew Talbert rightly notes that whatever view philosophers give of the prerequisites for moral responsibility, "very young children ... are generally taken to lack them" (Talbert 2019). In this short section, I cannot discuss all contemporary approaches to moral responsibility, so instead I merely highlight some points where Montessori's attention to the dignity of children should encourage revisiting commonplace assumptions not only about paternalism but also about (moral) responsibility.

As is evident in Schapiro's quotation above, philosophers often understand moral responsibility in a broadly penal way, in terms of an accountability for actions that might bring direct punishment and would at least warrant resentment and blame (or gratitude, praise, and possible reward). In his classic "Freedom and Resentment," P. F. Strawson defines moral responsibility in terms of "personal reactive attitudes," such that to be personally responsible is at least in part to be an appropriate object of such attitudes, and—as R. Jay Wallace puts it—"we must interpret the relevant facts [about responsibility] as somehow dependent on our practices of holding people responsible" (Wallace 1996: 89; cf. Strawson 1962; Schapiro 1999: 717). Strawson's main example of such a reactive attitude is "resentment" (or anger), such that to be responsible for some misdeed is for others to be justified in feeling resentment or anger toward one for that misdeed. Whether one adopts a specifically Strawsonian approach or not, penal accounts of responsibility, where responsibility is equivalent to deserving retaliatory attitudes, have three important features. First, they make moral responsibility primarily interpersonal or second-personal, something relevant first and foremost to what others can rightly expect of me or how others can rightly respond to my actions.

Responsibility ascriptions are part of something like a moral "conversation" (McKenna 2012) in which we engage in an "exchange of moral criticism and justification" (Wallace 1996: 164). We hold responsible when we "demand (require) certain conduct from one another and respond adversely to one another's failures to comply with these demands" (Watson 1988: 262, quoted in Talbert 2019). Second, penal accounts link moral responsibility with deservingness of various external harms (or goods), whether these be punishments (or reward) or social disapprobation or even just guilt or shame. Third, particularly given their widespread focus on resentment/anger, punishment, blame, and guilt, penal approaches lend themselves to what Martha Nussbaum has called the "magical thinking" wherein victims "think that inflicting pain on the offender cancels or assuages [their] own pain" (Nussbaum 2016: 24).

Montessori rejects the penal approach to responsibility. She objects to those who link "responsibility" and "duty" with "the idea of punishing ... like a judge before a guilty party" (Montessori [1931] 2019: 90). Consistent with Frankfurt, Wallace, and others, she sees ascriptions of personal responsibility as essential parts of ethical life, and agrees with Wallace's emphasis on formulating appropriate conditions of responsibility from our actual practices. Montessori's approach to responsibility differs from the penal model in several respects, however.

First, she does not take *adults'* reactive attitudes as paradigmatic, and she often notes that children given freedom in healthy environments treat one another in ways that diverge from the "natural law of the adult conscience" according to which "if somebody has done harm, he should pay the penalty" (24: 203). One feature of children's approach to responsibility involves a forward-looking focus on improving themselves and their world rather than a concern with punishment or blame.

> If a child breaks a vase, another child goes around and picks up the broken pieces and puts everything in order, consoling the child who has broken it. There is no question of who has broken the vase. Nobody questions the justice of the second child. There is no punishment for the person who has broken the vase. The questions of who, what, and why do not seem to arise. If in our social life, we thought in the same fashion, and we felt that we should remedy social disorders no matter who had committed them ...,social welfare programs today would not be in the sad state in which they are![36]
>
> (24: 204)

I will discuss children's alternative conceptions of responsibility and fairness in more detail in Chapter 4, and again in Chapter 6 when discussing the development of adult concepts of justice. My main point here is simply that contemporary philosophers' frequent appeal to "our practices" (e.g., Strawson 1962: 24; Wallace 1996: 89) require some specification of who "we" are, and Montessori is particularly alive to the possibility that communities of children can reveal healthier practices of holding responsible than adults.

Second, in her substantive view, Montessori rejects all three aforementioned features of penal approaches to responsibility. Consistent with her emphasis on character, Montessori's paradigmatic conception of personal responsibility is first-personal; *I* take responsibility for my actions, in ways that do not depend upon having a responsibility to or before others. Pre-eminently, I take responsibility to the perfectionist norms intrinsic to the work I am engaged in. When Sofia puts seven of the eight cylinders into holes and the final one does not fit, she not only recognizes that something is out of place, but takes responsibility for the failure and sees it as her responsibility to remove and replace the cylinders in order to complete the exercise properly. Each individual takes responsibility, through their effortful work, for their own processes of self-perfection.

Montessori thus replaces a punitive response to error—one that focuses on punishment, resentment, anger, and guilt—with a growth-oriented approach that focuses on improvement and change. Resentment or punishment is "superfluous" where someone has "set himself to work" toward improvement (1: 221). Instead, Montessori proposes that we look at responsibility in terms of one's role in correcting mistakes as part of normative self-governance:

> Everyone makes mistakes. This is one of life's realities, and to admit it is already to have taken a great step forward. If we are to treat the narrow path of truth ...,we have to agree that all of us can err ... So it is that we cultivate a friendly feeling towards error, to treat it as a companion inseparable from our lives, as something having a purpose, which it truly has ... The tiny child starts toddling uncertainly on his feet, wobbles and falls but ends by walking easily. He corrects his errors.
>
> (1: 223)

Consistent with her view of character, Montessori's model of responsibility emphasizes the "control of error," built into Montessori materials, which allows the child to "be aware of his own errors" and thereby "become interested in them" (1: 224). Through these materials, children hold themselves responsible in ways that patronizing adults often decline to do.

> The child is his own critic, and strives to carry out work perfectly controlling his error. While trying to become master of his own hand, he finds the object more severe than a teacher. A teacher would never have the heart to scold the child because he has not been careful ... The teacher has a great deal of compassion for the incapacity of the child, and will avoid giving him fragile things that will break ... .The object is a teacher that never forgives and reveals every little error that one commits. It is a scolding that the child does not mind.
>
> (24: 41)

To be responsible for an error is to be the one who committed or performed the error and who can correct it and improve. If Sofia put the cylinder in the wrong hole, the misplaced cylinder is her own error, and because she is attentively engaged in this work, it is hers to correct. Moreover, the misplaced cylinder is a symptom of a deeper error, a failure in Sofia's self-perfection. She has not yet developed perfections of visual acuity, memory, and manual dexterity to properly complete this work. So she must "recognize [her] own mistakes, and correct them!" (1: 224; cf. Vargas 2013).

Once we shift from interpersonal punitive responsibility to individual self-perfecting responsibility, the paradigmatic response to another's responsibility for her errors becomes respect and patience rather than anger or resentment. On contemporary penal theories of punishment, when a child fails to tie his shoes quickly, one either does not view him as responsible for this error or one is angry and blames him. By contrast, for Montessori, the proper response to a responsible agent's failures is to let him continue to work on self-perfection, to "never help another ... when he is making a constructive effort to do things for himself," or, if he really needs help, to "help [him] do it by [him]self" (24: 49; 22: 175). Of course, this respectful ascription of responsibility to another applies only to those who hold themselves responsible; cases of defiant and disorderly actions will be discussed in Chapters 4 and 6. The main point here is that Montessori's paradigm for responsibility is not the responsibility ascribed to offenders by their resentful victims but the responsibility agents ascribe to themselves when involved in attentive, norm-governed work.

There are things for which adults can be held responsible but children cannot (see Chapter 6), but children can and do hold themselves and one another responsible in an improvement-oriented way rather than penal way. This is a lesson Montessori thinks children teach us about the nature of responsibility, rather than an essential difference between how children ought to be treated and how adults ought to be treated.

11 Conclusion

Montessori developed her moral theory in and for the context of education. Educators should create environments that allow children to act freely and satisfy their needs, and in those environments, children take joy in developing and expressing their agency through a love of work focused on persistent, attentive, active engagement in normative self-governance oriented by ideals of perfection. The capacity for and tendency toward such expressions of agency is character, and it is the task of the educator to make room for character and its development. Children learn to button their coats and read and do math. They develop intellectual virtues like sensory acuity and intellectual humility. But the most important thing that children in Montessori classrooms develop is character, and they develop character simply by having a space where their character is not stifled, where they can proceed along their normal path of self-perfection.

This ideal of character as the highest good applies not merely to education, but to all aspects of ethical life. All of us should respect and express our own agency through engaging in attentive and norm-governed work. We should actively govern ourselves in accordance with norms intrinsic to the practices in which we engage and should strive for self-perfection through enhancing our own capacities.[37] Together, we should create a world within which character can be expressed and cultivated.

4

Respect for Others

1 The Second Part of Ethics: Respect

"Character," and the agency that one with character expresses, is the pre-eminent value within Montessori's moral theory. She bases her pedagogy on creating environments within which children can express their characters through attentive work they choose for themselves. However, individual character is only one part of Montessori's overall conception of ethical life: "Two things are necessary: the development of individuality [character] and the participation of the individual in a truly social life" (10: 52). Throughout her writings, Montessori emphasizes the twin tasks of cultivating individual character and cultivating social virtues that enable full participation in a just and healthy society. She refers to "a double development, that of the individual and [of] social relations" (14: 22). At times, Montessori even identifies "morality" with the social dimension of her theory:

> Morality, which is usually considered as an abstraction, we wish to consider as a technique which allows us to live together harmoniously … [M]oral and social teaching [consists of] teach[ing] [one] to respect other people, [and] to help all who need help.
>
> (14: 20, 25)

Montessori's approach to "social relations" emphasizes respect, help (as a form of respect), "solidarity," and social organization. In Chapter 5, I discuss solidarity, with its related virtue of obedience, and in Chapter 6, I show how respect, help, and solidarity all get enriched through articulated principles of social organization. The most basic form of social relation, however, is mutual respect. This respect addresses the fundamental social "problem" of "how all can be free in the same closed environment, when each can act in the way he wishes," solving that problem by proposing that each "leaves the others to be active so long as he also can be active. Each respects the work of the other" (14: 22).

"Morality" in this social sense is essentially a solution to a social coordination problem, a solution Montessori develops through creating contexts in which children address social problems for themselves. She vehemently rejects moral education that would "keep … children quiet to listen to someone who speaks … of morals" (18: 265).

Instead, children can and should learn by doing; they should be allowed to exercise agency within "an active community" where "if social virtues need to develop, they will do so at that moment when children must of themselves adapt themselves to these virtues" (1: 203, 18: 265). As with other pedagogical materials, where children begin with relatively simple exercises in constrained contexts and then develop more and more complex skills, so too socially they begin in a carefully constructed classroom designed to prompt certain sorts of coordination problems and then are gradually introduced to wider and wider fields of application for basic moral values: "We cannot teach this kind of morality to children of three, but experience can" (1: 202–3). Thus, Montessori constructed classrooms that encouraged everyday, child-proportioned conflicts to prompt awareness of the need to respect others (cf. Krogh 1981). She defends scarcity of materials, for example, in moral terms:

> There is only one specimen of each object, and if a piece is in use when another child wants it, the latter—if he is normalized—will wait for it to be released. Important social qualities derive from this. The child comes to see that he must respect the work of others, not because someone has said that he must, but because this is a reality he meets in his daily experience. There is only one between many children, so there is nothing for it but to wait. And since this happens every hour of the day for years, the idea of respecting others, and of waiting one's turn, becomes a habitual part of life which always grows more mature.
>
> (1: 202)

Given scarcity, there is "nothing for it" but to respect others' work. Respect enables and emerges from character-driven activity in community. "This experience of self-control teaches him that each person in the world has his own place and that we must respect the places of others. It is impossible to learn this fact by hearing it as a moral principle. It must be developed through experience" (24: 200).

While necessary in order for children to work peacefully in a community together, respect also becomes "cemented by affection" as children "come to know one another's characters and to have a reciprocal feeling for each other's worth" (1: 205). Consistent with Montessori's moral sense theory, children in social conditions of freedom, working alongside other children, come to recognize others' dignity and the propriety of treating them with respect: "spontaneously social sentiments come forth," not merely to solve social problems in an abstract or self-interested sense but also from genuine "sympathy" (24: 49; 9: 242). Children do not see respect primarily as a command from God or parents, an abstract requirement of practical reason, or a way to promote hedonic happiness; instead, through joy and peace in community, they rightly see respect as the basis for shared ethical life.

2 Character and Respect

The emphasis on both individual character and mutual respect might seem to introduce a tension in Montessori's moral theory. In fact, to many of her educationalist contemporaries and popular critics, the focus on individual development conflicts with socialization:

> I think that I need not repeat that our method considers the development of the individual and personality. When considering it under this light people often think that it lacks social education, because the prevalent idea is that, if one considers the individual, one does not consider society and vice versa. Therefore, they say that if our method is individual it cannot be social.
>
> (14: 19)

The problem of how to bridge the apparent "gap" from concern with self to concern with others is a classic problem within moral philosophy, from Socrates's attempt to vindicate justice against the egoistic skepticism of Thrasymachus in Plato's *Republic* or Confucius's claim in the Analects (e.g., 6: 30) that the virtuous/benevolent (*ren*) person does for others what he would have for himself, to Hobbes's *Leviathan*, which argues for principles of justice and solidarity based on the basic principle that each seeks his own advantage. Even if charges of a conflict between individual and social development are exaggerated in general, one might think that *Montessori*'s conception of individual character poses special problems. Montessori's account of agency focuses on following through on guiding instincts, persisting in work that interests oneself, and pursuing self-perfection. Moreover, in her emphasis on self-perfection, Montessori endorses the "Nietzsche[an]" ideal of "the superman," according to which "man can reinforce his own strength by ... powers which will urge him on upwards towards the infinite ... Yes, to be *more* than man" (9: 257; see too 2: 361–2). Given Nietzsche's own claim, made "at the risk of displeasing innocent ears," that "egoism belongs to the nature of a noble soul—I mean that unshakable faith that to a being such as 'we are' other beings must be subordinate by nature and have to sacrifice themselves" (Nietzsche 1966: 215),[1] Montessorian individualist perfectionism might seem inconsistent with a robust account of mutual respect for persons.

However, Montessori rejects the dichotomy between individual self-perfection and mutual respect. At the most basic level, she insists, "Now it is a fact that one cannot develop the individual outside society, and that one cannot have a real society unless it is formed by individuals" (14: 19). More pointedly, she critiques Nietzsche for his failure (or perceived failure[2]) to connect his *Übermensch* with genuine concern for others. This is not merely a failure of opportunity, but a blindness to the implications of Nietzsche's own ideal:

> To Friedrich Nietzsche, the superman was an idea without practical consequence...
> His conception offered no help in overcoming the ills of humanity; rather was it as a chain binding man to earth, there to seek means to create of himself the man superior to himself; and thus leading him astray into egotism, cruelty and folly.
>
> (9: 257)

Montessori accuses Nietzsche of an egotism that sets its sights too low, binding itself to all-too-narrow scopes for agency rather than taking on the work of overcoming the ills of humanity. When considering the attunement that active concentration requires, she asks,

> How could [those with character] live quietly amidst evil? If under the windows of our house people were piling up refuse until we felt that the air was being vitiated, could we bear this without protesting and insisting on the removal of that which was causing us to suffer? ... It is characteristic of "life" to purge the environment and the soul of substances injurious to health ... [T]his is the morality that springs from sensibility: the *action* of purifying the world, of removing the obstacles that beset life, of liberating the spirit from the darkness of death. The merits of which every man feels he owes an account to his conscience are not such things as having enjoyed music or made a discovery; he must be able to say what he has done to save and maintain life. These purifying merits, like progress, have no limits.
>
> (9: 256–7)

The drive for personal perfection that is constitutive of character also equips individuals with a "feeling" for the ills and potentials of others. The ideal of striving toward perfection, an ideal rooted in humans' deepest inner impulses, naturally realizes itself in a project of liberating others.

There are three main ways in which Montessori connects respect with character. First and most basically, while character is the primary good in Montessori's moral philosophy, respect is the primary attitude to take toward that good. Second, character, freely expressed and cultivated, gives rise to respect, both for others and for one's own character. Third and finally, respect for others is itself an activity in which one with character engages and is, in that sense, partly constitutive of that person's character.

2.1 Respect for Character

In Chapter 3, I articulated a Montessorian concept of the agency expressed by one with character and showed that this agency meets requirements for internality, activity, normative self-governance, and persistence, even if it does not include high-order reflection or deliberative rationality. I suggested there that agency in this sense satisfies the conditions for what Nomy Arpaly calls "moral autonomy" or what I called "respect-worthy agency." That is, character—and the agency that flows from it—is directly worthy of respect. While character is the fundamental value within Montessori's moral philosophy, respect is the basic moral attitude that one should take toward that value.

Why think Montessorian character is worthy of respect? Because children *do* respect it. As I noted in Chapter 2, "studying ... these children and their mutual relationships in an atmosphere of freedom, the true secrets of society come to be revealed" (1: 206). Adults have profound interests in the continued oppression of children, and it is all too easy for us to silence our consciences when it comes to asserting our wills over those of our children. But when attentive and loving teachers observe free children in healthy environments, they find that children value and express respect for one another as agents: "the child leaves the others to be active so long as he also can be active. Each respects the work of the other. This shows that the interest of these individuals is to be active" (14: 22; see too 1: 202). To see respect for others' characters as a moral practice just *is* to recognize its value through an uncorrupted moral sense, and children perceive more clearly than many adults both the immediate value of respect in interpersonal interactions and the broader necessity of respect for a moral community of peace and joy. Free from adult-centered prejudices, children also more rightly perceive the *sort* of respect that has moral value. In particular, the social coordination problem that children solve with mutual respect is the problem of how to sustain agency in social conditions (with scarcity of resources), where "agency" is understood by the children in terms of neither whim-satisfaction nor reflective deliberation, but rather in terms of the expression of character.

For example, one of the principles of mutual respect in Montessori communities is that "the material must be taken from its place, and not from another child" (24: 177), so that children must wait for others to finish before using a particular material. The logic behind this rule, which is generally developed by children even if articulated by adults, is respect for pre-reflective agency. Constant inquiries directed to a child at work—"can I use that?"—force him to step back from what he is doing and address the question of whether his use of the material is justified given another's desire for it. This reflective move interrupts his flow and thereby interferes with the expression of agency in attentive work. The anger a child (or even adult) expresses when interrupted, which differs in quality from negative emotions felt when one is unable to begin an activity, exhibits the awareness that interruption is a particularly acute violation of agency. As we will see in more detail in §4.2, children rightly seek protection from interruption; they seek, to slightly modify Virginia Woolf's famous phrase, "room of their own" (Woolf 1929; cf. Frierson 2016b). Once we see the importance for children of having space to engage in attentive work, we can see that such space is important for adult society as well. Even once we have capacities for sophisticated reflection, deliberation, and justification of one's activities, adults defend the importance of "private"[3] realms where we can immerse ourselves in activities that we find meaningful without defending their meaningfulness to others, or even to ourselves.

Montessori does not offer abstract arguments to prove that character is worthy of respect. She perceives, and sees that children perceive, the value of attentive work, through the joy and peace felt both by those involved in the work and those who observe their uninterrupted activity. She perceives, and sees that children perceive, the value of respect for that attentive work, in the joy and peace of those who show such respect and the remorse felt by those with otherwise well-developed characters who fail to show respect.[4] And she perceives, and sees that children perceive, the value of respect through the moral beauty of societies—even small ones such as classrooms—shaped by solving problems of social coordination through mutual respect.

2.2 From Character to Respect

Character is the proper object of respect, and respect the appropriate attitude toward character. *Self*-respect of some sort is constitutive of character. To be internally related to one's guiding instincts and to pursue self-perfection is implicitly to respect one's agency and the character that agency expresses. Respect for *others'* agency is not directly constitutive of character; the Nietzschean *Übermensch* concerned only for *his own* self-perfection is a logical possibility. In working with children, however, Montessori observed that respect for others naturally results from developing one's own character: "easy adaptation to the social environment" arises "as a result of the phenomenon of concentration" (17: 233).

> After these manifestations [of character] ... true discipline is established, the most obvious results of which are closely related to what we will call "respect for the work of others and consideration for the rights of others." Henceforward a child no longer attempts to take away another's work; even if he covets it, he waits patiently until the object is free ... When discipline has been established by internal processes ... there is a mutual respect ... between the children ... and hence is born that complex discipline which ... must accompany the order of a community.
> (9: 70)

The normal state of human society is one of mutual respect, so respect for others arises from the "normalization" that takes place when children are given freedom in environments conducive to the expression of their characters.[5]

At times, Montessori describes the transition from individual character to mutual respect as a straightforward "experimental fact" (9: 52). More recent philosophers have sought conceptual arguments for a connection between individual agency and respect for others. Alan Gewirth, for example, insists that "a claim on the part of the agent that he has a right to perform his action" is both "an essential feature of [one's own] action" and a claim by which "he is logically committed to the generalization of this right-claim to all prospective agents" (Gewirth 1974: 62–3). Christine Korsgaard argues that respect for humanity as such is a constitutive norm for human practical reasoning because our reflective endorsement of any reasons for action requires that we ascribe normative significance to reflection as such (Korsgaard 1996a; 2009). Thomas Scanlon argues for mutual respect as essential to what we mean by the notions of right and wrong (Scanlon 1998). Unlike these more abstract philosophical arguments, Montessori's essentially psychological claim lays out perceptions of moral sense as it develops in children in conditions conducive to its exercise (see Chapter 2). Like these philosophers, however, she highlights how striving toward perfection pushes beyond each individual. We naturally see others' pursuit of perfection as equal in value to our own, so we naturally come to respect and admire it. Moreover, like philosophers such as Scanlon, Montessori attends to how requirements generated by respect for others "are not just formal imperatives; they are aspects of the positive value of a way of living with others" (Scanlon 1998: 162). As character-driven individuals live in community, respect fosters ways of living with one another that have clearly recognizable value.

Several features of character lend themselves toward respect. Because character is a pursuit of perfection, it requires and fosters conceptions of what is admirable. Those with character must appreciate the value of norm-governed work toward ideals of perfection, and while initially oriented toward their *own* pursuits, they come to admire, respect, and be inspired by others' similar achievements of perfection or efforts toward satisfying challenging norms.[6] Montessori reports that often, when children wait for material they would like to use, "there is no sense of patient resignation in a child waiting his turn. The child enthusiastically watches what the other child is doing, how he carries out his actions" (24: 48). A child interested in a particular form of activity naturally finds himself interested in another mastering that activity, and children pursuing self-perfection in general develop interest in others' strivings toward their perfections.

Moreover, whether consciously or not, those with character ultimately strive not merely for *self*-perfection but for perfection of the species, the community, and the cosmos (see Chapter 3, §9). In following "a light that leads them on to a better world," they find that "all work is done not only for ourselves but also for others" (9: 256; 17: 166). Insofar as those with character seek the perfection of "humanity and society" (1: 191), they avoid activity that undermines others' capacities.

The focus of those with character on doing work well also cuts off many tendencies that would otherwise hinder mutual respect. Those with character pursue *perfection*, which displaces the *possessiveness* and *envy* that Montessori rightly sees as threats to respect. Insofar as one seeks materials only as means toward self-perfecting activity, one has little incentive to hold onto materials one no longer needs or waste energies taking materials from others. For one with character, "Freedom to take an interest in all kinds of things leads to focusing attention not on the things themselves, but the knowledge he derives from them. Hence his longing to possess undergoes a transformation" (1: 199; see too 10: 103). Relatedly, children with character, "free to choose their occupations ... did not show any sign of envy or competition, but ... help[ed] each other" (3: 27). Because those with character seek *progress* in perfection, rather than relative *superiority*, others' excellences become reassurance that progress is possible rather than threats to one's sense of self (1: 209; cf. Dweck 2006: 30). In environments free from oppression and rich with opportunities for agency, children also lack the fear and insecurity that prevent development of healthy forms of respect: "The social sentiments are born from the fact that each child is allowed by circumstances to carry out these actions with exactitude and to repeat them as often as he pleases" (24: 49). Since each knows that his own agency will be respected, nothing hinders him from respecting others. Finally, precisely because it focuses on *work*, character prevents competitive or hostile motives for disrespect: "the children ... [are] too much absorbed in their work to indulge in any of the disorderly actions which had marked their conduct in the beginning" (9: 70).

Montessori observed that when given the opportunity to engage persistently in effortful work that they choose for themselves, children develop character, and a natural consequence of such development in social contexts is respect for others. While she offers no conceptual connection between character and respect, she rightly shows that there is no conflict between them, and she highlights features of character that make its extension into respect natural.

2.3 Respect *as* Character

One final connection between character and respect is worth noting. Because character seeks perfection with an indeterminate object (Chapter 3, §9), practices of respect can and do become objects of attention. Those with character seek perfection not only in playing instruments or learning history but also in respecting others. They seek to know, conform to, and improve standards of excellence for social interactions, pre-eminent among which are norms of mutual respect. Children are attracted to lessons in "grace and courtesy" that help them more properly address one another, resolve conflicts, or negotiate situations requiring respect (Bettman 2003). Children actively take on potential classroom conflicts as problem-solving opportunities. Montessori gives an example based on an exercise where children walk around an elliptical line drawn on the floor, an exercise typically focused on walking skill, balance, and coordination, which in this case takes on an added challenge of mutual respect:

> When children are "walking on the line" one of them may go in the opposite direction to all the others, and a collision seems inevitable. One's impulse is to seize the child and turn him around. But he looks out very well for himself, and solves the difficulty—not always in the same fashion, but always satisfactorily. Such problems abound at every step, and it gives the children great pleasure to face them. They feel irritated if we intervene, and it provides constant practice in dealing suitably with situations that no teacher would be able to invent. The teacher, instead, usually intervenes, but her solution ... disturbs the harmony of the group.
>
> (1: 203)

As with other skills, children actively work at perfecting their abilities to respect one another. They take pleasure in solving social problems, just as they take pleasure in solving puzzles or rightly placing cylinders in a block. As in those cases, children make mistakes, but lack of peace in the community and natural sympathy with one another provide a control of error indicating that a particular "solution" has failed.

For both children and adults, participation in an active community provides constant opportunities to self-perfect through addressing increasingly complex problems of social coordination that require increasingly refined skills at respecting others. As we deal with various situations repeatedly, respect in those cases becomes easy and habitual, just as we effortlessly learn to write or type and then those activities become habitual. But as in the case of all other skills, mastering basic skills allows for attempting more complex skills. One who has mastered typing can try to compose a paragraph, and one who has learned how (and how long, and in what way) to wait patiently for others to move up a queue can try waiting patiently to raise an important question in a heated debate, or can work on designing processes or environments that facilitate patience. Social life presents endless possibilities for moral self-improvement, and those with character take interest in pursuing those possibilities.

3 The Priority of Respect

As §2 shows, and as I'll reiterate in §4.1, character holds priority over respect in that children typically manifest respect for one another once they have (already) begun to express character through free activity in a suitable environment. There are at least two other senses, however, in which respect has priority over character. While character is the fundamental value in Montessori's moral theory and while respect naturally flows from character, respectful behavior is required even of those for whom respect doesn't flow from character. This priority of respectful behavior plays out in two important contexts: supervision of those without character by relevant authorities (whether teachers in a classroom or coercive authorities in adult society) and self-governance in accordance with principles of respect.

When children (or other people) lack character-based motives of respect, teachers (or other authorities) must protect and promote character through ensuring that everyone respects others in their actions; the teacher "must not only not interfere when the child is concentrating, she must also see that [the child] is not disturbed," which requires that she "be a policeman" with those who interfere with others (17: 229). Montessori's reference here to police is a reminder that the practice of enforcing basic principles of justice is an appropriate and common part of adult society: "The policeman has to defend the honest citizens from the disturbers" (17: 229). For both children and adults, respectful behavior is required, whether or not it flows from character.

Nonetheless, even while allowing for the enforcement of respect, Montessori does not invoke penal or retributive concepts of responsibility: "We need not punish or scold or admonish when we stop bad behavior" (17: 230). The point is to end the disrespectful behavior, and Montessori ultimately looks to character development, rather than fear of punishment, as a means for promoting genuine respect. Relatedly, what is stopped here is "bad behavior." Enforcement alone fosters, not respect, but respectful *actions*. Moreover, even with respect to behavior, enforcement is primarily negative, that is, the prevention of actions contrary to basic norms of respect.

In general, externally enforced respectful behavior should be limited to contexts where people lack character-based motives of respect. Just as Schapiro claims that children can be treated paternalistically because the child "does not really 'have' a will yet" (Schapiro 1999: 730), so too Montessori claims that when children are still "prey to all of their different naughtinesses," that is, before they attend to work they choose for themselves, teachers may "do what ... your common sense dictates" (17: 229).

> [The teacher's] principle is never to intervene when the child is immersed in his work, when he is struggling with his little difficulties, when this infantile social life which is being organized presents some problem to be solved, as though she were leaving this little soul in a gymnasium where it is fortifying itself. However, if the child is disorderly, bothers his companions, or, when he is simply working imperfectly, then she intervenes and she redoubles her cares about such children until they have found the right path by which to enter into activity.
> (Montessori in De Giorgi 2019: 62)

Discerning when to intervene in children's social interactions requires judgment. As Montessori noted in the example of children "walking the line," adults have a general "impulse to ... intervene" when children are faced with social problems, but "Apart from exceptional cases, we ought to leave such [social] problems to the children" (1: 203). The challenge is discerning the exceptional cases (24: 199).

The problem with discerning when to intervene arises because, as I pointed out in §2.3, respect is an activity that children with character seek to do well, approaching social challenges as problems through which they can perfect their skills of respectful interaction. Unlike challenges children face in working with materials they choose for themselves, however, social problems generally arise uninvited. Even if children take interest in solving them, they did not choose to work on this particular problem at this time. This difference can be substantial and can generate ambiguity about whether a particular social difficulty is purely agency-inhibiting or whether it is an opportunity for children to exercise agency; in some cases, a social situation might even be an excellent opportunity for one child but agency-inhibiting for another.

While ultimately decisions about whether, when, and how to intervene in order to protect agency require well-cultivated moral perception, Montessori provides a few guidelines. She focuses on the case of teachers and children, but some of these guidelines can apply to social relations amongst adults as well. Generally speaking, adults should intervene when the children involved have not yet experienced the moments of intense concentration that "normalize" them and that come with attentive work. As with Montessori's deference to children's moral perceptions (Chapter 2), so here Montessori emphasizes that free children in healthy environments are adept at solving social problems well. For adults, this general guideline requires a different sort of application. To varying degrees, adults internalize oppressive moral structures, various deep-seated psychological fears and repressions, and deficient moral sensibilities. Thus, for adults, coercive enforcement of respectful behavior will be necessary and appropriate more often than for children. At the same time, as we will see in Chapter 6, adults have more refined conceptual and reflective capabilities, so we can and should organize coercive mechanisms and secure broad consent for them.

Montessori also points out that just solutions to social problems arise "where individual strengths are more or less equal" (24: 200); significant inequality can transform a situation from cooperative problem-solving to domination (24: 199). Montessori focuses on the significant power differential between teacher and students, but the point applies more broadly. When "solutions" to social problems emerge through the influence of privileged and more powerful agents over weaker and more vulnerable ones, the resulting situations may end up being unjust, contexts where the character of the weaker is sacrificed to the interests of the stronger.

Montessori also notes that "social experience and social organization will ... grow with the child and become more and more complicated" (24: 219). While she is always wary of underestimating children, intervention can also be called for when a social situation is simply too complex for children of a given level. Similarly, amongst adults, negotiating complex social realities may require complex organization when no single adult can properly discern what behavior would be "respectful" in a given context.

Throughout all of these cases, teachers and other enforcers of respectful behavior should be wary of over-enforcement and over-interference; agents with character naturally develop respect for others, and processes of solving social problems help to foster this connection between character and respect. Teachers and caregivers should provide children opportunities to solve social problems for themselves, and governments and institutions should avoid infantilizing adults through over-prescribing and over-enforcing social relations. At the same time, as we will see in more detail in Chapter 6, part of the process of growing into adults involves applying concepts, rules, and organizational structures to norms of respect, and ultimately, legitimate authorities have the responsibility to protect people's agency through ensuring basic respectful behavior.

So far in this section, I have focused on the priority that third parties—teachers or governments—must give to respectful behavior. A second important way that respect is primary is internal to each agent. While Montessori's character-based emphases on individuality, progress, and perfection resonate with Nietzschean perfectionism, her conception of respect, like Kant's, requires one to limit all one's actions—including one's pursuit of perfection—if and when required by respect for others. As one engages in particular projects and seeks self-perfection in various ways, she can never violate standards of respect. Just as for Kant, one ought to "so act that you use humanity, whether in your own person or in that of any other, always at the same time as an end, never merely as a means" (Kant [1785] 1996: 80), so with Montessori one must respect others' activities even while pursuing one's own. For this reason, the child interested in manifesting his character by working with a particular material waits patiently for another child to finish using that material (§2), and a child engaged in attentive work interrupts his own activity in order to help another in real need (see §4.3). Likewise, an adult whose pursuit of this or that personal perfection would violate anothers' rights either pursues different goals or finds respectful means for pursuing her goals. Admiral Byrd should not enslave or rob others in order to get to the North Pole.

There are at least four reasons one cannot legitimately choose to express character in ways inconsistent with respect toward others. First, there is no basis for preferring the agency of one individual over that of another, so at a systematic level, there is no reason to allow legitimate expressions of one's own character when those abridge another's freedom. Second, precisely because character is open-ended,[7] disrespectful manifestations of agency are never required in order to express character and pursue self-perfection. One always has the option of expressing character in various ways, so one must choose those that are consistent with respect. Third, because character involves pursuing not merely individual perfection but the perfection of the species, expressions of character that undermine others' agency are also self-undermining. And finally, as Montessori notes, expressing one's character naturally brings with it an interest in and respect for other agents. If one pursues work from a strong character and finds oneself disrespecting others, the infringement on others' agency will be disruptive to one's own ability to take joy in the work. Those "stronger types attracted by perfection" have a "true wish to become better" and are "no[t] ... tempted to acts of violence" (1: 189).

Unfortunately, most adults do not consistently have character in the fullest sense. Especially given this fact, each ought to bind herself to practice basic respect. Adults are generally attracted to perfection to some degree, but also suffer effects of unfree childhoods and their consequent repressions, deviations, and temptations toward passivity or aggression.

> [They] tend to slip toward the ... anti- and extra-social. These are always feeling tempted [away from perfection] and, unless they make constant efforts, feel they will become inferior. Therefore they need moral support to protect them from temptation ... The effort to resist evil is regarded as virtuous because it does in fact prevent us from falling into the moral abyss. These sufferers impose rules upon themselves to save themselves from falling ... More and more they cloth themselves in virtue, but it is a difficult life.
>
> (1: 189)

For most "virtuous" adult moral agents, respect shows up not primarily as an expression of character but as a constraint they must impose upon themselves. In that sense, even when it does not express character, respect is what Kant calls a "categorical imperative," something we ought to practice even if conflictedly rather than whole-heartedly. Just as external authorities must enforce respectful behavior when individuals do not practice it, so too individual agents can and should bind themselves to respectful behavior even when not wholeheartedly respectful.

In this section, I've repeatedly used the phrase "respectful behavior" rather than "respect" to refer to what must take priority over particular expressions of character. Ultimately, for Montessori, *true* respect *flows from* character, and thus there can't be a conflict between respecting others and one's character. In the context of this section, we can distinguish three levels of "respect," reflecting different degrees to which respectful behavior is internalized and flows from agents' wills. First, there is respectful behavior established through external enforcement of that behavior. In some cases, this behavior might be motived by fear of punishment, but often it will not even be motivated at all; one will treat others respectfully because, for instance, one simply lacks opportunities to treat them poorly, or one sees no need to do so, or one is distracted by a teacher. In some cases, disrespectful behavior might be prevented through literally picking up a child and putting him in another room, or (the adult equivalent) through imprisoning an offender. Here there is no "respect" in the proper sense at all, but rather *mere* behavior. Second, self-imposed rules of respect can constitute a reflective volitional stance rightly "regarded as virtuous." Here one reflectively endorses respectful behavior, even if one does not do so wholeheartedly because one remains tempted toward disrespect. This behavior might be said to be "respect" in a mitigated sense, but it falls short of Montessori's ideal of true, character-based respect. In that sense, Montessori rejects accounts of obligation that require inner conflict. In keeping with Romantic and later idealist critiques of Kant (e.g., Schiller, Hegel), she advocates a third sort of respect, wholehearted concern for others as an interest with which one wholly identifies. Those (adults) without this wholehearted respect ought to "impose rules upon themselves" (1: 189), and those who fail to impose such rules ought to be brought into conformity with community standards of minimal respect, but these are second-best measures, even if they indicate the moral necessity—and even priority—of respect.

4 The Nature of Respect

4.1 The Primacy of Character

In §3, I argued that respect is prior to character in that respect for others is categorically necessary, whether or not one has character. In another sense, however, character holds primacy in that the *reason* respect is morally required is because of the value of character and, relatedly, the proper *object* of moral respect is character. In emphasizing character as the locus of respect, Montessori differs from contemporary moral theories that emphasize happiness or preference-satisfaction (as utilitarianism does): "moral ... customs seldom arise merely to make life easier ... Social rules have aspects that are more contradictory than otherwise to this idea" (1: 167). Montessori also differs from those that emphasize respect for mere choice or end-setting (as Kantian ethics often does). For Montessori, we respect another's agency when we respect concentrated activity, his "tendency of interesting himself in exact things in an exact way" (24: 68): "society does not rest on personal wishes, but on a combination of activities which have to be harmonized" (1: 202); "the child leaves the others *to be active* so long as he also can be active. Each respects *the work* of the other" (14: 22, emphasis added). Respect secures harmony of *activity* rather than maximization of preference-satisfaction or even securing rights to choose as such.

Montessori's approach to respect thus differs from that of, say, Immanuel Kant, in important ways.[8] For Kant, one ought to respect others' capacities for choice and thus not interfere with or compromise their ability to pursue objects of their choice in ways they choose (as long as they do not wrong others). Furthermore, one ought to make some efforts toward positively advancing others' "happiness," understood as the sum of objects for which they "wish and will" (Kant [1788] 1996: 240). As we saw in Chapter 3, respect-worthy agency involves *activity* rather than mere passive enjoyment, so Montessori distinguishes, among "objects" of choice, between actions—particularly norm-governed, progress-oriented actions—and mere preferences for ends. Thus, she would distinguish a child's choice of a particular work from that same child's choice of a particular TV show or flavor of ice cream. One of Montessori's common descriptions of disrespect illustrates this difference between respect for chosen ends and respect for work.

> One day, the children had gathered themselves, laughing and talking, into a circle about a basin of water containing some floating toys. We had in the school a little boy barely two and a half years old. He had been left outside the circle, alone, and it was easy to see that he was filled with intense curiosity. I watched him from a distance with great interest; he first drew near to the other children and tried to force his way among them, but he was not strong enough to do this, and he then stood looking about him. The expression of thought on his little face was intensely interesting. I wish that I had had a camera so that I might have photographed him. His eye lighted upon a little chair, and evidently he made up his mind to place it behind the group of children and then to climb up on it. He began to move toward the chair, his face illuminated with hope, but at that moment the teacher

seized him brutally (or, perhaps, she would have said, gently) in her arms, and lifting him up above the heads of the other children showed him the basin of water, saying, "Come, poor little one, you shall see too!" Undoubtedly the child, seeing the floating toys, did not experience the joy that he was about to feel through conquering the obstacle with his own force.

The sight of those objects could be of no advantage to him, while his intelligent efforts would have developed his inner powers. The teacher *hindered* the child, in this case, from educating himself, without giving him any compensating good in return. The little fellow had been about to feel himself a conqueror, and he found himself held within two imprisoning arms, impotent. The expression of joy, anxiety, and hope, which had interested me so much faded from his face and left on it the stupid expression of the child who knows that others will act for him.

(Montessori 1912: 91–2; 2: 54)

Here a teacher "gently" sought to help a child get access to a good—seeing what the other children were looking at—that the child clearly sought. But she "brutally" interfered with the child's attentive work. The child's *character* was manifest not in wanting to see but in wanting to *act*, to perform a challenging task that has clear standards of success and that could be done well or poorly. By respecting the child's choice of end, the teacher failed to respect his *agency*.[9] In some contexts, as we will see in Chapter 6, we should respect individual choices of mere *ends*, but respect for others fundamentally requires respect for their *activity*, not mere choices. In that sense, Montessorian respect for others has a narrower—and different—focus than Kant's.

In another way, Montessorian respect has broader application than Kant's, in that one should respect *all* expressions of character, and not merely those endorsed by or based on reflection. While Kant requires respect only for agents with a capacity for reason-guided reflection, and—on some readings—only for those choices made or endorsed in the context of that reflection, Montessori specifically says, of the "tendency of interesting himself in exact things in an exact way," that "it is not a reasoning power that makes the child do this exercise, it seems almost an instinct" (24: 68). The child immersed in the project of moving a chair to get a peek over the heads of his peers need not reflectively endorse his project. He need not even be aware of what precisely his ends are. An adult who says "would you like to see the water-toys?" and who thereby prompts him to attend reflectively on his desires interrupts an activity that should be left undisturbed. And given the child's limited ability to deliberate, he might well answer this question with a "yes," which would seem to warrant the teacher's violent overthrow of his agency, an agency expressing itself in a task to which he is wholeheartedly and actively committed.

For Kant, there is a fundamental difference between a child's choice of ice cream, which need not be respected, and an adult's choice, which must be, because the adult, but not the child, makes the choice in the context of (a capacity for) reflection governed by a second-order faculty of practical reason (see Schapiro 1999; Grenberg 2018). Relatedly, for Kant, one ought to respect adults' deliberate choices made in the context of reflection more than (or even rather than) their immediate intentions, even when those immediate intentions are part of attentive work. As we will see in Chapter 6,

Montessori distinguishes between choices rooted in reason and reflection and those that are not, and she even allows that adult agency is fuller, in some respects, because it is guided by more abstract rational considerations. However, for Montessori, the bare capacity for norm-governed activity is nonetheless agency worthy of direct respect. We can and should respect children's character-driven work, and we should respect adults' unreflective activities, when—as in cases of "flow" (Csikszentmihalyi 1990)—these activities express character. Moreover, given the ways that adaptive preferences can come to have strong reflective endorsement (see Nussbaum 2000: 111–66), we can and should exercise judgment about whether a particular behavior, even when based on reflective endorsement of first-order preferences, constitutes an expression of respect-worthy agency. Even absent adaptive preferences, respectful people should exercise judgment about when to prioritize others' deliberate choices over their immediate expressions of agency in attentive work, and when to do the opposite. When you have expressed to me your reflectively endorsed desire to go to a movie, and you are now caught up in your work, like Montessori's "writer under the influence of poetic inspiration" (9: 16), respect may require that I set aside your reflectively endorsed desire for the sake of your current expression of agency, even without soliciting from you a further act of deliberation.[10]

4.2 Two Kinds of Respect

In Chapter 3, I pointed out that Montessori's account of agency connects respect-worthy agency and ideal agency. Another way to put this would be that the primacy of character links what Steven Darwall calls "recognition respect" and "appraisal respect." For Darwall,

> There is a kind of respect which ... consists, most generally, in a disposition to weigh appropriately in one's deliberations some feature of the thing in question and to act accordingly ... Since this kind of respect consists in giving appropriate ... recognition to some feature of its object in deliberating about what to do, I shall call it *recognition respect* ... [I]t just this sort of respect which is ... owed to all persons. To say that persons as such are entitled to respect is to say that they are entitled to have other persons take seriously and weigh appropriately the fact that they are persons in deliberating about what to do ... There is another attitude which ... we likewise refer to by the term "respect." Unlike recognition respect, its exclusive objects are persons or features which are held to manifest their excellence as persons or as engaged in some specific pursuit. For example, one may have such respect for someone's integrity, for someone's good qualities on the whole, or for someone as a musician ... Because this sort of respect consists in a positive appraisal of a person or his qualities, I shall call it *appraisal respect*.
>
> (Darwall 1977: 38)

Moral philosophy, generally speaking, emphasizes recognition respect; "respect [for people] simply because they are people ... is the sort of respect of special interest to moral theory" (Buss 1999: 518; cf. Darwall 1977). Montessori, too, emphasizes such recognition respect: "Children come to know one another's characters and to have a reciprocal feeling for each other's worth" (1: 205). At the same time, however, such children manifest an appraisal respect that consists in "admiration for the best. Not only are these children free from envy, but anything well done arouses their enthusiastic praise" (1: 209).

In line with a tradition of reflection on reflection that goes back at least to Kant, that "towering figure in the history of moral philosophy who appreciated [the importance of] respect for persons" (Buss 1999: 521), Montessori sees these two sorts of respect as closely linked with one another and with agency. On Kant's account, where "dignity" marks something out for recognition respect, "morality, and humanity insofar as it is capable of morality, is that which alone has dignity" (Kant 1996: 84); the "good will" is the only thing that is "good without qualification," but "the human being" as such "exists as an end in itself, not merely as a means to be used by this or that will" (Kant 1996: 49, 79). While the good will deserves unconditional appraisal respect, rational agency that falls short of the good will is a proper object of recognition respect.[11] For Montessori, to recognize another as an agent worthy of (recognition) respect is to recognize her as susceptible of appraisal respect, but this plays out not primarily in terms of a relation between the "good will" and "humanity," but between different degrees to which people actualize their characters.

Among those who regularly and (relatively) fully express character through attentive work, we can distinguish between three ways in which character expresses itself, each of which warrants a different mix of appraisal and recognition respect. On the one hand, when Montessori highlights that "anything done well arouses ... enthusiastic praise" (1: 209), she highlights the paradigmatic context for appraisal respect within her theory. Given that the pursuit of perfections is constitutive of character, those with character seek perfection for themselves and "respect"—in the appraisal sense—others who have achieved this or that perfection. Insofar as the agency worthy of (recognition) respect is an agency that *strives toward* excellence, however, already-accomplished excellence neither garners nor requires much recognition respect, except insofar as one pursues yet greater and higher perfections. On the other hand, one who falls far short of perfection but strives toward it demonstrates character in the paradigmatic sense; such striving most fully expresses each individual's agency and is precisely what most deserves recognition as something to take seriously and refrain from obstructing. Finally, one should adopt a posture combining recognition and appraisal when attending to virtues constitutive of character, such as confidence in setting ends for oneself, persistence in work, and attentiveness to norms governing one's activity. Because they are constitutive of agency, one recognition-respecting another's agency is in part recognizing the presence of these virtues and making room for their exercise. But because these virtues can be more or less fully realized in particular cases, one can also esteem and appraisal-respect another for, say, being particularly patient and persistent in carrying out work to which they are committed.

As Montessori often emphasizes, most people—both adults and children—lack character in the fullest sense. Due in large part to lack of freedom and poor environments, repression and deviations characterize much agency. Just as Kant needs an account of what sort of respect is owed to human beings who lack good wills, so too Montessori needs an account of the respect owed toward those without character. Since character is the ultimate object of respect, one might think that people without character do not warrant respect and can be treated however one chooses. At times, and to some extent, Montessori bites this bullet. She is willing to say that while teachers should not interfere with children at work, they may "do what you like with the rest of your class ... because this stage [prior to expressing character] is not important" (17: 229–30). Given her focus on children, moreover, she is sometimes quite pessimistic about adults (see 1: 161–2) and focused on creating environments that foster character, rather than providing a theory of respect to deal with its absence. Nonetheless, she offers some reasons for giving recognition respect to people with repressed or deficient characters. Respecting others requires respecting partial and incomplete strivings toward greater perfection. Alongside exhorting that we should "not admire, as the ancients did, the person born good, but educate him to be conscientious, strong, and useful," so too we should "not condemn the wicked but redeem him with education and with solidarity in our shared fault, which is the scientific form of forgiveness" (Montessori 1903: 331). Rather than emphasizing an essential difference between those with character and those without, Montessori emphasizes education for both, and solidarity with those who are relatively weaker.[12] Much of this effort, for Montessori, plays out in educational contexts, where all have the potential to develop character, but even amongst adults, we can work creating contexts where people can express and develop character. Montessori interprets the "Catholic dogma of the communion of sinners" in terms of the principle "In sociology—we are all guilty of the social causes of degeneration [of moral agency]—we all have a duty to contribute to improving the environment" (Montessori 1903: 330). Even for adults, we should respond to lack of character by creating rich environments and conditions of freedom that allow for the expression—and thereby cultivation—of character, and then we should respect manifestations of character when they arise, however rarely. Finally, as we will see in Chapter 6, because deliberation itself is an activity in which adults can engage, we ought to respect deliberate choices of other adults, when that deliberation is even relatively free and relatively wholehearted. While respect paradigmatically takes character as its object, we can and should respect agency even in its suboptimal forms as part of respecting each individual as an individual with the potential for character in the fullest sense.

4.3 Paradigm Vices: Interruption and Imposition

Montessorian respect focuses on harmony of activity; its primary object is individual character, expressed through self-directed activities of others. Montessori's paradigmatic forms of disrespect thus consist in violations of others' attentive work, which violations take two primary forms: imposition of tasks that another does not choose for herself, and interruption or interference with tasks on which another is concentrating. To respect a child requires that "he is left free to choose ..., without being forced at the wrong moment to any work, nor interrupted in his spontaneous occupations as long as they are useful" (Montessori in De Giorgi 2019: 50–2).

The first and most basic form of respect requires refraining from imposing one's will on another through coercion. When introducing the child to a new activity, "she [the teacher] must not use the violent authority employed in traditional schools, but must ask the consent of the children while offering them this material" (24: 111). To respect another person—whether child or adult—is to let *her* decide whether or not she wants to engage in a particular activity. Agency cannot be expressed when "the movement of [one person] obeys the will of [another]" (24: 113); it requires that one "depends upon his own will and not that of another" (24: 176).

A second form of disrespect—interruption—is all too often overlooked, and Montessori devotes extensive attention to warning against interruption. She warns that "too many teachers are inclined to ... interrupt [the child] continuously and teach continuously, instead of letting the children have their own experience" (Montessori 1949: 251). Interruption of children takes place in "the manner of masters to slaves who have no human rights" (9: 15), and "[h]e who interrupts children in their occupations in order to make them learn some pre-determined thing ... confuses the means with the end and destroys the man for a vanity" (9: 134). Even a trivial interruption can disrupt the concentration that constitutes children's expressions of their agency.

> When the child begins to show interest in [active work], the teacher must *not interrupt*, because this interest corresponds with natural laws and opens up a whole cycle of new activities ... The teacher, now, must be most careful. Not to interfere means not to interfere *in any way*. This is the moment at which the teacher most often goes wrong. The child, who up to that moment has been very difficult, finally concentrates on a piece of work. If, as she passes, the teacher merely says, "Good," it is enough to make the trouble break out all over again.
>
> (1: 254)

Montessori's approach to respect and agency shows why even these benign interruptions can be so harmful. Exercising effort toward achieving worthwhile goals is the core of character. In "those marvelous moments when their attention is fixed," children who are "roughly interrupted" can rightly object that their wills are thwarted (9: 16). When "interrupted ... they lose all the characteristics connected with *an internal process regularly and completely carried out*" (9: 74, emphasis original). Most basically, the respectful person must "never ... intervene when the child is immersed in his work" (Montessori in De Giorgi 2019: 62).

This "skill in not interfering comes with practice" (1: 255). Non-interference is a challenge, not least for epistemic reasons. It requires a cultivated moral sense to distinguish mere busy-ness from attentive work. Children also mature in their strength of will, making it possible to interrupt in some ways, as Montessori did in the case of Sofia, without violating a child's concentration. There can also be cases where interruption is required in order to facilitate other social goods (see §3 and Chapter 7), and it requires moral discernment to know when these cases hold. In the case of adults, deciding when to interrupt someone in a state of flow can be even more complex, and can require nuanced understanding of others' possible higher-order goals. Even beyond epistemic difficulties, it takes substantial willpower and "spiritual height" (Montessori 1912: 349) to resist helping someone struggling with a challenging task or to avoid unnecessary praise for a job well done. Adults plagued with egotism, impatience, and other vices have constant pretexts to interrupt others' effortful work for their own interests.

Imposition and interruption are two primary vices related to respect. Imposition directly forces another to conform her actions to one's own will. It directly violates the internality, activity, and *self*-governance that constitute another's agency. Particularly in cases of significant power disparity (such as between adults and children), those in power must take care to introduce proposed activities in ways that leave open the real option of refusal and thereby solicit genuine consent (or not). Interruption primarily violates the persistence condition for agency through cutting off self-governed activity. It forces someone to shift from activity to passivity and often undermines wholehearted commitment to the work in which one is engaged. For young children just beginning to develop their characters, even modest interruptions can be devastating to the child's agency both in the moment and long term (by eroding the child's confidence that he will be able to follow through on work he chooses, and thereby eroding his willingness to choose work). Even for adults and more mature children, interruption often undermines the flow in which agency partly consists, cutting off expressions of character in which they were invested.

4.4 Help

Given the danger of interruption and the importance for agents of effortful work on activities they choose for themselves, Montessori often warns against "excess of help," which she describes as "that which is most noxious to psychic life" (24: 62). In contrast to children with character who "respect one another's efforts" (1: 207),

> the mother who feeds her child without making the least effort to teach him to hold the spoon for himself ... is not a good mother. She offends the fundamental human dignity of her son,— she treats him as if he were a doll, when he is, instead, a man confided by nature to her care.
>
> (Montessori 1912: 98; cf. 2: 58)

Nevertheless, the same respectful children who let others work for themselves also "give help ... when ... necessary," such as when "there is a mishap, like the breaking of a vase," and "the child who has dropped it is desperate [and] ... feels ashamed" (1: 207–8). Children with character respect each other through non-interference, but also "help each other" (24: 111). As I mentioned in Chapter 2, the respect that flows from character development in children includes moral sensitivity:

> the children go to the aid of others only when there is a real need for help, for instance, when something has fallen down and is broken, or where there are too

many objects to put away and only a little time to do it. They never help another child when he is making a constructive effort to do things for himself. As if by instinct, they have it in themselves never to give what we call useless help.

(24: 49)

A teacher often intervenes at the wrong time. For instance, a teacher who sees a child transporting a heavy table, tells a second child to go and help. The child, if left to himself, would not have gone to help. In not going to do so, he would have done right because the child carrying the table was making the effort by himself.

(24: 202–3)

Here as elsewhere, Montessori's moral philosophy draws from children's moral sense, incorporating both an emphasis on help as part of mutual respect and a careful distinction between genuinely respectful help and the unnecessary assistance that undermines character.

To highlight the danger of unnecessary assistance, Montessori distinguishes "service" from "help." Service consists of doing something *for* another; it "suffocates their useful, spontaneous activity" by treating them like "puppets [or] dolls" (2: 58; Montessori 1912: 97). Such service "becomes a social disturbance and troubles the people to whom it is given" (24: 203). The disrespect and harm inherent in such service are not limited to children. She describes, for instance, how "one who has too many servants becomes increasingly dependent upon them and eventually their slave. His muscles grow weak through inactivity and eventually lose their natural capacity for work" (2: 58; cf. Montessori 1912: 98). Montessori particularly emphasizes how men degrade women by serving them: "She is not only maintained and served, she is, besides, diminished, belittled, in that individuality which is hers by right of her existence as a human being. As an individual member of society, she is … rendered deficient in all those powers and resources which tend to the preservation of life" (Montessori 1912: 99). Such service tends not only to inculcate "dependence" and "helplessness" but also the "domineering and tyrannical behavior" that "is the outward sign of the state of feeling of one who conquers through the work of others" (Montessori 1912: 100). While true "'valorization' of the individual is in close relation with [allowing that individual to engage in] maximum effort …, we [adults] have an instinct to give always an easier life" (14: 25), which ultimately disrespects those we purport to love. As noted in Chapter 3, what children and adults with character want qua agents is to *act*, not merely to attain the outcome(s) of action.

While service replaces the capacities of the one served and thereby demeans and diminishes her, respectful *help* cultivates others' capacities and honors their dignity, independence, and ultimately character. One who truly respects another "*help[s] him* to make a conquest of such useful acts as nature intended he should perform for himself" (Montessori 1912: 97, emphasis original; cf. 2: 58). Like respectful non-interference, the "desire … to help" is a "social sentiment, which one sees in [Montessori's] schools," that develops when children "are allowed by circumstances to carry out [character-driven] actions" (24: 49).

There are two primary contexts within which respect calls for actively helping others. First, there is the "very wise and simple way" that (Montessorian) children express their need: "help me to do it by myself" (14: 29; 22: 175; 24: 11; cf. 4: 6; 10: 97; 14: 29).

> The adult must help the child, but help him in such a way that he may act for himself and perform his real work in the world ... It is in this that our conception differs both from that of the world in which the adult does everything for the child and from that of a passive environment in which the adult abandons the child to himself.
>
> (22: 175)

As Montessori explains,

> This fundamental principle [to help the child act for himself] represents a guide for adults to follow, but it is not so simple to help the child do things for himself. It is easier for us, in fact, to do things for the child. For instance, if we want to help the child to wash and comb himself, a number of problems arise. [For example,] to teach the child how these actions are to be carried out takes much more time and patience on our part than it would take to do the actions themselves.
>
> (24: 11)

Relatedly, adults typically, "when they perform actions, do them quickly" (24: 10), not providing the slow and methodical precision of motion that the child needs to observe in order to properly imitate those actions and perform them for himself. In order to help children do activities for themselves, we need not only to avoid interference but also to provide clear instructions and models.[13] Adults also can and should help children through various forms of "indirect preparation" for activity, such that children engaging in one activity that interests them and matches their abilities (say, working on a puzzle) are also cultivating abilities that will help them perform more advanced activities later (say, holding a pencil). Such indirect preparation provides scaffolding to rise higher and higher, as children are "helped" to perform more challenging work without being "served" by having that work done for them.

The second sort of genuinely respectful help is what we might call "accidental" or "occasional" help: "if something untoward happens, if there is an accident when help is really needed, the child will ... leave all he is doing, no matter how important, in order to help" (14: 22). Montessori describes, for example, cases where "there is a mishap, like the breaking of a vase" or where "there is something interesting for all the children to do, and they find that one child is engaged in some long and tedious work" (1: 207–8; 24: 203). In these contexts, help does not necessarily promote agency directly, but it also does not undermine effortful work, and it serves other goods, ensuring that children avoid shame for mistakes or are able to participate in group activities. Given a sense of shared ownership over their environment and community, accidents such as the breaking of a vase also inspire help simply as a way of restoring that environment, in cases where dealing with this accident will be tedious or worse for the person principally concerned.

Respect for others can call for help of other kinds, including preparing an environment for others (see next section), the social solidarity akin to help I will discuss in Chapter 5, and other possibly appropriate forms of help discerned by those with character interacting in communities of mutual respect. Montessori primarily focuses, however, on the dangers of unnecessary help and the propriety of agency-enabling respectful help.

4.5 Respect and the Prepared Environment

Among the most important forms of help adults can and should provide is the construction of what Montessori calls "a *world for the child*" (22: 176). To work for themselves, children's preeminent need is the right kind of environment, "not an environment to be mastered and enjoyed, but an environment that will help him to establish his functions" (22: 175). Thus, for instance, "to comb himself, the child must have a comb which is suitable in form to the size of his hand" (24: 11). One of Montessori's most important contributions to early childhood education was this emphasis on providing appropriately sized materials so that children could carry about the operations of practical life for themselves, with suitably sized furniture, brooms, combs, shovels, etc.

An environment suitable for the child's agency must also include material that is inviting and attractive for children given their particular developmental interests and needs. Children depend upon a rich environment in order to exercise the agency available to them, but whereas adults are capable of and focused on shaping the external world, children are primarily capable of and focused on self-formation (see Frierson 2016b). Thus respect for children requires creation and maintenance of environments suited to the exercise of their wills. This point is not wholly unique to children. Adults have obligations to ensure that the world in which we live is one where all people's internal capabilities for self-governance have the minimal material conditions for expression. Just as "society has come to recognize [the laborer's] moral ... value and to accord him the means and conditions needed for his work as a matter of right," so too should "we carry this idea over to the child" (1: 12–3). For children, one has a special obligation to "give the child an environment in which everything is constructed in proportion to himself, and let him live therein. Then there will develop within the child that 'active life' which has caused so many to marvel ... [T]he environment ... in the schools ought [to] ... make such liberty possible" (9: 15, 55). Because children cannot create agency-conducive environments for themselves, adults have an obligation of respect to provide them a suitable environment.

5 Conclusion

Character constitutes the core value of Montessori's moral theory; it can and should be perfected, preserved, and realized, but most of all character should be *respected* as what gives each person "personal dignity" (12: 60). Just as character is the fundamental *value* in Montessori's moral theory, respect is the most basic moral *attitude* to take toward that value. Respect solves the social problem of how to create communities within which character can be expressed through individuals participating in work that they choose for themselves. For this reason, in disordered and abnormal societies, respect ends up being a categorical imperative, something the more prosocial members "impose ... upon themselves to save them from falling" (1: 189) and to which they bind other members through various enforcements. In healthy and "normalized" people, however, respect *flows from* and *expresses* character. Those with character naturally take interest in others' efforts toward perfection, and participating in a healthy community becomes itself a norm-governed activity in which each persists, striving for greater perfection.

5

Solidarity and Obedience

In Chapter 4, I described how mutual respect emerges when children begin to develop character, and how this respect becomes a second pillar of ethical life alongside character. Respect requires one not only to avoid imposition and interruption but also to help others. For Montessori, however, as children develop their moral lives, they embrace further social ideals of solidarity and obedience, which call for unity with others that goes beyond mere help. As with respect, solidarity and obedience extend rather than limit one's agency, but whereas respect preserves fundamental distinctions between individual agents, solidarity and obedience break down distinctions between agents, giving rise to forms of social agency that are irreducible to mere interactions amongst individuals. Respect involves "a discipline in which each has his different interests," "each person chooses his work," and "each must do different things... but... in harmony" (17: 235). Social solidarity, by contrast, involves "a true brotherhood ... cemented by affection" (1: 205), a "society by cohesion" (17: 233). "[V]italized by a social spirit," at this stage "it is normal for children to join together" such that they can be "compared to the ... cells in ... an organism" (1: 211; 17: 233; cf. 10: 22, 58). Similarly, while respect requires that one "leave [others] to follow their instincts of activity" (9: 113), an agent practicing obedience "can control his actions ... in accordance with the desires of another person" (9: 78; cf. 17: 79), where this is not mere submission but a "sublime spiritual obedience at present still unknown to the majority of mankind," one dependent upon "the construction of a strong internal life" (9: 162).

This chapter focuses on these further developments of Montessorian ethical life. I start with social solidarity, showing how solidarity develops from respect without being reducible to it (§1) and also how, like respect, solidarity grows from, supports, and complements individual character (§2). From there, I turn to the metaphysics of social solidarity, drawing on recent discussions of group agency within contemporary philosophy (§3), and briefly discuss the moral importance of social solidarity (§4). I then discuss obedience, which is like solidarity in developing from character and respect while going beyond the ways character and respect are still individualistic (§5). Finally, I discuss (§6) possible dangers of Montessorian solidarity and obedience and briefly describe how Montessori's view mitigates those dangers.

1 From Respect to Solidarity

Just as there is a close connection between character and respect, so too there is a close connection between respect and social solidarity. Over time, mutual respect, particularly when manifested in helpfulness, gives rise to something more. Thus after explaining that the "harmonious discipline" of children consists in mutual *respect*, where "each person chooses his work [and] do[es] different things," Montessori goes on:

> Little by little a development occurs in these new children ... Little by little a child absorbs the prevailing sentiments of his group. He is proud of the work of this group. This is an expression of social sentiment. The child is happy when his group or class is doing well ... This is a more complex kind of unity. It is a higher sentiment like the love we have for a city or a nation.
>
> (17: 235–6)

As with the relationship between character to respect, Montessori's claim here is fundamentally empirical and psychological. As a matter of fact, observed in classrooms around the world, children in societies of mutual respect come to feel "cohesion" or "social solidarity," a union *with* others rather than a mere respect *for* them. But as with character and respect, the connection between respect and solidarity is not merely an arbitrary fact; there are natural reasons that respect would give rise to solidarity in groups of character-driven people who relate to each other respectfully.

For one thing, some features of respect already go beyond mere non-interference to involve something like cooperation. When one person helps another, there is the beginning of a social bond. Moreover, affective dimensions of respect easily slide from mere valuing of another's agency and accomplishments to genuine affection for, interest in, and even sympathy with her. Both elements are reflected in Montessori's description of one of social life's "many aspects," which she calls "reciprocal help":

> The older children help the smaller ones and the small ones help each other. They show respect for and interest in each other. For example, when a child does something difficult for the first time ... [and] says "please stay and see that no one rubs it out," the second child will remain, like a soldier, in charge of the other's work ... No teacher could tell children to admire and be interested in each other's work.
>
> (17: 233)

> Our schools show that children of different ages help one another. The younger ones see what the older ones are doing and ask for explanations. These are readily given, and the instruction is really valuable, for the mind of a five-year-old is so much nearer than ours to the mind of a child of three ... There is a communication and a harmony between the two that one seldom finds between the adult and the small child.
>
> (1: 204–5)

Reciprocal help is fundamentally a matter of respect for others' work, but these examples of respect require more active interest than mere non-interference. In the case of the child who, "like a soldier," guards another's work, the guard becomes an integral part of that work. And the young teachers serving as guides directly facilitate cultivation of others' characters. Moreover, these helpers' emotions go beyond mere respect; they admire and take interest in others, and the young teacher actually shares in the younger pupils' aspirations for excellence. Likewise, from an absence of envy comes "mutual sympathy and pr[i]d[e in] each other's work" (17: 238). Thus even while primarily a matter of respect, the "goodness" of "reciprocal helpfulness" marks a nascent "unity derived from spiritual cohesion" (1: 220).

This spiritual cohesion becomes even more intense when individuals with character seek goods that cannot be accomplished without cooperation. The examples above are primarily cases of one individual helping another, but often a whole group works toward a good cooperatively:

> It is interesting to observe this society by cohesion of children. They engage in social activity for an external purpose. Children work in a group when the activity requires cooperation. They cooperate when they have something to do. I saw a little child who had taken out all the geometrical cards and figures and was looking at them when the music began. He wanted to put them away before joining in the music but this would have taken some time. The other children came to help him. This was spontaneous cooperation. They cooperate in laying the table, planting gardens, etc. Cooperation is the consequence of a free life with free activity.
>
> (17: 235)

In this case, there is a desire to help the boy with his cards, but given that the desire is to clean up the cards *very quickly*, the task can only be carried out by a group. Similarly, laying a table for a meal and caring for a garden require cooperation of many individuals. Working together toward a common end fosters social sympathy that grounds even more impressive forms of unity.

These cases of social solidarity involve uniting with others "when the activity requires cooperation" (17: 235). Kirk Ludwig explains two quite different senses in which an activity might require some sort of group action:

> group action extends what it is possible to do far beyond the powers of individual agents, and in two quite different respects ... In some cases, it is a matter of the greater causal powers of groups. Most people cannot lift a piano alone or carry a dresser up a flight of stairs, and massive construction projects like the pyramids or the Great Wall of China are far beyond the capacities of any individual. Nonetheless, it is a contingent fact that no individuals are powerful enough to do these things ... In contrast to these sorts of things, where as a practical matter we must work together to get something done ..., there are things that by their nature only groups can do, things which, if they are to be done at all, must be done with others. For example, no one can undertake an orchestral performance

of Beethoven's Ninth Symphony, carry on a conversation, play a game of chess or football, elect a new president, or get married, just by him or herself. By their nature these require other cooperating participants.

(Ludwig 2016: 3)

Cleaning up cards or laying out a table for a meal are examples of the first sort of group action, where individuals could do the relevant tasks in theory, but groups do them (better) in practice. The second sort of group action consists of tasks that, by their essential nature, require more than one person, such as a conversation or game of tennis. Montessori discusses many examples that exemplify the second sort of group action, one of the most important of which represents a final connection between respect and solidarity.

People can (and children do) transition from mutual respect to solidarity through growing investment in the community of mutual respect itself as a common project.[1] At first, children respect one another because "there is nothing for it but to" respect; it is a lived necessity of their life with others. Over time, the community formed through mutual respect becomes conscious of itself *as* a community.

> Little by little, [the children] become aware of forming a community … They come to feel part of the group to which their activity contributes. And not only do they begin to take an interest in this, but they work on it profoundly, as one may say, in their hearts. Once they have reached this level, the children no longer act thoughtlessly, but put the group first and try to succeed for its benefit.
>
> (1: 211)

In the right setting, character gives rise to social harmonies of mutual respect and periodic cooperation or assistance, and this mutual respect in turn enables each child to engage in work that cultivates her own perfections. As children become *aware* of these social harmonies, they make social life itself an object of attentive work. Just as a child might seek to become a better pianist, so she seeks to become a better member of society. Moreover, each becomes self-consciously aware of the benefits *to the group* of her activities, and she takes pride in individual activities for the sake not merely of individual perfection but also of group perfection. Thus even efforts to improve at piano are partly a matter of *the group* becoming a more accomplished community. Bennett Helm explains that "to identify with all or most of the values of a particular community is to identify oneself with the way of life that defines that community; it is, we might say, to identify oneself with the community itself" (Helm 2017: 232). Montessori gives an example of how children's pride in their community prompted one of many events that "forced upon us" the "idea of social cohesion":

> To give an example, it so happened that the Argentinian ambassador, hearing it said that in our schools children of four or five worked entirely on their own … and had an excellent discipline not imposed by authority, found himself unable to believe this. So he thought he would pay a surprise visit. Unfortunately, it happened to be a holiday, so he found the school shut. This was a school called

"The Children's House" in a block of working men's flats where the children lived with their parents. Just by chance, one of the children was in the courtyard and heard the ambassador's expression of annoyance. Guessing he was a visitor, the child said, "Don't worry about the school being shut. The caretaker has the key and we are all here." The door was soon opened and all the children went in and began to work. Here, then, was an example of action for the group. Each did his part without hope of reward. They cooperated for the honor of their community.

(1: 211–2)

Each child engaged in this or that character-driven work, pursuing excellence in their own activity. Each respected the work of the others. But each also pursued these individual and interactive goods *as part of* a shared good, from a shared commitment to the task of being a respectful and agency-conducive class.

With the transition to thinking about the social life of the community as a whole, genuine social solidarity is born. Here one conceives of goods as *group* goods achieved through *group* efforts. Moreover, unlike guarding another's work, caring for a garden, or helping someone quickly and neatly pick up his cards, the creation of a community of mutual respect depends upon the constant cooperation of the *entire* community. While there is *some* resilience to a well-ordered community, a single disruptive or disrespectful member has a significant impact on the perfection of the group. Ideally, participants' motivations cease to be purely individual and become social, namely a shared desire to be a more excellent community.

Children's identification with their communities of mutual respect is one *essentially* social activity, but ethical lives involve many and varied forms of solidarity, and Montessori's primary paradigm of such solidarity is an activity in which children with character took extreme interest, one that surprised Montessori at its ability to sustain attention and bind children into a group agent characterized by "perfect cooperation" and "unity" of agency (17: 234, 236). This activity—the "Silence Game"—grows more from character than from mutual respect, so I discuss it in the next section.

2 Solidarity and Character

In §1, I showed how social solidarity emerges from practices and feelings involved in respect, particularly within communities of mutual respect. In this section, I highlight four ways in which solidarity relates to character. First, it *requires* character, since the sympathy involved in solidarity requires that each have a strong will of his own. Second, it is, like respect, a natural *outgrowth* of character. Third, it helps *cultivate* (individual) character. Finally, it gives rise to a new conception of communal, social, or shared character.

First, social solidarity depends upon character. One might think that sympathy with and conformity to a group could come antecedent to or even conflict with one's own pursuit of personal perfections, but Montessori insists that solidarity as an ethical good *depends upon* character. This dependence is evident in her paradigmatic example of social solidarity, a game she stumbled upon in the course of her teaching and that is now a common component of Montessori education: the "lesson of silence" or "Silence Game" (1: 237; 2: 93, 115, 148–52, 325, 335; Montessori 1912: 212–3, 364). While this game has many variations, its basic element is the establishment, as a class, of the most perfect possible silence. The teacher directs the children—often with a whisper, or by writing a word on the board—to be silent, and silence gradually sweeps over the class of children, such that, in the end, "[f]ifty or sixty children from two and a half years to six years of age, all together, and at a single time, know how to hold their peace so perfectly that the absolute silence seems that of a desert" (Montessori 1912: 116; 2: 115; cf. 2: 148–52).

Montessori's silence exercise is quite unlike the "order" of "Silence!" given in "traditional schools" which is too easily "confuse[d] with a general reduction in noise" and a way of preventing children from acting out (7: 54). Silence among children is often seen as a necessary stifling of distracted impulses, a precondition for being appropriately receptive to instruction. For Montessori, silence has almost the opposite importance. Given her overall approach to education, the goal of silence cannot be passivity before an adult instructor. In fact, silence is not primarily a *precondition* for learning and development, but rather a *fruit* of such development. Silence requires strength of will, and the ability of children to be silent "offers a means of testing the children's will power" (1: 237).

> The silence discipline is connected with the child's own soul and not with the will of an outside person ... The discipline, the silence, the calm, all become free expression. The flowering of discipline is thus the result of growth; it is a spiritual development.
>
> (21: 58–9)

The Silence Game comes *after* children have had opportunity to develop character through sustained and self-chosen work (see 9: 127). Such children can already control distracting impulses through engagement in worthwhile activity. What the Silence Game provides is a *further outlet* for the will, rather than a limitation of it. In particular, it requires the utmost concentration and self-discipline, and thus gives a perfect opportunity to strive for greater and greater self-perfection.

> In order to have [perfect] silence, you must simply *not move*. And *in order not to move, you must think about everything that could possibly move*. So you must keep your legs and feet quite still, and your hands, and your whole body. You have to control your breathing ... Now this will be very difficult to do.
>
> (7: 52–3)

In traditional calls to be quiet, children are told to act *less*. In the Silence Game, they are called upon to a more thoroughgoing "activity," one that engages their entire body and is "very difficult"; this silence is "*interesting*" (7: 53, 55). It engages, tests, strengthens, and refines the will. And thus, unsurprisingly, "very young children of three or four ... *love silence to an extraordinary degree*" (7: 51).

While it provides an activity by which children can perfect themselves, the lesson in silence is unlike many other forms of work in that it cannot be done without the cooperation of every member of the class. Silence is essentially social, though not in quite the same ways as Ludwig's examples of chess or marriage (Ludwig 2016: 3). Unlike chess, one can in principle attain silence as an individual; silence is easier, in fact, than moving a heavy table by oneself, and individual silence is easier than silence in a group. The fascination of the Silence Game, however, depends upon its practice in a group.[2] Cooperation with others does not make the activity easier, but—partly by making it more difficult—cooperation makes the activity more interesting and changes its nature. The goal of complete silence depends not only upon *one's own* self-control, but upon the self-control of everyone, in unison. It is "an excellent *lesson in co-operation*" (7: 53) because—to a much greater degree than the establishment of a respectful class—"a single person can break it" (1: 237).

Second, the Silence Game illustrates how solidarity grows naturally from character. Pursuit of perfection in general naturally gives rise to a desire to be perfect as a member of society. As one comes to recognize feelings of unity that facilitate deeper forms of social cooperation, one with character naturally desires to perfect, strengthen, and refine these feelings. Moreover, the perfection toward which one with character aims is specifically a perfection *of agency*. Social cooperation, particularly cooperation in solidarity, makes human beings more capable of acting in and upon the world. Those with character seek these more impactful expressions of agency.[3]

Third, solidarity contributes to the cultivation of individual character. Those with character are driven by a desire for self-perfection, and being part of a group leads one to push oneself further than one might otherwise. The degree of self-control involved in the Silence Game is directly facilitated by the shared self-control of the group. Even beyond the Silence Game, one will often stick with a difficult project longer, work harder at it, and hold oneself to higher standards when one works as part of a group. Importantly, these benefits to individual character depend upon participation in a group being rooted in one's antecedent character and a genuine sense of solidarity. One who joins a group merely to gain some external good achievable by cooperation can be tempted with free-riding, aiming to get group goods with minimal individual contribution. But if one has character, one wants to do as much as possible as excellently as possible, and if one has solidarity, one wants the group to get as far as it can go. The standard benefits calculus according to which free-riding is "rational" no longer makes sense when one *identifies with* the group, sees excellent *activity* as the chief good, and sees the good(s) of the group as one's own.

This notion of identification with group goods gives rise to a fourth way that solidarity relates to character. In Chapter 3, I discussed character as an *individual* good, and for Montessori, any group goods must be built on and compatible with individual character. Nonetheless, from a group of strong-willed individuals, a new entity can emerge, a community or group with its own goods and its own "character." As individuals come to identify partly with character-driven groups, they expand their selves and thereby take on new forms of agency.[4] Just as strong organs within the body unite to form an even stronger body with goods distinct from those of individual organs, so too diverse individuals in a community unite to form a whole that pursues its own perfection. Like individuals, communities can be repressed or defective, caught up in infighting or pursuing merely external goods such as wealth or prestige. But healthy communities can have *character*, a norm-driven striving for increased perfections distinctive of the group. We can seek a more respectful and courteous community, greater harmony and sympathy amongst ourselves. We as a community can also seek to stretch our powers, developing technology to put people on the moon or discovering new facts about the universe or eliminating disease, poverty, or ignorance. We can seek peace and justice, externally as well as internally. Some of these goods can be accomplished by mere collections of individuals who happen to share goals or who agree to work together. But all will be *better* accomplished by strong and mutually respectful individuals who actually feel themselves bound together into a group by sympathy and a sense of solidarity, and some actually *require* this kind of unity.

3 The Nature of Solidarity

In the Silence Game, children make a "pool of wills," a "plural subject" made up of strong individual wills (Gilbert 1990: 7; 2006: 145; cf. Velleman 1997). Group "character" or "agency" raises issues about the metaphysics of groups that have become widely discussed amongst contemporary philosophers. Three main alternative approaches to group agency characterize contemporary philosophical discussions. First, "individualist" or "singularist" philosophers, such as David Lewis (1969),[5] argue that appeals to group agency can be wholly reduced to explanations in terms of individual agents. On such accounts, to say that "we had a conversation" or "we achieved silence" is really just to say something like that "I spoke to you and you spoke to me" or that "you and I were both silent at the same time." "Groups" are constituted by individuals whose behavior is shaped by individual preferences and individual expectations about the behaviors of others. Second, some philosophers argue that group agency should be understood in normative terms. Margaret Gilbert, for example, emphasizes the role of "joint commitment." Through a process wherein "each makes to clear to each his personal readiness to contribute to" the relevant goal in the relevant way, and thereby "the parties are *jointly committed*," where "their being jointly committed ... is a normative matter," that is, a matter of being *obligated together* to uphold the shared commitment, such that "if any one party ... does not conform, they, qua subject of the commitment, ... err" (Gilbert 2013: 7). Finally, various philosophers seek alternative accounts of group agency that do not reduce it merely to individual agents or normative concepts. Some of these remain more individualist. Christian List and Phil Pettit, for example, while giving an "individualistic account of group agency," nonetheless argue for a supervenience account according to which a group can judge and plan in ways not reducible to individual judgments or plans of its members (List and Pettit 2006: 86). Velleman defends a "joint making-up of minds [that] is not the making-up of a joint mind" (Velleman 1997: 49). Others, most notably Raimo Tuomela, claim that groups are "ontologically *emergent* (viz. involve qualitatively new features as compared with the individualistic basis) and in this sense *irreducible* to the individualistic properties," such that "joint intention [i]s a conceptually primitive notion, one ... not ... analyzable in terms of individuals' I-mode mental states" (Tuomela 2017: 26, 30; see too 2005: 358; but cf. 2007: 140 where he describes "we-groups" as "metaphorically ... agents").

Cutting across these divides in terms of how best to understand group agency, philosophers emphasize different sorts of group agents in their accounts. In her discussions of social solidarity, Montessori claims that "we must not confuse this natural social solidarity with the organization of adult society" (1: 213). In contemporary philosophy, many discussions of group agency focus on organized institutional forms of agency. Paradigm instances of group agency for Phil Pettit and Christian List, for example, are "committees and commissions, partnerships and companies ..., governments and courts" (List and Pettit 2006: 86). Others focus on examples that correspond to what Montessori calls "natural social solidarity." Michael Bratman, for instance, takes as paradigmatic cases where "we make a fresco together, or dance together, or converse together, or sing together, or build together, or experiment together" (Bratman 2013: 4), and Gilbert's main example is that of "walking together" (Gilbert 1990).[6]

Montessori discusses the organization of complex adult social structures, but she starts with natural social solidarity and particularly emphasizes natural forms of solidarity that arise among children. She conceives of social solidarity in terms of a felt sense of oneself as part of a whole, and because she focuses on solidarity in ethical life and human development, she is less concerned with its metaphysical status than its moral importance (see §4). Nonetheless, she develops philosophical resources that contribute to contemporary discussions, not least the importance of attending to children's felt solidarity in developing theories of group agency.

For example, many contemporary theorists of shared agency, including Bratman and Gilbert, draw on their accounts of the nature of individual adult agency as a framework for thinking about group agency. As noted in Chapter 3, Montessori's approach to individual agency emphasizes the agential capacities of children; she thus differs from most contemporary theorists of agency in seeing higher-order reflection and deliberation as unnecessary for the internality, activity, normative self-governance, and persistence that agency requires. Similarly, her approach to social solidarity differs from many contemporary accounts in highlighting pre-deliberative and pre-reflective forms of social solidarity. Bratman's account of shared intentionality, for example, requires "intentions on the part of each in favor of the joint activity, interlocking intentions, beliefs about the joint efficacy ... of the relevant intentions ..., [a] *connection condition* and ... *mutual responsiveness*" (Bratman 2009: 54, emphasis original; see too Bratman 2014). Montessori could—and does—affirm each of these elements, but for her (unlike for Bratman), none of them require reflective deliberation. Just as Sofia intends to work on the cylinder blocks by choosing that activity and attending to it, children form interlocked intentions by virtue of taking up the task of being silent together and attending to that task. Their beliefs about one another are implicit and enacted, like Sofia's "belief" that she erred when a cylinder remains that does not fit into the remaining hole. And they are connected and mutually responsive much as Sofia's intention connects with the tensions in her hand and wrist and responds to interactions between hand, cylinder, and perceived holes in the block. Similarly, the normative self-governance condition—what Gilbert describes in terms of joint commitment—emerges through a process that need not be deliberative; just as Sofia commits herself to doing the cylinder blocks activity well by attending to that activity, so too children, as a group, commit themselves to being silent by virtue of taking up that activity. Perhaps most importantly, the process of terminating commitment need not involve a separate deliberative act. Bratman rightly notes that all cases of shared agency—like all cases of agency—involve persistence, but his own examples of social agency highlight the role of non-reflective persistence in at least some of these cases. Simply stopping an activity or no longer taking interest in it can be sufficient to break off normative commitment to that activity in cases of both individual agency—Sofia's work with cylinder blocks or my casual flute-playing—and group agency—Montessori's Silence Game and Bratman's dancing together or singing together (Bratman 2014: 4).

At a basic level, Montessori remains strongly committed to individual agency. Solidarity depends upon "everyone's consent"; in the Silence Game, "the whole class must *want* to be silent" (7: 53). Moreover, for solidarity (as opposed to mere organization), consent requires *shared interest*: "The children all have the same aim and work together in order to achieve it. They all aim at perfect silence" (17: 234). As with Sofia's interest in cylinder blocks, *shared* interest delimits the commitments each has to the project of the group:

> you cannot achieve silence in a crowd unless every individual within the crowd *wants* to achieve it for a time. And after that the lesson is over ... You may have to begin again several times because it requires the effort of everyone, the *agreement* of everyone, because if one person doesn't want to do it, and makes a movement, the others can't enjoy the silence any more.
>
> (7: 53–4)

As we will see in Chapter 6, forms of organized shared agency can solidify agreement over longer time horizons and thereby establish different sorts of group commitment, but the most primitive sort of social solidarity consists of shared activity arising from a shared interest that partly constitutes joint commitment.

While solidarity requires individual agreement, consent, and interest, it also requires "cooperation" (7: 53). At times, Montessori's descriptions of solidarity describe the level of unification as quite minimal, as when she says merely that "Everyone does the lesson, all together" (7: 54). True solidarity goes beyond mere doing-alongside-one-another, however, at least in three respects. First, in solidarity, children are not merely engaged in tasks that happen to coalesce. Rather, "they all have the same aim and work together in order to achieve it" (17: 234). Each intends to bring about an aim through contributing to a process that depends upon others also working toward that same aim, and each intends to pursue that aim through pursuing it with others. Second, whereas cooperation can still be motivated by a desire merely to attain one's individual goals through working with others, social solidarity is a phenomenon within which each will "put the group first and try to succeed for its benefit" (1: 211). Montessori gives the example of "the Oxford and Cambridge boat race" where "every man rows his hardest for the boat, knowing full well that this will bring him no personal glory nor special reward" (1: 212, citing Carleton Washburne). Likewise, in the case of the Argentinian ambassador (cited in §1), children "cooperated for the honor of their community" (1: 212). Finally, social solidarity involves affective dimensions, including not only "sympathy" with one another and "a sense of solidarity" (17: 234; 1: 237; see too 7: 52–5), but also an affective unity that gets incorporated into each's individual character, as "little by little a child absorbs the prevailing sentiments of his group" (17: 235). Children (and adults) in solidarity *feel* united in a common task, and as they engage in it, they come to feel united as a common body. They work together, striving for perfection together.

These dimensions of solidarity can be understood in singularist or individual terms, such that each distinct person intends to pursue goals with others for the sake of benefits accruing to the group and with an awareness of the feelings of others. We have "perfect cooperation" that goes beyond merely game theoretic reductions of cooperation to individual self-interest, but it is not yet clear in what sense these forms of cooperation ontologically or metaphysically "unite the individuals" (17: 234). The "sense of solidarity" (1: 237) arguably goes beyond individualism to some degree, in that each *feels* united to others, but even this might be understood merely as a certain sort of feeling held by each individual, one that still allows for a reduction of group agency to attitudes of individuals.

In some contexts, however, Montessori discusses more profound sorts of unification in social solidarity, and she develops a metaphysical account of the development of individual agents that provides resources for explaining group agents as emergent entities—something like the "superagent" or "group mind" that many contemporary philosophers reject as "mysterious" (Bratman 1993: 99; Searle 1990: 404)—with powers that are irreducible to those of the individuals from which they emerge (or on which they supervene).

At the beginning of this section, I distinguished two sorts of "unity" on which Montessori focuses, namely natural social solidarity (as when people walk or dance or make silence together) and organized unity (as in political or corporate structures). In many of her writings on human history, she emphasizes a third sort of unity, that "unity—which is a fact in nature" (6: 47), that is, the simple fact that human beings are interdependent in such a way that we depend upon participation in social wholes in order to function.

> In the course of centuries, men have already organized themselves to work one for the other ... We have reached a state in our social organization that makes it impossible to live in [mere] nature; of necessity, each and every one of us depends upon the work of others and is obliged to work for others ... Man has accomplished a great feat in establishing a near-perfect system of exchange, similar to the circulatory system of the human body ... [U]nity is there already; it exists!
>
> (12: 85–7)

The social structures within which each person operates establish a real functional unity amongst human beings, such that, for instance, "the economy" adjusts prices, labor flows, and consumption without any particular individuals determining how these adjustments occur. Montessori even points out that our world has become so interconnected that, thanks in part to "economic mechanisms and communications" whereby "men have in fact managed to become united in their material interests," "we are all a single organism, one nation" (10: 21, 22). In terms of the metaphysics of agency, functional systematic forms of unity amongst human beings already manifest higher-order properties that emerge from the behavior of individuals who participate in those systems. In that sense, social groups, economies, and even humanity as a whole simply *are* unities.

This factual unification of individuals into social wholes can be compared with the way in which classrooms wherein children respect one another and pursue self-directed work are organized wholes. As I noted in §1, however, a shift occurs in such classrooms as children "become *aware* of forming a community ... [and] come to *feel* part of the group to which their activity contributes" (1: 211, emphasis added). Montessori makes a similar point about the human community as a whole (and about subsidiary communities):

> Although the necessity for material unity among peoples is universally perceived ...,the spiritual understanding, which alone can lead to unity amongst all men, continues to be missing ... It is useless to try to achieve unity amongst men [by] inviting them to work for each other, since this has been happening for centuries. Instead the question is [how] to bring about a radical change in the way we *view* human relations, endeavouring to influence men's *consciousness* ... World unity ... exists! The issue, therefore, is to do everything possible to help mankind become *conscious of this reality*, submitting to the perception of a need to create union amongst men by the revelation that ties of interdependence and social solidarity ... already exist, real and strong.
>
> (14: 85–7)

> When it is recognized that the world is already a living organism, its vital functions may be less impeded in their operation, and it may consciously enter on its heritage in the day towards which hitherto "all creation has been groaning and travailing together."
>
> (6: 47)

The challenge is not to *create* structured wholes with emergent properties that exceed the contributions of their parts. Such structured wholes already exist, in classrooms and social organizations and political bodies and the interconnected human community as a whole. The challenge is to make such wholes self-conscious.

> The living idea of the solidarity of all men, who come and go, from past to future, closely united by many bonds, generates a warmth arising from knowing we are part of something great, a sentiment surpassing even love of country. Our task as educators is to ensure that an intense consciousness of universal solidarity will flourish within our children.
>
> (14: 88)

This occurs partly through raising individual consciousness in group members, for instance through a sense of "profound gratitude" for the contributions of others or an "altruism" that focuses not merely on goods for individual others but for humanity as a whole (14: 86-7). Partly, the self-consciousness of social wholes emerges through deeper connections amongst its parts, such as a more profound "sympathy" of each with one another and that irreducible "sense of solidarity" present in everything from the small group of children playing the Silence Game together to those driven by the "profound passion" of connectedness with all humanity (17: 234; 14: 87).

Fully realized social solidarity requires both factual unification of individuals into a whole that exceeds the sum of its parts, and a consciousness of this unification. In some cases, such as the Silence Game, unification of individuals depends essentially on consciousness of unification. Part of what makes the Silence Game such a profound experience of solidarity is precisely this dependence. In other cases, such as participation in a community of character and respect, the fact of unification exists independent of the sense of unification, but even in these cases, the character of the whole changes when it shifts from an integrated whole consisting of individual decisions to an integrated whole with which individuals identify as parts. While a respectful community without solidarity would have been worth a visit from the Argentinian ambassador, the children's voluntary creation of that community for him occurred only because of felt solidarity.

4 The Moral Importance of Solidarity

The previous three sections highlighted how solidarity emerges from respect and character and what such solidarity consists of, but the most important question for Montessori's moral theory is why such solidarity should be seen as an important and valuable part of ethical life. Once human beings pursue their own perfection through activities that express their character, and once they do so in ways constrained by respect for others and inclusive of help and cooperation with others, one might think that further, more substantive forms of unity are at best unnecessary and at worst (see §7) dangerous.

Ultimately, Montessori's defense of the moral importance of solidarity draws from her moral epistemology. One can simply see that solidarity enhances human life. The perception of friends who feel genuine comradery with one another, citizens with patriotic allegiance, sports fans in a spirit of unity, and children achieving silence together gives rise to an immediate awareness that such forms of unity enhance human life. Montessori describes her own experience of how observation of children shifted her moral perceptions toward appreciation of solidarity. In discussing the Silence Game in particular, she highlights this point:

> Everything I say is the result of an experience, and experience has shown me some wonderful and surprising things. And that is why I say that *the child can teach us something*, that he can be a *guide or a light for us*.
>
> (7: 51)

Specifically addressing how to reconcile freedom with solidarity, she notes,

> If we have a set idea of what freedom is and what freedom must be, we end by becoming slaves of our idea of freedom. Instead, by living with children and observing their expressions of life, we must learn for ourselves what freedom really is. If we leave children free, we can observe what they do when they are free, and we can follow with them a certain law, by following which they come together.
>
> (24: 53)

When one pays attention to adults conversing or competing in group sports or playing music together, one can see the importance of group agency for ethical life, but Montessori rightly notes how the simple unity expressed in activities like the Silence Game provides a profoundly moving example of the nature and moral value of this sort of experience.

Beyond direct perception of its ethical value, Montessori highlights several articulable reasons that social solidarity plays an important role in ethical life. First, as the capacity of an individual for unity with others, and a capacity of a group for agency, it offers a focus for the self-perfecting powers of individuals and eventually groups. Work done in solidarity can be done with greater or less precision; it requires attention and work, involves internal norms, and increases agential efficacy at both the group and individual levels. As I become more unified with others, I become individually more perfect. As we become more thoroughly unified—while retaining individual character and mutual respect—we become more perfect as a community. Insofar as the pursuit of perfection is essential and solidarity provides a way of pursuing perfection, solidarity has ethical value.

Solidarity with others in groups also promotes further goods, both concrete external acquisitions—the silence we achieve, the bridges we build, and so on—and internal developments, such as intelligence or strength of will. Moreover, for Montessori, the ability to feel solidarity with others is necessary in order for social life amongst adults to truly flourish. Solidarity grounds successful states, organizations, and communities. As we will see in Chapter 6, adult moral life involves moral concepts and abstract principles. Society in particular depends upon formal laws, organizations, and structures. But for Montessori, there is a fundamental difference between societies where these formal structures merely manipulate isolated individuals into cooperative behavior and those where they articulate and structure individuals with practiced capacities for true solidarity and felt unity.

> Society does not depend entirely on organization, but also on cohesion, and of these two the second is basic and serves as the foundation for the first. Good laws and a good government cannot hold the mass of men together and make them act in harmony unless the individuals themselves are oriented toward something that gives them solidarity and makes them into a group. The masses, in their turn, are more or less strong and active according to the level of development, and of inner stability, of the personalities composing them.
>
> (1: 215)

Just as individuals without character can make their way through the world, pursuing various external goods in competition with others and preserving a dysfunctional and conflicted life, so too societies can exist and even amass great external goods without genuine social solidarity. But such societies will be plagued by internal tension and never rise to the perfection of which they could otherwise be capable. No refined laws or charismatic leader can provide a true unity of strong and independent personalities unless those personalities already have the psychical basis for unity. Healthy societies depend on a solidarity that "begins in infancy" and has "its roots in the unconscious creative zone of the mind" (1: 216). Montessori ascribes the failings of present forms of social organization precisely to the failure to cultivate felt social solidarity:

> If [social solidarity] became the rule in every social undertaking, from those which embrace the whole country down to the smallest industrial concern, and if all were moved by the wish to bring honor to his group rather than to himself, then the whole human family would be reborn. This integration of the individual with the group must be cultivated in the schools, because it is just this that we lack, and the failure and ruin of our civilization is due to this lack.
>
> (1: 212–3)

As we saw in §3, unity amongst human beings in the sense of interdependence is an empirical fact. As we will see in Chapter 6, social organization is an essential part of adult cooperative activity. Without true social solidarity, however, both are spiritless and mechanical.

Given humans' social nature, our need and desire to live in harmony with others, and particularly the current state of interdependence with countless others throughout the world, individual character is insufficient for complete moral virtue. And given that the full realization of our capacities for excellence depends not merely on being left alone and given occasional "help" but also on actively working *together* toward shared goals, mere respect for others is also insufficient. To be a morally excellent individual is always also to be capable of sharing in common projects, of exercising solidarity with others.

5 Obedience

For Montessori, social solidarity amongst equals is one form of unity amongst people. In many experiences of solidarity, individuals see themselves as equal (even if different) parts of a common project. But as social virtues develop, children also come to see themselves as part of hierarchies of excellence, and they naturally seek relationships of obedience to those they consider superior in one or another respect. The Silence Game itself is an example of "obedience [that] took on a collective aspect" (1: 237), and Montessori often emphasizes the role of the teacher as an authority figure in uniting children into silence (e.g., 7: 55; Montessori 1912: 116). She notes in general that "free children are singularly obedient," adding that, like solidarity itself, "Obedience must come from the formation of an individual['s character]" (17: 236; see too 1: 229, 249; 2: 335–8; 9: 78, 86–8; 17: 74). The capacity to obey, like social solidarity, is an important part of moral life.

Obedience might seem a peculiar virtue within Montessori's ethics. Montessori vehemently objects to a "[s]ociety [that] wants children to become adults based on our orders" (18: 251) and to those who tell children, "Suppress your impulse and do as I say" (18: 254). She warns,

> The obedience forced upon a child at home and in school ... prepares the adult to resign himself to anything and everything ..., instills in him an uncontrollable and irrational terror of public opinion ..., [a]nd through [this] sense of inferiority, the way is opened to the spirit of unthinking respect, and indeed almost mindless idolatry, in the minds of paralysed adults towards public leaders ... And discipline thus becomes almost synonymous with slavery.
>
> (10: 16)

It is easy to see why obedience to other people would be suspect within Montessori's moral theory. When I obey, I seemingly lose the internality essential for agency, literally being governed by an external will. Moreover, I become passively related even to my own "activity," merely taking on the role of an instrument of another. When I subordinate my choices to another's will, either through repressing my choices and instead doing what another says or (even worse) through forming my choice only in the light of the will of another, *my* self does not play any role in "my" actions. In contrast to command-and-obey methods of dealing with children, Montessori insists that "we must permit the *free, natural manifestations* of the *child*" (Montessori 1912: 8; cf. 2: 9):

> Life is based on choice, so [the children in Montessori schools] learn to make their own decisions. They decide and choose for themselves ... They cannot learn these things through obedience to the demands of another.
>
> (17: 236)

Cultivation of character and respect happens through command-free respect for children's independent agency.

Nonetheless, Montessori extols obedience. The child "who has reached a higher degree of evolution ... enters upon that characteristic phenomenon I have called the 'phenomenon of obedience.' He can ... direct [his actions] in accordance with the desires of another person" (9: 78; cf. 17: 74). Montessori describes in glowing terms the obedience of children to their Montessori teacher:

> When invited by a single gesture to come ..., they obeyed in a wonderful manner, leaving off work at once ...; they evidently felt pleasure in obeying, and an internal delight which came from the consciousness of ... being ready to leave something that they liked doing, at a summons to something of a higher order. They arranged themselves very carefully ... [W]hen any modification was necessary ..., it sufficed

to murmur a word in their ears and the almost imperceptible movement required was made with the utmost exactitude; ... they were able to translate the words they heard into actions.

(9: 87)

Montessori defends her high estimation of the value of obedience partly through appeal to the obvious joy that those with character take in obeying, but also through showing how obedience can—when properly structured—facilitate, express, and develop from character. Forms of obedience that relate to character in these ways are not oppressive but instead represent a higher evolution, an ideal of ethical life.

Obedience facilitates and expresses character in at least three important ways.[7] First, for those with character who actively seek norm-governed work, obedience is helpful and often even necessary in order to know appropriate norms governing one's work and to properly organize action within the world. Agents with character seek direction by others with more knowledge and experience, who can facilitate proficient, orderly, and informed expressions of agency: "It is as if the child had become aware that the teacher could do things beyond his own powers, and had said to himself, 'Here is someone so far above me that she can exert an influence on my mind and make me as clever as she is ...'" (1: 236). Given the centrality of normative self-governance, those with character seek clarity about appropriate standards of perfection for activities that attract them. Even if, in some sense, "every lesson infringes the liberty of the child," lessons nonetheless cultivate agency by providing "a determinate impression of contact with the external world" (9: 32). In contrast to "the mass of indeterminate contacts the child is continually receiving from his surroundings, [which] create chaos within the mind of the child," the "pre-determined contacts" articulated in lessons "initiate order [in the mind]" and thereby provide precise understandings of and actions within the world (9: 32). Such lessons that prepare the child for "subsequent free choice, and the repetition of the exercise, ... subsequent activity, spontaneous, associative, and reproductive" in which "the child will be left 'free'" (9: 32). "Obedience" facilitates orderly engagement with objects of work, which orient the child. Even for more mature children (and adults), norm-governed agency can require deference—and in that sense obedience—to others' guidance. As Roberts and Wood have explained in their discussion of intellectual autonomy, "some ways of receiving direction from another are compatible with, or even essential to, autonomy" (Roberts and Wood 2007: 261).[8]

A second role of obedience directly relates to the discussion of social solidarity in §1–4. In my primary example of social solidarity, the Silence Game, children together pursue the goal of total silence. This group agency is solicited through the invitation of the teacher. Montessori describes the "marvelous and quite unexpected unity" of the Silence Game as one wherein "a whole group of children almost identified itself with" the teacher they obeyed (1: 237). Here we find "obedience [with] a collective aspect," and correlatively, a collective organized by obedience. As the term "identified" suggests, obedience is a kind of social solidarity, one in which multiple agents form an organized whole. As in all solidarity, the unification represents genuine agency when it arises from the voluntary coordination of strong wills; in obedience, one with a strong will subordinates that will to another for the sake of fuller expression of agency. Obedience is intrinsically a form of solidarity. At the same time, as a contingent matter, obedience helps *facilitate* broader forms of social solidarity; when a group jointly obeys a recognized leader, this obedience often consists of participation in shared activity, which generates solidarity amongst members of the group. Particularly when solidarity arises without shared deliberation, the voice of an authority often catalyzes joint commitment in a group.

Finally, a third role of obedience becomes evident when obedience directly expresses one's character. Montessori notes that "will and ... obedience ..., in the minds of most people, are opposed ideas," and ascribes this to the fact that "education is so largely directed toward the suppression or bending of the child's will, and the substitution for it of the adult's will, which demands from the child unquestioning obedience" (1: 229). As most people rightly see, autonomous agency is not present in the discipline and obedience typical of most adult-child interactions, or in forms of obedience rooted in external rewards, or even in the response of pre-normalized children to "policeman" teachers seeking to preserve order and guide students toward work. In these cases, obedience arises as something external to one's agency, a limitation on activity, a constraint with which one does not identify. One might "voluntarily" obey for the sake of external rewards, but even in such cases, one's specific actions are governed by another *rather than* by oneself. By contrast with these sorts of obedience, Montessori describes an obedience in children that *arises from* individual agency.

> We think of freedom and obedience as being two contrasting things. Instead, these free children are singularly obedient. Obedience must come from the formation of an individual—otherwise it is a repression. It can be the manifestation of the perfection of an individual. Only one who is master of himself can obey. If we do not have this inner discipline it is difficult to obey. Children who are happy obey the teacher ... who asks but does not command. The children are proud to be able to obey.
>
> (17: 236)

Where other forms of obedience repress the will, this obedience is an *accomplishment* of a strong and free individual. When it comes to thinking about the role of obedience in education, "[t]he basic error is to suppose that a person's will must necessarily be broken before it can obey, meaning before it can accept and follow another person's directions" (1: 232). By contrast, Montessori articulates a sense of obedience that *expresses* character, one that depends upon a *strong* rather than weakened will.

The connection between character and obedience is evident in the joy with which children obey:

> When invited by a single gesture to come and be measured, they obeyed in a wonderful manner, leaving off work at once, and moving with smiles, as if fascinated; they evidently felt pleasure in obeying, and an internal delight ... [O]bedience [had become] a fascinating acquisition"
>
> (9: 87–8)

The joy of obedience is *not* a joy in passively abdicating to another's will, but rather joy in successfully and freely accomplishing an effort of will. The "internal delight" in obeying

> came from the consciousness of being able to work, and of being ready to leave something that they liked doing, at a summons to something of a higher order ... [T]hey could control their voluntary movements and direct them; they were able to translate the words they heard into actions: *this enabled them* to obey, and this constituted for them a fascinating internal conquest.
> (9: 87, emphasis original)

The "phenomenon of obedience" arises when the child "becomes a personality who has reached a higher degree of evolution [and] ... begins to be 'master of himself' ... He *can obey*, that is, he can control his actions, and therefore can direct them in accordance with the desires of another person" (9: 78, emphasis original; cf. 17: 74).

Such obedience *depends upon* character. It "includes a training of both intellect and will" and requires "exercise of the will" (2: 335–6; 9: 127). Without a capacity to govern oneself, one cannot joyfully submit to another. When describing the "genius" as "the man who has burst his bonds asunder, who has maintained his liberty," Montessori's first example of such liberation is "that sublime 'spiritual obedience,' at present still unknown to the majority of mankind, with the exception of monks, who, however, often recognize it only in theory, and contemplate it only in the examples given by the saints," an obedience that depends upon "the construction of a strong internal life" (9: 162; cf. Nietzsche 1966: 61–2). To be *able* to obey depends upon having achieved the self-control intrinsic to character, and obedience that proceeds from this foundation *expresses* that character.

6 Conclusion: Solidarity, Obedience, and Totalitarianism

In §2, I suggested that there is a prima facie tension between Montessori's emphasis on individual character and her affirmation of solidarity as an ethical ideal. Similarly, in §5, I highlighted an apparent tension between freedom and obedience. In both cases, Montessori's specific approaches to solidarity and obedience show how these pillars of ethical life can emerge from rather than conflict with individual freedom. Even setting aside theoretical philosophical concerns, however, there are apparently serious practical problems with an ethic that emphasizes the centrality of solidarity and obedience, and particularly one that focuses on cultivating children to be capable of experiencing profound group solidarity and enthusiastic obedience to authorities. When discussing the Silence Game, Montessori even describes it as a "totalitarian" solidarity, referring there merely to the fact that it requires total participation, but alluding to the danger that practices of solidarity and obedience can be directed in authoritarian ways, which undermine rather than support human dignity. When discussing the importance of solidarity for uniting people in ways that go beyond mere organization, she explicitly refers to "Mussolini and Hitler" as among "the first to grasp that rulers who wish to make sure of a new social order surviving, must train people to it in infancy … These heads of the state felt the need to have a 'cohesive society' as a basis on which to build, and they prepared its roots accordingly" (1: 216). One concerned primarily with individual character and respect for persons might reasonably see solidarity and obedience as fundamental threats or at best unnecessary and risky addenda to ethical life.

As her references to Mussolini and Hitler make clear, Montessori recognizes the danger arising from misuse of humans' capacities for obedience and social organization.

> Those nations that want war have managed to recognize and give scope to the powers hidden in children and young people to further their own interests, to organize them socially, to make them an active force in society. It is a tragedy that this truth has thus far been recognized only by those powers that seek war.
> (10: 29)

Most basically, Montessori responds these dangers by reiterating the centrality of individual agency, even for solidarity and obedience. Solidarity can and should develop from "the realization of *one's own* value," which "urges to association because he who is conscious of his values is … an energy" that seeks a higher and more effective outlet (12: 83–4, emphasis added); "society by cohesion … does not come from any imposed behavior, or even from imitative behavior" (17: 233). Likewise, "Obedience is no mechanical thing, but a natural force … intimately related to the will … [A]n obedience … which is not the natural consequence of an awakened and exercised will, brings whole nations to disaster" (6: 77). The cultivation of solidarity and obedience should go hand-in-hand with the cultivation of individual character.

When solidarity and obedience emerge through cultivation of individual agency, they bring internal mechanisms for preventing the disasters that can arise from *blind* obedience. Montessori explains that when children work and develop character, not only does "naughtiness disappear … without correction" but "[a]long with naughtiness, other characteristics also disappear which are usually considered to be good in children—extreme obedience…, submission, etc." (17: 188). The psychological changes that make for internal discipline and awaken interest in solidarity and obedience also prevent the submissive and extreme obedience that characterizes totalitarian societies. Moreover, these protections against obsequious or mindless solidarity strengthen rather than weaken social wholes:

> Good laws and a good government cannot hold the mass of men together and make them act in harmony unless the individuals themselves are oriented toward something that gives them solidarity and makes them into a group. *The masses, in their turn, are more or less strong and active according to the level of development, and of inner stability, of the personalities composing them.*
> (1: 215, emphasis added)

Grounding group agency on enduring individual agency not only prevents "disaster" in the misuse of solidarity but also generates "strong and active" social wholes. Organized societies within which individual agency is crushed might be stronger (albeit in a disastrous way) than mere collections of individuals, but an organized whole arising from and supporting strong individual personalities is stronger still.

Beyond showing how solidarity, properly cultivated, prevents destructive totalitarian excesses, Montessori also insists that solidarity in the cause of peace, mutual respect, and human dignity is needed to combat enemies of those values. Immediately after grieving the "tragedy that [the value of solidarity] has thus far been recognized only by those powers that seek war," Montessori goes on:

> But the fact that a truly powerful organization of humanity cannot be improvised overnight is a reality that has great practical value. The groundwork for such organization must be laid in childhood, at the very roots of life. Society can be organized, in short, only if education offers man a ladder of social experiences as he passes from one period of his life to another. Those who want war prepare young people for war; but those who want peace have neglected young children and adolescents, for they have been unable to organize them for peace.
>
> (10: 29)

The solution to bad solidarity is not the rejection of solidarity, but the utilization of solidarity for the purposes of respectful and peaceful human cooperation. Ultimately, solidarity in the cause of peace and justice will be stronger than solidarity in the service of war and injustice because the former enhances the character on which true solidarity is built and does not require stifling the respect for others that naturally flows from strong characters. But precisely because unjust and violent regimes generate a social strength that needs to be resisted, just and peaceful societies need to recognize the value and power of felt solidarity.

6

Adulthood, Abstraction, and Reflective Deliberation

The preceding three chapters (3–5) outlined core features of Montessorian ethical life: character, respect, and solidarity.[1] In each case, I showed how these features of ethical life can be and often are present in children. Children have character and thereby exercise an agency worthy of respect. They should, can, and often do govern themselves by standards of respect for others, which includes offering agency-enhancing help to others. And they are capable of substantial social solidarity. Children participate in these features of ethical life when granted freedom in environments conducive to their development, and they are able to do so without higher-order reflection, self-conscious deliberation, or applying principles of Reason. Montessori rightly points out, "Morality has been considered something abstract concerning adults, not concerning children. Instead we must consider morality as a fact of life, which can be studied in the developing child" (14: 20–21).

Immediately after mentioning the presence of morality in children, Montessori goes on: "It is a fact of life which has different phases following the phases the child passes through" (14: 21). Chapters 3–5 focused on features of ethical life present in children under the age of five. Those reading this book, however, are not such children. As we grow into adults, the form of ethical life changes. On the one hand, pre-reflective forms of character, respect, and solidarity remain central in adults' lives. Adults often feel most themselves when engaged in immersive activities in which they seek to excel and perfect themselves and to which they wholeheartedly commit. In sport, sex, conversation, music, teaching, problem-solving, or countless other activities, intense immersion in the flow of effortful activity gives meaning to adult lives. Respect, too, is often a matter of waiting patiently in line rather than pushing one's way to the front, or adopting a non-imperious tone of voice, or stepping aside to let someone pass. In many such cases, adults need not deliberate or reflect in order to engage in respectful behavior. And adults feel solidarity with one another, even without reflective deliberation, when in contexts—such as religious gatherings, sports, or concerts—that foster a sense of unity and foci for shared agency.

On the other hand, however, adults have capacities that young children lack, capacities that affect their ethical lives.[2] For example, Montessori discusses older children's "felt need to escape the closed environment" (12: 7). Young children flourish in carefully prepared environments, but as children mature, they seek to "go out," to "escape from the house" and "succeed in adapting [themselves] to the outer world" (12: 11, 12). Such changes have implications for the nature of ethical life, such that, for instance, older children and adults who "go out" also extend their interests (character), respect, and solidarity beyond the walls of school and home. In this chapter, I focus on two specific and particularly salient capacities that emerge in adolescence and have significant implications for agency and ethical life. The first—a capacity for "abstraction"—corresponds to the development of Reason as an abstract faculty of thinking about the world. As children mature into adults (starting around age seven), they begin to conceive of moral relations in abstract terms. Rather than merely waiting patiently for work because there is "nothing for it but to wait," they abstract from these lived experiences and seek general principles of right and wrong, justice and injustice. As we mature into adults, we become capable of governing ourselves through the application of these concepts. Second, as we saw in Chapter 3, deliberation and reflection are central components of many contemporary accounts of agency, shaped as they are by an effort to characterize *adult* agency as paradigmatic. While I argued in Chapter 3 that such reflection is not essential for agency, I acknowledged that reflective deliberation can enhance agency. In §1, I discuss the role of abstraction in adult ethical life. In §2, I take up the ways that deliberation changes Montessori's overall account of character and agency, noting both the value and the limitations of reflective deliberation.

1 Abstraction

1.1 The Passage to Abstraction

For Montessori, "the passage to the second level of education is the passage from the sensorial, material level to the abstract" (12: 5).[3] This "power of abstraction belongs exclusively to man," distinguishing him from mere animals and allowing him to "further create ideas in his mind through which something new arises" (24: 150; cf. 1: 165; 17: 194; 24: 190). The increased interest in abstraction that arises in later childhood and adulthood permeates every aspect of human life. In general, abstraction is the capacity to take, "from the millions of things that we can see around us, ... a quality from many objects which possess that quality," and thereby "form an idea" (24: 78). Children who have worked in sensorial ways with various materials come to formulate words and concepts that extend application of the principles they understand in an embodied way. Montessori notes with respect to mathematical principles, which she teaches first through the manipulation of concrete objects such as sets of beads or shapes, that "The child knows the rules already through experience and practice" but as they mature, they come to express them abstractly (24: 298). More generally, for very young children, the materials with which they work constitute "materialized abstractions" (24: 81) with norms for self-governance—"control of error" (1: 224)—built directly into them. As children mature, they internalize these materialized abstract norms.

For development in general, abstraction has several important effects. It allows older children and adults to extend knowledge beyond the world that is immediately present to their senses. Rather than placing cylinders in their proper holes or building a tower with blocks, older children can investigate the life cycle of the polar bear or try to figure out the volume of water that passes from the Ganges into the ocean each year or study dark matter and black holes. The capacity to abstract also frees thought and action from reliance on specific features of the physical environment. Adults no longer need careful arrangements of beads to perform arithmetic operations, but can do them "in their heads." The capacity to extend knowledge also enhances one's interest, curiosity, and ambitions. Montessori notes, "the [older] child needs to enlarge his field of action" (12: 3); he seeks to go into the world, both physically—leaving the confines of his classroom—and also through his imagination, inferring from "a few details ... [to] a classification of the Whole" (12: 21). Abstraction also serves an important role in extending the time horizons over which children govern themselves, providing a non-material focus of attention that can be sustained longer than children are able to remain focused on sensorially given material. Long-term planning, a sense for one's life as a whole, and commitment to principles that apply to a range of situations all require abstraction. And abstraction enables the application of rules and principles to contexts where one does not have the relevant sensorimotor habits.

These effects are general and not limited to ethical life, but they also extend the scope of ethical life. Our extension of knowledge and interest beyond what is present includes an extension of *moral* considerations beyond what is present. Rather than merely avoiding bumping into one's neighbor, one develops concern for how this or that class of people in general is treated in this or that general context. The ability to free thought and action from concrete particulars allows agents to initiate new projects, including new moral projects, and to pose for themselves abstract considerations of justice or excellence. The ability to form long-term plans and abstract principles makes it possible to commit oneself to principles with what Christine Korsgaard calls "provisional universality," in that one commits to follow those rules throughout life and one applies them to all cases that fall under them. Abstraction thereby changes the structure of character, respect, and solidarity.

1.2 Abstraction, Agency, and Character

For both children and adults, character is a capacity and tendency to exercise agency, where agency consists of normative self-governance through persistent activity in accordance with interests with which one identifies. In both children and adults, these aspects of character are present in ways that do not depend upon abstraction. When Sofia invests in her cylinder blocks or Alex Honnold climbs a rock face or Jonathan Biss plays a Beethoven sonata, they express character through direct engagement with concrete, sensorially present, materially realized action. When Sofia, as an older girl, decides that she will study more algebra so that she can better investigate the possible effects of climate change on coral formations, or when Admiral Byrd "undertook the humiliating task of collecting money in order to explore the South Pole" (1: 192), or when Denis Papin turned from having his "attention ... arrested by the sight of the lid of a saucepan of boiling water raised by the steam" to investigate "steam [a]s a force which could lift a piston" (9: 167), these expressions of character require abstraction.

Abstraction can be involved with character in superficial ways that do not change the essential structure of agency. To use one of Montessori's examples, when "Galileo ..., standing in Pisa Cathedral, ... watched the oscillations of a hanging lamp [and] ... observed ... the isochronism of the pendulum" (9: 166), his observations were not *mere* observations; Galileo conceptualized the hanging lamp as a pendulum and its regular movement as isochronism. In that way, his cognitive work depended upon abstraction. More generally, Csikszentmihalyi describes a "flow of thought" that takes place in the development and exercise of "symbolic skills" (Csikszentmihalyi 1990: 127, 6). As in other cases of flow, the self loses consciousness of itself while immersed in these symbolic activities, and they do not necessarily require exercise of agency extending beyond moments of flow. The skills being exercised are skills that involve abstracting in particular ways and/or manipulating abstract objects, so expression of character in these cases requires abstraction, but only because of the specific content of the activity in which one is engaged.

Abstraction can also change the nature of character in more significant ways, corresponding to each dimension of agency discussed in Chapter 3. Self-governance in accordance with norms changes. Lacking a developed capacity for abstraction, Sofia engages with norms as they are present in the material with which she works; "control of error" is built directly into classroom materials. Agents who abstract are able to follow norms that are abstract, conceptual, and even "universal" rather than merely material, sensory, and immanent.

Philosophers of agency describe various ways that universality and consistency are essential to agency (see, for example, Korsgaard 2009). For Montessori, universality and cross-situational consistency are not intrinsic to agency as such, but they are intrinsic to abstraction. For "red" to be an abstraction is for the concept to apply consistently to every instance of red. I do not have the concept "red" if I apply it only to those red things to which I feel like applying it. If I agentially engage myself in working on a given set of cylinder blocks, that agency requires that I persist in my activity for some time period, but my commitment to work with these blocks does not commit me to work with other similar blocks or even with these blocks at another time. By contrast, if I commit myself to "work on cylinder blocks" in the abstract, this commitment applies universally to all relevantly similar blocks (subject to various ceteris paribus qualifiers).

Moreover, Sofia's self-governance primarily involved control of her body in accordance with norms to which she committed herself, along with the enhancement and inhibition of impulses in accordance with those norms. Those with capacities for abstraction can explicitly and directly order not only their actions and impulses but broad commitments, all in accordance with (abstract) principles of (abstract) reasoning. In terms of specifically "moral" self-governance in the traditional sense, only an agent who abstracts can pursue the greatest good for the greatest number (see Mill 1863) or "act only in accordance with that maxim through which you can at the same time will that it become a universal law" (Kant 1996: 73). More broadly, agents capable of abstraction can explicitly govern themselves by basic norms of practical rationality. Sofia governs herself by the norm of consistency, without formulating "consistency" as an abstract principle, because she literally cannot put two cylinders in one hole or a single cylinder in two holes at once, but adults can explicitly establish structured hierarchies of values and evaluate the consistency of the elements of those hierarchies. In that sense, only with abstraction do we get the "established constitution" Schapiro identifies as necessary for having a will of one's own (Schapiro 1999: 729).

The *persistence* essential for agency also expands as abstraction enables longer time horizons of self-governance. When I comprehend an activity abstractly, I can commit to and engage in it for hours, days, or even years. When Sofia worked with her cylinder blocks for forty-four repetitions, her agency coalesced around a sensorially given project to which she remained committed for a time, after which she returned the material to its place. She may have persisted for as long as an hour in this activity, though it was likely shorter. Some young children can persist even longer, counting long chains of beads or completing elaborate LEGO structures, for example, and can return to this work after having had to break at the end of the day. While children orient agency around interests in sensorially given materials, however, the temporal extent of self-governance is constricted, for at least two reasons.

First, the interest must always be *in* something sensory and given. In contrast to forty-four repetitions with cylinder blocks, one who abstracts can commit to a month-long research project or an expedition that takes years to plan and execute. These sorts of long-term commitment are possible only when the task that one engages in is largely a matter of realities not sensorially and materially given but imagined or conceptualized.

Second, the interest itself is sensorial rather than abstract. A young child must *feel* interested in an activity in order to *be* interested in it. An adult can take herself to be interested in something even when she does not currently feel that interest. Just as Sofia's present interest in the task of placing cylinders can govern her bodily habits and passing interests, so an older child or adult can have an abstract commitment to a principle or course of action, and, on the basis of the commitment, bind herself to engage in an activity even in the absence of presently felt interest in it. Admiral Byrd can spend time in fundraising that he doesn't enjoy for the sake of his interest in the South Pole, and when, after a long week of fundraising, a unique fundraising opportunity arises, he can decline an appealing invitation to a relaxing dinner with friends in order to pursue that opportunity, even if at that particular moment his commitment even to the expedition shows up to him merely abstractly, as something he knows he wants but is weary of at the moment.

As noted in Chapter 3, those with character strive not only to engage in norm-governed activities, but to pursue perfection, and abstraction also expands the scope of perfections toward which agents can explicitly aim. While very young children aim at various perfections, both in terms of doing the work "perfectly" and in terms of improving (or perfecting) themselves, they directly experience these perfections as desirable without *conceptualizing* them *as* perfections. Part of Sofia's fascination with the activity of manipulating cylinder blocks comes from the expectation (and then experience) of improving her manual dexterity, visual acuity, and fine motor strength. In that sense, Sofia sets manual dexterity and visual acuity as goals of her activity. But she does not value dexterity or acuity *in the abstract*. By working with cylinder blocks, she does not, for instance, commit herself to engage in other activities that would enhance these same capacities. When agents become capable of abstract concepts, however, they can set particular forms of self-perfection as explicit goals; they can aim to become stronger or better at mathematics or more attuned to the needs of others, and they can then choose activities that support the pursuit of those abstract goals.

Agents can also form an abstract concept of perfection in general, seeking to perform specific tasks "for the sake of the fine," as Aristotle puts it (Aristotle 2002: 141 [1120a23–24]), and explicitly aiming to cultivate themselves into more perfect human beings, taking specific efforts as part of a broader commitment to this overall—abstract—goal. As a person matures, "he begins to ask: What am I? What is the task of man in this wonderful universe?" (6: 4). As he develops into adulthood,

> The individual should be the man who knows how to make his own choice of action, having passed to perfection in the preceding phases. He should be as a live spark and aware of the open gate to the potentialities of prospective human life and of his own possibilities and responsibilities.
>
> (14: 37)

Rather than merely seeking to refine movements of her hand in order to place this cylinder perfectly in its hole, an older Sofia seeks to be an excellent person and to engage in activities that cultivate capacities toward that end. Abstraction facilitates self-direction as human beings shift from shaping activities in accordance with given standards of perfection to pursuit of wider and more explicitly open-ended applications of agency: "Unless man could imagine and make abstractions ... his intelligence would resemble that of the higher animals, that is to say, it would be rigid and restricted to some particular form of behavior, and this would prevent its expansion" (1: 165). Moreover, as we become more capable of abstraction, we can more explicitly see our specific work and individual perfections as contributions to the development of our society, species, and cosmos: "It is in this stage that 'vocation' and 'militancy' occur. These [adolescent] children want to make a direct contribution to society" and, even more, "The aspiration of such a man cannot limit itself to personal advantage ... the tendency must be for the whole of humanity" (14: 35, 37).

Finally, abstraction affects the sort of internality available to agents. In asking "Who am I?", an agent formulates an abstract sense of self, one toward which she can intentionally orient self-perfecting activities. Rather than merely *being* an agent internally related to various desires and forming herself through her commitments to act on certain guiding instincts, she now sees herself *as* a "self" who is committed to various principles and who has various desires. She is thus capable of directing attention self-consciously to consider explicitly whether such-and-such a desire or value reflects herself. From this process of considering herself as a self, she becomes capable of formulating higher-order reflective desires to be such-and-such a kind of person with such-and-such sorts of desires, or to act in the light of principles to which *she*—a transtemporal agent of whom she now has a concept—is committed. In that way, abstraction not only generates abstract values and principles that can figure in deliberation but also the abstract concept of oneself that (often) plays an orienting role within reflection and deliberation.

This capacity for relating to oneself, one's desires, and one's values through abstraction also makes it possible to integrate extrinsic motivation into genuinely "internal," autonomous action. Confirming many of Montessori's key claims about character and agency, psychologists Richard Ryan and Edward Deci have emphasized in their "self-determination theory" that "intrinsic motivation"—a "natural inclination toward assimilation, mastery, spontaneous interest, and exploration that is ... essential to cognitive and social development and that represents a principal source of enjoyment and vitality throughout life"—leads to and supports various positive psychological outcomes, while "extrinsic motivation"—where an activity is done not for its own sake but for some separable result such as avoiding punishment or getting a reward—can lead to adverse outcomes (Ryan and Deci 2000: 69–70; cf. Ryan and Deci 2017). Nonetheless, and despite the risks of extrinsic motivation particularly for younger children, Ryan and Deci acknowledge that "intrinsic motivation is not the only type ... of self-determined motivation" (Ryan and Deci 2000: 71; cf. Deci and Ryan 1985). For young children, extrinsic motivations cut off the self-direction essential for agency. In adults, however, extrinsic motivation can be internalized and made autonomous when an individual incorporates an external motivator into their sense of self, such as when one studies mathematical concepts one is not directly interested in, so that one can carry out experiments in physics that one is directly interested in (Ryan and Deci 2000: 72–3). As in the case of intrinsic motivation, "more autonomous extrinsic motivation was associated with more engagement, better performance, lower dropout, higher quality learning, and better teacher ratings, among other outcomes" (Ryan and Deci 2000: 73). A child may continue to work on a basic mathematical skill, for example, for the sake of being able to learn something more complex in which they are more interested. Here the motive for the particular act in which they are engaged is extrinsic, but they can be wholeheartedly committed to that act through their commitment to its end. These changes, too, enable rational and reflective deliberation, which takes interests and desires as instances of a general kind and assesses them in the light of abstract normative ideals and an abstract sense of oneself.

In Chapter 3, I emphasized that children have an agency that is not only worthy of respect but a legitimate aspiration for self-perfection. This agency manifests internality, activity, normative self-governance, and persistence, and it does not depend on second-order reflection or deliberation. Abstraction adds important new dimensions to the exercise of this agency. The adult who sets out to explore the South Pole or cure cancer or make the world more just manifests her character insofar as she persistently and actively pursues goals that are genuinely her own, seeking perfection in her activity. In that way, her agency is like that of the child. But her goals are largely imagined and abstract, the norms according to which she pursues them are principled, and her persistence is structured by abstract commitment (Ryan and Deci's "autonomy") rather than persisting, occurrent, first-order desire. We should aspire not only to develop the agency that characterizes young children—by engaging in activities that involve flow, for instance—but also to develop forms of agency made available through our powers of abstraction. We should also respect not only the agency present in young children but also that agency made possible through abstraction. In Chapter 7, I discuss in more detail how these forms of respect might differ for children and adults. In the next subsection, I turn to other ways that abstraction changes the nature of respect.

1.3 Abstraction and Mutual Respect

In addition to its impact on character and agency, the development of abstraction changes the nature of *respect* in three important ways. First, because those capable of abstraction can exercise agency in new ways, respect for agency can have new objects. Given that the proper object of respect is character, when people become capable of expressing character abstractly, they deserve new sorts of respect. Longer time horizons of activity, for example, make it more disrespectful to, say, discard a fellow students' notes than to interrupt them as they are taking those notes. While young children focus on particular tasks without regard for their final products, the product of activity for an older child or adult is often part of a broader more abstract task with a longer time horizon. Relatedly (and a point I return to in §2 and Chapter 7), respect for persons does not generally require that one respect others' mere preferences, but as self-governing tasks become more abstract, mere preference can become increasingly integrated into character.[4]

Second, beyond new forms of agency that require respect, abstraction also gives rise to an awareness of one's own dignity as something abstract that can be threatened by behavior that does not directly undermine one's agency: "If, up to the present, it is important not to bump someone in passing, it is now considerably more important not to offend that person" (12: 7). Once people are capable of engaging not merely with sensorially available, material givens but also with abstract concepts of dignity and self, they are vulnerable to harm and disrespect through offensive or demeaning actions that do not directly compromise their pursuit of concrete goals. A child can ignore the fact that another does not step aside to let them pass, as long as they do not actually require the accommodation, but an adult feels insulted at such disregard. Adolescents are vulnerable to insult and mockery in ways that very young children cannot understand (or that they even find amusing). Once the shaping of a socially situated self becomes an explicit (abstract) goal, agency is vulnerable in new ways, and new forms of respect are required.

Third, the structure of respect itself adds deliberate principles to what had been an embodied and pre-reflective adaptation to one's social environment. As children mature into adults, moral development "is not a question of training his movements; we begin the introduction of moral relationships, of those that awaken the conscience" (12: 7). The child's "habits and customs," which arise from lived realities of social life, develop into a "fixed system" when "abstraction ... supervenes to simplify and unite, so that the mind can succeed in expressing infinite immensities in a determinate form" (1: 169). At this stage in moral development, the older "child begins to be conscious of right and wrong, this not only as regards his own actions but also the actions of others. Problems of right and wrong are characteristic of this age; moral consciousness is being formed" (1: 175).[5] Only once a child abstracts can he act on general *principles* of fairness. Relatedly, as children mature and ask themselves about their identity and role in the world, they increasingly seek work that not only cultivates individual perfection but also serves others, and not merely particular others they encounter in daily life, but other people in general: "He passes from feeling for himself in relation with those with whom he is in contact, to feeling for others whom he has never seen. It is an abstract love" (14: 35). Respect, consideration, and help expand. Thus, "the acts of courtesy, which he has been taught with a view to his making contacts with others, must now be brought to a new level. The question of aid to the weak, to the aged, to the sick, for example, now arises" (12: 7). Just as the child comes to see respect as requiring more than merely not bumping into another person, so too he comes to see respect as owed to those into whom one could not bump because they are not in his immediate environment. The adolescent shifts from skills of practical life such as tying shoes or washing hands to "economic independence" (12: 62) and the "joy [of] feeling one's own value being appreciated ... [through] feeling useful and capable of production" (12: 82). Respect for others thus not only becomes an explicit aspiration, by what was formerly respectful "help" and "non-interruption" expands to include a desire that one's actions contribute in tangible ways to the good of unknown and "abstract" others.

1.4 Abstraction, Solidarity, and Organization

Just as abstraction expands opportunities for individual agency and respect, so too it creates new opportunities and a different quality for social solidarity. Superficially, abstraction makes possible new shared projects around which people can unite. As young children experience solidarity in the Silence Game, so physicists and mathematicians unite in the shared flow of working through a hard conceptual problem. Adults can conceptualize and explicitly strive for "justice" in social relations, while children strive together for that justice which is directly experienced through the peace and harmony of mutual respect in a particular classroom or home. In these cases, the *object* of social agency requires conceptualization, but the quality of social solidarity is the same as that for young children.

More significantly, abstraction changes the *scope* of social solidarity. Just as older children and adults come to experience respect for distant and abstract others, so too they can come to experience solidarity beyond those directly present to the senses. Abstract communities of respect can become objects of solidarity, as in patriotism or the sense of unity with humanity as a whole, and such communities also provide contexts within which deeper forms of union can occur.

In the Silence Game, children form a social whole through immediate sensory feedback with one another in a concrete situation. Abstraction (and the related faculty of imagination) makes it possible to experience oneself as part of an abstract whole. Among the most important examples of this social solidarity is patriotism; as children who have practiced small-scale social solidarity form abstract concepts of their country and nation, "the love of country is born, the feeling of belonging to a national group, and of concern for the honor of that group" (1: 175). Just as the young child was proud when he saw one of his classmates accomplish some challenging task, so too the older child and adult can be proud of the accomplishments of his "country," a corporate whole the reality of which depends essentially upon abstractions. Montessori even emphasizes the cultivation of a sense of solidarity with past and future human beings. The study of history, for example, should emphasize ways human beings depend upon one another and contribute to goals that go beyond any given individual. "If human unity—which is a fact in nature—is going at last to be organized, it will be done only by an education that will give appreciation of all that has been done by human co-operation" (6: 47). Human cooperation does not require felt solidarity, but as children come to understand cooperation in its historical importance, they come to feel a part of broader social wholes and eventually of "humanity" in the abstract.

> The children pass from sentiment towards the numerous individuals that surround [them] in [their] second vaster environment, in which [they] witnessed how the physical world and human society functioned, to an abstract social sentiment for Man in general. They may feel and demonstrate for the class or people, for instance, but generally they try to understand man's behavior in the world as a whole, including the past.
>
> (14: 35)

The experienced union of agency in social solidarity involves "profound emotion and enthusiasm," and while this feeling begins with one's immediate social environment in childhood, abstraction allows it to expand to embrace broader collectives and even "the holy cause of humanity" as a whole (6: 47).

Most significantly, abstraction makes it possible for solidarity to graduate from felt unity of intention to *organized* unity. The social cohesion present in children doing the Silence Game is sufficient to establish united agency, but mere sensory, felt unity cannot tie together the social wholes needed to accomplish adults' perfectionist goals. Because "cohesion alone is not enough to set up a society which can play a practical part in the world, evoking therein a civilized life of work and thought" (1: 215), we need an "organizational and conscious part of society" (1: 216). Just as abstraction transforms respect from regularized behaviors that enable harmony in society to explicitly articulated principles of justice and fairness in the light of which children self-consciously self-regulate, so too abstraction transforms social solidarity from mere felt unity to forms of unity with explicitly articulated processes and principles for acting together as a whole. "For a group to act together ..., they need only share a plan" (Schapiro 2014: 282, following Bratman 1987), and while—for Montessori—children can form plans (albeit not in Bratman's or Schapiro's sense) to create silence, organization in terms of abstract concepts and procedures makes it possible for larger groups of individuals with more diverse interests and motivations to share plans together and retain solidarity for longer time (see further discussion in §2.3).

2 Reflection and Deliberation

2.1 Reflection, Deliberation, and Agency

In Chapter 3, I argued that reflection and deliberation are not essential for respect-worthy agency, or even for the sort of ideal agency encapsulated by Montessori's concept of character. There I noted, however, that Montessori recognizes a special place for reflection and deliberation in adult agency, and I promised to discuss the role of reflective deliberation in adult agents. It is time to make good on that promise. Montessori does not emphasize "reflection" or "deliberation" in quite those terms, but she highlights that, alongside abstraction, older children and adolescents ask "why" questions with increased seriousness.

> The [older] child ... enters the abstract field; he wishes to know reasons. It is curious to notice that one of the things which preoccupies these children is what is ethical in life; what is good, what is bad. If you tell the little child that he is bad or good, he just accepts it. Whereas the seven-year-old wants to know why he is bad, and what it is to be bad, etc.
>
> (14: 32, see too 12: 10)

Sofia with her cylinder blocks confronts a material that has a right way of completing it; she governs herself in accordance with straightforward norms intrinsic to her work. When, the next day, she wants to work on the cylinder blocks again, but another child has it, she waits patiently for the other child to finish, since there is "nothing for it but to wait" (1: 202). As Sofia matures, however, she does not simply need norms in accordance with which she can self-govern. She needs to know why those norms are *good*. Through abstraction, seeing particular desires and norms as particular instances of general kinds of desire and value, Sofia enters into the sphere of reflection, capable of deliberating not only about how to do this or that well, but about whether to follow through on her desires to do this or that and about whether her standards of excellence in this or that activity are legitimate. She has "a desire to distinguish good from evil by her own powers" (6: 2); she engages in reflective, rational deliberation.

My goal in this subsection is threefold: (1) to show how deliberation enhances agency, (2) to elucidate the limits of deliberation, and (3) to highlight how agency-enhancing deliberative capacities are continuous with and emerge from non-reflective and non-deliberative forms of agency. The first task coheres well with contemporary adult-centered approaches to agency; it shows what is distinctive and valuable about reflective, adult agency. The next two tasks continue the argument of Chapter 3, showing why reflective deliberation cannot be taken to be either necessary or sufficient for agency. First, however, I say a bit about what reflection and deliberation *are*.

2.1.1 What Are "Reflection" and "Deliberation"?

Three-year-old Sofia working with her blocks reflects and deliberates in a sense. She picks up a particular cylinder, looks at the available holes, looks at the cylinder, "reflects" on where the cylinder should go, "deliberates" about whether to place it in this spot or that one, and then places the block. When she finds herself with a cylinder left over that doesn't fit in the remaining hole, she reflects on what went wrong, deliberates about where she should try to place cylinder now, takes out some cylinders and re-places them, and shifts her strategy so that she can find a spot for each cylinder. Montessori even uses the term "reflective [*reflessivo*]" to describe this engagement in attentive work (22: 80). Likewise, when Csikszentmihalyi explains how one can be an agent even when there is "no room for self-scrutiny," as in cases like "the sailor holding a tight course feels when the wind whips through her hair" or "the painter ... when the colors on the canvas begin to set up a magnetic tension with each other," even these agents-in-flow, however, like Sofia with her cylinders, respond to changing water conditions with different tack and choose one color rather than another, reflecting on how best to bring out the tensions amongst them (Csikszentmihalyi 1990: 64, 3). Neither Sofia nor other agents in flow, however, engage in what contemporary philosophers typically mean by "deliberation" or "reflection."

Within contemporary philosophy, several different accounts of what distinguishes adult agency from that of animals and children are prevalent, most of which appeal in one way or another to higher-order reflection and/or "deliberation." As philosophers have sought to direct attention to what is unique about this (adult) human agency, they typically highlight one or more of the following features. For one thing, reflection is typically understood to take one's own desires, inclinations, or other mental states as its objects. For Frankfurt, deliberation is the context for forming second-order desires, that is, desires about one's desires, such as the desire to stop craving cigarettes. For Schapiro, "being inclined is the starting point, rather than the ending point, of deliberation" (Schapiro 2021: 99; see too Korsgaard 1996a, 2009). In reflective deliberation, we take first-order desires and inclinations as proposals for how to act, reflect on them, deliberate about whether they are worth acting on, and then decide. Schapiro and Frankfurt differ in how they treat this basic feature of reflection, but they share the idea that reflection takes desires as objects of consideration and assesses whether or not to make them decisive for action.

For another thing, reflective deliberation, insofar as one is engaged in it, is "free" in the important sense that for any affirmation made in deliberation, one can ask of that affirmation whether one endorses it or not, and for any reason given in favor of some consideration, we can ask whether that reason really counts as a good reason. Some philosophers think that some reasons considered in reflection might be unconditionally valid, such that when we reflect on, say, whether to "act as our humanity requires" we have "no option but to say yes" (Korsgaard 1996a: 123). Even in these cases, however, we can *ask* of our humanity whether it is really worth acting on, and for Korsgaard, the unconditionality of humanity is precisely a function of the nature of our freedom, not a limitation on it. Others claim that once having made a decision (through deliberation), "reopening the question without a further reason" "makes no sense" (Schapiro 2021: 79), but even here, the reflective stance leaves open the possibility of revisiting prior decisions, and insofar as we follow through on decisions rather than reflect on them, our decisive choice to act has brought deliberation to an end. In itself, deliberation is free relative to any consideration that comes before it.

These two features of reflective deliberation distinguish Sofia's agency in working with cylinder blocks from deliberative adults. Sofia "deliberates" about whether this block should go into this hole or another, but she does not take her own "guiding instincts" as objects of reflection. She deliberates *from within* her commitment to her activity, not *about* that commitment. Moreover, even if there is some sense in which, say, she considers her inclination to lie down and rejects it because it doesn't give her a good view of the cylinder holes, any reflection on first-order desires lacks the open-ended freedom of adult reflective deliberation. For all of her ability to persist in her chosen activity, she doesn't—and can't—persist in questioning whether her inclination toward the activity really warrants working on it.

Finally,[6] a third feature of deliberation emphasized by Schapiro (and others, such as Korsgaard (1996a: 101–2)) is that the deliberative perspective is essentially "first-personal," that is, a perspective *from which* I act, rather merely a perspective *on* human action from the outside. As Schapiro puts it, her question is not "what happens when someone acts" but rather "what am I doing, insofar as I am acting?" (Schapiro 2021: 19). Particularly for Kantian moral philosophers, the point of talking about reflective deliberation is not to isolate a mechanism by which human beings generate complex behaviors, but to look at what people are committed to from the stance of one reflecting about what to do. Deliberation is a stance from which one looks at one's actions as possible actions, looks at desires or impulses as proposals, and considers one's values and whether to remain committed to them. Throughout my discussion here, and indeed even in Chapter 3, I share this commitment to investigating agency from within the standpoint of an actor rather than merely as an external observer of behavior. The emphasis on the first-person perspective is not relevant, however, to the concerns of this chapter, precisely because my prior discussion of agency also treated adults in flow and actively engaged children from a first-person perspective. As Schapiro elegantly explains, what it means to investigate first-personally is to investigate the "guiding conception" of the activities that we undertake, where this "guiding conception is a description of an activity under which the participant chooses it and finds it worth engaging in ... Its role is to specify the aims and methods in which the activity consists, as well as to identify what is at stake in doing it successfully" (Schapiro 2021: 21). Schapiro rightly uses the example of "playing chess" as one for which there is a "guiding conception" that specifies "what [one] must be taking responsibility for, insofar as she is undertaking to play chess" (Schapiro 2021: 25), and in the same way we can and should look at Sofia's engagement with cylinder blocks from a first-person perspective. Schapiro also refers to an "activity [of] acting as such," the topic of her own first-personal investigation, and also, crucially, the topic of my investigation of Sofia's agency in Chapter 3. In laying out the necessity for internality, activity, normative self-governance, and persistence in the agency of young children, I presented a first-person account of the constitutive requirements for acting as such. There is *also* a first-person perspective on reflective deliberation, and reflective deliberation has its own guiding conception, but this is not "the" guiding conception for agency as such.

2.1.2 How Reflective Deliberation Enhances Agency

Alongside our ability to act in the light of abstract principles, adults' capacity for reflection sets us apart from other animals. This capacity also enables adults to attain levels of self-regulation, cooperation, and efficacy that children—with their more direct, first-order agency—cannot achieve. For all of my insistence in Chapter 3 that agency does not require reflective deliberation, we should not underestimate its importance.

Most basically, there is a distinct *sense* of agency present in reflection and deliberation. Experiences of flow are often those in which we feel most alive and most ourselves, but reflective deliberation can generate profound experiences of identification and agency that are qualitatively different from those experienced in flow. Philosophers like Sartre and Korsgaard highlight these feelings of responsibility for oneself when they describe our situation as one in which we are "condemned to choice and action" (Korsgaard 2009: 1; cf. Sartre 1993). Schapiro describes the "moment of drama" where one is "inclined but not thereby determined to act" (Schapiro 2021: 10).[7] In reflection, we identify with the reflecting agent and take particular interests and desires as objects of consideration, asking "What will *I* do with or about this inclination?," and precisely because it is self-conscious and takes its "own" desires as objects, the reflective sense of self instantiates a kind of agency and self-governance not present in Sofia's unreflective engagement with cylinder blocks.

Relatedly, because abstraction enables us to explicitly form a concept of self, reflective deliberation provides a context to *explicitly* see decisions as made by my*self*. When Sofia identifies with the guiding instincts she expresses through choosing to work with cylinder blocks, she does not form for herself a concept of self against which she measures her activity. When I reflect, however, I can and often do consider whether acting on this or that desire would be true to who I take myself to be. This attention to self is not always the focus of deliberation. Generally speaking, even when I reflectively deliberate, considerations for or against acting on this or that desire directly appeal to reasons in the world, not considerations about who I want to be. I might feel like insulting the person who just cut me off in traffic, but then I consider what effects my outburst will have on my passengers and the fact that the offending driver will likely not even notice my outburst, so I refrain. Or I wonder whether to stop grading these papers because I feel like watching a movie, and I resist on the grounds that the students really need my comments before they submit their next assignment. All of these deliberations involve some implicit appeal to my identities or sense of self, just as Sofia's interest in her cylinder blocks involves some implicit appeal to her sense of the manual dexterity or spatial sense she wants to cultivate, but none of them *explicitly* attend to myself or identities as factors in deliberation. Still, deliberation at least sometimes provides a context for considering reasons that explicitly appeal to myself, a context absent from non-reflective action.

Deliberation enriches each of the aspects of agency discussed in Chapter 3. While Sofia's immersion in her work expresses her wholehearted and internal relation to her guiding instinct, reflective deliberation provides for enhanced internality. When I reflectively endorse a guiding instinct through choosing to take that instinct as providing good reasons for action, I identify with that instinct in a threefold way: (1) through acting on the values proposed by the instinct, (2) through seeing the instinct as an instinct with which I identify, and (3) through identifying with the higher-order standpoint from which I endorse the instinct. In that sense, Frankfurt, Schapiro, and others are right to think that reflective endorsement in deliberation gives rise to a sort of internality that is not present in Sofia's engagement with cylinder blocks.[8]

Reflective deliberation also allows me to take a different kind of active stance toward my desires. Sofia's agency is active in that the instincts on which she acts are literally instincts toward activity, and what it means for her to identify with them is to act on them. But the presence of those desires in her is not something that she sees as an activity of hers. She acts *from* her desire but doesn't *actively desire*. When the desire comes to have the efficacy that it does through her consideration and endorsement *of* that desire, however, she sees the desire itself as the product of her activity. Just as the completed cylinder blocks work expresses her agency as its product, so too the deliberately initiated activity of working on the blocks expresses her agency *both* in being her own newly initiated activity *and* in being the product of her now concluded deliberative agency.

Reflective deliberation also makes it possible to self-govern in accordance with more abstract values that bind across a wider range of contexts and that depend less upon one's environment. Sofia's normative self-governance relies on norms intrinsic to the materials with which she works, namely the cylinder blocks. The adult "accustomed to making decisions in all matters pertaining to [her] daily round" (9: 136) makes quick decisions in the light of established habits of choice, attending to what each situation demands but not reflectively deliberating about her overall orientation of activity. But when faced with situations for which they do not already have norms or habits of choice, adults must—and can—deliberate about what to do, creating new norms or discerning how old norms apply to new situations. Particularly when they have reason to think that instinctive reactions to a situation might lead them astray, they need not only to deliberate but to deliberate *reflectively*, considering whether to follow first-order inclinations. If they are adults or older children committed to abstract goals or principles, they must consider how those apply to the situation.

Children self-governing in the light of a guiding instinct, or adults immersed in flow, adhere to norms of the activity they choose, and when they have "completed" their activity,[9] they move on to other activities with other norms. When one can formulate abstract goals and principles of action, one can commit to abstractions one explicitly takes to apply beyond any particular cycle of activity. Just as the concept of the self becomes efficacious in governing conduct through reflective deliberation, so too in order for any abstract goals or principles to be efficacious, people require a mechanism by which abstractions can override particular desires that may arise in particular contexts. As a young child, Sofia's Catholicism can express itself in direct sensorimotor engagement with materially present ritual practices; she can light candles, kneel and stand, and so on. But the abstract values to which this Catholicism commits her become volitionally efficacious only when she can govern herself through subjecting particular desires to reflective consideration in the light of those values. The volitional importance of abstract values thus relies on our capacity to reflect on particular desires and weigh them in the light of abstract commitments.

Deliberation also provides the context within which we can question our abstract goals and commitments and revise our sense of self. Even as a three- or four-year-old, Sofia regularly challenges her understanding of her situation. When she ends the cylinder blocks exercise with one cylinder left over, she recognizes that she must have made a mistake, and she goes back to try doing her work a different way. But she doesn't—and can't—directly challenge her interest in the activity itself. As deliberation becomes more reflective, however, we can increasingly challenge our commitments and agential strategies at higher levels. An eight-year-old Sofia could ask whether working with cylinder blocks is as valuable as practicing piano, given her interest in cultivating both her musical and mathematical senses, and she can suspend both of these activities to do more research on horses, given her desire to give her friends a presentation on horses. Eighteen-year-old Sofia can ask whether math, music, horses, friends, or Catholicism have any value; she can inquire about the overall point of life and whether this or that set of values makes sense as a whole. This sort of revision of values requires a capacity not only to reflect on whether some action works for the task to which I am committed, but also whether that commitment is warranted in terms of other values, and even whether those higher-order values are justified *tout court*.

The possibilities of acting on abstract values and of revising them are related. Sofia's commitments to friendship and Catholicism are at *risk* in deliberation because only in deliberation do they have the strength and influence that they do. Without reflective deliberation, Sofia can pursue projects in solidarity with others, but she can't self-consciously bind herself to these projects for the sake of "friendship." If solidarity is broken, she no longer governs herself in accordance with her earlier desires and feelings, but she does not lose a commitment to an ideal or a friend. Without deliberation, Sofia can light candles and spend time in contemplative prayer, but she does not bind herself to these activities for the sake of an abstract commitment to Catholicism, so when she ceases to pray, this reflects no crisis of faith but only a shift in interest and attention.[10] Once Sofia becomes capable of governing her behavior through reflective deliberation in the light of ideals—say, rejecting her immediate impulse to spend the morning painting and instead going with her friend Mario to church because of her friendship and her religious convictions—she also becomes capable of asking whether this friendship and these convictions should have the weight she accords them.

These reflective enhancements of agency also rely on and contribute to an increased time horizon for agential persistence. As shown in Chapter 3, guiding instincts can structure activities with sufficient persistence to constitute people as agents. Working with her cylinders, Sofia governed herself by subordinating other impulses to an interest to which she committed herself. However, such interests do not persist uninterruptedly for years, days, or even hours. Schapiro may exaggerate the time-horizons of adult agential commitments when she describes the need for an entire "plan of life" (Schapiro 1999: 729–30), but adults do govern themselves with long-term goals, plans, values, and ideals. To sustain consistency over long time horizons, we need to be able to commit to values in such a way that we can act on those values even when we do not immediately feel like acting on them.[11] Reflective deliberation provides a mechanism for extending agential commitments through interruptions in activity and even felt desire.

Reflective deliberation provides other benefits for agency. It facilitates autonomously motivated efforts toward merely instrumental goods.[12] Particularly in its social form (see §2.3), it allows for cooperative planning, reliance on others, and commitments to which we can legitimately be constrained by ourselves and by others.[13] It allows for proactive shaping of desires in oneself and others, and it facilitates the work of constructing environments conducive to long-term human development. Through deliberation, people are better able to make use of theoretical insights for orienting activity. And so on. While not essential for agency, the reflective deliberation that emerges as children grow into adults enhances agency in countless ways.

2.1.3 The Limits and Insufficiency of Reflective Deliberation

Reflective deliberation opens up whole new spheres for character, degrees of self-control, foci of agency, ways to form a sense of self, extensions of agency over longer time, and other agential goods. In that sense, contemporary theorists of agency are right to emphasize its importance. However, when philosophers argue that reflective deliberation is necessary or sufficient for agency, they go too far. I addressed the necessity claim in detail in Chapter 3, where I showed that pre-reflective children have an agency that constitutes a form of human excellence and that is worthy of respect, but this subsection adds further reasons to reject deliberation as necessary for agency. I further address whether reflective deliberation is *sufficient* for agency, arguing that we not only *can* be excellent agents without reflection but that ethical life—and even deliberative agency itself—*requires* non-deliberative agency.[14]

For one thing, excellence of deliberative agency is insufficient for overall excellence as an agent because flourishing ethical life—even for adults—requires participation in activities where deliberation inhibits one's ability to perform the activity well. Csikszentmihalyi's studies of optimal experience find that flow states, where "attention is invested in realistic goals ... [and] because a person must concentrate attention on the task at hand ... [they] momentarily forget everything else," are not only "the secret to happiness" but also moments where "instead of beings buffeted by anonymous forces, we feel in control of our actions [and] masters of our own fate" (Csikszentmihalyi 1990: 6, 3; 1996). Even Schapiro, while defending the centrality of reflective deliberation for agency, acknowledges the importance of non-deliberative activities:

> There are lots of situations in which it makes sense to try to shut down our deciding minds—to "loosen up," to "let ourselves go," or to "go with the flow." You might aim for this when you are making art, playing with small children, dancing, or having sex. In all of these activities, and in many more, it is common to fall into overthinking. We become too self-conscious, too deliberate, too reflective, and in the end, we lose our ability both to take proper pleasure in what we are doing, and to do it well.
>
> (Schapiro 2021: 149)

Among athletes, the phenomenon where "athletes become so ... self-focused ... that their ability to execute a skill ... is impaired" is often called the "yips" (Mayo 2021). The same phenomenon shows up in art, music, and even daily conversations. In any activity involving flow, deliberation *on* the activity in which one is engaged distracts from participation *in* that activity and can compromise performance. For similar reasons, as Schapiro notes, reflection can inhibit pleasure in an activity.[15] Insofar as one takes pleasure in active engagement—whether making art or playing games or having sex—deliberation distracts from that engagement and thereby reduces one's pleasure in it.

Non-deliberative exercises of agency are also essential when there is simply not time for deliberation, when even momentary reflection can slow one's reaction and inhibit one's ability to respond appropriately.[16] Montessori highlights that when important decisions need to be made quickly, the capacity for non-deliberative but self-directed agency is essential:

> [T]he mechanism of the habit of decision give[s] us a sense of liberty ... [W]hen an actual conflict arises in such a consciousness, and the decision has to be instantaneous, ... [t]hat which gives strength to resist [temptation] is ... the *exercise of will-power*; and this exercise is to be found in the routine of life itself ... [such as with] the mother of a family, much occupied in her mission of domestic work, and accustomed to decide in all matters pertaining to the daily round.
>
> (9: 136)

Decisions that must be made too quickly for deliberation play essential roles particularly in three important contexts. First, as noted above, activities involving flow often require rapid decisions. If the tennis player deliberates about whether to run to the net, her decision will be moot before her deliberation has even properly begun. She must make decisions, and make them *for herself*, even without reflectively deliberating. Second, as Montessori notes in her example of the "mother of a family," everyday life is filled with decisions. Some are relatively urgent, such as whether to rush to my crying baby when the water on the stove is boiling over. Some are made in the context of daily flow, such as whether I really need to put the attachment on the vacuum cleaner to reach that corner. Others are not urgent and even involve some degree of reflective deliberation, such as whether to fold laundry or buy more eggplant for dinner, but the deliberation can remain essentially first-order, and a well-developed agent can attend to this decision in much the way Sofia attends to the choice of where to place the next cylinder. For all of these everyday decisions, Montessori emphasizes not only that they exercise the agent's will, but also that they can be routine and unreflective.[17]

A final context for the importance of fast decision-making comes with urgent decisions in unfamiliar contexts. Montessori considers the "moment of peril" where someone faces an unforeseen temptation to violate their moral values, arguing that more important than any "moral vision" is the "power to exercise their own wills," a power developed precisely in the routine choice-making of daily life. We can see the importance of non-deliberative agency even in Schapiro's own paradigmatic example of the "moment of drama," taken from a poem that starts, "What do you do with the mad that you feel?" (Schapiro 2021: 9, quoting Rogers 1997). Schapiro's gloss on the poem emphasizes the centrality of reflective deliberation:

> In the poem, the protagonist is angry, and being angry makes her *feel like* doing "a thing that's wrong." ... The protagonist feels like fighting back, in [a] harmful way. But she also has a choice whether to fight back or not. Although she is inclined to fight back, she is not determined to do so. She is *having* an inclination to fight back, but she is not yet *acting on it*, and it is still up to her whether to act on it or not. I will call this, "the moment of drama." You are in the moment of drama

when you are *inclined, but not thereby determined, to act*. The moment of drama is the focus of this book.

(Schapiro 2021: 10)

One important point to highlight here is that even from the first-person perspective, our lives are typically not lives filled with moments of drama; much of life is spent following through on inclinations that we don't pause to call into question.[18] For the present discussion, however, what's more important is that these moments of drama are often settled, and often *must* be settled, by choices that do not leave room for reflection. The case of anger on which Schapiro focuses provides an excellent example. While anger can be a response to ongoing insult or mistreatment, it often arises in situations that require an immediate response. Someone pushes me or insults me, and I get angry, and I will either lash out (with fists or stinging words) or not. Even taking a moment to step back and reflect is a choice that, in the context, involves giving up certain possible responses toward which my anger prompts me. Often, in such situations, the moment of drama is settled without conscious reflection or deliberation; I'm insulted and I clench my fists and turn away, or reply with a vicious slur, or punch the person. What I do expresses who I am and what my commitments are, but it often does not express any "decision" made through reflective deliberation. Even if I subdue my inclination to strike back, I do so not by reflective rejection but through immediate and pre-reflective identification with a contrary inclination. Even the poem on which Schapiro comments focuses more on *feeling* than on principles:

> It's great to be able to stop when you've planned a thing that's wrong. And be able to do something else instead, and think this song—"I can stop when I want to. Can stop when I wish. Can stop, stop, stop anytime ... And what a good *feeling to feel like this*! And know that *the feeling is really mine*. Know that there's something deep inside that helps us become what we can. For a girl can be someday a lady, and a boy can be someday a man."
>
> (Rogers 1997, quoted in Schapiro 2021: 9, my emphasis)

The power to refrain from doing a thing that's wrong is often not a matter of reflective deliberation but of contrary feelings, feelings that are "really mine," feelings that even the young children who were Mr. Rogers's primary audience were able to have.

Non-deliberative action is important in ethical life because it often enhances agents' efficacy, pleasure, and speed, but the final reference to feelings that are "really mine" brings out the most important feature of non-deliberative action, one that Montessori and Csikszentmihalyi both emphasize: deliberation can inhibit one's sense of *agency*. When the "artist whose mind has just conceived the ideal image which it is necessary to fix upon the canvas" (9: 17) is interrupted in her flow—whether by another person or even by her own second thoughts—she not only does a poorer job painting and experiences less pleasure; she feels as though her agency over her work has been interrupted by something alien to that agency. As she attained maximal expression of her*self*, she suddenly lost control, precisely by being brought to exercise too much control. The deliberative self in this context shows up as a threat to the full exercise of the agency to which she was committed in her craft. Similarly, when conversing with a friend on a long walk, my attention might shift from the conversation itself to reflection on why I am engaged in this conversation at all, whether I can afford to be spending so much time on it, whether this friend is really worth my time, or whether friendship itself is really valuable. These shifts toward a more second-order reflective perspective inhibit my ability to fully inhabit the conversation, and if the conversation is one I care about with a friend I care about, this inhibition caused by reflection interferes with my agency, even if it is prompted by "my" higher-order thoughts.[19]

Beyond these ways in which non-deliberative agency contributes to ethical life as a whole, deliberation *itself* requires non-deliberative agency in several ways. One way deliberation depends upon non-deliberative agency can be elucidated by comparison with a critique made by Joseph Butler of those who claim that all are motivated only by self-love: "if self-love wholly engrosses us, and leaves no room for any other principle, there can be absolutely no such thing at all as happiness or enjoyment of any kind whatever; since happiness consists in the gratification of particular passions, which supposes the having of [those particular passions]" (Butler 1726: Sermon XI, ¶9). Butler defends benevolence as a "particular passion" no more in conflict with self-love than pride or jealousy or any other passion. He asks, rhetorically, "Is desire of and delight in the happiness of another any more a diminution of self-love than desire of and delight in the esteem of another?" (Butler 1726: XI, ¶10). Butler's overall point, however, is not unique to benevolence. The point is that self-love tells a person to satisfy their own desires, so they require desires *other than* self-love in order for self-love to operate.[20]

Similarly, reflective deliberation considers whether to act on this or that inclination or value or goal. Insofar as I constitute myself through reflective endorsement, however, I cannot see myself as *simply* my deliberative self, since I need particular practical identities, desires, projects, etc., to endorse. Just as self-love must satisfy particular passions other than self-love, so too reflection must endorse particular goods other than mere reflection. (Moreover, for Montessori, at least part of what one should consider in reflecting on any given action or inclination is whether it is really something *I* want to do.)

Even in the context of Butler's objection, we might still say (as Korsgaard and Schapiro do) that considerations we endorse in deliberation, and even endorse *because* we see them as expressing our agency, only *really* have value (or really express our agency) insofar as they are endorsed through deliberation. Until then, they are at best provisionally one's own.[21] This description does not ring true to many of my own experiences of deliberation. In *some* cases, I consider different options, and I decide on this or that option, and I then commit myself to it because I have endorsed it. In other cases, however, I consider different options and I consciously commit myself to this or that option because I find that it *already* reflects my agency. In some cases—say, Jonathan Biss's dedication to Beethoven—one might reflectively endorse a commitment because one sees it as one's own, even while continually struggling in reflection to figure out *why* it is one's own (cf. Biss 2020).

Even more serious problems for the sufficiency of deliberative agency arise from further ways that deliberation depends upon non-deliberative agency. This reliance is apparent when one attends in a fine-grained way to the process(es) of reflective deliberation itself. Deliberation requires that one stand back from particular interests and consider what to do with one's inclinations in this context. It then requires considerations of reasons for and against various courses of action, and if sufficiently reflective, considerations of reasons for or against the legitimacy of those reasons. Finally, it requires completion; at some point, one must decide that deliberation has gone on long enough; one must choose and act. None of these elements of deliberation are typically under deliberative control.

Deliberation typically *begins* from a process that is non-deliberative; whether a human being steps back and deliberates cannot generally be the result of a choice that follows *from* taking a step back: "beginning deliberation is itself something [one] does not deliberate upon" (Arpaly and Schroeder 2014: 48). We deliberate when desires or habits are insufficient to motivate, when we face conflict or novel situations, or when we find ourselves in environments unconducive to work in accordance with our guiding instincts. We do not generate Schapiro's "moment of drama" through choice but simply find ourselves in such moments, reflectively deliberating. If to be "under volitional control" is to be an *effect* of deliberation, then the beginnings of deliberation are not generally under volitional control.[22]

Likewise, *within* deliberation, we do not exercise direct control over what considerations occur to us.

> [E]xtended deliberative actions are made up, not just of... basic exercises of agency over thought, but also of the occurrence in consciousness of thoughts and feelings that serve as inputs to deliberation but which are not brought to consciousness through exercises of [deliberative[23]] agency.
>
> (Arpaly and Schroeder 2014: 25)

Considerations weighed for and against various policies strike the deliberator as relevant based on her underlying interests, convictions, commitments, deliberative habits, or attentiveness to others' reasons. When deciding whether to continue smoking, I consider effects of smoking on long-term health and on the welfare of those around me. If these considerations do not arise, if it just doesn't occur to me to think about health or about others, I can't simply make myself consider them by an act of (deliberative) volition. Moreover, we can be (and are) held responsible for failures to take seriously the effects of our actions on others, not only when we take such effects into deliberation and reject them as irrelevant but also—indeed, often especially—when we don't consider them at all (see Smith 2005).

Even if considerations *do* arise, there is a limit to how far I can make various reasons "live options" (cf. James 1896) for me. In a sense, I can deliberate about whether to begin worshipping Greek gods, but through no force of mere will can I bring myself to take this possibility seriously. Other people at other times have been able to take it seriously, and yet others can't take seriously options that I *can* take seriously (say, whether to worship God as understood by the Greek Orthodox Church). Whether an option is a live one must be settled antecedent to its role in my deliberation.

Finally, deliberation cannot bring deliberation to an end. Reflection is free and open-ended, to the point that even having reached a seemingly unassailable conclusion—perhaps Korsgaard's recognition that she has "no option but to say yes" to "act[ing] as ... humanity requires" (Korsgaard 1996a: 123)—one can still call into question whether one has fully thought through every possible error in one's deliberation, a condition that—at its worst—can generate what Montessori calls the "mania of doubt," consisting of an "impossibility of taking a decision, and which produces a serious state of distress" (9: 138).[24] The end to deliberation can't itself be the outcome of completed deliberation at risk of a regress (wherein we endlessly deliberate about whether we have good reasons to end the most recent deliberation).

2.1.4 Deliberation as Work

Deliberation depends upon non-deliberative forms of agency because deliberation itself is a form of work, an activity in which a person engages, and it can fail *as* an activity in the same ways that other behaviors can fail to be genuine actions. We can fail to be internally related to the interests requisite for deliberation: the interest in initiating deliberation, in continuing to deliberate in this or that way, and in ending deliberation. Our deliberation can be passive rather than active. It can fail to adhere to norms of deliberation; we might seek to adhere to those norms and fall short, or we might ignore or dismiss such norms. Deliberation can fail the persistence condition when we simply lack the patience or constancy to follow through on the deliberative task we've set for ourselves. For all of these criteria, a sufficiently serious failure disqualifies the relevant activity from being considered "reflective deliberation," even if it involves certain aspects of reflective deliberation. Just as Sofia isn't doing the cylinder blocks activity if she is just throwing cylinders around the room, Michael isn't reflectively deliberating, even if he notices his desire and his capacity to stand back from it, unless he attends to the task of deliberation with at least some degree of persistence and some attention to some norms of reflection.

We can fail to be internally related to our own deliberation when we are forced to deliberate by someone else, or when in the course of deliberation we rehearse arguments we've picked up from those around us and that we know are "right" but that we don't actually identify with, or when we conclude deliberation with a "decision" that feels alien. In extreme cases, we may find ourselves neurotically obsessed with certain considerations in deliberation while wishing that we were not so obsessed. Montessori describes one such clinical case:

> The patient was a man whose business it was to go round to houses collecting refuse; he was seized with misgivings lest some useful object should have accidentally fallen into the rubbish-baskets, and that he would be suspected of appropriating it. Hereupon the unhappy man, just when he was about to go off with his load, climbed all the stairs again, and knocked again at all the doors, asking whether something valuable might not perhaps have chanced to be in the baskets. Going away after assurances to the contrary, he would return and knock again, and so on. In vain he applied to the doctor for some means of strengthening his will.
>
> (9: 138–9)

Even in more ordinary cases, many are familiar with the case where "a person who is going out... locks the door and shakes it; but when he has gone a few steps he is assailed by doubt: did he fasten the door?" (9: 139). In these cases, we deliberate when we want to have decided, and we cannot help but take factors into consideration that we want to have dismissed. We can't shake certain deliberative tendencies, but we also don't identify with them. Even when we are not subject to irrational doubts of this sort, we can engage in a process of reflection wherein we do not identify with the higher-order considerations that arise in deliberation. The compulsive door-locker, for example, keeps asking whether he is really sure that he locked the door, but he doesn't want to be asking this again and again, so his higher-order consideration (am I really sure?) is one he doesn't identify with, and even the yet higher-order consideration (do I really want to be a compulsive door-locker?) is yet a further aspect of compulsive self-questioning that he sees as not really himself. As Frankfurt notes, "Someone does what he really wants to do only when he acts in accordance with a pertinent higher-order volition. But this condition could not be sufficient unless the higher-order volition were *itself* one by which the person *really wanted* to be determined" (Frankfurt 1988: 166). If I "decide" not to smoke because of a second-order health-based desire not to smoke, but I don't really identify with that second-order desire, my reflective deliberation itself lacks internality.

In related ways, we can be passively related to our own deliberation. We might find ourselves unable to immerse ourselves in flow activities, constantly deliberating despite ourselves.[25] Passivity can be particularly clear when others influence our deliberation. In some such cases, "the provision of reasons [can] preempt the other person's own deliberative activities such that her decisions about important life questions cannot then be seen as flowing from the independent exercise of her capacities to canvass and weigh reasons" and "the result can be a form of loss in being unable to see herself fully as a self-directing agent realizing purposes of her own" (Tsai 2014: 79). When another asks me to consider this or that reason, I often can't help but consider it, and I may find myself passively deliberating, merely following along as another guides me to a practical conclusion. Even if another is not physically present, I might "deliberate" in passively following a script written by a haunting voice inside my head, a parent or friend or teacher whose patterns of thought I can't shake, don't really identify with, and passively follow to a decision. Deliberation can also *end* passively, if I find myself forced to decide prematurely, perhaps by the urgency of the situation, the pressure of others, or environmental factors that interrupt my deliberative work.

We can fail to self-govern in deliberation. Weakness of will is a classic case where a person engages in deliberation but fails to self-govern insofar as the "decision" made upon terminating deliberation fails to direct behavior. Self-governance also fails when one lets oneself ignore (or give excessive weight to) this or that consideration, or prematurely terminate deliberation, or even prematurely enter into deliberation, in response to mere whims or passing feelings. Even if we self-govern in some sense, deliberation can fail to adhere to its internal norms. As Korsgaard explains, "the activity of reflection has rules of its own, rules which ... are constitutive of it" (Korsgaard 1996a: 257–8).[26] For example, "the hypothetical imperative [namely, 'whoever wills the end, wills the means'] is constitutive of action" in the way that "the presence of both a noun and a verb in an English sentence is constitutive of its being a sentence," and practical deliberation is further committed to governing itself by some general principle directing us to "promote our own good" (Korsgaard 2009: 30, 52–3). Similarly, Michael Bratman shows how various "norms of consistency, agglomeration, means-end coherence, and stability" govern planned (intentional) activity (Bratman 2009: 43). Someone who simply mentally runs through a series of considerations that seem vaguely relevant to a course of action, but without governing his deliberative process in accordance with at least some norms of practical rationality, isn't deliberating at all. By virtue of deliberating, the deliberator necessarily aims for the right (or a right) outcome of deliberation and thus commits herself at least implicitly to the norms that give rise to good choices.

Finally, as with all work, deliberation requires persistence. As I pointed out in §2.1.2, deliberation enhances the temporal extension of agency, a point Bratman's "planning theory of agency" emphasizes (see Bratman 1987; 2013). But it must be possible to extend agency across time in a way that does not depend upon deliberation because deliberation itself is a form of activity that requires temporal extension. For deliberation to be a context within which I implement plans and values again and again across time, I have to be able to sustain each episode of deliberation long enough for those plans to show up as relevant and be affirmed. This persisting in deliberation cannot itself be the product of a process of deliberation where I implement a plan to deliberate, at least not in general, on pain of an infinite deliberative regress. Deliberation, as work performed by an agent, requires pre-deliberative, agential persistence.

Because deliberation is a sort of work, agents engage in deliberation from interests to which they are internally related, which they express actively and persistently through self-governance in accordance with relevant norms (of practical reasoning).

Beyond these constitutive connections between reflective agency and agency as such, agential deliberation depends developmentally upon prereflective agency in at least two senses. First, as Montessori emphasizes, agency develops through use. Children able to engage in activities they choose for themselves strengthen their capacity to choose for themselves, and when such children grow into adult deliberators, they choose to deliberate, to consider this or that in deliberation, and to end deliberation, for themselves. Like Sofia's choice to repeat her cylinder blocks work, these choices are not themselves consequences of deliberation, but they nonetheless express agency, and it is *because* these non-deliberate choices express agency that deliberation itself is agential. Those whose agency is repressed in childhood learn to either lash out or passively await direction, manipulating themselves and others without purpose. Children repressed in these ways grow into adults overly quick to judge themselves or others, overly inhibited through excessive deliberation, and/or unable to deliberate without guidance from another. For such adults, even deliberation itself often falls short of being genuinely agential.

Second, as noted in §2.1.1, *reflective* deliberation is a particularly self-conscious and complex form of a broader sort of deliberation intrinsic to all agency. When Sofia works with her cylinder blocks, she "deliberates" about where to put this particular cylinder, paying attention to its size and the sizes of the holes in the block. She may even be aware of her inclination to put it in the closest hole but override this inclination because that hole is clearly too big. This deliberation operates on a small scale. She overrides micro-inclinations to move in this or that way, but not her overall inclination to do this work. She deliberates almost instantaneously and in ways primarily directed by her attention to the material. As she matures, Sofia's task-oriented deliberation takes on longer time horizons, more abstract considerations, and broader arrays of inclination. When an older Sofia decides not to work on the cylinder blocks because she knows she wants to finish her research on horses,[27] she subordinates an immediate inclination to a higher-order interest. Her deliberation continues to expand as she considers the value of book-learning itself, the value of school vs. work vs. play, the value of friendship, and so on. Eventually, the task of living her life and finding her "task ... in this wonderful universe" (6: 4) requires deliberation in the broadest and most reflective sense, the sort of deliberation that provides what Schapiro calls a "plan of life" (Schapiro 1999: 729).

2.2 Deliberation and Respect for (Adult) Persons

Because Montessorian respect is a form of agency wherein one values others' agency, when deliberation expands the scope of agency, it also changes the nature of respect, and that in three primary ways. First, as children become more capable of stepping back from their own inclinations to consider whether acting on those inclinations conforms to their other goals and ideals, they also become capable of reflecting on the inclinations, goals, and ideals of others. Respect thus comes to include not merely letting others pursue projects of value to them through, say, waiting patiently for a fellow child to finish his work, but also explicitly taking into account others' goals and values, responding to reasons they proffer and considering the effects of one's actions on their good. Respect involves letting others' reasons into one's deliberation and taking those reasons seriously.[28]

Second, given that respect requires that one refrain from interrupting another's agential work, and given that deliberation itself is a form of agential work, respect for others requires allowing them to engage in their own processes of deliberation. Human beings have considerable power to influence or side-step others' decision-making processes, and as noted in the previous paragraph, respect even involves opening oneself up to this influence. There are corresponding duties of respect, however, to avoid misusing this power to prevent others from deliberating for themselves.[29] As in the more basic case of "help" (see Chapter 4, §4.3), knowing when to assist another in her deliberation and when to let her deliberate for herself requires moral judgment; respect requires both offering needed help and avoiding unwarranted interruption.

Third and finally, as reflective deliberation opens up possibilities for explicitly engaging in long-term projects of self-formation and self-expression, people increasingly need to respect what might otherwise have been non-agential features of one another. For example, respecting adults' deliberation can often involve respecting their arbitrary choices, preferences, and even whims, not directly for the sake of those preferences or whims but for the sake of the broader projects of which they form a part. The teenager who works to earn money for a car needs to have her choices about what car to buy respected, not because consumer choice *as such* is worth respecting—a toddler who wants this or that toy car would not need his choices respected—but because *her* choice of this car is part of a broader project of money-making and consumption, a part of becoming someone who is good at getting the resources to make arbitrary choices and prudent in how she makes them.[30]

2.3 Solidarity, Organization, and Group Deliberation

Children participating in the Silence Game act together but do not deliberate together (because they do not deliberate at all). When those children grow up and plan a group trip, they act together in part *by* deliberating together. Patriotic citizens singing their National Anthem act together but do not deliberate together. Those same patriotic citizens, when they establish a national health care system or consider appropriate reparations for injustices their nation has committed, act together in part by deliberating together. Deliberation—whether informally conducted as part of a group or carefully organized through structures and procedures for reaching group decisions—adds new dimensions to group solidarity.

Just as individual deliberation provides a means by which abstract values are able to exert influence over time, so too shared deliberative processes within a group provide mechanisms for the formation, ongoing influence, and revision of abstract values within the group as a whole over time. By virtue of her ability to reflectively deliberate about inclinations and values, Sofia's Catholicism could both exercise influence over her behavior and be subject to scrutiny and reassessment. So too the Catholic Church as a whole, through processes of shared deliberation, is able to sustain commitments to some abstract ideals and to revise commitments to others. These *shared* abstract values can be assessed by each individual as she decides whether or to what extent to identify with the group, but they can also have force within the group as a whole and be evaluable through processes of shared deliberation that define the group.

One way to think about how deliberation helps constitute various forms of social solidarity remains focused on individual-level deliberation and its associated commitments. Bratman, for example, emphasizes what he calls "meshing sub-plans":

> By requiring that my intentions both interlock with yours, and involve a commitment to mesh with yours, the theory ensures that rational pressures on me to be responsive to and to coordinate with you—rational pressures characteristic of shared intention—are built right into my own plans, given their special content and given demands of consistency and coherence on my own plans. And similarly with you. So there will normally be the kind of mutual, rational responsiveness in intention—in the direction of social agglomeration, consistency, and coherence—that is characteristic of shared agency.
>
> (Bratman 2009: 55)

Bratman provides for a sort of deliberative solidarity built from but going beyond basic respect for others' reasons, as each agent deliberates in such a way that she incorporates a commitment to shared plans. Through each restricting her own actions in the light of this commitment, the group of agents "agglomerates" plans in ways that constitute shared agency.

Other forms of shared deliberation draw on organized deliberative structures in order to generate intentions of the whole that exceed and even diverge from any intentions of individual members. Much contemporary philosophical work on social agency focuses on how principles of organization generate forms of agency that transcend mere collections of individual choices. Christian List and Philip Pettit, for example, show how groups of individuals with clearly worked-out group decision procedures can reach decisions that none of the individuals would reach on their own; their approach focuses on how organized decision-making structures combine individual choices such that results are not reducible to a "simple function of the attitudes of its members" but are nonetheless a result of individual attitudes given "various forms of coordination" (List and Pettit 2011: 8, 10; cf. Pettit 2012). Peter Galison has documented how scientific laboratories function as highly structured group agents with rules for how different members should perform various roles within the system of creating and disseminating scientific knowledge (Galison 1997, 2003; cf. Heubner 2014: 25–35). Political bodies in well-organized states—ranging from town councils to political parties to the state as a whole—operate in accordance with mechanisms for generating group decisions and group goals from the contributions of individuals. And countless other associations, corporations (profit-seeking as well as non-profit), clubs, and other groups make up organized wholes that bring individuals together toward the pursuit of shared goals or projects.

In all of these cases, organization can bring about agential unity. List and Pettit even explain how different forms of organization give rise to group agents with different degrees of *rational* agency, that is, different degrees to which agency consistently adheres to basic norms of practical rationality. For example, they contrast a structure wherein each decision is made purely democratically with one that decides on "premises" democratically but where conclusions follow as rational implications of those premises. To illustrate this point, consider a case where one must decide, by a majority vote of six jurors, whether a defendant is liable for some action for which they must pay compensation. To be guilty, it must be the case that (1) there is convincing prima facie[31] evidence that the defendant performed the action, (2) the defendant has no convincing alibi to cast doubt on that evidence, and (3) the deed wronged the plaintiff, such that the plaintiff is due compensation. Now consider two different organizational structures. For one, jurors vote only on the issue of liability, based on their individual judgments about the other issues. For the other, jurors decide each of the three issues collectively, and the judge then issues his verdict based on their decisions and formal decision-making procedures. Now imagine that two jurors affirm (1) and (2), but not (3). Two jurors affirm (1) and (3), but not (2). And two jurors affirm (2) and (3), but not (1). Under the first system, the jury as a whole will vote (unanimously) that the defendant is not liable. Under the second system, the jury as a whole will vote to affirm (1), (2), and (3), each by a 4–2 margin, and the judge will find the defendant liable. List and Pettit focus on cases of this sort in order to show that in the first case, the behavior of the jury as a whole is at best imperfectly agential, since the jury-as-agent believes a set of premises (1–3) that imply a practical conclusion, but it does not affirm the conclusion. The "group" functions as a set of interacting individuals making their own decisions and merely collating those decisions. In the second case, by contrast, there is a group rationality that is distinct from the rationality of any of its members.

Montessori does not enter in the details of group organizational structure to the degree that List and Pettit do. Like them, however, she rightly points out that organization makes it possible for individuals to assemble into groups that deliberate in ways the individuals do not. The capacity for abstraction makes possible organizations based on abstract principles, and such organizations can implement decision-procedures not located in the agential capacities of any one of their members. In that way, abstract organization opens up new forms of cooperation with great potential to effect changes in the world.

However, while Montessori shares an appreciation for the power of organized solidarity, she warns against the reliance on *mere* organization that characterizes (much of) List and Pettit's approach, and that Montessori (rightly) sees characterizing much of modern life. Organized unity, for Montessori, properly grows *out of* pre-organized unity and remains related to it. Montessori compares the development of social cohesion to weaving, in an analogy that applies more generally to the relationship between pre-reflective and reflective forms of ethical life:

> When a piece of cloth is to be woven, the warp is prepared first. All the threads lie close together, but parallel to each other. This is like the society by cohesion ... The second stage is when the shuttle attaches all the threads together. This is like the work of the leader who connects all the people together. Yet it is necessary to have the warp, the society by cohesion, as a basis—or we could not weave a strong piece of cloth. These phases ... can form the study of the embryology of society.

(17: 237–8; see too 1: 216–7)

Many political philosophers (Hobbes, Locke, Kant, Rawls, and others) assume a conception of human beings as relatively isolated individuals united by laws and institutions into a common whole. Montessori affirms that the ascent to abstraction makes it possible to construct laws and institutions with this function, just as this ascent makes it possible to impose moral rules on oneself if one lacks character properly speaking. Moreover, not only might such laws be necessary, but given each person's ability to understand the function of the laws and even to play a role in their creation, there is a sort of political autonomy in following laws that constrain one's behavior for the good of the whole. But trying to build moral unity through reflective, concept-driven processes *alone* is like a weaver trying to bind together a bundle of imperfectly aligned threads. The resultant unity will be messy and unstable, the instantiated autonomy half-hearted; at best, each will understand and rationally accept how and why laws are necessary, but still *feel* constrained rather than liberated by those laws. By contrast, for Montessori, laws and institutions—whether for uniting society or for unifying one's will—should take an antecedent capacity for unconscious and felt unity and transform it into a consistent, firm, determinate, self-conscious unity. With this transformation, felt unity can expand to wider social wholes. From the Silence

Game amongst peers in the classroom, one can rise to an organized and felt solidarity with fellow members of associations, citizens, and ultimately with the global society of which we are parts.[32]

3 Conclusion

In Chapter 3, I showed how Montessori interpreted the lives of children living in freedom in conditions conducive to development and thereby articulated a concept of pre-reflective agency worthy of direct respect, susceptible to cultivation through exercise, and central to flourishing ethical life. Chapters 4 and 5 expanded on Montessori's conception of ethical life. In Chapter 4, in addition to further defending the importance of respect for pre-reflective agency, I showed how and why respect for others is a central feature of Montessori's moral philosophy. In Chapter 5, I laid out the important roles of social solidarity and obedience. All of these features of ethical life— agency, character, respect, solidarity, and obedience—can occur without reflective deliberation, and all are present in the lives of children in conditions of freedom.

Adults, however, are not children. In this chapter, I focused on two important dimensions of adult agency that set it apart from the agency of children, namely adults' capacities for abstraction and reflective deliberation. These developments increase the scope and temporal horizon of agency, respect, and solidarity, and they alter the phenomenology of those features of ethical life. Even in adults, deliberation is not the sum of all that is good or agential in life, but it plays a central role in self-governance, respect, and solidarity for mature human beings.

While adding an important dimension to Montessori's conception of ethical life, this chapter also completes and nuances the argument (begun in Chapter 3) that children have an agency worthy of respect. In Chapter 7, I turn to a further implication of this argument, namely a direct refutation of asymmetrical attitudes toward paternalistic behavior when directed toward children as opposed to adults. In addition to arguing that such asymmetrical attitudes are unjustified, I also address seemingly intractable practical problems that might arise from a moral theory that requires as much respect for children's agency as for that of fellow adults.

7

Paternalism

Over the course of this book, I have laid out basic values of Montessori's moral theory, which she based on insights gleaned from respectful attention to free children living in conditions conducive to their development. In Chapter 3, I showed how children demonstrate a form of agency susceptible of respect, and in Chapter 4, I argued that this agency is the proper locus of respect. Throughout Chapters 3–5, I emphasized that adult forms of deliberation and reflection are not necessary in order to live flourishing ethical lives, and Chapter 6 showed how adult agency both differs from and depends on the agency of children. In adults as well as children, character, respect, and solidarity are the pillars of ethical life, though adults have deliberative and reflective forms of these key pillars alongside pre-reflective and non-deliberative forms. My overall goal has been to depict a form of ethical life that puts at its core an agency that consists of active, norm-governed, persistent expression of interests with which one identifies, an agency that sometimes—but not always—involves reflective deliberation.

In Chapter 3, I pointed out that one important motivation for the standard, adult-centered approach to agency is to justify paternalistic behavior toward children. Schapiro makes this connection explicit when she claims, "The philosophical task is to ... explain ... why children are proper objects of paternalistic treatment" (Schapiro 1999: 717, 724). Other philosophers often implicitly treat as a discussion-stopping reductio ad absurdum the argument that if such-and-such counts as agency, then even very young children have agency. Schapiro offers a particularly pointed—because so common and so seemingly clear—case of this general tendency, the case of the obstinate daughter, where "it is thought appropriate that children, however deeply loved by their parents, are not their parents' equals when it comes to having a say in how their lives are to be lived" (Schapiro 2003: 576):

> Consider, for example, a father who, when putting his two-year-old daughter to bed, asks her which pair of pajamas she'd like to wear ... [I]n the background of such an interaction there is likely to be some restriction on the range of discretion accorded to her ... For example, should she refuse to wear pajamas at all, or should she insist on wearing pajamas which are too lightweight, given the cold weather, the father will usually be ready to force her to make a different choice ... To see that this is a distinctive feature of adult-child relations, consider what would happen if the same man were to fail to dissuade his wife from wearing uncomfortable

pajamas to bed. Were he to try to force her to wear different pajamas, she would appropriately object that he was treating her like a child.

(Schapiro 2003: 576)

In this and myriad other common cases, mutual respect prohibits adults from treating each other in ways that we typically—and without apparent fault—treat children.[1] Dworkin explains the basic position, articulated by Schapiro and widely shared by most discussants of paternalism:

> [T]he burden of proof is different depending on who is being treated paternalistically. If it is a child then the assumption is that, other things being equal, the burden of proof is on those who resist paternalism. If it is an adult of sound mind the presumption is reversed.
>
> (Dworkin 2020)

If the argument of Chapters 3 and 4 is correct, then children have agency worthy of direct respect and Dworkin's asymmetry claim cannot be straightforwardly maintained. In this case, everyday practices of apparently good parenting and caregiving seemingly require radical revision, and we seem left with an unworkable and morally irresponsible kind of laissez-faire approach to childcare. Beyond examples like the obstinate daughter, strict anti-paternalism regarding children might seem to rule out seemingly essential interventions with children's agency, as basic as preventing a toddler from running into a busy street to recover a ball or requiring that children participate in some sort of schooling.

In this chapter, I defend symmetry in our treatment of children and adults when it comes to paternalism. Against Dworkin and Schapiro, I argue that differences between children and adults do not warrant fundamentally different standards for determining whether paternalism is appropriate. Because most of this argument has already been laid out in Chapters 3, 4, and 6, the bulk of this chapter focuses on articulating everyday implications of Montessori's conception of children's agency. In particular, I consider alternatives to paternalism that allow adults to practice legitimate care for children and briefly discuss when paternalism toward children (and adults) can be justified, if—contra Schapiro—children already have a will to respect. Throughout, I discuss how differences between children and adults, while not relevant to *whether* paternalism is prima facie impermissible, are relevant to when, how, and why anti-paternalism is essential for moral respect.

1 What Is Paternalism?

Paternalism is a way that people treat one another. To treat another paternalistically is to override or coerce another's agency solely for the sake of promoting that other's good. Different accounts of paternalism differ with respect to what precisely counts as agency, what counts as "overriding or coercing," and how to define the relevant goods. For example, the relevant "goods" might be moral goods (such as when one bans pornography because watching pornography is a moral vice) or spiritual goods (forced conversion or Sabbath laws) or goods of objective well-being (banning smoking to preserve health) or subjective goods (requiring seatbelts to preserve people's lives, on the assumption that people want to remain alive). Often, such as with laws banning smoking, paternalism focuses on the relationship between a state/government and people living under the jurisdiction of that government, but a broader concept of paternalism addresses any interactions between persons, including smaller-scale personal relationships, such as when one regularly hides a friend's cigarettes for their good. Philosophers often distinguish—albeit not in consistent ways—between so-called "soft paternalism" and "hard paternalism," generally using "soft paternalism" to refer to one or another form of acceptable paternalism (see §5 below). As we will see in §4, the past decade has also seen a rise of interest in so-called "libertarian paternalism," whereby one modifies others' "choice architecture" in such a way that one "alters people's behavior in a predictable way without forbidding any options" (Thaler and Sunstein 2008: 6). And in recent years, consequentialist philosophers have increasingly argued in favor of broad paternalism even with respect to adults (see, e.g., Conly 2012 and Hanna 2018).

All of these discussions are ultimately relevant to when, how, and why paternalism or anti-paternalism expresses respect for others, whether those others are children or adults. For the purposes of this chapter, however, I require only the relatively straightforward concept of paternalism as deliberate interference with another's agency solely for the sake of promoting that other's good.

2 What's Wrong with Paternalism?

Because my primary goal in this chapter is to defend symmetry between adults and children when it comes to paternalism, I largely ignore general pro-paternalist arguments. If paternalism is justified in general, such that the burden of proof always lies with one who would argue *against* a particular paternalistic intervention, then there is no principled difference between adults and children when it comes to such interference.[2] While I present a partial defense of paternalism in §5 below, my overall strategy in this chapter accepts that paternalism is prima facie impermissible, so I start in this section with three broadly Montessorian arguments against paternalism. First, paternalism is wrong because individuals are generally better at promoting their own interests than those who would seek to intervene. This "proficiency argument" (Schapiro 2003) is affirmed by Montessori, who adds an important dimension of subconscious guiding instincts by which people pursue perfection in ways that even they do not fully understand. Second and more importantly, paternalism is wrong because it infringes on the dignity that individuals have by virtue of being agents. Character, and the agency expressing and perfected in character, is the highest human good, so infringing on another's agency infringes on something each of us must take to be unconditionally valuable. Finally, paternalism is developmentally destructive. Character develops through exercise. By inhibiting its expression, paternalism represses, perverts, and erodes character.

2.1 Paternalism, Proficiency, and Well-Being

One of the most prominent and widely discussed anti-paternalist arguments is John Stuart Mill's defense of "liberty" in *On Liberty*. There, Mill argues that "the only purpose for which power can be rightfully exercised over any[one] ... against his will, is to prevent harm to others. His own good, either physical or moral, is not a sufficient warrant" ([1859] 1989: 13). In defense of this principle, Mill appeals only to "utility" as "the ultimate appeal on all ethical questions" ([1859] 1989: 14). The details of Mill's utilitarian argument are beyond the scope of the present discussion, but roughly speaking, there are three main utilitarian arguments for liberty, all of which boil down to the notion that individuals are better at pursuing their own well-being than others are at directing them toward it. First, because each individual has a stronger *interest* in their own welfare than any other person does, each will pursue that interest for themselves more effectively than others will pursue it for them.

> [Each person] is the [one] most interested in his own well-being: the interest which any other person, except in cases of strong personal attachment, can have in it, is trifling, compared to that which he himself has.
>
> ([1859] 1989: 76)

Second, because each individual has a greater *knowledge* of their own situation than others do, they will pursue their own advantage more effectively than others can. For example, "with respect to his own feelings and circumstances, the most ordinary man or woman has means of knowledge immeasurably surpassing those that can be possessed by anyone else" (Mill [1859] 1989: 76). Third, because liberty itself is partly *constitutive* of well-being, people's freedom to choose for themselves must be preserved in order for them to maximize overall well-being: "the free development of individuality is one of the leading essentials of well-being" (Mill [1859] 1989: 57).[3]

Montessori explicitly endorses these broadly utilitarian arguments against paternalism, particularly the last, referring to denials of liberty as "miseries" and specifically endorsing the truth that "we know that enjoyment depends upon being at liberty" (9: 13, 15). She tells a clever parable to help adults see how this principle applies to everyday paternalistic interference in the lives of children:

> What should we do if we were to become the slaves of a people incapable of understanding our feelings, a gigantic people, very much stronger than ourselves? When we were quietly eating our soup, enjoying it at our leisure..., suppose a giant appeared and, snatching the spoon from our hand, made us swallow it in such haste that we were almost choked. Our protest: "For mercy's sake, slowly," would be accompanied by an oppression of the heart; our digestion would suffer. If again, thinking of something pleasant, we should be slowly putting on an overcoat with all the sense of well-being and liberty we enjoy in our own houses, and some giant should suddenly throw it upon us, and having dressed us, should in the twinkling of an eye, carry us out to some distance from the door, we should feel our dignity so wounded, that all the expected pleasure of the walk would be lost. Our nutrition

does not depend solely on the soup we have swallowed, nor our well-being upon the physical exercise of walking, but also upon the liberty with which we do these things. We should feel offended and rebellious, not at all out of hatred of these giants, but merely from our recognition of the innate tendency to free functions in all that pertains to life ... It is this love of freedom which nourishes and gives well-being to our life, even in its most minute acts. Of this it was said: "Man does not live by bread alone." How much greater this need must be in young children, in whom creation is still in action!

(9: 15–6)

In this story, the giant fails to promote the well-being of the main character, partly due to failures of *knowledge*: he does not realize, for instance, that the main character is happily thinking of something pleasant while slowly putting on her coat, or that she needs time to enjoy her food. Partly, though this is only implicit in the story, the giant rushes the main character because he is more *interested* in himself, and particularly his own time frame, than her, and thus fails to really be attentive to what is better for her. Largely, the failure is due to an underestimation of the value of liberty itself as *constitutive* of well-being (and even of raw pleasure itself).

The first two of these arguments—based on interest and knowledge—boil down to what Schapiro has aptly called "proficiency" arguments, which claim that individuals are typically more proficient at pursuing their own good for themselves than others are at pursuing that good for them (Schapiro 2003). Schapiro rightly notes that antipaternalists such as Mill typically allow paternalism with respect to children. As Mill puts it, "It is, perhaps, hardly necessary to say that this doctrine is meant to apply only to human beings in the maturity of their faculties. We are not speaking of children" ([1859] 1989: 13).[4] Insofar as Mill relies on proficiency arguments, paternalism toward children can be justified because "children lack reason" in that "they are incapable of deliberating *well*," say because of an "incapacity to make choices which protect and advance their own interests" or an inability "to make well-reasoned choices generally" (Schapiro 2003: 580).

Schapiro rightly rejects proficiency arguments as bases for distinguishing children from adults, partly on the grounds of her more robust argument against paternalism toward adults (see §2.2) and partly on the grounds that any such difference between adults and children would be only a difference of degree and should be dealt with the same way in both cases. If an adult who tends to make bad choices should receive support and advice but not coercive interference, so too for the case of a child (see Schapiro 2003: 581). More generally, proficiency-based arguments against paternalism for adults are subject to empirical disconfirmation, given the widespread evidence of deliberative and reasoning errors in adults. Adult reasoning is influenced by cognitive biases, peer effects, and framing effects (see Kahneman 2011; Hanna 2018), and many adults lack relevant knowledge or simply make decisions in a hasty or habitual way. If paternalism is precluded only because people decide better for themselves than others decide for them, then paternalism is allowed whenever we have good reasons to think that our decision for another will be better than the reasons they make for themselves.

While adults' tendency to deliberate badly erodes the adult-child distinction from one direction, Montessori would add an important further point that erodes the distinction from another direction. Many proficiency-based defenses of antipaternalism focus on *conscious* interests and knowledge. Consistent with her broader approach to agency, Montessori often highlights *unconscious* interests and knowledge. A child's "love of work" orients him toward tasks that are particularly important for his specific "sensitive period" of development: "The child is richly endowed with powers, sensitivities, and constructive instincts that as yet have neither been recognized nor put to use. In order to develop, he needs much broader opportunities ... Society must fully recognize the social rights of the child" (10: 24). Children (and adults) work in ways that give them immediate pleasure in activity, prepare them for joyful rest after activity, and develop them in ways necessary for future well-being. Not only do caregivers usually fail to understand the complete function of these activities; often agents themselves are aware only of their desire to engage in this or that work. When in flow, human beings focus on their activities, not on broader purposes for those activities nor even on the role of those activities in their well-being. And yet such activities—in adults and especially in children—are expressions of individual liberty and necessary for complete human well-being. Paternalistic interference subverts individuals' investment in activities the value of which they know only unconsciously: "It is something within us which man does not recognize, which God alone knows, a something which manifests itself imperceptibly to us to the end that we may complete it" (9: 16).[5] Adult interference often inhibits the natural and wise self-direction of children because children are at work on tasks and in ways that adults do not fully understand.

Beyond proficiency arguments, one can oppose paternalism given the intrinsic value of liberty as partly constitutive of well-being. This argument resonates with Montessori's emphasis on character as the fundamental value of ethical life. In relations with one another, respect—including respectful help—takes as its object the agency of others. Because genuine help assists agency, one should never compromise agency for the sake of other goods. On its own, the constitutive value of agency does not unconditionally preclude paternalism. Interfering with someone's agency in a particular case might facilitate their agency overall (see §5 below). Mill himself allows paternalistic interference with adults who engage in activities—selling themselves into slavery—that directly threaten their agency. We might enhance a child's agency, similarly, by interfering when he wants to chase a ball into a busy street, and we might (and often do) similarly justify coercing or undermine children's choices for the sake of ensuring that they learn what they need to know in order to exercise agency effectively as adults. As these examples suggest, however, whatever paternalism such an argument allows can apply to both children and adults. The father who forced his daughter to wear comfortable pajamas was (probably) not doing so for the sake of facilitating her future agency, and an adult who prevents another adult from chasing a ball into a busy street is unlikely to be condemned as unduly paternalistic.[6]

2.2 Paternalism, Humanity, and Agential Authority

In *On Liberty*, when opposing paternalism on the grounds of utility, Mill explicitly "forego[es] any advantage which could be derived to my argument from the idea of abstract right" ([1859] 1989: 14), indirectly alluding to a tradition of opposing paternalism on the grounds that individuals have a general right of self-governance intrinsic to them as agents (or human beings). Even when introducing the intrinsic value of liberty, Mill treats it as a constitutive *part* of well-being rather than as what Allen Wood calls an "existent end" worthy of direct respect. Schapiro puts this in terms of Kant's "humanity principle":

> Humanity [that is, agency] is not a positive end to be produced or promoted; rather it is a negative end, one which serves as a limiting condition on all of our choices ... [T]he power of choice is ... something that puts a direct constraint on permissible forms of interaction. On an even stronger interpretation of the humanity principle, certain forms of treatment are ruled out regardless of the end to be promoted thereby. More specifically, the principle rules out forms of interaction which, by their nature, deprive others of the opportunity to exercise their capacity for choice with respect to the specific proposals with which they are faced.
>
> (Schapiro 2003: 583)

For Kant, one must treat "humanity, whether in one's own person or in the person of any other, always at the same time as an end and never merely as a means" (Kant 1996: 80). On most readings of Kant,[7] the "humanity" one must treat as an end is precisely each agents' capacity to set and pursue her own ends, and treating this humanity as an end requires that one never infringe upon the authority of each agent to make her own choices.[8] Kant's argument for this requirement is that whenever I make choices, I necessarily treat my own choice-making capacity as having legitimate authority over my actions, "but every other rational being also represents his [similar capacity] in this way consequent on just the same rational ground that also holds for me," so I ought to see his choice-making as authoritative for him just as much as mine is for me (Kant 1996: 79). Unlike the consequentialist arguments in §2.1, Kant need not claim that giving others authority over their choices leads to choices with better outcomes. Rather, his point is that agents have authority to make *their own* choices, something that we commit ourselves to whenever we choose (including when we choose to act paternalistically toward another). To behave paternalistically is thus a sort of contradiction, where a person says both that I (the pro-paternalist) can rightly make decisions based on my own judgment because I am an agent, but also denies that agents in general can be trusted to make decisions based on their own judgment.

In Chapter 4, we saw that Montessori makes a similar argument for the requirement that each respect the agency of every other. Once one develops character, one comes to recognize the centrality of agency for ethical life. Children with character naturally respect expressions of character in others and develop a sensitive attunement to those expressions, avoiding interruption (even with unnecessary "help") and providing genuine help when truly needed. Children's respect grows from their awareness of their own agency. From the "sense of personal dignity" grows a corresponding "sense of justice" (12: 60). Unlike Kant (and Kantians), Montessori does not propose any logical consistency argument from valuing one's own agency to valuing the agency of others. Consistent with her overall moral epistemology, her argument is natural and psychological rather than conceptual. As human beings develop into well-functioning agents, they directly perceive the value of agency as something not to be interfered with, and they perceive this value both in themselves and in others.

As we saw in Chapter 3, Montessori differs from Kantian arguments in rejecting the necessity of reflective deliberation for agency. For Kantians, the "humanity" that warrants respect requires higher-order reflection and rational deliberation; it is from within the standpoint of rational deliberation that one commits oneself to the value of one's (deliberative) agency and thereby to the value of others' (deliberative) agency. Insofar as what we necessarily endorse in our own choices is our reflective or deliberative self, and insofar as children's agency is pre-reflective, Kantians justify treating children paternalistically because we do not thereby violate in them what we must value in ourselves (see Schapiro 1999; 2003). However, if we identify with our prereflective agency and prereflectively commit ourselves to its authority, and especially if we identify with and endorse our deliberative activity only insofar as we identify with and endorse our more basic capacity to select activities for ourselves and persistently engage in those activities,[9] then that which we necessarily value in ourselves is also present in children. Montessori's anti-paternalism calls us to "admire and serve the inner forces of the child and humbly set ourselves aside with the intention of cooperating so that the personality of the child with its inner presence is always before us" (7: 97). Deliberation itself proceeds from "inner forces" with which we (adults) identify, so by virtue of acting at all, whether deliberatively or not, we commit ourselves to have respect for these "inner forces," that is, to respect for agency as such, whether deliberative or not.

This non-consequentialist argument justifies Montessori's dignity-based and rights-based rejections of paternalism. Montessori refers to the child as the "forgotten citizen," who "must be appreciated in accordance with his true value. His rights as a human being ... must become sacred" (10: 34).[10] She insists that when children's agency is interrupted, "something precious is lost" and children are "depreciated [*diminuiti*]" (9: 16), made less, undermined in their personhood. When Montessori discusses "the fact that [adult society] has neglected and indeed forgotten the rights of the child" in ways that "should arouse the conscience of humanity in a most vehement manner," she identifies this neglect for rights with society having "failed to recognize [the child's] value, his power, his essential nature" (22: 188). Throughout these and similar discussions, she appeals not merely to negative consequences, but to something *intrinsic* to the child that is directly wronged in the violation of their rights, work, and agency.

This sort of anti-paternalistic respect distinguishes Montessori's approach from that of some recent moral philosophers who endorse a strong connection between reflective deliberation and agency, but who nonetheless defend the notion that we have direct duties to non-reflective beings who are "agents" in the sense of "beings for whom things can be good or bad" (Korsgaard 2018: 20–1).[11] This sort of defense of duties to non-reflective agents still assumes an essentially paternalistic stance toward them. Montessori's claim about children's agency is different. It is not merely that various things are good for children—such as food, sleep, shelter, and play—or perceived by them as good—such as candy, ice cream, or television. In these respects, children, adults, and animals all have instinctive orientations toward natural goods. But human beings,[12] whether children or adults, also "play a particularly active and responsible role in constituting our selves, our own minds and identities" (Korsgaard 2018: 35). Paternalism undermines this self-constituting capacity. When one behaves paternalistically, one looks out for natural goods of a person while not allowing that person to constitute herself by herself. For Korsgaard and others, active self-constituting depends upon second-order reflection and/or Reason-guided deliberation, and thus is not (fully) present in (young) children. For Montessori, however, self-constitution happens whenever one exercises self-governance in accordance with constitutive norms of activities to which one commits oneself, whether reflectively or through wholehearted interest. As I showed in Chapter 3, children's agency—governed by prereflective choices and actions—can be oriented toward self-constitution rather than merely toward the satisfaction of instinctive desires, so duties to children cannot merely focus on what is good for them but must also treat them with anti-paternalistic respect.

2.3 Paternalism and Development

Section 2.2 focused on how paternalism threatens agency as an existent good. Insofar as someone is an agent, their capacity to make choices for themselves ought to be respected because making choices for oneself, however well those choices turn out, is an essential—and perhaps the most essential—good of human life. Whereas §2.1 raised concerns about the consequences of paternalism for one's welfare, §2.2 rightly highlighted the disrespect intrinsic to interference with another's expression of their agency. For Montessori, the most important objection to paternalism combines features of both arguments. As we saw in Chapter 3 and again in §2.2, Montessori sees agency (particularly as the expression of agency) as the supreme value of ethical life. Paternalistic interference is wrong in part because it directly interferes with expressing this agency. But as an educator focused on human development, Montessori also—indeed preeminently—focuses on effects of paternalism on the *development* of agency. Thus when she refers to cases where one "roughly interrupt[s]" "those marvelous moments when attention is fixed," she adds that such moments are also cases where the "process of organization which is to develop them begins in their souls," and goes on: "Perhaps at the very moments when we were about to create ourselves, we were interrupted and persecuted, and our spiritual organization was left rickety, weak, and inadequate" (9: 16). When highlighting the problem of replacing "the disorderly movement of the child ... [with] the will of the adult," she asks, "And what happens to the child's mind?" (24: 113). The evils of society having "neglected and forgotten the rights of the child" include not merely the direct injustice, and not even just the "torment," but also that it "has, maybe unconsciously, ... broken him down" (22: 188).

As one would expect from an educator focused on human development from infancy through adulthood, Montessori's arguments against paternalism emphasize how it corrupts or prevents the development of character, and, by extension, of agency, virtue, and ethical life.

Montessori's basic argument is quite simple. Character develops through exercise. To be an agent capable of making choices for oneself and persistently following through on those choices persistently requires that one's efforts to make and persist in choices be permitted. Moreover, like most human capacities, character has sensitive periods of development. Throughout childhood, one builds a well-formed adult character through exercising increasingly complex forms of agency. Young children are particularly adept at choosing activities that satisfy fundamental inner needs, and they excel at persisting in such self-chosen tasks for as long as necessary to accomplish requisite inner growth, and they naturally set aside work that no longer serves an inner need. These features of agency develop and grow through exercise, and all are essential to fully virtuous and authentic adult agency. As children mature, they become increasingly capable of setting aside short-term inclinations for the sake of longer-term goals, of setting for themselves abstract ends, and of participation in artificially constructed forms of agential organization at both individual and social levels. They gradually develop reflective capacities and higher-order deliberation. And so on. All such capacities require exercise and even error in order to properly develop. Paternalistic interference prevents such exercise. Montessori explains the need for volitional exercise by analogy with physical exercise:

> It would certainly never occur to any one that in order to educate the voluntary motility of a child, it would be well first of all to keep it absolutely motionless, covering its limbs with cement (I will not say fracturing them!) until the muscles become atrophied and almost paralyzed; and then, when this result had been attained, that it would suffice to read to the child wonderful stories of clowns, acrobats and champion boxers and wrestlers, to fire him by such examples, and to inspire in him an ardent desire to emulate them. It is obvious that such a proceeding would be an inconceivable absurdity.
>
> And yet we do something of the same kind when, in order to educate the child's "will," we first of all attempt to annihilate it, or, as we say, "break" it, and thus hamper the development of every factor of the will, substituting ourselves for the child in everything. It is by *our* will that we keep him motionless, or make him act; it is we who choose and decide for him. And after all this we are content to teach him that "to will is to do" (*volere e potere*).[13] And we present to his fancy, in the guise of fabulous tales, stories of heroic men, giants of will, under the illusion that by committing their deeds to memory a vigorous feeling of emulation will be aroused and will complete the miracle.
>
> (9: 140–1)

By repressing a child's choice of this or that activity, one not only prevents that child from practicing an essential agential power, but one acculturates the child to conform his will to those of others. Children come to expect that trying to make their own choices will prove fruitless; they expect choices to be overridden by others and stop even trying to find activities that are intrinsically appealing to them. As adults, they reflect and deliberate in accordance with what they think is expected of them, without even being aware of whether they really care about the reasons they take to be decisive. Their adult agency, whether in flow or deliberation, is always tepid, shaped by the sense that it's not worth being too personally invested in what they are doing since it can so easily be overridden by those who purport to "know better."[14]

3 Interference without Paternalism

In §2, I offered three arguments against paternalism and for symmetry between children and adults. This might sound well and good in theory, but also "philosophical" in the pejorative sense that implies being out of touch with practical realities of life. Children's vulnerability and ignorance seem to require paternalistic treatment. The next three sections show how we can avoid paternalism in relation to children without leaving them to eat candy all day long and chase balls into busy streets instead of going to school.

First, given the definition of paternalism in §1—intentional interference with another's agency solely for the sake of promoting that other's good— it should be clear that some forms of interference with others are not paternalistic. For one thing, non-intentional interference is not, strictly speaking, paternalistic. While I will not discuss this form of interference in detail, it is worth noting complexities about what precisely counts as intentional. The relevant "intentionality" should be taken to excuse the case where, say, I clean up an apparent mess on the floor not realizing that this is a handmade "puzzle" that a child was working on. By contrast, the caregiver who feeds her year-old baby rather than letting that child sloppily maneuver food into his own mouth interferes with his agency even if she does so with the "intention" only of ensuring that he gets enough food. Insofar as one intentionally engages in behavior toward another while disregarding their agency, one exhibits a disrespect for agency that can be considered paternalistic, whether or not one specifically intends to disrupt that agency. Even careless "bumping into others," for Montessori, is a form of disrespect that can compromise another's agency (as we will see in more detail in Chapter 8).

Beyond fully unintentional behavior, there are two important non-paternalistic forms of interference with other people. First, one might interfere with others' agency for some reason other than promoting the good of that other. In some cases, such interference will be especially disrespectful, such as if I were to interfere with your agency solely for the sake of showing my dominance over you; but in many such cases, interference will be for the sake of other goods, and the moral issue at stake is not paternalism but the relative weights of a given individual's agency and those other goods. Among the most important such other goods are harm to others and/or the infringement of others' agency. Both Mill and Kant, for example, allow for interfering with the liberty of one who threatens harm to someone else. I discuss the importance of these sorts of non-paternalistic interference in §3.1. Second, one might interfere with other persons, but not with their *agency*. In §3.2, I discuss precisely what this means, how it is possible, and how it applies to children. Then, in §4, I consider ways of non-paternalistically influencing others in ways that foster their own (or others') goods, and in §5 I consider possible cases where paternalism in the strict sense might be justified for both children and adults.

3.1 Interference for the Sake of Others

Paternalism requires interfering with another's agency *for the sake of the person herself* (see, e.g., Dworkin 1972; 2020). Many interventions with others' agency are for purposes other than the good of the agent.[15] Mill's prohibition on paternalistic intervention specifically contrasts such intervention with power "rightfully exercised ... to prevent harm to others" ([1859] 1989: 13), and the central concept of Kant's political theory is that "coercion that is opposed to [actions that wrong others] (as a *hindering of a hindrance to freedom*) is consistent with freedom in accordance with universal laws" (6: 231). Montessori, too, in the midst of insisting that the "fundamental" rule for interacting with children "is not to interfere," adds that the teacher "must not only not interfere when the child is concentrating, she must also see that [the child] is not disturbed," where this obligation will require that she "be a policeman" with respect to children interfering with others (17: 229).[16]

This basis for interfering with agency provides some permissibility[17] for interference in the lives of children. The child's demand for this or that toy is an imposition of his will over the parent's, not a mere exercise of will. Throwing a ball inside the house is an expression of agency that is also a direct threat to the homeowner's agential right to property. In such cases, parents have a non-paternalistic justification for interfering with agency. And this point is highlighted by the similarity in adult cases; one could prevent another adult from throwing a ball in one's house, and one need not give adults whatever they ask for.

Intentional interference with another's agency can be permissible, even for anti-paternalists, when such interference is not solely for the sake of promoting that other's good, and pre-eminently when such interference is needed to prevent violations of others' agency, whether these violations are direct (as when a child disturbs another child's work) or indirect (as in destruction of property). Specifying the limits of such non-paternalistic interference is far from simple; much modern political theory is precisely oriented toward delimiting justified non-paternalistic uses of coercion. The situation is particularly complicated under conditions of dependence, such as between children and their caregivers, where children are dependent upon caregivers for various needs, and caregivers have an obligation to those under their care to provide for their needs. Consider the obstinate daughter. If she goes to sleep with pajamas that are too lightweight for the weather, not only will *she* have a poor night's sleep, but her *father* will have to wake up at night to help her change, and/or deal with his grumpy daughter in the morning, etc. Her dependence on him, and his obligation to care for her, constitutes a situation within which her harm to herself can infringe on *his* agency. Thus he might, in something akin to self-defense, pre-emptively prevent situations that will cause such infringements. Moreover, the lightweight pajamas that the daughter chooses to wear, and even the bed in which she chooses to sleep, are the property of the father, not of her. Even from the standpoint of his own (property) rights, the father can set the terms under which she uses goods that are his. The famous line—"You'll follow my rules as long as you live under my roof" (cf. Warnick 2015)—is testament to this broadly property-based assertion of rights over the child.

Montessori frequently warns about the danger of making use of these sorts of justifications for interference with the lives of children, noting how the "utter social inferiority" of the child puts him in a state of "complete disadvantage" (22: 59). Given children's dependence, adults could justify almost any intervention in the lives of children on the grounds of the adult's own personal rights over their time or property. Fortunately—and appropriately—a (typical) caregiver's love for children and conscious sense of duty toward them rightly call forth a reluctance to appeal to personal rights in order to oppress children's freedom. The sense of justice that children demonstrate with each other and that morally attuned caregivers employ recognizes a general need to subordinate one's personal goods for genuine needs of those under one's care, and this recognition limits even interpersonally justified interference. Moreover, caregivers' status as both interested party and judge in such cases can and should give them pause when defending their own rights at the expense of the weak children under their care. Defending one child against the infringements of another is quite different from forcing one's daughter to wear warm pajamas for the sake of one's own improved sleep. As a result, parents typically disguise self-interested motives for infringing on children's freedom, appealing instead to paternalistic justifications:

> The repression of inconvenient acts on the part of the child in the environment where the adult reigns becomes inevitable through the fact that the adult is not aware of his own defensive attitude, and is conscious only of love and generous self-surrender ... The subconscious instinct of defense appears consciously in another guise; the proprietary sense that makes the adult anxious to defend things he cherishes from the child becomes at once, "the duty of training the child so as to teach him good habits" and fear of the small disturber of his comfort becomes "the need to make the child rest a lot for the good of his health."
>
> (22: 59–60)

Rather than admitting the self-centered but at least prima facie legitimate grounds for restricting the child's behavior, adults prefer to believe that paternalistic interference is morally justified due to a categorial difference between children and adults.

This sort of reasoning becomes particularly salient when comparing the cases of the obstinate daughter and the obstinate wife. Schapiro rightly notes that in our everyday attitudes, we treat the child as though her right to wear the pajamas of her choice is "doled out to her as ... a mere privilege," while the wife has a genuine right to wear the pajamas she chooses, to "lead her own life" (Schapiro 2003: 577). Strikingly, even in this context, Schapiro adds that this right to lead one's own life applies only "with regard to matters affecting only her welfare," which opens the whole set of interpersonal justifications presented earlier in this section. How would we respond if the husband, once he "fail[ed] to dissuade his wife from wearing uncomfortable pajamas to bed" (ibid.), pointed out to his wife that she tends to wake him up in the night when wearing uncomfortable pajamas and to ruin his day when she doesn't get enough sleep? I suspect that we would be reluctant to grant these justifications sufficient weight to warrant giving him sartorial authority at bedtime. The wife may well be more likely to wake him up and ruin his day, and once she is grumpy because she was uncomfortable in bed, she may be no more able to control these infringements than the child. But because the wife—at least in much of twenty-first-century American society—is more socially and politically powerful than the child, she has the ability to stand up for her rights in ways that the child does not. The husband's claims of his personal rights sound selfish and disproportionate in both cases. Paternalistic justifications, clearly patronizing when directed toward the wife, sound plausible when directed toward the politically voiceless child, but they are no more legitimate.

3.2 Interference with Non-Agential "Choices"

As noted in §1, most anti-paternalists allow for apparently paternalistic behavior directed toward those who lack "the maturity of their faculties" (Mill [1859] 1989: 13). So-called "soft paternalism involves intervention on behalf of people who are ill-informed, impaired, or otherwise incapable of voluntary choice" (Hanna 2018: 20). Schapiro's alternative to proficiency arguments trades on the notion that "actions caused by children fail to be their own" because "a child [is] incapable of making her own choices, whether good or bad," so that a child "does not really 'have' a will" (Schapiro 2003: 586, 579; 1999: 730). The key point is that there is nothing prima facie wrong with infringing upon *mere desires* or even "choices," if those desires or choices do not express the *will* of an *agent*.

On some accounts, the relevant distinction is between different sorts of *people*, such as between adults and children or between adults with and without "sound mind" (see Hanna 2018: 1). In Schapiro and many others, agency applies to adults of sound mind, those with an established character based on principles of Reason arrived at through reflection. The choices of such agents ought to be respected. Based on her example of the obstinate wife, choices of agents ought to be respected by others regardless of the extent to which those choices proceed from the agent's established character. Even if the wife's refusal is a mere whim, because she is a reflective agent, she has authority over herself and her choices must be respected. By contrast, because children are not yet agents in this sense, Schapiro does not consider infringing on their choices to constitute paternalism.

For Montessori, however, agency is a concept that most fundamentally applies to particular behaviors, where we should distinguish behavior that expresses *agency* from what we might call "mere" behavior. A particular choice can be agential, or merely whimsical, or even the expression of weaknesses of will that one deliberately rejects. In contemporary philosophical discussions, cases of weakness of will are often used to highlight actions, even of adults, toward which paternalism might be justified.

> A classical example is given in the Odyssey when Odysseus commands his men to tie him to the mast and refuse all future orders to be set free, because he knows the power of the Sirens to enchant men with their songs. Here we are on relatively

sound ground in later refusing Odysseus' request to be set free. He may even claim to have changed his mind, but since it is just such changes that he wished to guard against, we are entitled to ignore them.

(Dworkin 1972: 77)

More mundanely, we might consider someone who gives her friends the car keys and tells them not to let her drive if she's been drinking, or who recognizes a tendency to stay up too late watching Netflix and asks her partner to disconnect the Wi-Fi after 11 p.m. In these cases, the relevant party specifically asks for (and thereby consents to) behavior that would otherwise be paternalistic, but we might say that even without such express consent, it is impossible to interfere with the "will" of a person whose choices are controlled by Sirens or alcohol or Netflix-stupor rather than by themselves.

The examples of Odysseus and others suggest some privileging of reflective deliberation as constitutive of agency, but for Montessori, as we saw in detail in Chapter 3, the difference between agential behavior and mere behavior is not primarily a matter of the amount of reflection, deliberation, or influence by Reason. Choices can be agential when they proceed from careful reflection, but also when they manifest loves and cares with which we identify or when they are part of one's attentive work;[18] and they can *fail* to be agential, even when deliberate and reflectively endorsed (as Odysseus illustrates, and see too Chapter 6). As in the case of Schapiro, however, Montessori's distinction between mere impulse or desire and those choices that reflect agency gives rise to a distinction between two kinds of interference, a problematically paternalistic interference with agency and a prima facie permissible interference with non-agential "choice."

The distinction between choices that are genuinely agential and those that are not allows for interference that might otherwise seem paternalistic, for just the reasons that Schapiro highlights in distinguishing children from adults. When someone's behavior does not express their agency, interfering in that behavior does not infringe upon their agency, so it can't be paternalistic. In the case of children, this distinction implies that many choices need not be respected because they are non-agential. Thus while insisting that teachers generally not interfere with children's attentive work, Montessori adds, "But do not apply the rule of non-interference when the children are still the prey of all their different naughtinesses. Don't let them climb on the windows, the furniture, etc." (17: 229). The point here is not just that one may need to interfere to protect others (as in §3.1), but also that there is no interference with *agency* at all in these cases.[19] Precisely for this reason, "the teacher should have an acute intuition which enables her to understand inner manifestations as distinct from ones that are not manifestations of the spontaneous inner life of the child" (18: 106), and the criteria for agential choice laid out in Chapter 3—internality, activity, normativity, and persistence—help distinguish cases of agency from mere choice. Children's desires to be entertained, watch television, engage in whim-driven play, or avoid going to sleep generally lack one or more of these criteria. The case of the obstinate daughter illustrates this distinction. The "choice" of pajamas is generally[20] neither the expression of an agential love nor an impulse toward attentive work. It is more like a "willful" expression of mere impulse or preference. By contrast, the child intensely interested in some task who wants to continue his activity rather than go to bed *is* expressing agency worthy of genuine respect. Even if a caregiver needs to stop that activity, there is agency to infringe upon, and any infringement comes at real cost to the child. This distinction between agential and non-agential choices does the same work as Schapiro's distinction between adults and children, allowing us to justify interventions when agency is not at stake that would be precluded (because paternalistic) when agency is at stake. But by focusing on particular choices and broadening the scope of agency, it rejects any general permissibility of paternalistic treatment of children as such.

Moreover, by focusing on particular choices, Montessori's account of non-agential behavior includes adults as well as children. Most straightforwardly, she can distinguish, even in adults, between choices that reflect agency and those due merely to weakness of will, inattentiveness, or whimsical and frivolous desire. When Odysseus, hearing the Siren's call, demands that his compatriots cut him free of his bonds, they do him no wrong by refusing to do so. His particular choices are at odds with his agency; they conflict, and obviously so, with his "established constitution." In this case, Odysseus explicitly instructed his compatriots not to listen to his subsequent pleas, but the general point holds: particular "choices" are rightly disrespected when they do not express a person's agency.[21] To the extent that the obstinate wife's choice of pajamas is just as non-agential as her daughter's, it is no worthier of direct respect; the mere fact that she is an adult is insufficient to make that choice agential.

However, adults have capacities for agency that children lack. Schapiro is correct that adults are capable of choosing in the light of reflection on their life as a whole, and that such reflection is generally sufficient for agency (though see Chapter 6, §2.1.3). Insofar as the wife's insistence on wearing uncomfortable pajamas involves reflective endorsement of her sartorial inclination in the light of her character, it is agential and deserves direct respect. Moreover, as noted in Chapter 6, respect for adults' deliberation can require that one respect otherwise arbitrary choices because of how those choices figure into adults' broader projects of self-constitution. Even if her choice of this or that pajama is wholly whimsical and not directly reflective of her agency, the wife's choice of her overall situation—her marriage, her ownership and control over various material resources, and so on—includes authority over nighttime wardrobe choices. These specific choices need not even be reflectively endorsed or consequent upon deliberation; they fit into her longer-term project of securing domains within which she can express herself through preferences and passive pleasures, where the securing of these domains—rather than appealing to what she does with them—directly expresses agency. Insofar as she endorses some general principle of self-expression in arbitrary preferences, she can assert her agency in defense of *that* principle, rather than some specific feature of her impulse.[22] That assertion of agency, rather than the particular whim it hinges on, is worthy of direct respect. This sort of assertion is particularly pronounced where it is still under construction, as in the adolescent who earns money for herself and establishes herself under a roof of her own, in large part in order to secure a domain for arbitrary exercises of choice, even of otherwise non-agential choice. Reflective deliberation thus does make a difference in the sorts of paternalism that are unjustified, and it vindicates some degree of adult-child distinction. Since the young daughter's whim is not integrated into a broader agential project of this sort, it stands alone as a *mere* preference.

Despite the important role that deliberation plays in distinguishing adult choices from those of children, these distinctions should not be exaggerated, and they do not always warrant more protection for adult choices than for those of children. For one thing, for both adults and children, agency can be expressed in non-deliberative ways, and interruption of these prereflective forms of agency, even for an agent's good, is prima facie wrong. Such is the case, discussed in Chapter 3, of the "writer under the influence of poetic inspiration" or "mathematician ... perceive[ing] the solution of a great problem" (9: 16). Montessori rightly notes, however, the flipside of the special privileges granted by reflective deliberation, namely that non-deliberative agency in children has a special sanctity that it lacks in adults. Whereas adults interrupted in the midst of flow have grounds for complaint that their agency has been compromised, "the child in like case does not lose some single production; he loses himself" (9: 17). The adult can reflectively engage with his paternalistic intruder; one form of agency can be replaced with another. The child's agency is simply cut off. The adult's flow activity takes place within a broader context of long-term agential projects, while the child's whole self is invested in this or that particular activity (see too §5). Rather than this warranting disregard for children's agency, the fact that adults have forms of agency that children lack warrants taking what agency children do have all the more seriously.

4 Libertarian Paternalism, the Prepared Environment, and Positive Discipline

In §3, I discussed two forms of interference with others that do not constitute paternalism. In the first case (§3.1), there was real interference with another's agency, but this interference was not *paternalistic* because it was for the sake of some good other than the welfare of the agent. In the second case (§3.2), interference might well be for the sake of the one interfered with, but the interference was not paternalistic because it does not actually infringe on the other's *agency*. In recent years, philosophers and others have become increasingly interested in a third form of intervention in the choices of others, which its primary proponents (Cass Sunstein and Richard Thaler) dub "libertarian paternalism." Unlike non-paternalistic interference with choices, libertarian paternalism leaves agents free to choose but seeks to influence behavior without coercion or imposition.

Sunstein and Thaler's approach begins from psychological findings showing that human choices (and cognitions) are influenced by various "biases and heuristics," such that the contexts of choice—what Sunstein and Thaler call the "choice architecture"—shape agents' decisions. For example, if employers sign employees up for a retirement plan as a default, most employees will remain signed up, while if employees are required to proactively enroll, many will not. Patients offered an operation with a "90% chance of survival" are more likely to choose the operation than one with a "10% fatality rate." Smaller plates and cups decrease food and drink intake. And so, too, countless other environmental conditions and framing effects predictably lead to different choices. Choice architects construct circumstances to influence—or "nudge"—people to make better choices:

> Choice architecture and its effects cannot be avoided, and so … the golden rule of libertarian paternalism [is]: offer nudges that are most likely to help and least likely to harm … A good system of choice architecture helps people to … select options that will make them better off.
>
> (Thaler and Sunstein 2008: 74, 94)

Sunstein and Thaler describe their view as paternalistic because it involves "self-conscious efforts, by private and public institutions, to steer people's choices in directions that will improve the choosers' own welfare" (Sunstein and Thaler 2003: 1162), but this paternalism is "libertarian" because it does not compel or override individuals' choices: "A nudge … alters … behavior in a predictable way without forbidding any options or significantly changing … economic incentives … Nudges are not mandates. Putting the fruit at eye level counts as a nudge. Banning junk food does not" (Thaler and Sunstein 2008: 6).

Properly speaking, libertarian paternalism is not paternalism. As Dworkin has put it, "Basically, the definition of paternalism in Libertarian Paternalism is focused solely on the fact that nudges are being used to make the agents being nudged better off" but "nothing … in the definition" corresponds to the notion that "the action … interferes with the liberty or autonomy" of an agent (Dworkin 2020). Rather than a form of paternalism or—as in §3—a sort of intervention that doesn't count as paternalism, so-called "libertarian paternalism" describes a set of intentional strategies that can affect people's choices in ways that make them better off without in any way interfering with their freedom. Long before Thaler and Sunstein proposed such strategies in politics, Montessori emphasized their importance for pedagogy.[23] Even for the cases described in §3, where intervention is permissible, infringing on choices should be avoided when possible, so Montessori develops alternatives that alleviate common concerns about not interfering with children's choices. Montessorian choice architecture arises in two primary contexts, what she calls the "prepared environment" and the "discipline" in which caregivers invite children to positive activities rather than preventing, coercing, or even bribing them away from negative ones.

4.1 The Prepared Environment

One of the most important alternatives to direct infringement on children's choices is what Montessori calls "the prepared environment." As she explains,

> The mistake which has been repeatedly made in education when envisaging the liberation of the child has been to think that this can be achieved through a hypothetical independence from the adult, and to disregard the appropriate preparation of the environment.
>
> (Montessori 1997: 70)

> Today, he who speaks of liberty in the schools ought at the same time to exhibit objects—approximating to a scientific apparatus—which will make such liberty possible.
>
> (9: 55; see too Montessori [1910] 1913: 14)

Children depend almost entirely on adults for their physical and social environments, so we can shape the options available to them in ways that promote their goods *through* their enhanced agency rather than against it. This shaping of environment is both unavoidable—since we will shape their environment in one way or another whether we are deliberate about it or not—and morally unobjectionable. Adults can exercise considerable control over children through preparation of environment, control that does not depend upon overriding or disrespecting children's agential choices within that environment. A pajama drawer that includes only suitable pajamas can prevent many conflicts over poor choices.[24] Moreover, because children (at least very young children) lack capacities for long-range planning and for constructing their own environments, such indirect influences compromise agency for children even less than they might seem to for adults.

In fact, Montessori's libertarian paternalism is even less paternalistic than Thaler and Sunstein's. Hausman and Welch explain that libertarian "nudges such as setting defaults seem ... to be paternalist" because "in addition to or apart from rational persuasion, they may 'push' individuals to make one choice rather than another" (Hausman and Welch 2010: 128). Within Montessorian prepared environments, however, children are offered attractive opportunities to express agency. Even if these opportunities do not "take the form of rational persuasion" (Hausman and Welch 2010: 128), which Hausman and Welch seem to think is essential for autonomy, they do directly appeal to children's *agential capacities*. Thaler and Sunstein's libertarian paternalism can be focused on any of a variety of goods (happiness, productivity, etc.), and primarily involves channeling an agency already assumed to be operative in the directions that they prefer. For Montessori, by contrast, the primary purpose of prepared environments is precisely to increase the exercise of agency, both in the present—so that children make more agential choices and are less the prey of mere impulse—and in the future—so that children develop the capacities that will make them more effective agents as adults. Thus, while Montessori can make use of the general concept of libertarian paternalism to reconcile her prepared environment with strict Kantian respect for persons, her agency-centered and agency-enhancing approach is less susceptible than other forms of libertarian paternalism to critiques that accuse libertarian paternalists of insidiously manipulating people's choices.

For Montessori, the preparation of the environment focuses on three elements. First, because agential choice for the young child primarily involves attentive work, an environment must be rich in developmentally appropriate opportunities for such work: "the freedom of the child can only [be] realized through an environment suited to the child, in which he can find what he requires to develop his own functions" (Montessori 1997: 70).

> The child needs to have something to do, to have objects on which to act ... *We must construct an environment for the child in which he can be active!* ... These little beings, who cannot speak on their own behalf, are nonetheless saying to us, "We have a right to a world of our own."
>
> (10: 48–9)

Second, the environment can and should provide materials that *both* provide occasions for attentive work *and* cultivate other goods for children, particularly the skills and capacities they will need to be well-functioning adult agents. For example, while any aesthetically pleasing cylinder blocks could hold the attention of an appropriately aged child, Montessorian cylinder blocks have pencil-diameter knobs by which they are lifted, preparing students' hands for the future exercise of agency through writing. By crafting an environment with inviting material that indirectly prepares for future development, caregivers accomplish pedagogical goals without coercion, punishment, or bribery. Finally, as noted in Chapter 4, the prepared environment is carefully structured socially to allow exercise of skills of respect for and solidarity with others. By providing an environment in which social problems and opportunities arise in simplified form, Montessori classrooms call on children to develop healthy social practices through their own free recognition of the necessity for such practices. In addition to fostering these abilities, this context transforms what might otherwise seem to be bare paternalism into legitimate enforcement of the mutual respect necessary for a functional community.

4.2 "Positive" Discipline

An important supplement to—or part of—the prepared environment is the social environment, and particularly the teacher, parent, or other caregiver. The teacher plays many roles in the environment, among which one of the most important is to help children escape the tyranny of passing whims and begin to express genuine agency.[25] In this capacity, even when she acts as "policeman" involved in "discipline," she "need not punish or scold or admonish when we stop bad behavior; we can ask the child to come and pick flowers in the garden or offer it a toy as an occupation that will appeal to it" (17: 229–30). Even with an entire class of disruptive children, rather than bribery, punishment, or authoritative declaration of authority, teachers "prepare [children], ... eliminating their uncontrolled movements [through] preparatory exercises ... such as ... to make a row of chairs and sit on them [or] to run from end to end of the room on tiptoe" (1: 244). The general strategy of the teacher in these cases is to offer children something immediately appealing but also active and norm-guided. Rather than suppressing or interfering with bad choices, caregivers first and foremost invite children *into* genuine agency and/or good choices. In the case of the obstinate daughter, challenging her to put on longer pajamas is better than telling her she cannot put on short ones. And importantly, offering mere choices—"how about trying one of these new pajamas?"—is less effective at eliciting agency than invitations to work—"do you think you could put these longer pajamas on by yourself?" At one level, positive discipline relies on classic techniques of libertarian paternalism; for instance, alternative ways of getting children to wear longer pajamas make use of so-called "framing effects" where identical courses of actions presented in different ways appeal differently to choosers. However, unlike some framing effects—such as the classic example where people choose surgery with a 90 percent success rate over surgery with a 10 percent failure rate—Montessori focuses on frames that specifically invite exercises of agency. These can be direct—as in asking children to *do* something rather than to merely *refrain* from doing something—or indirect, through presenting materials in ways that children naturally find to invite their active engagement. The general principle underlying both positive discipline and the prepared environment is that one best attains "[d]iscipline ... indirectly, that is, by developing activity in spontaneous work" (2: 326).

As in §3, the difference between children and adults with respect to libertarian paternalism is merely a matter of degree. Husbands do not generally have as much control over pajama options available to their wives as parents do over their children. Adults are often less susceptible to positive discipline than children. And because adults also have at least partial responsibility over shaping their own environments, usurping this responsibility may be less permissible with adults than with children. But various forms of libertarian paternalism—including both prepared environments and positive encouragement toward good options—are increasingly and rightly recognized as important ways of facilitating social goals while respecting adult agency. Crafting children's learning or home environments toward enabling and cultivating their agency should be no less constrained by respect for humanity than similar constructions of social spaces in the adult world. Crucially, too, these respectful ways of influencing one another for the better provide non-paternalistic alternatives in cases where paternalism might otherwise seem required.

5 Allowable Paternalism

§3 highlighted seemingly paternalistic interventions with agency that are legitimate but only because they are not genuinely paternalistic. §4 showed two important alternatives to genuine paternalism in shaping others' choices toward their good. In both sections, I argued for symmetry, in general if not in each specific case, between children and adults, and in none of these cases is paternalism strictly speaking justified. However, there seem to be at least some cases in which genuine paternalism toward children *is* permissible, cases where one is justified in interfering with the most agential of choices for the child's own good and without their consent. Parents routinely prevent children from chasing balls into the street, force them to wear sunscreen, and make them go to bed at night.[26] And adults often do so even when the child's chasing the ball is part of concentrated activity or when they must cut off activity for the sake of sunscreen or bed. Even if such paternalism could in principle be avoided with a well-prepared environment (that prevents balls from going into the street, for instance), positive discipline, or just caring anticipation of needs (putting sunscreen on before or after the child is rapt with attention, or gently redirecting a child toward evening activities that will end quickly or be easy to set aside), the real and imperfect world in which real and imperfect caregivers function often presents occasions in which paternalist interference is the only way to protect or promote essential goods for children. Even with all of the provisions in §3–4, children's weakness and vulnerability seem especially to require that one usurp agential rights for their benefit. Strict prohibitions on paternalism toward children would put caregivers in an untenable position.

Caregivers' position would be untenable, *if* a reasonable anti-paternalistic moral theory absolutely prohibited *all* infringements on others' agency for their benefit. But such anti-paternalism is also untenable for adults, all of whom, like children, depend upon others' love and care, not to mention effective political and social institutions. Even most political liberals endorse paternalistic laws requiring seatbelts or involuntary contributions to state pension systems such as Social Security, and allow that consent can be insufficient for allowing oneself to be used in various ways (such as medical research, cf. Kerstein 2013). Even anti-paternalists like Mill allow intervention in cases where an agent wants to sell themselves into slavery or engage in actions that would result in their unintentional death.[27]

While Montessori generally focuses on cases where adults are wrongly and overhastily paternalistic, her view is equally important in cases where paternalism might be required in order to preserve the health, safety, or even agency of a child. In these contexts, her theory shows why such cases need to be treated *as* instances of paternalistic intervention in agents' choices, and thus as prima facie objectionable, rather than as mere discipline of non-agents. This perspective shifts the burden of proof from paternalism being default-acceptable for children to a standard according to which it must be justified in particular cases. As I noted in the introduction to this chapter, Dworkin's differential "burden of proof" for "a child" and "an adult of sound mind" nicely articulates what has become the standard approach to paternalism (Dworkin 2020: 8). Schapiro's defense of paternalism toward children similarly emphasizes the distinction between "justifying particular paternalistic actions one-by-one" and "justifying a general practice which sanctions an asymmetrical distribution of authority between occupants of different positions"; her goal is the latter, namely to justify the "practice as a whole," that is, the practice of seeing children's choices as lacking "authoritative force" and requiring "final ratification by a higher, adult authority" (Schapiro 2003: 579, 576; see too 1999: 715). Given Montessori's account of children's agency, this standard view is mistaken. The burden of proof in instances of paternalistic intervention in agential choices should be the same for children as for adults, and decisions about whether this or that paternalistic intervention is justified cannot be answered simply by saying that the one intervened with is a child. Interference with children's agency cannot be evaluated merely on the basis of *consequences* for the children involved but must also consider the direct wrong of infringing on their agency.

Nonetheless, cases can arise for both adults and children who require paternalism. A full discussion of the appropriate range of paternalistic intervention in general is far beyond the scope of this chapter, but a few basic principles highlight how a symmetrical structure for evaluating appropriate intervention can provide sufficient leeway for caregivers without unduly limiting freedom of either children or adults. The fundamental principle governing paternalism lays burden of proof on one who would intervene with the agential choices of another to show that the harm (or lost good) of non-intervention sufficiently outweighs the prima facie disrespect inherent in intervention. Some factors that might contribute to meeting this burden would include:

1. **Consent** to paternalism. Odysseus specifically requested paternalistic interference (Dworkin 1972: 77). Students who enroll for a course or clients who hire a weight-loss coach turn over some decision-making authority to another. Members of an organization or citizens in a democracy might impose paternalistic policies on themselves. In all of these cases, higher-order consent to paternalistic policies or practices mitigates the disrespect inherence in those practices.
2. **Harm** (or good) **to agency**. Respect for agency includes not only deference to existent agency but also the promotion of future agency. Agential choices that undermine future agency—suicide, selling oneself into slavery, use of agency-undermining drugs, etc.—are more susceptible to paternalistic intervention than choices that merely affect other aspects of a person's welfare.
3. **Degree of harm**. Paternalism is more justified when interference can prevent a particularly severe harm. Seatbelt laws, limits on (excessive) gambling, and required contributions to medical insurance arguably fit into this category. Stopping an inattentive child (or adult) from chasing a ball into a busy street fits.
4. **Degree of interference with agency**. Choices can express agency to different degrees, and the interference with those choices can be more or less severe. Given a particular degree of harm prevented through paternalistic interference, it is easier to justify such interference with a person's pajama choice than with their choice of religion. Even the same interference—say, interrupting someone in the middle of working on a puzzle in order to ask whether they'd like to go for a walk—can be more or less justifiable depending upon how important the interrupted activity is for the person's agency. If an adult has just picked up a puzzle out of boredom and is starting to work on it, it's barely paternalistic to interrupt her. If a child is in the midst of concentrated activity, especially if such activity is rare for that child, interrupting the puzzle for the offer of a walk may be completely unjustifiable.
5. **Irreversibility**. If the harm prevented is irreversible or the opportunity for good is irrecoverable, paternalism is more prima facie justified. Interrupting someone so that she can see a solar eclipse is more justified than interrupting her to see a passing school bus.
6. Choices based on **ignorance**, misinformation, or cognitive deficiency. As Dworkin puts it, "If a man believes that when he jumps out a window he will float upwards, would we not detain him, forcibly if necessary?" (Dworkin 1972: 79).[28] Paternalism is easier to defend when it forces agents to take appropriate means to their ends or prevents them from activities with consequences they are ignorant of and want to avoid, though Montessori's emphasis on the importance of error[29] will mitigate this justification in cases where other factors are not present.
7. **Post hoc consent**. Relatedly, we can partly defend paternalism by means of justified conjectures that the person toward whom we behave paternalistically will come to endorse the choices they were forced to make and even the paternalism that forced those choices.

These considerations provide only some factors that help justify paternalism in particular cases, and one or more proposed factors may be mistaken.[30] My purpose here is not a definitive list of criteria for allowable paternalism. Rather, I aim to sketch prima facie plausible criteria that apply to both children and adults, and to briefly discuss how symmetrical principles might play out differently in practice for different sorts of agents.[31]

Given the set of criteria above, paternalism will sometimes be easier to justify toward children than toward adults. Children are generally more ignorant than adults of the implications of their actions (criterion 6). Combined with other factors (such as 2, 3, or 5), this difference becomes particularly salient. Generally speaking, anyone about to drink a glass of paint thinner or chase a ball into a busy street should be stopped, regardless of whether that person is a child or an adult, but children are much more likely to make these kinds of choices than adults, and such choices are more recognizably the result of ignorance in children than in adults. Even in the case of the obstinate daughter, her choice likely reflects ignorance about the effects of sleeping without pajamas, and this ignorance provides at least some justification for paternalistic intervention.[32] Moreover, because children lack long-term foresight and heavily depend upon environmental conditions created by others in order to exercise agency, factor (2) comes into play particularly often in the case of children. Adults have both responsibility and ability to act in the present in order to preserve their long-term capacities for agency. But young children lack the ability for explicitly self- and future-oriented action. Adults' special obligations to assume this responsibility can justify, for instance, requiring that children eat appropriate food, get appropriate amounts of sleep, and spend time in agency-conducive environments.[33]

At the same time, the criteria above will often justify paternalism toward adults when comparable paternalism is not justified toward children. Criterion (1), for example, can never justify paternalism toward very young children, precisely because they lack the capacity for long-term planning that would make it possible for them to consent to future paternalisms.[34] Moreover, given their lack of higher-order deliberative capacities and the "established constitution" by which they identify with long-term plans and goals, children's immersive flow activities express their agency in more essential ways than comparable flow activities of adults. An adult intensely concentrating on solving a puzzle can rightly be interrupted so that they will not be late for the performance they have looked forward to for weeks. Here one feature of the adults' agency—their agential engagement with the puzzle-task—is compromised for the sake of another. A young child in a similar situation cannot have integrated the interest in the performance into their agency in the way that the adult has, so interrupting their immediate activity is extinguishing one agency without furthering any other. For related reasons, criterion (4), and even criterion (2), can preclude interruptions of young children that would be permitted for adults. While the (adult) "artist at work" can complain that her "inspiration is lost" when rudely interrupted, "the child ... loses himself ... because ... he is composing ... the new man" (9: 16–7). At the same time, criteria (3) and (5) will often require more serious intervention in adult agency than in the agency of children. Particularly in a well-prepared (and basically safe) environment, children's capacity to cause themselves serious and lasting harm is quite limited. As Rousseau puts it, "It seems that children are little and weak only in order that they may get ... important lessons without danger. If the child falls down, he will not break his leg; ... if he grabs a knife, he will hardly tighten his grip and will not cut himself very deeply" (Rousseau 1979: 78). Adults have more strength, more resources, more access to harmful behaviors, more responsibilities, and thereby more potential to do serious and lasting harm to themselves through their bad decisions.

The criterion that applies the most differently to adults and children is (7). Adults can have what Schapiro calls an "established constitution" based on reflective endorsement of principles governing their lives as a whole. Thus, on the one hand, it can be relatively easy to justify paternalistic interference, particularly in activities grounded in weakness of will or even in flow, based on knowledge of a person's constitution. On the other hand, it should be difficult to justify paternalistic interventions that prevent someone from acting in accordance with their established constitution by claiming that such people will endorse those interventions later. Because young children's agency expresses itself in temporally limited forms of self-governance and children are constructing the characters from which they will—but only much later— evaluate paternalistic interferences, it can be easier to justify paternalistic intervention. However, because excessive paternalism can create slavish mentalities that approve paternalism in retrospect only because they have lost the capacity for self-assertion, interventions grounded on criterion (7) must be justified with care, and only in conjunction with other criteria (particularly (2) and (4)). Moreover, the possibility of justifying paternalism in terms of long-term preference shaping can apply to adults as well; Martha Nussbaum, for instance, has emphasized the role of adaptive preferences even in adults as grounds for paternalistically imposing education on women who do not (at the time) desire it. Such possibilities further emphasize the similarities between adults and children, and the care with which we should employ justifications in terms of *long-term* post hoc consent for adults can and should guide the extent to which we regard these justifications as legitimate for children.

One context within which paternalism is particularly appropriate toward children relates to protection against paternalism itself. Children cannot defend themselves from paternalistic interference, partly because of a contingent "utter social inferiority" (22: 59) that children today share with women and other oppressed groups in the past (and today), but also partly because of an inability—based on their developmental stage—to organize, think in terms of abstract concepts, shape their environment, and participate in adult social life. Among the most important forms of allowable "paternalism"[35] toward children is thus precisely the safeguarding of children from paternalism:

> The defense of the [child] citizen can come only from adults who see things clearly, because the children cannot organize everything by themselves ... There ought to be a body or an institution for the protection of children, something like a "Ministry for Children."
>
> (7: 80–1)

> [A]dults make many efforts to obtain certain rights for their citizenship. You have certain parties and trade unions and you have speakers and representatives of Parliament as well as newspapers and magazines and all these intelligent people do just one tiny part of speaking about one small right of man. And tell me where there is to be found a meeting for the cause of the freedom of children, for the freedom of the only being who is incapable of defending himself and incapable of speaking for his own rights.
>
> (7: 81)

Older children and adolescents can, should, and do advocate for their own interests, but younger children will always need—whether they choose it or not—advocates who fight for their rights to be free.

6 Conclusion: Paternalism as Non-Ideal Theory

In §5, I allowed that the imperfect world in which imperfect caregivers function presents occasions that require paternalistic interference. In §4.1, I pointed out that adults have responsibility for creating the environment within which children grow up. One implication of this responsibility is that any instance of paternalism—or even, arguably, of non-paternalistic interference (§3.1[36])—reflects a failure to properly create an environment within which children (or even adults) can flourish. Adults only "must" behave paternalistically because we have failed to create an environment in which paternalism is not necessary. Any violations of another's agency imply moral fault, even if they are the best we can do. Particularly for teachers, parents, and other caregivers who have considerable power over the environments of those in their charge, an instance of paternalism calls for reflection on which prior failures of responsibility resulted in the need for this particular paternalistic intervention. Rather than complacency about interfering with children's agency, such an approach calls for constant recognition of adult culpability for failing to provide safe, agency-conducive spaces.

In that sense, paternalistic interference falls into what has come to be called "non-ideal" moral theory, distinct from "utopian or idealistic" theories but also having the character of a "transitional" theory that can help achieve these ideals (Valentini 2012: 654). Ideally, society should provide environments such that from infancy through adulthood, people are able to express their characters in ways that are free, safe from serious and irrevocable harms, and conducive to development. Well-constructed environments throughout childhood would safely cultivate the careful use of agency in adolescents and adults, who would then be able to co-create their environments in such ways that they would not need paternalistic interference from others. Unfortunately, we live in a world where many children's environments do not invite exercises of agency, and where allowing children to freely exercise their agency can lead them to death or serious injury.

In that sense, a paternalistic society is an unjust society, and every instance of paternalism—whether directed toward children or adults—is a symptom of injustice, even if not every instance of paternalism makes a society more unjust. In conditions unconducive to freedom, paternalism may be required in order to create opportunities for agency or force individuals who lack character to take the first steps into cultivating their agency. In conditions where exercising agency is excessively dangerous, paternalism might be required to protect essential aspects of individuals' well-being. Paternalistic interference exhibits avoidable injustice on the whole, but having created an environment within which exercising agency in developmentally appropriate ways can cause irreparable harm, interfering with dangerous uses of agency may be the least unjust thing one can do.

Even in the imperfect world in which we live, however, children's freedom should be more respected than it is. Children are—or can be—agents expressing their characters through their work. We can and should avoid interrupting them or coercing them to replace their own wills with ours through punishments and rewards. We can and should pursue alternative means for protecting them from harmful choices, most notably through environments and explicit suggestions that invite children to exercise agency, and to do so in ways that are safe, developmentally beneficial, and conducive to overall well-being. Given our historic indifference to creating such environments and our cultural complacency about repressing children's agency, we will need to make use of *some* interventions in children's lives, partly to deal with children who disrespect others, partly to deal with cases where children endanger themselves or others without real agency, and partly in fully paternalistic ways, protecting children from choices that could have sufficiently bad and lasting effects. Particularly in the case of paternalism, such interventions are non-ideal, and we should work toward a world within which they are unnecessary.

Most importantly, while there may be differences in how and when paternalistic justifications apply to children and to adults, there is no fundamental difference between the legitimacy of paternalism for these two classes of persons. Both children and adults have forms of agency worthy of respect. In both cases, we should respect that agency through deference and non-interference (and, as noted in Chapter 4 though not emphasized here, positive help). And in both cases, there might be extreme contexts where, due to a poorly constructed physical and social environment, we need to paternalistically interfere with choice. However, given the vast power differences between adults and children, and our historical complacency toward paternalism directed at children, we should be *at least* as careful in granting ourselves paternalistic license in the case of children as other adults. Dworkin, Schapiro, and others, who endorse an asymmetrical burden of proof, are wrong.

In practice, the contrast between Montessori's approach and standard approaches like Schapiro's may not be as dramatic as their alternative visions of paternalism suggest. Partly the reasons for this are due to the points I make in this chapter about ways in which, even on Montessori's view, interference may be warranted in particular cases. Partly, too, the contrast will not be as sharp in practice because advocates of the standard approach need not allow just *any* paternalistic interventions, and the fact that young children's agency is not worthy of direct respect does not imply that one can simply treat them in whatever ways one chooses. Schapiro's own work is particularly thoughtful in this regard, qualifying the scope of paternalism in several important respects. With as much vehemence as anything in Montessori's writings, Schapiro insists,

> Our ... obligation as adults ... [requires] not treating children as if they belonged to a distinct and permanent underclass ... [W]e are not to treat them as anything other than practical agents, creatures who share with us the problem of finding reasons for actions. We are not to treat them as if they were mere objects to be possessed, manipulated, and exploited; nor may we treat them as if they were wild animals, creatures of instinct who have no potential for reason.
>
> (Schapiro 1999: 735)

Even for Schapiro, adults do not have a right to assert their wills over children in general, but rather "adults are only entitled to govern children on the condition that they act like adults" (Schapiro 2003: 593). Moreover, we adults can exert paternalistic control only insofar as we "do what is in our power as adults to help children work their way out of childhood," particularly by developing those capacities for agency that are at present latent, merely provisional, or limited in scope. And this means, among other things, that

> Negatively, ... [w]here [children] have achieved sovereignty over some domain of discretion, we are not to subject them to our control. Positively ... we must strive as far as possible to make them aware of their natural authority and power over themselves and its proper exercise.
>
> (Schapiro 1999: 736)

Schapiro's paternalism is not the tyrannical imposition of one's will on children in one's care, but a careful and limited disciplining and governing role of a caregiver seeking to raise future agents.

In that context, Montessori's approach might seem to differ from the standard approach merely in emphasis or tone. In practice, a thoughtful Kantian caregiver and a Montessori caregiver will often behave the same way, letting children make choices where those choices express budding agency and/or where they would not be overly destructive, but constraining choices that reflect merely a domination by unruly impulses, particularly when those choices have the likelihood of serious or lasting harm.

However, differences between Montessori's approach to children's agency and the standard approach remain significant, even in the context of careful and nuanced versions of that standard approach. For one thing, what *counts* as having "achieved some level of sovereignty" will be significantly different for Montessori and for Schapiro. For Schapiro, we should "be willing to allow children *to make rules for themselves* when they are capable of doing so" so that they can learn to develop "principles of deliberation" (Schapiro 1999: 736, emphasis added). For Montessori, this principled, Reason-guided, reflective form of agency is neither the only form of agency, nor even—particularly for children—the most important. We owe children's *other* expressions of agency direct respect. More generally, Schapiro's focus on childhood as a developmental predicament leads her to emphasize a consequentialist approach toward children, such that even our respect for their emerging agency is in the service of helping them to work their way into adulthood. By contrast, Montessori legitimately draws attention to the way that children's already-existent agency, as expressed in love and work, requires direct respect. This means that for Schapiro, but not Montessori, paternalism is still the background condition of adult relationships with children; the fundamental *attitudes* toward children are diametrically opposed, in the same way that sophisticated consequentialist ethical theories and Kantian theories have similar implications for treatment of adults, while differing in their fundamental attitudes.

8

Embodied Agency, Embodied Ethics

In the *Secret of Childhood*, Montessori writes, "one day I thought of giving a rather humorous lesson on how you blow your nose." As she explains,

> After having imitated various ways of using a handkerchief for this purpose, I ended by showing how it can be done discreetly, so as to make as little noise as possible, slipping out the handkerchief so that the action remains more or less hidden. The children listened and watched with the keenest attention, and did not laugh, and I wondered to myself what could be the reason. But hardly had I finished when there came a burst of applause ... Then indeed I was utterly amazed ... It occurred to me that perhaps I had touched on a sensitive spot in the social life of this little world. The question I had treated was one that children associate with a kind of continual humiliation, a permanent derision; they are always being scolded about blowing their noses. Everyone shouts at them, everyone insults them (they are habitually referred to as "snot-nose" ...), and, in the end, especially in schools, handkerchiefs are pinned visibly to their overalls ... like a stigma and badge of shame. Yet no one had ever taught them without attacking him or her directly how they ought to blow their noses.
>
> (22: 113)

Thus far, this book has articulated and defended a concept of agency lying at the core of ethical life, one that involves choosing meaningful activity for oneself and pursuing that activity in a self-governed and persistent way. In Chapter 2, I outlined a moral-sense-based moral epistemology, and Chapter 3 showed the sorts of character and agency that Montessori perceived to be morally good. Chapters 4 and 5 extended this moral philosophy to show how and why respect and solidarity contribute to ethical life, and Chapter 6 showed how the abstraction and deliberation adults are capable of contribute to our agency. Chapter 7 then drew implications of this overall approach for adult attitudes toward children. Throughout this discussion, I—like most moral philosophers today—have treated choice as though it takes place through a purely mental power of volition, at best merely applied to the world through a body to which that power is attached. Internality, self-governance, and other characteristics were treated in ways that could seemingly be present even in disembodied spirits. In this chapter, I turn to the crucial role of the body in agency and ethical life.

Montessori's lesson on blowing one's nose highlights how easy it can be for adults to overlook the bodily motions involved in actions necessary for participation in polite society, for respecting others, and for garnering basic respect from others. Leaving aside issues of public health, snot provokes a natural disgust-reaction,[1] such that concealing one's snot is a virtually universal sign of respect. Montessori's specific attention to "showing how it can be done discreetly" reflects a heightened sensitivity toward both others' possible disgust and the complexity of bodily motions involved in practicing this act of propriety particularly well. She rightly sees—or came to see—politeness and mutual respect as tasks requiring bodily movements of the sort that, like all character-driven activities, can be attended to, exercised, and done increasingly well.

While the children's rapt applause and serious attention surprised her in this case, Montessori's pedagogy already gives central importance to various "exercises of practical life" consisting of various forms of "reconstructive work ... [that] tends to the co-ordination of the psycho-muscular organism" through activities such as "dusting or washing a little table, sweeping the floor, laying or clearing the table, cleaning shoes, spreading out a carpet" (9: 113). In such activities, a child "will gradually perfect his movements without fatigue, acquiring grace and dexterity" (9: 114).

Montessori often emphasizes "graceful" or "proper" bodily movement. Contrasting her approach with that of traditional schools which (at the time) had children work at desks that were either bolted to the floor or too heavy to move, she notes how light furniture cultivates graceful bodily self-control:

> Immobility and silence ... *hindered* the child from learning to move with grace and with discernment, and left him so untrained that, when he found himself in an environment where the benches and chairs were not nailed to the floor, he was not able to move about without overturning the lighter pieces of furniture. In the "Children's Houses" [Montessori schools] the child will not only learn to move gracefully and properly, but will come to understand the reason for such deportment. The ability to move which he acquires here will be of use to him all his life. While he is still a child, he becomes capable of conducting himself correctly, and yet, with perfect freedom.
> (Montessori 1912: 84; cf. 2: 49, emphasis original)

> [Such a] child has not only learned to move about and to perform useful acts; he has acquired a special grace of action which makes his gestures more correct and attractive, and which beautifies his ... body now so balanced and so sure of itself.
> (Montessori 1912: 353)

In these discussions, Montessori begins with a relatively mundane and physical sense of "graceful" movement, a way of carrying oneself without knocking over furniture or bumping into others. But she slides from this apparently merely bodily self-control to the notion of "correct conduct," "freedom," and a person—that is, a body—"sure of itself." Montessori further emphasizes this connection between body and will— between bodily "grace" and moral virtue—by explicitly tying "exercises" of the will to grace of *action*:

> The will, like every other faculty, is developed and strengthened through methodical exercises. In our schools, exercises for the will are to be found in all of a child's intellectual exercises and his exercises in practical life. A child seems to be learning to carry out his movements with grace and accuracy, how to sharpen his sense perceptions, and how to read and count, but actually he is becoming the master of himself and laying the foundations for a strong and ready will.
>
> (2: 336; see too 17: 139)

The bodily coordination necessary for "movement with grace" also partly constitutes self-mastery and a strong will.

Bodily coordination is essential for moral virtues, which Montessori aptly compares to learning the piano:

> we give these children the opportunity to *exercise* their patience, make choices, and persevere—every day of their life. They must have the opportunity to *exercise* all these virtues that, together, form character ... They learn patience and adaptation to another's needs. It is not enough for them to have these things explained ... —*they must practice them*. Otherwise it is as though you explained a piano to a child, explained in detail how it worked and then told him to play. It is not enough to understand. If he is to be proficient, he must spend hours and hours practicing ... Character formation cannot be taught. It comes from experience ... Everything needs extensive preparation and much practice.
>
> (17: 236–7, emphasis original)

Learning the piano not only requires repetition and practice; it requires *bodily* repetition and practice. Someone who "practices" piano by reading and rereading a score, or meditating on the proper technique for piano-playing, will never learn to play. Part of learning to play the piano is training the *body*—particularly though not exclusively the hands—in certain movements. Likewise, for Montessori, part of the "exercise" of patience is cultivating habits of literal bodily self-restraint. A child who must "wait for [a work material] to be released ... every hour of the day for years ... respecting others and ... waiting one's turn," engages in certain bodily practices: standing, diverting attention, speaking softly, and lifting the replaced material with care and without rushing or bumping into the student who has just finished working it. Over time, these postures and habits of movement "become a habitual part of life which always grows more mature" (1: 202). Because "the will must manifest itself in actions which the body must carry out effectively" (9: 139), moral virtue—as an excellence *of will*—requires a body capable of and cultivated toward virtuous practice.

For Montessori, perfection of movement intertwines with all three features of ethical life—character, respect, and solidarity—as well as with myriad specific virtues such as patience, compassion, or humility that partly constitute those core elements. In that sense, Montessorian ethical life is thoroughly and constitutively *embodied*: "it is neither by philosophizing nor by discussing metaphysical conceptions that the morals of mankind can be developed; it is through [embodied] activity" (14: 83). In §1, I touch on a sense of "embodiment" prominent in some recent feminist philosophers and affect theorists, namely emphasis on the importance of emotions (conceived as embodied states) in ethical life. In the rest of the chapter (§§2–4), I outline some more literally bodily practices and competences on which character, respect, and solidarity rely. My conclusion raises further issues for work in embodied moral theory and briefly addresses how this embodied approach relates to various forms of "disability."

1 Embodiment and Emotion

While mainstream moral theorists still largely downplay the role of embodiment in ethical life, others increasingly introduce the notion of the "body" to contrast with overly rationalistic conceptions of agency, often in the context of feminist critique; thus some "feminists trouble a mind-body distinction by engaging affect and emotion in their work" (Huseyinzadegan et al. 2020; cf. e.g. Ahmed 2004). Robin May Schott, for example, glosses the notion of a "split between an embodied and a reflective self" as equivalent to "rational consciousness becom[ing] detached from feelings or desires," and she aims to resuscitate attention to the body via emphasizing eros, affect, and emotion (Schott 1988: 183).[2] Within contemporary philosophy, integration of emotion and embodiment takes many different forms, and some philosophers who prominently feature emotion within their moral work do not tie it in any special way with embodiment (see, e.g., Nussbaum 2001: 58; Sherman 1999). Moreover, as I will emphasize in §2, attention to affect and emotion are not the primary ways in which Montessori's own emphasis on embodiment plays a role in her moral theory. Nonetheless, because of the connection between emotion and embodiment in much recent literature, and because Montessori's moral theory features emotion as an important dimension of ethical life, I take the present section as an occasion to briefly highlight the role that emotion plays within her moral theory.

All three core features of Montessori's moral theory—character, respect, and solidarity—feature emotional dimensions.[3] With respect to character, for example, she explains, "This fundamental quality, when it embraces the sentiment [*sentimento*] of the individual …, his whole personality, is what we have called *character*. The man of character is … faithful to … his own convictions [and] his own affections [*affetti*]" (9: 133). The authenticity essential to acting from character requires not only making choices for oneself and actively persisting in governing oneself in accordance with those choices; one's actions and attitudes must also be faithful to one's ownmost sentiments and affections. People of character *feel* authentically and for themselves, so character cultivation requires not only giving children freedom to act but also enabling and facilitating their freedom to affectively respond to their environment. Montessori emphasizes that the prepared environment should be "lovely and pleasant" with a "beauty [that] invites activity" (8: 41); children should work not begrudgingly or merely from principles, but from a sense of joy and felt love for their activities and the environment within which those take place. The child engaged in work, Montessori notes, is "remarkable for his sweetness and delicacy of feeling," particularly "in his joy when he had learned or completed some task" (9: 89).

Likewise, in her discussions of respect and solidarity, Montessori emphasizes the affective dimensions of children's attention to each other. Children come to have "love and admiration," "true brotherhood," and a "*feeling* for each other's worth" (1: 205). Respect is "cemented by affection" (1: 205), and a respectful person comes to not only "defend and value" but also—and foremost—to "love ... his ... group" (1: 211). Within ethical life, "true relations between man and man ... are established in sympathy ... with our fellows, comprehension of their sorrows, [and] the sentiment of justice: the lack of these sentiments convulses normal life" (9: 242). In summarizing the importance of emotion for ethical life, Montessori exhorts her readers to

> set yourselves free from all bonds and all measurements and lay hold of the one thing needful: to be alive, *to feel* ... What is the use of knowing all the moral laws and even practicing them, if the heart be dead? It is as if we should whiten the tomb of a corpse. The moral, self-satisfied man, without a heart, is a tomb.
>
> (9: 245–6, emphasis added)

One might think that however important emotions are to ethical life, they cannot express *agency* because we do not directly control our emotional responses to situations. Kant famously says that "love as an inclination cannot be commanded" because it does not "lie in the will" (Kant 1996: 55). Nancy Sherman rightly notes both the common moral practice of "hold[ing] people morally responsible for their emotions" and the "doubt among both lay and philosophical observers about the legitimacy of [this] moral practice" on the grounds that "we are unsure just how emotions involve agency and control" (Sherman 1999: 294; see too Smith 2005). Like Sherman's, however, Montessori's overall approach to agency provides a context within which to see emotions as both results and forms of agency, and also to call into question the myth of total control even over the sorts of deliberate choices taken as paradigmatic of activity. In Chapter 3, I noted Sherman's recognition that "the requirement for immediate control, even in the case of actions, is suspect" because even, say, "the simple act of snapping a finger can be, for the novice, a painstaking project that builds upon incremental willings," so just because "we cannot start a specific sort of emotion on a dime ... does not make it so terribly different from being able to perform ... actions" (Sherman 1999: 300–1). In Chapter 6, I expanded on this argument by showing that reflective deliberation itself requires engaging oneself in ways about which one cannot antecedently (or even consequently) reflect. To make a deliberate choice requires recognizing that I am in a condition for choice, beginning to reflect, recognizing this or that as salient to my choice, and bringing deliberation to an end. All of these steps involve emotional attunements, and on pain of regress, they cannot all be results of other acts of deliberate choice.

Given Montessori's attention to non-deliberative and non-reflective forms of agency, she has ample room to recognize emotions as expressions of agency. And given her recognition of the role of exercise in the cultivation of volitional capacities, she can straightforwardly explain how pre-reflective forms of emotional agency can be taken up and exercised, repressed, or modified in the light of reflective decisions, and then how this exercise or repression, or modification, then shapes how we respond emotionally to new situations. Teachers should provide children with opportunities not merely to *act* respectfully and with solidarity but to *feel* respect and solidarity. Such opportunities elicit feelings that both express and shape through exercise children's agency. Likewise, teachers should not only provide opportunities for children to choose work for themselves, but also the space to *feel* joy in work well done, frustration in failure, excitement about new discoveries, and the whole range of emotions tied to active engagement with the world.

2 Embodied Agency, Embodied Character

The centrality of embodiment for Montessori goes beyond merely incorporating emotion into moral philosophy.[4] She specifically attends to movements of literal, physical bodies as partly constitutive of agency. Even her account of the role of emotion in moral life includes attention to "muscular emotion" that is akin to "muscular memory" (18: 172).

In this focus on embodiment, Montessori's moral philosophy intersects with the growth of interest in so-called "embodied" or "enacted" cognition in contemporary philosophy of mind. John Haugeland argues that "Mind ... is not incidentally but *intimately* embodied" (Haugeland 1998: 236). Psychologist Esther Thelen explains that "cognition ... arises from bodily interactions with the world" (Thelen 2000: 4). Philosophers like Andy Clark and Alva Noë emphasize the essentially "sensorimotor" nature of cognition (Clark 2011; Noë 2004, 2009). George Lakoff and Mark Johnson claim that cognition "is not disembodied [nor even merely neuronal] ... but arises from the nature of our brains, bodies, and bodily experience" (Lakoff and Johnson 1999: 4). Embodied cognition theorists oppose not only Cartesian dualists who see the mind as some immaterial substance, but also more common contemporary theories that treat the mind as wholly instantiated in states of the brain (and other neurons) or who treat cognition as essentially a matter of conscious representations. Instead, embodied cognition theorists argue that cognizing the world involves bodily activity in that world, and the "organ" of the mind includes (at least[5]) the entire body. In this section, I briefly discuss how the body and bodily coordination partly constitute moral character; in the following sections I turn to embodied features of respect and solidarity.

Strikingly, within the contemporary embodied cognition research program, there has been relatively little work on what we might call the "embodied will," namely the extent to which not only cognition but also choice and action depend upon and are instantiated in the configurations and dispositions of one's body. Just as traditional philosophers of mind have treated the mind as the sort of thing that could exist independently of a body, or at best as something that happens to connect to a body that it "uses," so too moral philosophers typically treat moral agents as disembodied deciders of this or that whose decisions play out through the medium of a body. As Anne Reichold puts it,

> In ethics ..., the concept of a person is characterized by mental ascriptions only ... The moral character of a person is justified by pointing to consciousness, reason, memory, and autonomy. Reflections on the role of the body can hardly be found. The embodiment of persons does not see to be important in ethical reflections on the nature of persons.
>
> (Reichold 2007: 169)

As it applies to both the contemporary research program in embodied cognition (which largely ignores ethics) and to much mainstream moral theorizing (which largely ignores the body), Reichold is basically correct.[6] While some proponents of embodied cognition in the broadest sense explore the role of the body in *moral cognition* (e.g., Lakoff and Johnson 1999: 290–334), contemporary researchers in embodied cognitive science still devote only scant attention to the embodied nature of *agency* and *virtue*.

For Montessori, however, agency is constituted through forms of bodily coordination. To have a "will," Montessori insists, "some mastery of the body is also necessary" because "movement is the ... purpose of the nervous system" (9: 137; 5: 37); further, "[v]oluntary action ... increases in degree as its dependent muscles perfect themselves and so achieve the necessary conditions for seconding its efforts" (9: 140). Thus, when children "practice the gymnastics of the will in the daily habits of life" (9: 129; see too 17: 139), this gymnastics includes literal stretching and strengthening of muscle groups that enable children to have strong wills.

The body is essential for moral agency because such agency consists not merely of internal resolutions but also of *realized capacities for virtuous activity*.

> There can be no manifestation of the will without completed action ... To think and to wish is not enough. It is action which counts. "The way to Hell is paved with good intentions." The life of volition is the life of action.
>
> (9: 127–8)

One who makes excellent resolutions, but lacks the coordination to do what is required, is not morally excellent. Moreover, the importance of the body is not merely that of an instrument for the will; as we will see in more detail below, bodily capacities open up new ways of seeing the world, new "affordances," such that otherwise irrelevant features of the world show up as (morally) salient for volition.

As we saw in Chapter 3, character consists of a capacity and tendency toward fully expressing one's agency. Unlike many philosophers, whose discussions of agency would be compatible with "agents" being disembodied souls interjecting choices into the world, Montessorian agency is essentially embodied: "there is a perfect parallel between the formation of the will and the co-ordination of movement of its physiological structure, the straited muscles" (1: 139[7]). Because musculature is the material structure of the will, "the will and refined movements must grow side by side" (24: 177). Montessori particularly emphasizes the refined movements of the hand as connected with development of character: "the child who has used his hands invariably has a stronger character ... [T]he child who can use his hands shows firmness of character" (5: 40).

In *Intellectual Agency and Virtue Epistemology*, when I argued for the importance of physical dexterity as an intellectual virtue, my argument hinged upon the connection between intellectual virtue and character (Frierson 2020: 149–60). For Montessori, movement is necessary for intellectual development because movement is necessary for development as such, and movement expresses and facilitates intellectual agency because movement is constitutive of agency as such. Mental development might seem to be the most difficult context for defending the importance of bodily capacities. Unlike one who "wishes to devote himself to sport or to dancing" (9: 140), for whom the centrality of the body is obvious, "when mental development is under discussion, there are many who say, 'How does movement come into it? We are talking about the mind.' And when we think of intellectual activity, we always imagine people sitting still, motionless" (1: 126). That even "mental development must be connected with movement and be dependent on it ... because mind and movement are part of the same entity" (1: 126) shows the centrality of the body for the expression of character in all its forms. Through "doing work far beyond our dreams ... provided his hand was allowed to work," the "child has revealed" his "secret," namely that "personality is one and indivisible"; in particular, the working child shows the absurdity of the theory that "a cultivated mind consorted with manual helplessness" (6: 7).

Montessori's point is not merely that the will requires muscles to carry out its tasks, though she affirms that "the will must manifest itself in actions which the body must carry out effectively" (9: 139). Her more basic point is that in order even to perform an act of will, one must have a body capable of carrying out that act: "the performer wishes to devote himself to sport, or to dancing, or to the arts of self-defense ... but in order to *will* this it is necessary that he should have practiced continually, thus making ready the apparatus on which the volitive act will finally depend" (9: 140, emphasis original). Character requires choices among activities seen as possible activities for an agent like me, an agent with my motor capacities. We might see this in terms of James Gibson's notion of "affordances" (Gibson 1979); what the environment offers as possible activities depends on sensorial capacities essentially linked with my body. The norm-governed and self-perfecting work that expresses character is always constrained by and formative of bodily capacities. As I discuss elsewhere, even work that might seem purely intellectual ultimately depends upon refined muscular coordination (Frierson 2020: 155–6).

Montessori also regularly links the open-ended perfectionism of character with humans' capacities to shape and reshape our bodies.

> The coordination of all the muscles comes through work in human beings. The animals acquire their particular movements by heredity. Squirrels run up trees quickly, tortoises move slowly, some animals jump, etc.—all these movements are hereditary. Man, in contrast, must construct all the coordination of all his movements.
>
> (17: 166–7; see too 18: 167)

Open-ended perfectibility arises from the open-endedness of the human body. Perfection can be open-ended because human muscular coordinations (especially in tongue and hand) are so flexible, and the coordination of movements children seek expresses their unique forms of engagement with the world: "the muscles of man are not directed just by instinct, as are those of other creatures. The individual himself must animate his motor powers ... [to] ... prepare for his own individuality" (7: 95). How I move and what my body is like express who I am; the flexibility of a dancer or the relative inflexibility of a long-distance runner (see Barnes 2016: 86) are features of their character, aspects of bodily comportment that both open sets of possibilities for them and express who they are.

> A gymnast is not born with a special set of muscles to help him, nor a dancer born with certain refined muscles for his art; both develop them by will. So nothing is established, but everything is possible, under direction of the will; and men do not all do the same things, as animals of a single species. Each man has his own path to follow, and work is a chief expression of his psychic life ... Though muscles are too numerous for all to be exercised, there is a certain number below which the psychic life will be endangered.
>
> (5: 39)

Insofar as character involves self-governance according to norms intrinsic in our activities, the formation of character in Montessorian prepared environments requires adapting our muscular capacities to the requirements of our world, including our cultural world. We come to have our own individual character through bodily motions in a particular context shaped by our environment. As Pierre Bourdieu points out, we develop a "habitus" that consists in part of a "bodily hexis," that is, a "durable manner of standing, speaking, and thereby of feeling and thinking," a "logic which is acted out directly in the form of bodily gymnastics" (1977: 93–4, 117).[8] For Montessori, part of coming to have character requires shaping one's bodily motions to conform to norms and standards intrinsic to the activities in which one engages, whether writing with a pencil or keyboard, sweeping the floor with a broom or Swiffer, or eating properly with fork or chopsticks or hands. More complex activities like playing piano or writing a novel or developing a new mathematical theory or voyaging to the South Pole or experimenting with electricity all build off basic bodily capacities to perform elementary tasks, and all involve new bodily coordinations of various kinds.

At the same time that character requires conforming oneself to norms built into one's environment, mature practices of self-perfection increasingly shift from the self-formation involved in conforming to pre-given norms, toward, as Montessori puts it, "add[ing] a point to the circle which fascinate[s]" us (1: 191). Those with character not only pursue increased individual perfection but ultimately seek to contribute new forms of excellence to humanity as a whole. In that context, the cultivation of bodily coordination involves developing wholly new ways of engaging bodily with the world. Bodily innovation is clearest in the context of those like dancers or athletes who develop visibly novel ways of moving their bodies in order to accomplish new goals or to reach familiar goals in new ways. Consider Diego Maradona's refinements and innovations in dribbling and ball control, or the way that Kazuo Ohno's Butoh dance form opened new dimensions of bodily emotional expressivity in post-war Japan.

Other cases—such as Admiral Byrd's voyage to the South Pole or various astronauts' accomplishments in space travel—require the development of countless less obvious new bodily capacities in order to cope with the conditions faced on such journeys. Even Montessori's examples of more "intellectual" geniuses—writers, mathematicians, artists, or scientists (9: 16–7)—require *at least* using familiar bodily capacities fluently in order to accomplish new goals, and often (as with the development of new techniques in painting or new experimental apparatuses) require cultivating specific, new forms of bodily dexterity. Most radically, the body can provide a site to contest widespread social norms, such as when Judith Butler describes how embodied performativity provides contexts where, for example, "woman" can be seen as "a term in process, a becoming, a constructing that cannot rightfully be said to originate or end … it is open to intervention and resignification" (Butler 1990: 45). Where one might initially learn cultural-bodily hexes as norms to which one seeks to conform one's body, each can (and should) also approach those norms from the perspective of their own open-ended pursuit of perfection in the "circles which fascinate" them, and, through new forms of bodily engagement with the world, "add a point to the circle" of human possibilities.

3 Embodied Respect

In Chapter 4, I pointed out that respect for others is something that can express character; it is a norm-governed form of activity, a sort of perfection, a skill (§2.3). Like all other skills, respect for others involves training our bodies to move in certain ways in response to problems posed by our environments. Moreover, just as respect in general grows from and partly expresses character (Chapter 4, §2.2), so too Montessori's appreciation for the essentially embodied nature of agency extends to an awareness of the essentially embodied nature of respect for (and solidarity with) others.

Consider three dimensions of respect for others: (1) non-interference with others' choices, (2) cooperation and help offered to those in need, and (3) basic "politeness" that avoids "anything which may offend … others, or which is impolite or unbecoming" (9: 130; 2: 50). Non-interference is arguably the minimum level of basic respect for others, present not only in Montessori's account of respect (Chapter 4, §4.2) but also in Mill's basic harm principle—"the sole end for which mankind are warranted … in interfering with the liberty … of any of their number is self-protection" (Mill [1859] 1989: 13)— and Kant's claim that "if my action … can coexist with the freedom of everyone …, whoever hinders me in it does me *wrong*" (Kant [1797] 1996: 387).[9] The obligation to help others, too, is not only an important feature of Montessori's theory (Chapter 4, §4.3), but also widely affirmed by moral theorists from Kant (1996: 75) to Peter Singer (Singer 1971). As Singer puts it, it is "uncontroversial" that "if I am walking past a shallow pond and see a child drowning in it, I ought to wade in and pull the child out" (Singer 1971: 231). The moral importance of politeness is less widely affirmed, and by many even rejected, but Montessori affirms that culturally specific forms of grace and courtesy are important, embodied features of respect for others, and this view has recently gained support from various moral philosophers, most notably Sarah Buss

(Buss 1999). In the rest of this section, I show how each of these elements of respect requires bodily refinements; in §3.3, I also briefly discuss why politeness is essential for respect.

3.1 Non-interference

While theorists disagree about the scope of the obligation to non-interference, ordinary moral judgment and philosophical theories concur in seeing respect to require that I not interfere with others' choices or activities without good reason. As we saw in Chapter 4, this obligation not to interfere lies at the heart of Montessori's moral theory, and she rightly sees interruption as a paradigmatic form of interference. To pick up on the quotations above from Mill and Kant, the point of non-interruption is to allow each to carry on their activities, so long as they carry out those activities in ways that allow others to be active as well. As Montessori says, "society ... rest[s] ... on a combination of activities which have to be harmonized" (1: 202). What Montessori's embodied ethics adds to this general account of mutual respect is the recognition that harmony of activity requires patterns of movement and specific forms of muscular coordination: "children who cannot utilize coordinated movements for an intelligent purpose destroy everything ... because the active muscular movement and the mind are not connected" (17: 139). In describing children's development of mutual respect, Montessori explains,

> When he begins to respect the work of others; when he waits patiently for the object he desires instead of snatching it from the hand of another; when he can walk about without knocking against his companions, without stamping on their feet, without overturning the table—then he is organizing his powers of volition, and bringing impulses and inhibitions into equilibrium.
>
> (9: 129–30)

Restraining oneself from snatching material from others might seem to require mere strength of will, but it also requires patterns and habits of bodily movement. Even more clearly, walking through a room of busy children without bumping into others or knocking over tables requires practiced sensorimotor capabilities at least as much as—and indeed as conditions of—intentional choices to let others do their work. Thus, Montessori offers these practices of respect specifically as examples of how the child "makes a selection among the muscular coordinations of which he is capable, persists in them, and thus begins to make such coordinations permanent" (9: 129). Even with respect to (adult) teachers, Montessori emphasizes that "skill in not interfering comes with practice" (1: 255).[10]

Because mutual respect partly consists of bodily competencies, Montessori cultivates it through spaces that encourage exercise of respectful muscular coordination. The description of the child who "begins to respect ... others" continues,

> It would be impossible to bring about such a result by keeping children motionless, seated side by side; under such conditions "relations between children" cannot be

established, and the social life of children[11] does not develop. It is by means of free intercourse, of real practice which obliges one to adapt his own limits to the limits of others, that social "habits" may be established.

(9: 130; see too 17: 139)

Thus, for example, she explains,

> Our little tables and our various types of chairs are all light and easily transported, and we permit the child to *select* the position which he finds most comfortable ... And this freedom is not only an external sign of liberty, but a means of education. If by an awkward movement a child upsets a chair, which falls noisily to the floor, he will have an evident proof of his own incapacity; the same movement had it taken place amid stationary benches would have passed unnoticed by him. Thus, the child has some means by which he can correct himself, and having done so he will have before him the actual proof of the power he has gained: the little tables and chairs remain firm and silent each in its own place. It is plainly seen that the *child has learned to command his movements* ... [T]he child will not only learn to move gracefully and properly, but will come to understand the reason for such deportment. The ability to move which he acquires here will be of use to him all his life. While he is still a child, he becomes capable of conducting himself correctly, and yet, with perfect freedom.
>
> (Montessori 1912: 83–4, emphasis original; cf. 2: 49)

Montessori's basic point, as her critique of "stationary benches" implies, is that learning respect for others is not merely a matter of learning *that* others matter and that one ought to limit one's activity to allow them to carry out theirs. Even verbal or merely conceptual appreciation of how to moderate one's activity in conformity with respect for others is insufficient. Children—and adults—need to *practice* respect *in embodied ways*. Whether moving through crowded spaces, eating with others, working in libraries, standing on subways, cheering at sports events, dancing socially, or myriad other sorts of interpersonal interaction, one needs bodily habits and capacities of respect for others. Even sitting around a table conducting a department meeting requires a capacity to control the volume of one's voice, the posture and movement of one's body, the focus of one's gaze, all in ways that depend on cultivated muscular coordination. Lived respect requires moving one's body in ways attentive to others' spaces and others' needs.

3.2 Help

Helping others, too, requires bodily competences. Singer's scripted example carefully avoids requiring of the would-be rescuer an ability to swim: "if I am walking past a *shallow* pond and see a child drowning in it, I ought to *wade in* and pull the child out" (Singer 1971: 231, emphasis added). Even here, however, saving the child depends on the strength, balance, and coordination to wade effectively into a pond, grab a struggling child, and wade back out. To give this help *well*, one also needs to be able to speak in a tone of voice sufficiently firm to gain the child's compliance but also soothing enough to offer comfort, and one needs to be able to grab and hold the child without harm, offense, or inappropriate contact. Many of these requirements—ability to walk, wade, carry awkward objects while wading, etc.—involve bodily skillfulness constitutive of character-driven activities distinct from respect. Others, such as knowing how to hold and interact with the bodies of other persons, including children, may be specifically honed as part of developing one's capacity to offer respectful help to others. One can expand one's repertoire of help, and thereby of respect, through learning to swim—and to rescue as part of learning to swim—or learning CPR, or learning bodily competences associated with attentive listening or comforting or exerting authority or a host of other forms of interaction. To help others, I need a body that can move in the ways others require.

Within Montessori's pedagogy, one of the more important applications of this principle comes in the help teachers offer children.

> When a child is ready to start ..., the lessons are given individually. A teacher makes an almost timid attempt to approach the child whom she believes is ready ... She sits down by his side and picks up an object that she thinks will interest him ... The lesson is a call to attention ... Words are not always necessary. Very frequently all one has to do is to show the child how the object is used. But when the teacher has to speak and show the child how to employ material ..., the instruction should be brief.
>
> (2: 109)

The words should be spoken with precision and the right tone of voice, and the "timid" approach requires carrying one's body and using one's voice to focus children's attention on the environment rather than the teacher and to promote the child's activity. Teachers help children not merely through the content of what they say, but through the ways they move their bodies.

Bodily competence does not merely enable *implementation* of choices to help and respect others; as noted in §2, "the will and refined movements must grow side by side" (24: 177). We can think of this point in terms of what Barbara Herman has called "rules of moral salience" that "structure an agent's perception of his situation so that what he perceives is a world with moral features" (Herman 1993: 77). Alternatively, we might use the term "moral affordances," drawing on James Gibson's suggestion:

> The affordances of the environment are what it offers the animal, what it provides or furnishes, either for good or ill ... I mean by [affordance] something that refers to both the environment and the animal in a way that no existing term does. It implies the complementarity of the animal and the environment ... [Affordances] have to be measured *relative to the animal* ... They are not just abstract physical properties. They have unity relative to the posture and behavior of the animal being considered.
>
> (Gibson 2015/1979: 119–20)

We perceive the world in general in terms of our interests and capacities, what the world "affords" as possible avenues for action. Likewise, what features of a situation are morally salient depends in part on where I am located and what I am able to do in that environment. I recognize another's sadness as morally salient—for that matter, I recognize it at all—only insofar as it provides some possible action-guiding importance for me. My capacities for action not only affect the extent to which I can carry out what I choose to do; those capacities constrain what options for choice I even see, what I can even choose. To show help to others, I need to develop skills of helping; only thereby are others' genuine needs recognizable as possible factors in my choice.

3.3 Grace and Courtesy

While Montessori often emphasizes the importance of respect, dignity, and help, she equally often discusses social relations in terms of "grace," "courtesy," or "politeness," each of which is connected with ways of moving the body. Thus, after learning to "move about the furniture with poise and care," "we have a series of exercises in which the children learn to move gracefully, ... to salute each other, ... to receive various objects from each other politely" (Montessori 1912: 123). In discussing the need to limit liberty for the sake of mutual respect, she includes norms of politeness alongside general principles of respect such as not harming others.

> A child's liberty should have as its limit the interests of the group to which he belongs. Its form should consist in what we call good breeding and behavior. We should therefore prevent a child from doing anything which may offend or hurt others, or which is impolite or unbecoming. But everything else, every act that can be useful in any way whatever, may be expressed. It should not only be permitted but the teacher should also observe it.
>
> (2: 50; Montessori 1912: 87)

Montessori illustrates what is "impolite or unbecoming" with cases such as children with "fingers in their noses" (2: 54) or adults who "pay a visit" to a friend when it is "not her day for receiving" (9: 128), and what is polite includes verbal courtesies such as "please" and "thank you" but also—and more importantly—the proper speed and posture when handing something to someone (Montessori 1912: 123) or the practice of "ris[ing] to our feet" when "a venerable person enters" (9: 128). Montessori classrooms now regularly include various lessons in "grace and courtesy," not merely "Blowing one's nose" but also such things as "Passing by a tight space," "giving and receiving a gift," "opening a door for another," "offering help to a friend," "passing a platter of food," "introducing two friends," "giving comfort to a friend," or "apologizing for calling a wrong number" (Bettman 2003). For all of these lessons, the adult carefully presents physical motions (and, if necessary, words) associated with polite behavior and then gives children opportunities to exercise these motions, both in real situations and in role play with one another.

While many moral theorists sharply distinguish norms of polite society from moral norms of respect, Montessori treats politeness as essential for socially situated respect, part of how individuals "adapt to life with other people" (Montessori 1984, quoted in Sackett 2003: 4). Some of these norms of politeness are virtually universal, but many reflect culturally specific practices that specify and make precise otherwise general and vague requirements of social life, making what would otherwise be neutral forms of activity—say, extending a hand in greeting or bowing one's head—into normative requirements of polite society in a particular context. And just as children in healthy conditions naturally absorb a particular language and make it their own, so too they seek to learn and practice their particular society's norms of propriety.

Like Montessori, contemporary moral philosopher Sarah Buss affirms that "acknowledging a person's intrinsic value—treating her with respect—also requires that one treat her politely (considerately, respectfully). If we treat someone rudely, then we fail to treat her with respect—even if we do not prevent her from pursuing her most fundamental goals" (Buss 1999: 797). The heart of Buss's argument is that there are direct forms of respect, ways in which individuals acknowledge one another's dignity through conformity with norms of polite interaction. To respect others is not *merely* to allow them to carry out their choices, but to show them that they are respected through accepted forms for expressing respect. In explaining why we should care so much about politeness, Buss notes that the answer, "simply," is "that we believe we are worthy of respect, we believe that because we are respect worthy we deserve to be *treated with respect*, and we believe that being treated with *courtesy*—being *treated respectfully*—is a very important way—indeed, a necessary condition for the possibility—of being treated with respect" (Buss 1999: 802).[12] Buss describes,

> for example, what is required to acknowledge that someone (A) is an expert on some topic (X). When doing a research project on X, one ought to look up A's papers. But surely this indirect acknowledgment is not sufficient. If, for example, when one is discussing X with A (and others), one repeatedly interrupts A's attempts to explain something about X or responds to her comments with a sniff of the nose, a roll of the eyes, or a "That's what *you* say," then one has failed to acknowledge her expertise (or has not acknowledged it enough, which comes to the same thing where giving people their due is concerned).
>
> (Buss 1999: 803)

Various forms of *direct* acknowledgment of another's status—whether as an authority or even, in more ordinary cases, as simply a fellow human being with dignity—are partly constitutive of what is required in order to treat that person with appropriate respect. Montessori—in something of an inverse to Buss's example of authority—discusses the ideal of the "scientist [who] is humble," illustrating this humility through a series of conventional behaviors indicating equality of status with his students: "descending from his professional throne to work standing at a little table, ... taking off his robes to don the workman's blouse, [laying] aside the dignity of one who states an authoritative and indisputable truth to assume the position of one ... seeking the truth together with his pupils" (9: 101). Likewise, Nancy Sherman argues that "Playing the role of the good person ... has to do with ... socially sensitive behavior—how we convey to others interest, empathy, respect, and thanks through the emotional expressions we wear on our faces (or exhibit through our body language and voices) ... We spoil kindness ... if our reluctance is betrayed in inappropriate 'furrowed brows'" (Sherman 2005: 286).

Buss's and Sherman's descriptions of disrespectful behavior, like Montessori's examples of impoliteness, highlight the important role of the body. Bodily behavior matters for politeness because patterns of movement have social meanings that communicate respect or disrespect, and directly communicating such respect or disrespect is part of what is required in order to actually respect others. The sniffing of the nose, rolling of the eyes, and even saying "that's what *you* say," which may well happen without deliberate intention or even self-conscious awareness, all communicate disrespect. Buss rightly goes on to emphasize these "subtlest gestures (the curl of the lip, the raised eye-brows)" and "slightest differences in vocal tone" as significant aspects of "respect in the most ordinary interactions" (Buss 1999: 814). Similarly, Yuriko Saito, in an insightful analysis of a scene from *The Pillow Book of Sei Shōnagon*, points out how in certain contexts, "bodily movement accompanied by loud noise and hurried and fidgety motion communicates thoughtlessness or indifference, while a gentle and elegant bodily movement implies a caring and respectful attitude" (Saito 2016: 229, discussing Sei Shōnagon 1982). Nancy Sherman rightly observes, "To show the proper gaze toward another, to bear oneself physically in a certain way, mindful of what would offend, insult, or shame are in many cultures simply the ways we acknowledge others as worthy of respect" (Sherman 2005: 274). Drawing on Cicero, she lists "specific material elements of decorum—in particular ... bodily comportment, facial demeanor, and tone of voice," where those include such things as the need to avoid "languidness in our gait, lest we look like 'carriages in solemn procession' or show a kind of frantic haste lest it betray (or encourage) a lack of equanimity within" (Sherman 2005: 282).

At times, philosophers emphasizing the importance of politeness suggest that what really matters morally is the *effort* to be polite, rather than success in that effort. Thus, Buss claims, "people who are boorish or sulky or obnoxious ... are morally deficient precisely because they make so little *effort* to please" and another "fails to treat me with respect if she makes no *effort* to hide her disinterest in, or contempt for, my feelings" (Buss 1999: 798, 804, emphasis shifted; cf. Darwall 1977: 43). Buss is correct that in some cases one might find fault with impoliteness because it shows a lack of effort. In other cases, however, excessive effort is itself a sign of impoliteness. To use Buss's example, the person who visibly holds themselves back from interrupting the supposed authority might be preferred to the boor who rudely interrupts, but the signs of effort to avoid interruption—the tensed muscles in his neck, the subtle leaning-in and fidgeting, and the slight shaking of his head that he can't quite hold back—all represent failures of (appraisal) respect. Even if he does not consciously choose to comport his body in these ways, and even if he wants to be someone who shows respect to the authority in his presence, his body expresses disrespect. Likewise, even if we give some credit to a person who is trying to use a more respectful tone of voice or bodily orientation with all of those around him, and who explicitly affirms their equality and advocates for them in a variety of ways, if we find that he regularly talks to members of certain groups with a babying tone of voice and adopts a posture indicating superiority around them, we can rightly accuse him of failing to satisfy fully the requirements for equal respect.[13] To use one of Montessori's examples, we exercise polite respect when "the sweetmeat to which our neighbor helps herself is just the one we desired, but we are careful to give no sign of this [such that] all the movements of our body are not merely those dictated by impulse or weariness; they are the correct expression of what we consider decorous" (9: 128).[14] Here *effortful* self-restraint would undermine the expressive function of decorum; what is needed are habits of interaction whereby our bodies move (or remain at rest) in ways that allow others to enjoy goods to which they are entitled, even if we would also like to enjoy those goods. Just as children, in waiting patiently for another to finish work with a desired educational material, must learn to wait in ways that avoid distracting fidgety movements, so too they come to comport their bodies in ways that "we consider decorous."

3.4 Bodily Habits of Respect

Non-interference, help, and politeness all express respect, and all require complex muscular co-ordinations, which arise through exercise but, once mastered, lie beyond completely conscious control.

> The will stores up its prolonged efforts outside the consciousness, or at its extreme margin, and leaves the consciousness itself unencumbered to make new acquisitions and further efforts. Thus, we cease to consider as *evidences of will* those habits in which we nevertheless see the consciousness [*conscienza*][15], as it were, hanging over and watchful of each act, that it may accord with the perfect rule of an external code of manners.
>
> (9: 128)

Even if "only disease can ... induce a [well-formed] man of society to cease to act in a becoming manner," the young child is "an unbalanced creature" "making his first trial of arms," so caregivers need to provide children contexts where, "together with other children, [they can] practice the gymnastics of the will in the daily habits of life" (9: 129).

> Th[e] reciprocal equilibrium between opposite motor forces [impulse and inhibition] is the result of prolonged exercises, of *ancient habits* within us; we no longer have any sense of effort in performing these, we no longer require the support of reason and knowledge to accomplish them; these acts have almost become reflex. And yet the acts in question are by no means reflex actions; it is not Nature but habit which produces all this.
>
> (9: 128, emphasis original)[16]

The habits formed through deliberate effort in childhood inscribe themselves in our bodily patterns of movement. We come "naturally" to move in ways that conform with requirements of mutual respect, and this second nature expresses our embodied agency.

Embodied habits of virtue are essential partly because they make it possible to focus on "new acquisitions" (9: 128). One who no longer needs to think about typing can devote attention to constructing and expressing more and more complex thoughts in writing, and one who can move around a room without upsetting others' work can devote his attention to cultivating more acute sensitivities to others who may need help. These further sensitivities, in turn, are largely a matter of patterns of bodily movement—regular movements of head and eyes to survey the room, appropriately moderated gait in moving toward a potential beneficiary of aid, and so on—that, in turn, become habituated and no longer conscious, so that one can further refine moral character.

Embodiment is also essential because it is more *reliable* than intentional respect. As Montessori explains,

> We know well how the person who has not been brought up to observe certain rules, but has been hastily instructed in ... them, will too often be guilty of blunders and lapses, because he is obliged to "perform" there and then all the necessary coordination of voluntary acts, and there and then direct them under the vigilant and immediate control of the consciousness; and such a perpetual effort cannot certainly compete with the "habit" of distinguished manners.
>
> (9: 128)

In one way, the susceptibility to blunders and lapses might be a matter of giving into temptations to violate norms of respect, but Montessori's example suggests something more common and more basic. Respectful interaction requires countless small adjustments of demeanor and comportment, adjustments beyond any individuals' capacity to keep track of. It is simply impossible consciously to attend to every requirement of respectful interaction, consciously and deliberately to avoid interrupting or bumping or looking askance at others, intentionally to shift one's gaze and bodily orientation to be aware of others, modulate tone of voice based on audience and appropriate affect, and so on. Social life depends on "bodily hexes," whereby "behavior [can] be regulated without being the product of obedience to rules" through a process in which "the social game [becomes] embodied and turned into a second nature" (Bourdieu [1987] 1994: 63, 65).

Many acts of moral virtue are almost entirely bodily. On accounts of the good will such as Kant's, any action, to be morally estimable, must be done "for the sake of duty," which, even if it does not involve specific contemplation of the moral law, at least requires some degree of reflection and deliberate control by conscious volitions. In a famous argument against this Kantian account as involving "one thought too many," Bernard Williams explains that when a man saves his wife (rather than a stranger) from drowning, some—"for instance, his wife"—might hope that "his motivating thought, fully spelled out, would be the thought that it was his wife, not that it was his wife and that in situations of this kind it is permissible to save one's wife" (Williams 1981: 18). Williams accuses Kant of requiring too much reflection at too abstract a level. Arguably, however, even Williams' alternative involves too much thought; in many cases—particularly in emergencies like people fallen overboard—any thinking at all will likely make one's responses too slow. Some, not least the man's wife, might hope that he would save her first and think about what he did later. To draw on an example mentioned by Philippa Foot of a "rescue in a swift flowing river": "It was the head tracker's marvelous swift response that captured my admiration ..., his split second solicitousness when he heard a cry of pain, his finding in mid-air, as it were, the only way to save the injured body" (Hershey 1956, quoted in Foot 1978: 4). Foot rightly says that such examples do not show "that it is wrong to think of virtues as belonging to the will" but rather that "what [they] ... show is that 'will' must here be understood in the widest sense" (Foot 1978: 4).

We can make an analogy here with non-moral cases of action. The tennis player who thinks "hit it because it's a ball" is little better off than one who thinks "it's a ball, and in games like tennis, one should try to hit the ball." To play tennis excellently, one needs to stop thinking altogether, to trust immediate reactions of one's body, which perceives (often unconsciously) nuances of the ball's motion. Similarly, much of moral life consists in cultivated bodily responses to situations, such that one need not think at all in order to do what is morally required. Montessori illustrates how respectful behaviors "no longer require the support of reason ... [but] have almost become reflex" with her paradigmatic example of social courtesy: "we may be comfortably seated in a corner of the drawing-room, but a venerable person enters, and we rise to our feet" and although "we are not much attracted by this lady, nevertheless we also bow or shake her hand" (9: 129). Young children or those adapting to a new culture may need to be reminded of what respect requires, but for morally excellent and culturally situated agents, rising at the sight of a venerable person can and should be etched into muscle memory. Just as one learns tennis by training one's body and learns to write by training one's hands, so too one learns virtue by cultivating habits of muscular movement that facilitate respect for others. And just as, for Montessori, muscular training (such as in writing) is not a mere *tool* of one's cognitive processes but partly constitutive of them (see Frierson 2020: 52–4), so too respectful habits of movement and muscular control are partly—and indeed largely—constitutive of moral virtue. To return to the example of Onorado (Chapter 1), the respect exhibited in his "exquisite sensibility, which manifested itself in the affectionate expression of his moved[17] face, and in the effusion of a general tenderness which looked for no return," also required physical comportments of his eyes as he "glanced at his neighbor ... to regulate himself ... by" him and of his hands, mouth, and body as he "tried to eat his bread very slowly" (9: 89).

These habits of control are not merely mechanical, rote repetitions. Despite the apparent rigidity of some of the lessons in grace and courtesy, the general training in embodied virtue includes facility in adjusting one's body to perceptions of moral sense about what respect requires in changing environments. For example, children learn coordination needed to properly replace materials on shelves in ways that do not disturb others and that leave the materials in good condition for future use. In one case Montessori describes, however, a shelf "was too narrow, and ... often ... children in selecting the pieces which they wished to use would allow [the material] to fall to the floor, thus upsetting with great noise all the metal pieces which it held" (Montessori 1912: 84–5; 2: 49). While the teacher "intended to have the shelf changed," the children, with well-cultivated habits of muscular coordination, adapted to the changed situation and "learned to handle these materials so carefully that in spite of the narrow and sloping shelf, the [materials] no longer fell to the floor" (Montessori 1912: 85; 2: 49). This small example illustrates a broader point, namely that the cultivation of virtuous bodily comportment primarily consists not of narrowly specified motions conducive to respect in particular contexts, but of habits of bodily self-control adaptable to changing situations.

4 Embodied Solidarity

The embodied nature of solidarity is often hidden in plain sight. In Margaret Gilbert's classic "Walking Together: A paradigmatic social phenomenon," she discusses theories emphasizing "common knowledge" or "shared person goal[s]" and develops her own account of solidarity in terms of joint "commitment" (Gilbert 1990: 3, 7), but she does not draw attention to the obvious fact that, as Judith Butler puts it, "nobody goes for a walk without a technique of walking" (Butler and Taylor 2010: 3, 50).[18] More importantly, as Butler and Taylor illustrate, no pair of people go for a walk *together* without developing an embodied technique for moving in ways that keep them at the same pace, with an appropriate distance between them, and so on.

Having discussed the role of embodiment in character and respect, the extension to solidarity is relatively straightforward. There are several dimensions of embodied solidarity. Most basically, in order to join with others in shared agency, one must have well-cultivated capacities—including bodily capacities—for agency as such. In discussing the Silence Game in particular, Montessori often emphasizes forms of bodily self-control intrinsic to that game:

> In order to have [perfect] silence, you must simply *not move*. And *in order not to move, you must think about everything that could possibly move*. So you must keep your legs and feet quite still, and your hands, and your whole body. You have to control your breathing ... Now this will be very difficult to do.
> (7: 52–3, emphasis original)

All forms of shared activity require bodily coordinations, not only of each individual participant but of the group of participants together. To play football as a team or violin as part of a quartet or to build a respectful community together, one requires specific bodily capacities.

Solidarity in a particular activity requires bodily capacities distinctive of that activity—remaining silent or throwing a football or playing violin—but also specific embodied capacities for working *together*. Beyond playing violin well, a member of a quartet requires specific sensorimotor coordinations in order to hold one's instrument in ways that facilitate awareness of others, to move head and eyes to attend to others, perhaps even to breathe in a staccato burst that indicates that it is time to start playing and/or to nod and shift one's body in just the right subtle ways and at precisely the right times in order to communicate. Moreover, just as each's gait needs to adjust when walking together, the quartet members' otherwise individual muscle coordination and memory of how to play a piece needs to shift in order to play well with others. While I might move my fingers with a particular tempo playing solo, I subtly change this tempo while practicing with others, in order better to play together. When groups have sufficient time to practice together, the muscle memory of a musical piece is essentially shared, as each plays in a way they would not have developed on their own, and all play together through attention to movements organized specifically to the group.[19]

Language itself involves a complex set of muscular coordinations that enable shared agency among members of a linguistic community. Among the earliest muscle development in infants is the training of muscles in the mouth and tongue in order to communicate. Later, and a major focus of Montessori's early pedagogy, we learn to hold and manipulate pens or pencils—or, today, keyboards or touchscreens—to write the alphabet(s) of our group. While language is neither necessary nor sufficient for solidarity in the strict sense, the muscular skills required for language use are paradigmatic means for shared agency.

Solidarity also provides an excellent context for seeing how new forms of embodiment can transform possibilities for human agency. Again, spoken and then written language are particularly vivid examples of this. The invention of writing (or, earlier, of painting) required retraining the human hand to perform new kinds of movements, and this retraining made it possible to unite together with people in new ways, and to unite with new sets of people, distant in space or time. Similarly, religious rituals foster solidarity: "The congregation at the Mass do not merely look on; they are actors in the drama. When the priest speaks, the people answer him ... They all become one thing together, one single voice, lifted up to Heaven" (19: 28). This unity is accomplished not only through the activity of speaking and listening but also through specific bodily motions carried out in coordinated ways, such as when all in unison "beat their breasts three times" or when all kneel together and "rise up again" (19: 62).

More recently, a particularly interesting example of bodily innovation as a means for opening new sorts of solidarity is the contact improvisation movement, started in the 1970s by choreographer Steve Paxton and others, which not only inspired new forms of dance, but also specifically created new ways for people to dance *together*. As Paxton (with others) describes it,

> Contact Improvisation is an evolving system of movement ... based on the communication between two moving bodies that are in physical contact and their combined relationship to the physical laws that govern their motion—gravity, momentum, inertia. The body, in order to open to these sensations, learns to release excess muscular tension and abandon a certain quality of willfulness to experience the natural flow of movement. Practice includes rolling, falling, being upside down, following a physical point of contact, supporting and giving weight to a partner. Contact improvisations are spontaneous physical dialogues that range from stillness to highly energetic exchanges. Alertness is developed in order to work in an energetic state of physical disorientation, trusting in one's basic survival instincts. It is a free play with balance, self-correcting the wrong moves and reinforcing the right ones, bringing forth a physical/emotional truth about a shared moment of movement that leaves the participants informed, centered, and enlivened.
>
> (Paxton et. al. 1979: 35)[20]

Within this dance form, partners learn to share a center of gravity, moving together and supporting one another so that they constitute a single body-in-motion. The attention to shared motion here heightens features of all embodied solidarity, namely how solidarity requires sensorimotor adaptation to the group of which I am a part. But contact improvisation creates new forms of solidarity. While solidarity in motion is present in many dance forms, contact improvisation's emphasis on sharing weight and moving naturally together has opened spaces for new sorts of work together as partners. One often-cited implication of Paxton's approach is a shift from traditional gender roles within dance forms like ballet, where men lift women, to a more egalitarian form where sheer strength is de-emphasized relative to balance and attentive coordination, and where women regularly lift men and relatively light and weak dancers lift relatively heavy dancers.

Contact improvisation and religious ritual accentuate embodied elements present in all practices of solidarity. Even the most abstract solidarity of large corporations or political bodies requires bodily capacities to communicate and adjust behavior in the light of requirements for acting together. Like respect for others and character-driven individual activity, social solidarity is embodied movement in the world.

5 Conclusion

This chapter has only scratched the surface in terms of thinking about how embodiment relates to agency and ethical life. In §1, I showed how ethical life for Montessori includes affective dimensions, such that to be a moral agent is not merely to think and choose in certain ways but to *feel* in certain ways. Beyond the role of affect, Montessori also emphasizes literal bodily movement in ethical life, from the muscular coordinations essential to various character-driven activities to specific bodily comportments constitutive of mutual respect in a given cultural context and the precise forms of bodily attunement and physical readjustment that occur in solidarity with others.

There are further issues of embodiment that I have not discussed in this chapter and that are topics of current discussion within philosophy and worth further investigation in Montessori. Beyond the ways that we must learn to move our bodies in order to conform with social standards of mutual respect, I have not discussed the ways individuals' bodies shape social perceptions of them. Race, sex, disability, obesity, and other forms of the body can affect how one is treated by others and thereby strongly influence one's capacity for agency in a given context. I have only indirectly addressed issues about an individual's rights over their own body and the ways in which the "body" functions as a site of coercion and political negotiation. I have not talked about pain. And I have only obliquely raised issues about the relationship between the positive sense of "normalization" that Montessori employs to describe individual's authentic self-immersion in structured activities they choose for themselves and the more problematic "normalization" that cultural theorists such as Judith Butler (see too Foucault and Bourdieu) criticize as partly constituting social structures that overly regiment human behavior and reify arbitrary cultural values. I have not discussed the important roles the body plays even in abstract moral reasoning, for instance, in the metaphors used for moral concepts and categories (see Lakoff and Johnson 1999).

One of the most important lingering issues about the role of the body in Montessori's moral philosophy, one with connections to many of the aforementioned themes, relates to the status of (physical) disability within a Montessorian moral philosophy (cf. Bergoffen and Weiss 2011, 2012; Hellbrügge 1982). A moral theory that requires bodily coordination for full participation in ethical life risks further marginalizing those with physical disabilities. Relatedly, one might raise a broad concern about the relationship between "ought" and "can"; if I am not capable of a particular bodily coordination, it seems as though that coordination cannot be required as part of, say, a morally obligatory respect for others.

With respect to the general issue of whether one can be morally obligated to move in ways that one is not currently physically capable of, I would highlight four key points. First, notions of "ought" or "obligation" do not play significant roles within Montessori's moral theory. While there are ways of doing things more or less excellently, and there is room for a sense of constraint and obligation within non-ideal theory, Montessori's conception of moral excellence is development-oriented rather than punitive or even abstractly evaluative. Second, the notion of possibility implied by "can" in "ought implies can" is vague. When Sofia begins to work on her cylinder blocks, she "cannot" place the blocks in the correct places, in that she often misjudges what the correct hole is and/or has trouble manipulating the blocks to slide them into the holes properly. But in another sense, she corrects herself and identifies her mistakes as mistakes because she can place the blocks correctly, in that she can make herself the sort of person who will place them correctly. So too with the child who bumps into their companions or the adult who speaks with a disrespectful tone of voice. Both are capable of becoming people with different bodily habits and capabilities, even if they fail to have those capabilities at a given time. Third, Montessori remains open to the reality of inevitable moral failures and even moral tragedies. Mistakes and errors are part of ethical life because they are part of life, and it may well turn out, for instance, that one has developed a body that expresses disrespect toward others despite one's best intentions. Changing one's moral theory to make this disrespect not count as a real moral failure just papers over a real problem in our shared ethical life. Finally, one of Montessori's core pedagogical insights is the important role of environment in shaping human potentials. As noted in Chapter 7 (particularly §6), moral failures are always failures of a person in a context, and the purpose of moral failure is to identify locations for improvement, both in person and context. When someone "can't" coordinate their body in ways necessary for expressing respect, that person should strive toward self-perfection, and we all should seek to create an environment within which improvement is possible and moral failures are correctable.

Many of these general points also apply to physical disability, but one with what Elizabeth Barnes has called a "minority body" (Barnes 2016) may also face specific moral challenges. I have discussed disability in the context of intellectual virtue elsewhere (Frierson 2020: 161–74), and most of what I say there applies to moral agency as well. For one thing, rather than providing a reason to discount the importance of the body, disability studies helps show how important bodily engagement actually is for ethical life. In a beautiful depiction of the mutual respect and solidarity involved in walking together, Judith Butler and Saunaura Taylor converse while walking through the streets of Berkeley, and one can observe each's (polished) adaptation of their movement in order to walk *together*, maintaining an appropriate distance apart, moving at the same pace, shifting their gaze from road ahead to their walking and conversation partner, and so on. That Sunaura Taylor is in a wheelchair highlights rather than diminishes the truth that "nobody goes for a walk without a technique of walking" (Butler and Taylor 2010: 3, 50), and both Taylor and Butler have to organize their bodily movements in order to enact their solidarity and respect. Moreover, both enact those movements in an environmental context and with appropriate technology, including the sidewalk, shoes, and wheelchair that make the walk together possible. Similarly, in her revisioning of ethical values in the light of—among other things—disability studies, Alexis Shotwell emphasizes the importance of "understanding ethical decisions resulting from our embodied being" and, while being "*against*" various forms of normalization, her approach is, "in ... againstness ..., [also] very much *for* ... optimism ... [about] collective determination of how to get on together" (Shotwell 2016: 203). Shotwell recognizes that we are embodied, and that embodiment matters for ethics, and that the way to move forward is to take that seriously while also going to the root of mutual respect, namely our need to live and move and have our being together with others, while also relying on social solidarity in order to evolve our social structures to make it possible for all to be respected and respectful, thriving and flourishing in our embodied life together. Disability studies does not point toward devaluing bodily components of mutual respect but toward re-visioning those bodily components to take even *more* seriously the task of constructing ways of moving together.

Different people have different bodies, and all of us cultivate our bodies in some ways rather than others. As I quoted in §2, "Each ... has his own path to follow, and work is a chief expression of his psychic life ... Though muscles are too numerous for all to be exercised, there is a certain number below which the psychic life will be endangered" (5: 39). Those labeled as disabled may have some different potentials than others, but none of us actualize all of our potentials, and all must—to live well—actualize some, where this actualizing involves movement of the body that one has. Moreover, and this is a key point as we move together into a better future, the norms of respect and solidarity are social constructions built from our attunement to one another as we seek to live and act together in society. Insofar as some members of that society have been ignored or marginalized, often because of their different bodies, norms of respect will fail to produce the "harmony of activity" that defines what respect is. Moral agents all—as participants in shared humanity—need to work toward the creation of social and physical environments that make it possible for each individual to develop into someone who can participate in ethical life, including the fully embodied cultivation of individual character through self-chosen work, enactment of practices of mutual respect, and full participation in practices of social solidarity.

Several years before her experience with Sofia, Montessori had worked with children labeled as "deficients" by her society, and precisely through her work with such children, she was able to identify, among other things, the importance of training in bodily movement in order to express agency and participate in ethical life. Those early lessons attuned her to realities that were only reconfirmed through work with a broader range of young children. Throughout her pedagogy and philosophical reflections, her attention to the developmental realities of young children made the role of the body in moral formation impossible to ignore. As children pursued their own individual expressions of agency and self-perfection, they had to refine their movements, and as Montessori sought to prepare children to do this well, she developed extensive sets of materials that indirectly prepare the bodily motions children need to draw on for more advanced expressions of agency. As children sought to live together in active communities, they had to adjust their bodies to one another, and Montessori's attention to cultivating these bodily graces led her to create learning environments where the negative effects of clumsy or careless motions would be readily apparent to those moving poorly. And the paradigmatic experience of solidarity among young children in Montessori classes—the Silence Game—brings with it a particularly heightened attunement to the physical self-control required for acting together. While this chapter has barely scratched the surface of the issues and potential within embodied moral philosophy, it at least offers a Montessorian provocation toward such inquiry and a start toward its defense.

9

Love

Man has devoted so much intelligence to the study of other natural facts ... Why not spend a little of this vigor in the study of a force that might unite mankind? Every contribution able to bring out the latent power of love, and to throw light upon love itself, should be welcomed with avidity and considered of paramount importance.

(*The Absorbent Mind*, 1: 263)

1 The Philosophy of Love

In *Creative Development in the Child*, Montessori offers a description of the life of a child in an "environment ... prepared in such a way as to offer the child free activity" (24: 237). Consistent with the importance of character in her moral philosophy, she starts by outlining the emergence of character through norm-governed and persistent work:

> In this environment, the child comes into contact with some objects upon which he concentrates. The special characteristic of this activity, which is a cycle of laborious work without rest, is calm. Throughout this activity the child slowly builds up his personality and gradually acquires special characteristics. He becomes a serious person and learns to finish the activity which he has begun.
>
> (24: 237–8)

She goes on to incorporate further aspects of her moral philosophy, offering samples of the social life—including respect, help, and obedience—that emerges in a community of free, character-driven agents:

> He shows a very special ability to offer help when help is really needed, and to show respect for those who are occupied in an activity. He shows special sympathy and understanding for smaller children. He shows that kind of obedience which, we might say, is a consent of the spirit to other people, and he acts according to the will of another in serenity and calmness.
>
> (24: 238)

In these few sentences, Montessori summarizes much of her moral philosophy. She then concludes her summary with a remarkable claim: "All these things may be considered as manifestations of love" (24: 238). As the sum of ethical life, "the 'law' of love [*amore*] ... comprises within itself all legislations and moral codes" (9: 250), and "all is nothing unless love is there" (1: 268).

In this book, I have explained how Maria Montessori's moral-sense-based moral theory makes agency its central value and character, respect, and solidarity its three central components. I showed how these are enriched through abstraction and embodied in ethical movement. Consistent with the title of this book, Montessori describes her overall account in terms of "the moral question" (9: 205) and explicitly seeks to develop a new approach to "morals" (17: 207). However, Montessori also expresses concern about a society that "is very concerned with morals" such that "morality ... become[s] a study in and of itself" (17: 206). Just as her mentor Giuseppe Sergi "substitute[d] the human individual taken from actual life in place of ... abstract philosophical ideas" (Montessori [1910] 1913: 14), so too Montessori is less interested in moral philosophy than in "spend[ing] a little ... vigor ... to bring out the latent power of love" (1: 263). Her moral theorizing arises from a loving observation of children's lives. Character, respect, and solidarity all express the power of love. Abstraction itself is a way in which human beings raise love to a moral universal scope. The embodiment of ethics manifests the centrality of love as a form of life. What I have called the moral philosophy of Maria Montessori could equally be called "Montessori's philosophy of love."

First and foremost, for Montessori, "love [i]s the force that preserves life" (9: 245), and Montessori particularly emphasizes that an education that proceeds from "love [of] humanity" must "look to the life of man and serve it" (17: 10). As she puts it in the *Absorbent Mind*,

> Love and the hope of it ... are a part of life's heritage. It is life that really speaks, not just the poets and the prophets. Love may be considered ... from the point of view of life itself. Then we see it not only as something imagined or desired, but as the reality of an eternal energy that nothing can destroy ...
>
> But love is much more than we have said so far. In man's mind it has been exalted by fantasy, but in us it is no other than one aspect of a very complex universal force, which—denoted by the words "attraction" and "affinity"—rules the world, keeps the stars in their courses, causes the conjunction of atoms to form new substances, holds things down to the earth's surface. It is the force, which regulates and orders the organic and the inorganic, and which becomes incorporated into the essence of everything and of all things, like a guide to salvation and to the endlessness of evolution. It is generally unconscious, but in life is sometimes assumes consciousness, and, when felt in man's heart, he calls it "love."
>
> (1: 264, 266)

At times, Montessori identifies love with basic forces of attraction or affinity, whether conscious or not, such that "all creation is the fruit of love" (24: 369). She says that "gravity ... is like universal love," "Water ... hurries in love to the ocean bearing gifts," and "chemical attraction only occurs between ... elements that have an affinity" (24: 368; 6: 27; 24: 366). In other contexts, she specifically links love with certain forms of (animal) life: "Nature evolved by strengthening what had been a weak point in animal behavior, bestowing [on mammals and birds and some other animals] the new energy called Love ... a powerful passion ... able to make a small bird forget fear and care for self" (6: 35; cf. 9: 243). Here love refers not to a general principle of affinity but specifically to the tendency of some living things to de-prioritize themselves in order to attend to the needs of others, particularly their offspring. More specifically, as noted in the quotation above, Montessori calls "love" the conscious affinity felt by human beings, and it is this sense of love that plays the most prominent role in Montessori's moral philosophy. In this sense, "the whole labor of life, which fulfills itself subject to its laws and brings beings into harmony, reaches consciousness under the form of LOVE" (22: 83). As experienced by human beings, love finds expression through full participation in ethical life, that is, in agential work, mutual respect, and social solidarity.

Most generally, love consists of not "patronizing charity ... but a reverent consciousness of [the] dignity and worth" of its object (6: 15–6).[1] Montessori eulogizes the geologist and philosopher Antonio Stoppani[2] as someone who reveals "what love is in the world, in the soul of man" because Stoppani was "a man who loved the environment and saw it with prophetic eyes," who "loved the things of science from the point of view of work and of spiritual directives" and "thought there were some things [so] lofty and beautiful that they must be given to the public" (Montessori [1936] 2009: 33). Reverently conscious of the value of "lofty and beautiful" ocean currents, coral formations, and ecosystems, Stoppani was also deeply attuned to the dignity and value of those whom he taught about these things.

Whether expressed toward one's environment, particular objects of study, other persons, or humanity as a whole, love as reverent consciousness of the dignity and value of something contrasts sharply with "patronizing charity" (6: 15), "attachment" (10: 84), or the sort of "love" that manifests in possessive desire for something. As Montessori explains,

> There is a constant interaction between the individual and his environment. The use of things shapes man, and man shapes things. This reciprocal shaping is a manifestation of man's love for his surroundings. Harmonious interaction—when it exists, as in the child—represents the normal relationship that should exist between the individual and his surroundings. And this relationship is one of love. Love impels the child not toward the possession of the object, but toward the work he can do with it ... This great revelation we owe to the child. Two paths lie open in the development of his personality—one that leads to the man who loves and one that leads to the man who possesses. One leads to the man who has won his independence and works harmoniously with others, and the other to the human slave who becomes the prisoner of his possessions as he tries to free himself and who comes to hate his fellows.
>
> (10: 53; see too 1: 196–8; 10: 85)

True love, which recognizes others' value, seeks to work with them in a relationship of mutual independence and mutual harmony. Onorado loves himself and his fellows, seeking to moderate his behavior to preserve his dignity while recognizing theirs. Sofia loves her cylinder blocks, engaging with them with recognition and appreciation of their own internal norms and structure. Neither seeks merely to dominate or possess the materials with which they work or the people with whom they interact.

Tying together the focus on life with the reverent consciousness of value, Montessori in one work describes "love" as "that ardent fire ... which keeps life kindled and gives value to all things" (9: 214). In the rest of this concluding chapter, I draw together the themes of this book and show how such love permeates every aspect of Montessori's moral philosophy, starting with the epistemic source of moral claims, manifesting in the substantive values of Montessori's theory, and including the embodied nature and conceptual development of ethical life.

2 Love as the Source of Moral Epistemology

In Chapter 2, I explained the important role of the "moral sense" in Montessori's moral philosophy. Like other senses, the moral sense provides the epistemic basis on which further knowledge can be built through abstraction and reasoning. For Montessori, moral philosophers best glean "absolute" moral insights, as opposed to those due merely to "laws of society, public opinion, [or] material well-being," through application of the moral sense and especially through careful attunement to children's application of their moral sense in conditions conducive to their freedom.

As in her description of ethical life from *Creative Development*, where Montessori identifies the sum of ethical life with love, so too in *Spontaneous Activity in Education*, she identifies the moral sense itself with love:

> Positive science includes in the term 'moral sense' something complex which is, at the same time, sensibility to public opinion, to law and to religion; and multiplying it thus, it does not clearly define in what "moral sense" consists. We talk of it intuitively; each one has within himself something that "responds" to the appellation; and by this internal response he must understand and decide in what this "moral sense" consists. But religion is simple and precise: it calls this internal sense which lies at the root of life, Love.
>
> (9: 242)

She introduces a later discussion of the "internal sense" by which "good and evil may be distinguished" by referring to Christ's substitution of the "'law' of love" for the Decalogue, and she contrasts this internal sense with "cognitions of morality" (9: 250). Only such an internal *sense*—that is, love—would be "bound up with life itself" and thus "absolute" (9: 251). Unsurprisingly, then, "it is only through love that this sensibility [of conscience] can be perfected" (9: 253).

Montessori elaborates on the ways that the moral sense is properly called love: "the 'moral sense' ... is to a great extent the sense of sympathy with our fellows, the comprehension of their sorrows, the sentiment of justice: the lack of these sentiments convulses normal life" (9: 242).³ As I noted in Chapter 2, Montessori often identifies our "inner sensation" of good or evil with a particular sort of "joy [and] peace" or "remorse and lack of peace" (18: 261). But such sentiments can be obscured or fabricated when we overlay ideological views about life onto our perceptions of our situation. In moral appraisal, adults have a tendency of "merely wanting to apply a preconceived plan," against which the only remedy is "to love humanity" (17: 10). Through a love that is attentive to others' dignity, we focus on their own perspectives and their own life.

> Love gives us a deep knowledge of the people we love, and a close spiritual relationship with them ... The tie of love gives the mother the capacity of understanding the meaning of her child's language ... by empathizing with her beloved child's needs.
>
> (24: 182)

When Montessori goes to say that "to keep a person alive, we have to understand him through this great love" (24: 182), her concept of "life" here is that full Nietzschean sense of life, life as vibrant fullness, not mere persistence of organic form. To keep another truly alive, we must reverently attend to their value and dignity, thereby coming to recognize what is genuinely conducive to their flourishing. And to recognize what is genuinely conducive to the flourishing of human life just *is* to have a moral sense, to see what is absolutely *good*. In the sense, the "judgment of love is the judgment of [moral] knowledge" (9: 91).

Equally importantly, Montessorian moral philosophers must attend not only to their own moral perceptions but to those of the children they care for and observe. What Montessori says about scientists and teachers applies even more forcefully to moral philosophers seeking to learn from children: "the *soul of the scientist* is entirely possessed by a passionate interest in what he sees ... [and] so [too] in the teacher interest in the phenomenon observed [the child's agency] will be the center round which her complete new personality will form spontaneously" (9: 99). In the case of one seeking to learn from children,

> vision ... should be at once precise like that of the scientist, and spiritual like that of the saint. The preparation for science and the preparation for sanctity should form a new soul, for the attitude of the teacher should be at once positive, scientific, and spiritual. Positive and scientific, because she has an *exact* task to perform ... Spiritual, because it is to man that h[er] powers of observation are to be applied.
>
> (9: 104)

This spiritual and exact engagement with children from whom one seeks to learn requires love. One who seeks "deeper knowledge," to know "the secret of childhood" more than mere "superficial facts" must have "a new kind of love" (1: 256). Only thereby can she really *see* the new moral truths that children are ready to reveal. And only then, "when the children show her their real natures," does she understand "perhaps for the first time, what love really is" (1: 256).

3 Character as Love

In Chapter 3, I laid out Montessori's approach to agency and her emphasis on the centrality of character for ethical life. As I showed there, agency requires the persistent engagement in norm-governed work toward which one is internally motivated. Character, present already in children but cultivated through exercise, consists of a tendency to express agency that strives for perfections of various kinds. Often, however, when describing the "personality entirely different from the one we had previously taken into consideration" that was exhibited in children of character like Sofia, Montessori describes it in terms of a "passionate love of ... work" (10: 15). For Montessori, character—and indeed agency as such—is ultimately grounded in love, and especially in what she calls "love of environment." About children's inner drives, she says,

> Indeed it is as love of his environment that we may envisage the irresistible urge which, throughout the sensitive periods, unites the child to things. It is ... a love of the intelligence which sees and assimilates and builds itself through loving.
>
> (22: 84)[4]

More generally, she asks, "How can we term by any other name, the great interest, the great enthusiasm, of the man who has begun to observe and take in reality in an exact fashion, except by the name of love" (24: 82). In general, the "joy and enthusiasm in work" exhibited by one with character arises from "love of his surroundings" (10: 54).

I have already discussed important roles that intellectual love plays in epistemic excellence (see Frierson 2020: 107–33). More generally, all forms of excellence, for Montessori, proceed from children's love for their environments and efforts to engage with those environments in more precise and refined ways, ways that better recognize and harmonize with the value of the beloved objects. Such love-motivated activities, in fact, better satisfy the internality requirements for agency than more reflective, principle-based accounts of agency (see Frankfurt 2004; Jaworska 2007; Seidman 2009). In Chapter 3, I mentioned that Montessorian agency lacks the felt conflict implicit in many accounts of self-control. The grounding of character in love emphasizes even more strongly the ways that Montessorian agency is wholehearted and fully invested rather than dutiful and conflicted. While character-driven action requires "*serious work*" with "*maximum effort*" (9: 77), one motivated by love is wholeheartedly "attracted by perfection" because "it is in their nature" (1: 190):

> There is no force of gravity [against which they must struggle], but a *true* wish to become better. Often there is aspiration without the prospect of absolute perfection, but in any case these people are drawn towards perfection, naturally and without effort ... Their search for it is not sacrificial, but is pursued as if it satisfied their deepest longings.
>
> (1: 189–90)

While pursuit of perfection is not *easy*—and in fact the "work" that agents love is precisely *challenging* work—its challenge consists in overcoming difficulties of the work itself, not overcoming conflict amongst volitions, concerns, or loves.

Sufferers [motivated by duty rather than love] impose rules upon themselves to save them from falling. They attach themselves to someone better than themselves. They pray Omnipotence to help them in temptation. More and more they clothe themselves in virtue, but it is a difficult life.

(1: 189)

By contrast, those with character "love ... order and work" and fully identify with this love (10: 15).

The child has given us striking revelations of different kinds of love, all of them directly related to work ... It is not simply tender affection. I assure that I have seen this love, I have been amazed by it; I have called it 'love for one's environment' ... Love of the environment inspires man to learn, to study, to work ... It leads to intimate contact between the thing that is loved and the human spirit ... [,] an interchange between an object and a man's spirit ... Love is the instinct that guides our actions.

(10: 85–7)

As noted in §1, love as a reverential consciousness of the value of something leads to "intimate contact" with that thing. Objects in the environment call out to the human spirit and provoke learning, study, and work. In other words, objects of love, the value of which we recognize, provoke expressions of character.

Montessori connects the role of love as a force of life with the open-ended perfectionism intrinsic to character to highlight the role that love plays in humans' "cosmic task," the forward progress in culture and in life made possible through character-driven activity.

The love of one's environment is the secret of all man's progress and the secret of social evolution

(10: 86)

Progress is possible only due to a new kind of love which enters the heart of man ... The discoveries which have arisen out of this feeling of love are not for the scientist himself, that he might sleep peacefully or eat better ... but for the service of the whole of humanity.

(24: 83)

The scientist who "had a love ... for snakes" (10: 85) focuses her energies on these animals and thereby expresses her character through study of and work with them,[5] as Admiral Byrd's journey to the Poles expresses his love of the Arctic. Consistent with Montessori's account of character, however, the pursuit of their individual loves through an open-ended pursuit of perfection contributes not only to their own individual progress toward deeper understanding and interaction with the objects of their love, but also to the progress of humanity toward a fuller engagement with the world.

4 Love in Respect

In Chapter 4, I turned from individual character to respect for others, describing how those with character come to respect one another. There I emphasized that "respect" is the proper attitude to take toward character in both oneself and others, and that character is the proper object of respect for others. Consistent with Montessori's concept of love as reverential consciousness of another's dignity, she rightly sees respect for individual others, when fully developed, as equivalent to love of them. She regularly links "love and respect" (9: 98) or "love and justice" (10: 86) and often insists on the centrality of love for proper help (see §7).

As in the case of respect, love for other persons primarily takes others' character as its focus. Particularly with respect to children, Montessori distinguishes "two levels of love." The first "refer[s] to the care we take of them, the caresses and affection we shower on those we know and who arouse our tender feelings" (1: 257). In the second form of love, one feels like "one is serving the spirit of man, a spirit which has to free itself" (1: 257). When it assumes the form of mere affection, love can devolve into possessiveness, treating another as an object of one's amusement (see §7). Even at its best, however, when one with love of the first kind focuses on "care" for others, they can care for trivial whims or wishes or care in line with some dogmatic view about what is best for them. True love, the second and higher form of love, arises when interactions with others are governed by reverential consciousness of their dignity, their inner spirit seeking to free itself. To love another with this higher love is precisely to respect them properly, to acknowledge and attend to them as agents with their own characters, their own ways of striving for perfection for themselves and ultimately contributing to the advancement of the world.

Just as I argued in Chapter 4 that respect for others emerges from character, so too love for others emerges from a more general love of one's environment. On the one hand, Montessori makes clear that the love of environment by which children love their work is not *identical to* love, concern, or respect for other persons: "a love for science and art, and all that mankind has created, will not suffice to make men and women love one another" (6: 15). On the other hand, however, other persons are part of one's overall environment. Thus, in describing the love of children for special adults in their lives, Montessori says, "*In the child's environment*, the adult is a special object of love" (22: 84, emphasis added). Love of this or that object within the environment does not in itself imply love for the *people* in one's environment, but love for other people is *part of* a broad love of environment as a whole. Most importantly, respectful love for others arises precisely when children are given the opportunity to express their environment-directed love. Montessori contrasts the false love that arises in a world of adults hiding themselves from each other with the true love that comes when one's ability to love objects of attention gives rise to a natural love for others in society:

> People try to teach children nice manners. But children who are allowed to develop normally are loving creatures who are naturally kind and polite to one another ... Outward rules of behavior are necessary only when man is insensitive and unfeeling. Everything must then be taught; everything becomes a burden to

us. We are slaves... Our will to power and possession enslaves us, and instead of a human society based on love and justice we have a society in which all men must hide behind masks in order to love.

(10: 86)

Just as character is not identical with respect, so too love for one's environment is not identical with love for other people. But just as character allowed to express itself in freedom gives rise to respect for others, so too when one is able to freely follow through on one's love for this or that feature in one's environment, that love naturally grows to encompass the human persons who are also part of one's environment, and one approaches others with a well-cultivated capacity for respectful attention, that is, for love.

Moreover, the general account of love in §1 applies to *both* love of non-persons (cylinder blocks or geological formations) *and* to love of other people. In both contexts, such love is an expression of and aid to life, and in both contexts, such love involves reverent consciousness of the value (in the sense of dignity) of its object. In the case of other persons, however, consciousness of another value generates "sympathy" with others, whereby we are able to pay attention to the developments of their spirit. In earlier work (Frierson 2020: 117–22), I drew on J. David Velleman and Iris Murdoch, both of whom highlight—like Montessori—the close connection between love and a "reverence ... that stands back in appreciation of the rational creature [another] is, without inclining towards any particular results to be produced," and I highlighted the connection between "the capacity to love" and "the capacity ... to *see*" (Velleman 2000: 358; Murdoch 1970: 65, emphasis original). To love another, that is, to be reverentially conscious of the dignity of another, is to really *see her*, to look past her superficial characteristics and even superficial desires and to recognize her character, that innermost spirit striving to express itself in freedom.

As usual, Montessori uses children as exemplars of this sort of love. In a description of how to shepherd young children through the process of learning to speak a language well, Montessori contrasts the "adult" who "instead of giving patient help ... often speaks quickly and carelessly" with "an older child, perhaps one who is four years old, who is full of love, help, and admiration for the small child. This admiration and approbation help the soul of the small child enormously" (17: 66). The older child genuinely admires the process at work in the younger child, a process whereby that child acquires language for himself. The older child already recognizes her role as one of supporting the agency of the younger. This love, with its own open-ended attentiveness to the others' disclosures of agency, goes beyond any principles or logical rules of respect.

> Logic is frozen. In love there is no logic. We may think that someone is stupid, that someone is indifferent, and yet we may love him. If the person who is loved feels our love for him, he becomes alive. Logic makes us judge other people by our own standards. We set ourselves up as the standard. This is logic and not love, and with logic we kill.
>
> (24: 182)

The logic that Montessori primarily criticizes here is the logic of what in Chapter 4 (following Darwall), we called "appraisal respect," namely a sort of respect whereby one values another's accomplishments. Even "recognition respect," however, which respects all others by virtue of their humanity, can fall into lifeless formulae. True respect for others is *loving* respect, a reverential consciousness of the dignity of another that remains open to the others' disclosure of her value.

5 Solidarity through Love

While respect for others is the customary and essential form of love for other persons within Montessori's moral philosophy, solidarity with and obedience to others express even deeper degrees of love. There are two primary ways in which solidarity expands and heightens the love already described in §§3–4.

First, true solidarity is a form of love. Sometimes, Montessori uses love as a near-synonym for solidarity, referring to "solidarity and love" as though these are twin concepts (14: 88). More often, she describes solidarity as emerging from love or as a particular kind of love. Thus she explains that "society by cohesion … is a characteristic of little children, for they are naturally full of love and sympathy … for others" (17: 237), and she describes "patriotism"—which elsewhere is a paradigm of social solidarity—as a "special love" (17: 95).[6] Moreover, as already noted in Chapter 5, Montessori regularly emphasizes that social solidarity has affective dimensions, so she invokes "love" to distinguish genuine *solidarity* from mere understanding of structural unity. For example, in talking about unity with humanity as a whole, she says,

> The fruit of this understanding [of unity] can never be a cold, conventional brotherhood. The living idea of the solidarity of all men who come and go, from past to future, closely united by many bonds, generates a warmth arising from knowing we are a part of something great, a sentiment surpassing even the love of country.
>
> (14: 88)

Elsewhere, she explicitly references "love" as "the one thing that will forge true human unity" (10: 20). Importantly, as in §4, the relevant "love" here need not involve sentimental affection or patronizing care for others; instead it is a reverential awareness of others' value and responsiveness to them. Even in the Silence Game, the paradigm of felt solidarity, the love of each child toward the other is a form of *sympathy*, an attunement to each's expression of agency, rather than cuddly fondness for one another.

While social solidarity is partly constituted by unifying love *toward* others, it is also partly constituted by *shared* love *with* others. In *The Absorbent Mind*, for example, Montessori describes the remarkable solidarity present at gatherings of Montessorians, wherein the most diverse groups "all mingled together, and none of us felt it in the least bit necessary to regulate or direct these groups" because "despite our differences of race, or religion, or of social position, we felt during our discussions of the child a fraternal union growing up between us" (1: 261–2). What made this remarkable solidarity possible was the child, who provided "a point on which there converges from everyone a feeling of ... love" (1: 262). In its context, Montessori's focus in this discussion is the unique role of the child in fostering unity amongst human beings by virtue of the natural love adults feel for children, but the discussion highlights a more general point about solidarity. Just as individual character governs itself through love, so too solidarity—that form of group character—arises when many individuals come to share a common love, not merely all loving the same thing, but loving that thing as a single lover. In Montessori gatherings, diverse persons unite around the love of the child. In the Silence Game, classrooms of children unite around the "love of silence" (7: 51). Various other forms of solidarity unite in other shared loves.

6 The Expansion of Love through Imagination and Abstraction

In Chapter 6, I showed how different dimensions of ethical life, while not essentially abstract or reflective, develop through adolescence and into adulthood, in large part through incorporating more abstract concepts and higher order reflective and deliberative capacities. Love, too, develops through adolescence and into adulthood in at least three important respects.

First, older children and adults become capable of loving abstractions, or loving things for the sake of abstract qualities of those things. In her advice to elementary teachers, Montessori reiterates her general claim that "the child should love everything he learns, for his mental and emotional growth are linked ... Dante has said ... 'The greatest wisdom is first to love,'" but she then specifically applies this "Intellectual Love" to abstractions: "Children can and do love abstract subjects, such as mathematics, so love can exist for the mental work [of adolescence]" (6: 14–5). Montessori's praise of Stoppani (see §1) emphasizes the great scientist's love of abstract objects (Montessori [1936] 2009: 33), and in her *From Childhood to Adolescence*, she gives detailed examples of how to inspire, for example, the love of "water," where water refers not to some particular sensorially given instance but to water in general:

> Certainly one would like to be able to penetrate the mysteries and the majesty inherent in water. In this way the desire to celebrate it in verse is also born. Its mode of action, its intelligent aim, its grandiose mission cause its maternity to be suspected. Is it not, in fact, the mother of all these living beings, the agents of Creation? Saint Francis of Assisi understood this well for, in an outburst of fraternal love for the elements, he sang the praises of "Sister Water who is very useful and humble and precious." It is loved by all because all living beings—plants and animals—are thirsty and cannot live without it. Why would we not admire it and feel gratitude for it as well as the desire to know more about it? The study of water, then, can become a passion, and the precise conclusions reached by a direct knowledge of it elucidate such a study.
>
> (12: 35)

As elementary children stretch their imaginations beyond what is immediately and sensorially given, they become capable of love for "water" or for "carbon" (cf. 6: 39), or for various kinds of things, forces, and relations. What was love of a particular insect or butterfly becomes a love of insects and butterflies in general. Sofia's love for her cylinder blocks becomes a love of geometry. In order to facilitate the child's "passage to abstraction," Montessori emphasizes that the teacher herself must not only have a desire to help her students but must "love and understand the universe" in order to "present … the world" to "the child which finds itself in the world of the abstract" (12: 18–9).

Among the most important transformations in the object of love are the transformations in respectful love of fellow human beings. Beyond love of particular individuals in our sensed, immediate environment, we become capable of love for imagined individuals distant from us in time and space, and eventually we can love humanity as such.

> Most of us experience the kind of love that causes us to be deeply attached to others; but this is a passing love. There is ample reason, however, to believe that the human spirit is inherently capable of another kind of love that is not transitory, that does not change, does not die. Man expresses this by saying that he loves something that transcends his family—he speaks of his love of his country, of his love of God.
>
> (10: 84)

Broader forms of love are based on capacities that develop during adolescence. "Love of the homeland is based on imagination," that is, on abstraction. Montessori even describes her own activism, her "fight on behalf of children" as something that "needs imagination, because we ourselves know only very few children" (12: 19). Through being able to imagine others that we are not in direct contact with, and to emotionally engage with those abstractions, our love comes to extend beyond our immediate sphere. For Montessori, this expansion of love through abstraction is one of the most important qualities that human beings bring to the world. As one "passes from feeling for himself in relation to those with whom he is in contact, to feeling for others whom he has never seen," the child develops an "abstract love" that makes him "want to make a direct contribution to society" (14: 35).

Love undergoes another transition as well, due largely to the increased desire for consistent *principles* of action and organized social *structures*. As Montessori explains it, the first step in this transition looks like a diminution of felt love: "Little children between three and six years of age have a special psychology. They are full of love … This is the first step …, but … by seven years of age, the child … is interested in distinguishing between good and bad" (17: 204–5). Onorado's sense of his own dignity and love for his companions, and even Sofia's love for working with her cylinder blocks, undergo a transformation. As seven- or eight-year-olds, Onorado wants to articulate principles of justice that ensure that each person gets his fair share, and Sofia wants to know how her work contributes to greater goods for the social whole. These more mature and reflective agents want to know the "why?" behind their loves, and they want principles that are abstract and general.

Montessori endorses this more reflective turn as part of the cultivation of a higher, more abstract love, but she also describes a crucial third stage in development, one within which the desire for abstraction is again subordinate to a broader sense of love: "If we look at adults, we will see many who are always considering whether their actions are good or bad..., [but] those who are concerned with looking at the good and the bad forget humanity... There must be something greater. Then comes the adolescent. He is full of generosity. He saves humanity" (17: 206). In this third stage, a rule-following morality that emerged as a healthy development from the spontaneous love of the infant returns to a new and higher spontaneous sort of love—generosity—that seeks not so much what is due to others as what can be done for the sake of humanity from one's overflow of life. This love marks that culmination of character that Montessori, from her earliest published book, described as the "ideal love" which "Nietzsche has embodied... in the woman of Zarathustra," a love by which she "desires a son better than herself" and seeks to "create a son... better, more perfect, more courageous than has yet been born," from whence "new generations... begin their triumphant march in time towards eternity" (2: 361–2).

This highest form of love—generosity—emerges after abstraction, once one with character is able to see themselves self-consciously as promoting new degrees of perfection that outstrip anything heretofore imagined and thus anything articulated in laws and principles already laid down. At one level, each individual adult seeks to *be* this more perfect son himself, following through on his ownmost loves in pursuit of "add[ing] a point to the circle of perfection which fascinated him" (1: 191). At another level, each individual seeks to respect others and thereby create—or allow to emerge—sons more perfect than heretofore. And at yet another level, those with this highest form of love have come to love humanity as such, a love that requires abstraction but allows individuals to push beyond mere abstraction toward a felt unity with humanity in which each sees her own achievements as achievements on behalf of the progress of the species and ultimately of the universe. Through abstraction, Sofia's love of environment and Onorado's love of his companions rise into the love felt by those geniuses inspired to contribute "poem[s], artistic masterpiece[s], [and] useful discover[ies]" to "humanity" (9: 17).

7 Paternalism

Within the context of her philosophy of love, paternalistic behavior toward children represents a failure of love, and in particular, a failure to see that love essentially consists of respectful attention to another. Montessori rightly observes that adults today explicitly, even emphatically, affirm love for children: "[P]eople speak only of the grown-up's love for the child. This is said not only of parents but of teachers, 'Teachers love children!'" (22: 85). When criticizing her contemporaries for failing to "recognize that the child is a personality with great human value and sacred social rights," she notes,

> This statement will dumbfound many people and strike them as a vast exaggeration, an absurdity. They will immediately object, 'How can we be accused of lack of

awareness of the child when he is the apple of our eye, our hope? How we be accused of lack of concern when we are such conscientious parents, keenly aware of our responsibilities?'

(10: 45)

Paternalism itself, in fact, is by definition a form of conscientiousness, and in that sense a sort of love. The paternalist overrides another's agency solely for the sake of promoting that other's good, solely—we might say—out of "love" for the other.

When applied to children, the notion that we override their agency out of love for them still has an air of commonsense, but Montessori rightly compares paternalism in this context to the paternalistic assertion of patriarchal power against which she struggled from her own elementary years (when she sought entrance into a traditionally male engineering school) through her explicit participation in feminist political organizing over the course of her life. As she puts it,

> Some time ago, a very important question arose—that of the role of women ... The same kinds of things were said at that time about women as are now being said about children and their role in society. In those days, too, it seemed absurd to speak of women as forgotten human beings. "We've neglected women, you say? How can that be, when we do everything possible for them, when we love them so much, when we protect them and are ready to die for them, when we work all our lives for them."

(10: 45)

Just as this patronizing, paternalistic treatment of women wore a veneer of love while utterly failing in reverential consciousness of the dignity and value of women, so too with children:

> Yes, of course, we all love children, we love them a great deal, but we do not appreciate them for what they really are. We love our children or believe we love them, but we do not understand them. We do not do what we should for them, because we have no idea what it is we should do, what place they should occupy in society ... The adult commits a serious error when he takes himself for the child's creator and believes he must do everything for him ... The adult believes he is the child's creator, while what he should rightly be is the servant of creation. And all he succeeds in being is a dictator, whose wishes the child must blindly obey. The adult has considered this very kind of dictatorship to be one of his own social problems, but he has never regarded it as a social problem of children.

(10: 45–6)

These adults who so "love" their children are the same who "put down all [the child's] spontaneous manifestations to naughtiness and who think of defending themselves and their possessions against him" (22: 85). Having lost "the sensitivity that we have called 'the intelligence of love,'" such adults cannot recognize the agency of the child, the life within him that loves the world and seeks to expand harmoniously into that world (22: 85). They perceive only "an empty vessel" needing to be filled, protected, and cared for (10: 46).

In her more generous moments, Montessori allows that adults have genuine albeit misguided love toward children, but she also warns that supposed paternalism often actually covers over essentially selfish motivations. Particularly "In ... societies ... where certain forms of feeling, such as love ... are taken for granted, such instincts [towards avarice, anger, and selfishness] must be camouflaged" (22: 60). As noted in Chapter 7, there might well be non-paternalistic reasons for, say, preventing children from throwing balls in one's house. At the very least, there are windows to protect. But adults have a tendency to conceal their own selfish reasons for suppressing children's activities, preferring instead to pretend that such suppression is for children's own good. Ultimately, while "the good manners and the education we instill upon our children are for the sake of the sanctimonious, selfish adult," "the adult is not conscious of his own defensive attitude, and is conscious only of love and generous self-surrender" (17: 134; 22: 59). Somewhat jokingly, Montessori quips that "We say we love children very much, but we do not love them at six in the morning" (17: 134), but this jibe conceals a quite serious example of such false paternalism, namely adults' tendency to say that "children need their sleep" when really adults want "to stop the child from getting out of bed and running around the house because this disturbs our selfish way of life" (17: 133). We want to show affection and care for children on our timelines, in our ways, and without disrupting the rest of our lives.

In two respects, then, paternalism is a false love. First and most egregiously, many in Montessori's time and today are uncomfortable with the idea of adults forcing behavior from children merely for the convenience of adults but quite comfortable with forcing behavior from children for the child's own good. As with patriarchal structures of old, we are complacent about infringements on children's dignity and rights as long as those infringements are excused as part of "love" or "care" for the child. Thus, we falsely pretend to paternalistic interference when such interference is really, essentially, selfish. Secondly, however, even when adults are motivated by genuine care and affection for children, such affection is falsely called love because it does not sufficiently *respect* children or recognize their *dignity*. Even at its best, paternalistic interference with children's agency fails to be truly loving.

There is one final way in which love is important for thinking about paternalism. In Chapter 7, I discussed alternatives to paternalism, ways that adults can protect children and promote their development without undermining their agency. In that context, I left out one important alternative, namely reliance on children's love for adults. Montessori often emphasizes that "The child wants to obey and loves us" (22: 85). Particularly in healthy relationships where adults support children's free activity, "the child is disposed to obey the adult, in the very roots of his spirit" (22: 85). Even in dysfunctional contexts, the child has a strong love and admiration for adults.

> Only when the adult asks him to deny the commands of the inner impulse urging him to creation ... does it become impossible for the child to obey ... The fits of temper and disobediences of the child are the expressions of a vital conflict between his creative urge and his love for the grown-up who does not understand him.
>
> (22: 85)

When adults direct children in ways that support their development, children do not need to throw fits or disobey; they can and readily do follow direction from adults, and do so from a heart-felt love for the adults.

Adults have a responsibility to engage in the "delicate work of love towards the child" (9: 248), but the right sort of love requires respect for the child as an agent. Thus, for example, when a child is engaged in work, "we ought not to call [the child] by name, and offer him our affection, inviting him to accept our help" (9: 247). This does not mean that we should be cold toward children, but rather "we ... should wait; not coldly, but ... ready ... Our 'response' to the child should be ... full, ... prompt and ... complete," and when we respond, we should treat the child with dignity, with a warm response that also "give[s] an upward impetus to the ... life of the child" (9: 247). True love toward the child includes respect that does not interrupt or interfere with agency, even in the name of love, and that at the same time provides an environment to support it, seeing one's own presence as a crucial part of that environment, and responding in love to the "love of environment" exhibited by the child.

8 Embodied Love

In Chapter 8, I showed how Montessori develops an ethics for embodied agency, one that takes seriously how character, respect, and solidarity all involve literal movements of the body. Because agency as such consists of bodily interaction with one's environment, ethical life is essentially embodied. Having now seen that character, respect, and solidarity are forms of love, it should be clear that and how love itself is an essentially embodied feature of human life. At one level, love motivates the cultivation of bodily coordinations. Sofia's love of her cylinder blocks cultivates strength in fingers, dexterity in her hands, and attuned eye-hand coordination. Montessori explicitly says that children's "love [of] useful objects" leads to a condition where "instead of knocking against furniture and breaking objects, they perfect their movements" (9: 224), and she emphasizes how "love for his environment makes the child treat it with great care and handle everything in it with the utmost delicacy" (1: 198). As we saw in Chapter 8, her accounts of respect and solidarity involve the cultivation of specific bodily capacities to express those forms of love. Whether expressing love for others through non-interference or attentive help or norms of politeness, one enacts love through bodily capacities; a loving body is one attuned to the needs of others and capable of the delicacy of movement and voice required of love in various contexts. So too, loving solidarity requires orientations of body, whether for the particular tasks one engages in with others—keeping one's body still in the Silence Game, for instance—or in the subtle movements of body involved in attending to and communicating with others (see Chapter 8, §4). Not only does Montessori take seriously "embodiment" through placing the emotion of love at the core of her moral theory, but her specific understanding of love includes substantial focus on the literal movements of body that arise from and partly constitute that love.

9 Love and the Child

I end this book where it began, with a focus on the child. While my book's title acknowledges Maria Montessori as the author from whom these moral insights emerge, Montessori herself repeatedly stresses that the moral and pedagogical insights she presents were taught to her by the children with whom she worked. With respect to love in particular, Montessori stresses that "the study of love and its utilization will lead us to the source from which it springs, The Child" (1: 268).[7] How does the study of love lead us to the child?

Children "need ... love" (17: 112). The vulnerabilities of children are not first and foremost about being hit by cars or falling from heights or being eaten by bears, nor even primarily in their need for food or shelter; rather, children essentially "need *love* in order to grow" consistently with their true nature. "The child does not need a bell, he needs a person full of love and sympathy for him ... Their joy in life depends on the love ... of ... the people around them," since by nature "children are full of love," but "they are only without love if they are ill-treated" (17: 112, 204). Moreover, children's need for love—particularly given that "the child ... loves us" (22: 85; see §7)—readily elicits love from others. Not only do "all mothers naturally love their children," but "all humans of every race and every country ... have children," so "the child can become the focus of universal interests and ends" (17: 204; 10: 70). Children are proper and natural objects of love and thereby provide a locus for reflection on the nature of love.

Children also exemplify love: "little children ... are full of love" (17: 204; cf. 9: 248). Unlike the reflective but often conflicted agency of the adult, the love of a child in a healthy environment is an unmixed love, a love that expresses itself through self-governed and persistent work with the objects of his love. "The child ... seems to work miracles when we realize how eagerly he seeks independence and the opportunity to work, and he possesses great treasures of enthusiasm and love" (10: 18). Such love *is* agency, and the tendency to act in accordance with one's loves, oriented toward perfection in oneself and one's environment, constitutes character, the pre-eminent virtue in Montessori's moral philosophy. This love in agency overflows into a respectful love for others, a love characterized by respect for others' work, recognition of their need to pursue their own loves, and help when (and only when) necessary. Beyond respect, the child's love of others includes admiration for them, solidarity with them, and an eagerness to obey. These three forms of love—character, respect, and solidarity—are essentially embodied and, partly for that reason, are susceptible of being exercised pre-reflectively and independent of deliberation. All three are enhanced through processes of abstraction, reflection, and deliberation that expand the scope of love and thereby allow for more complex and temporally extended expressions of agency, more universal forms of respect, and vaster and more organized forms of solidarity. When the teacher, and the moral philosopher, can adopt an "attitude of humility, which is after all an attitude of love toward the child" (24: 28), we can learn *from* the child what love is and can be in the world, and thereby promote, in theory and in practice, ethical lives of love.

Notes

Chapter 1

1. For an example of a child working with a similar material, see https://www.youtube.com/watch?v=B1NXgGVw6Iw (accessed September 1, 2021).
2. Montessori notes that Onorado's "father, who was very poor but also neglectful, denied the child bread; the child did not resign himself, did not cry, but struggled constantly, with all the means at his disposal, to obtain his portion of bread" (9: 88).
3. See Chapters 3 and 7, which include further citations.
4. For discussion of various editions of this work, see Trabalzini 2003 and 2011.
5. Moreover, these basic moral values show up in every cultural context in which children are given freedom in a healthy environment, "not only in almost every nation that shares our Western heritage, but also among many other widely divergent ethnic groups: American Indians, Africans, Siamese, Javanese, [and] Laplanders" (10: 15).
6. In addition to objecting to the ascription of this philosophy to *Montessori* (rather than Sofia and Onorado), one might also object to the notion that Montessori is a *philosopher*. Despite her insistence on drawing from the lives of children to illuminate every "branch of ... philosophy" (22: 1), her name is virtually unknown within academic philosophy. Among Montessori educators, she is best known as a pedagogical innovator, a medical doctor, and even an early developmental psychologist, but not as a philosopher. The general public often knows the name "Montessori" only as part of the expression "Montessori school." It is true, too, that she never wrote a *Treatise Concerning the Principles of Morals* or a *Metaphysics of Morals* or even a book entitled *Moral Agency and Ethical Life*. For most of her life, the primary focus of her work was on issues of pedagogy, particularly for children under the age of six. She sometimes even seems to deprecate "philosophy" in favor of empirical scientific investigation or real life, such as when she praises her mentor Giuseppe Sergi, who "like the scientists who preceded him ... was led to substitute (in the field of pedagogy) the *human individual* in his lived reality, in place of general principles or abstract philosophical ideas" (Montessori [1910] 1913: 14, translation modified). Like Sergi, Montessori's pedagogy puts actual individuals—particularly children—ahead of abstract philosophies. Nonetheless, as I will show throughout this book, she is a philosopher of the first rate.
7. I offer a slightly longer account of Montessori's life in Frierson 2020: 9–13. For more detailed discussions of her life, see Babina and Lama 2000, Foschi 2012, Kramer 1976, Moretti 2021, Standing 1984, and the regularly updated biographical overview at https: //montessori-ami.org/resource-library/facts/biography-dr-maria-montessori, most recently accessed 6-3-2021.
8. See Matellicani 2007; Trabalzini 2011: 39.
9. See Cimino and Foschi 2012; Foschi 2012; Foschi and Cicciola 2006; James 1906; Santucci 1963.

10 See Shapiro 2016 for the significance of genre and gender in marginalization of earlier historical philosophers.
11 The closest hooks would be James or Bergson, and anyone interested either of these philosophers would do well to engage with Montessori.
12 On children's marginalization, see Gopnik 2009: 3–6.
13 Lessons in "grace and courtesy," for example, can become attempts at communicating one's own moral insights to children, rather than ways of giving children language for their own insights and a context to exercise skills of interaction.
14 I here bracket a seventh, namely "Autonomy as personal efficacy, or having the ability to get along well in the world without requiring the help of others. In this sense of 'autonomy' a person can make herself more autonomous by learning how to drive, becoming rich, becoming knowledgeable, or gaining physical strength" (Arpaly 2003: 119). This sort of autonomy is anticipated by Montessori's emphasis on the "conquest of independence" (e.g., 1: 75f.), but it is not directly relevant to the argument of this chapter.
15 Arpaly adds to her definition of ideal autonomy that it refers to "states that are supposed to be desirable and only attainable by the few" (Arpaly 2002: 124), and the notion of this autonomy as "heroic" builds that elitism into its concept. For Montessori, as for contemporary philosophers such as Korsgaard and even Arpaly's own examples of Freud and Jung, ideal agency is attained only by a few at present, but it is attainable *in principle* by everyone. Thus I prefer the terminology of "ideal" over "heroic."
16 Arpaly also rejects this view (see Arpaly 2002: 33–66, 125).
17 I discuss this sense of agency in Chapter 3, §10.
18 Montessori would likely have been familiar with this work, at least indirectly, given her instruction by Antonio Labriola.

Chapter 2

1 For discussion of Montessori's empiricist epistemology, see Frierson 2020: 17–34.
2 Others affirm "particularist" moral theories, according to which each situation has appropriate responses, but there aren't universal moral rules (e.g., Dancy 2004; Hooker and Little 2000).
3 In Chapter 6, I discuss moral effects of the transition from sensation in early childhood to abstraction in adolescence. One of those effects is a capacity to develop moral distinctions through reasoning rather than merely through perception. The point here is that such distinctions are initially made by inner sensation, and even later reason-based distinctions are based on abstraction from and imaginative reconstruction of data provided by inner (moral) sense.
4 The Italian word *conscienza* is ambiguous between the English terms "consciousness" and "conscience." In the Montessori-Pierson English translation, the translator has opted for "conscience."
5 Cf. Hume ([1751] 1975) and Smith ([1759] 1982) for traditional sentimentalist accounts, and for neo-sentimentalism, see deSousa 1987; Döring 2007; Goldie 2007; Helm 2001; Prinz 2004, 2007; Tappolet 2011; Zagzebski 2003.
6 The ellipses here conceal a qualifier, namely that this is the moral sense "of which positive science speaks." In the context, Montessori distinguishes the complex

7 Strikingly, Montessori does not emphasize one of the more important moral emotions among many contemporary moral sentimentalists (and even in Adam Smith), namely anger or resentment. Montessori generally rejects anger as a disordered emotion, both in children—"one of the characteristics of children ... who have not organized their minds or movements, is to get angry. Three things go together: disorderly minds, disorderly movements and anger" (4: 55)—and in adults—"The deadly sin that arises within us and prevents us from understanding the child is Anger. But since no deadly sin acts alone, but always in combination or company with another, so Anger summons and combines with a sin of more noble appearance and hence more diabolical, Pride" (22: 96; thanks to Joke Verheul for these references). For discussion of resentment as a paradigmatic "reactive attitude," see Strawson 1962. For a critique of anger with which Montessori would likely be sympathetic, see Nussbaum 2016.

8 "Normalization" is a technical term that, as noted in Chapter 1, refers to the condition of a child left in freedom in an environment conducive to independent activity, that is, a child who has not been subject to neglect or oppressions that cause psychological deviations.

9 As this passage indicates, Montessori is at least a moderate internalist about moral sense (but not about abstract cognition of moral principles). Insofar as one senses the good by means of feelings of peace and joy, one is motivated to pursue or preserve it. For discussion of internalism in moral psychology, see Rosati 2016.

10 Note that Hutcheson is raising this concern only to address it.

11 See especially Chapter 3, §9.3.

12 Strictly speaking, these deviations do not corrupt the moral sense itself but only atrophy and displace it: "the laws of society, public opinion, material well-being and threats of peril [are in themselves] powerless to produce these various sensations" of "serenity ..., enthusiasm, [and] remorse" (9: 251). When moral terms are misapplied—say, by identifying passivity as good and activity as evil—children do not actually come to *feel* or *perceive* serenity in passivity and genuine moral remorse about activity, but they come to feel the ease of not suffering others' disapproval or punishment when they are passive, and they feel socially induced anxiety, fear, and shame about being active. Because of the similarity between these non-moral feelings and the moral sense, children come to misapply moral terms, and if never given the opportunity to exercise their genuine moral sense, that sense can fail to develop or even atrophy (much like external senses; see Frierson 2020: 135–48). As a shorthand for this displacement and atrophying of moral sense, I here refer to the process whereby people confuse non-moral feelings with moral perceptions as corruption or deviation of the moral sense.

13 In this respect (but cf. §3), Montessori's is more like Reid's moral sense theory than Hume's (see Reid [1788] 2010; Cuneo 2011; Roeser 2010).

14 See Foschi 2012; Cimino and Foschi 2012.

15 The theorists to whom she appeals for these accounts of evolution are Carl Wilhelm von Nägeli and Hugo Marie de Vries, both important figures in the development of genetics and the eventual Darwinian synthesis, as well as Léon Laloy (a Belgian biologist), whose *Evolution de la vie* (Laloy 1902), she cites as

particularly helpful for understanding the fundamental principles of biology to which she adheres (see PA 40).
16 A full explication of the metaphysics underlying Montessori's claims here would take us too far afield, but the notion of life is a central metaphysical category for Montessori, one that she sought to articulate in various different ways over the course of her life. For more details, see Frierson 2018.
17 For a more metaphysically loaded conception of life and its normative importance, see Evan Thompson 2007. On his account, "life" is not an irreducible category with normative implications but an isolation of certain kinds of systems in the world—those with what he calls an "autopoeitic" structure—where autopoiesis itself involves "the two-fold purposes of identity (self-production) and sense-making (adaptivity and cognition)" (Thompson 2007: 153). For Evan Thompson, as for Michael Thompson and Philippa Foot, "vital structures have to be comprehended in relation to norms" (Thompson 2007: 74) according to which they seek to conform to "optimal conditions of activity" (Thompson 2007: 147, quoting Merleau-Ponty 1962: 148).
18 The naturalist and relatively metaphysically thin reading of teleology in this section might seem to be at odds with other of Montessori's writings that suggest a more theologically loaded metaphysics of morals. While her moral sense theory is *compatible* with theological accounts of moral values, it does not require any such account. Even where she appeals to the importance of religion for moral life (e.g., Montessori [1929] 2000: 14–15) or promotes what might seem to be a divine command theory of morals (Montessori [1929] 2000: 14; 7: 93–7; 10: 27), the function of her invocation of God is to shift attention from one's own sense of what is right for the child to *what children themselves reveal*. Thus "To discover the laws of the child's development would be the same thing as to discover the Spirit and Wisdom of God operating in the child" (Montessori [1929] 2000: 14). The point is not that one should look to any specifically religious source for ethics. Rather, the appeal to "God" should orient us toward children. Montessori likely did ascribe a theological origin and focus to the moral sense, but such a focus is not essential to her moral epistemology or pedagogy as such.
19 Though cf. Varela, Thompson, and Rosch 1991; Noë 2004.

Chapter 3

1 Because Montessori sees development as cultivating abilities and interests together, there are no capacities that are not also tendencies. If one never acts in some way, then there is a reason one does not. If that reason is internal, then one does not fully have the capacity since one lacks its motivational component. If external, one has both the capacity and a thwarted tendency (but see Frierson 2016b and Nussbaum 2000: 84–5). Put another way, part of being able to do X is being able to motivate oneself to do X in appropriate circumstances, which is nothing other than actually motivating oneself in those circumstances.
2 According to Schapiro's reconstruction, the romantic view posits that "our passions direct us towards what is truly good for us [and] are determinative of our 'true selves'" (Schapiro 2021: 13–14). Arguably, the rejection of this romantic view of *agency* arises from the rejection of an equally "romantic" view of children. Montessori's

elevated sense of children's dignity brings with it a view about the dignity of non-reflective agency; Schapiro's rejection of the former brings a rejection of the latter.

3   The attitude that sees proper relations with children as fundamentally paternalistic is prevalent not only among philosophers who work on paternalism (e.g., Dworkin 1972: 76f.) and childhood (e.g., Brighouse 2002, 2003), but also in contemporary discussions of agency (e.g., Frankfurt 2006: 6; Velleman 2000: 104). Even beyond those who explicitly appeal to the need to legitimate paternalism as a partial basis for their accounts of agency, most moral philosophers, who are adults, reason about agency in ways that take the kind of agency that adults (mostly) have and children (mostly) lack as paradigmatic of agency worth respecting.

4   Often Schapiro identifies these alien forces with one's "inner animal" where one is "governed purely by instinct" (Schapiro 1999: 730–1; cf. 2021: 85–116). The notion that identification is essential to agency is pervasive in contemporary philosophy. See, for example, Frankfurt 1988: 58–68; Jaworska 2007.

5   Recently, Schapiro has taken activity and passivity to be better than identification for distinguishing full-blown agency from mere impulse: in "having an inclination…, you identify with [your condition] as being in some sense your response to your situation … But it is also a condition in which you are distinctively passive in relation to that activity" (2021: 128–9).

6   See Bratman 1987 and 2007: 28ff; Korsgaard 1996a: 60–3; and 2009: 75–6; but cf. Schapiro 2012: 349.

7   Throughout, while I reject a certain sort of reflection, reason, deliberation, and persistence, I continue to affirm more modest variations of these meta-cognitive capacities, and in particular, forms of them that can be present in even the youngest children. Even the newborn infant trying to get a good latch on his mother's nipple must reflect on what is working and what is not as he manipulates the muscles in his mouth and tongue.

8   On Montessori education and flow, see Rathunde and Csikszentmihalyi 2005a, b; Shernoff and Csikszentmihalyi 2009.

9   In §8, I also show how flow also meets agential standards for persistence; here Montessori describes agency's temporal locus better than Csikszentmihalyi, who occasionally overstates how much flow requires one to "find rewards in the events of each moment" (1990: 19).

10 I'm leaving aside (for now) Montessori's appeal to the good of humanity served by these geniuses. I discuss the importance of striving for the perfection of the human species in §9.

11 Some of Montessori's points about agency apply to more mundane sorts of choice and decision than those involved in attentive work, but taking attentive work as a paradigm highlights general features of agency that are evident throughout ordinary life. For example, Montessori explains that most decisions in everyday life, like most decisions within flow states and attentive work, are unreflective, but they involve the same sort of agency that arises reflectively in more complex cases:

> Now a *decision* is always the result of a *choice*. If we have several hats, we must decide which one we will put on when we go out; it may not in the least matter whether it be the brown hat or the gray, but we must choose one of them. For such a choice we must have our motives, whether they be in favor of the gray or the brown; but finally one of the motives will prevail and the choice will be made. Obviously, the habit of taking a hat and going out will facilitate our choice; we are almost unconscious which of the motives stirred and struggled

within us. It is the question of a minute and leaves no impression of effort. Our knowledge as to which hat will be suitable for the morning or the afternoon, for the theater or for sport, saves us from any mental conflict. But this will not be the case if, for instance, we are about to spend a certain sum of money on a present. What shall we buy among the various objects from which it will be possible to choose? If we have no very definite knowledge of the things, our task may become an anxiety.

(9: 134–5)

12 See especially Frankfurt 1998: 159–76. Several philosophers recently have also developed accounts of internality tied to love or care. Frankfurt describes "reasons of love" as reason with which we fully identify (Frankfurt 2004, 2006) and Agnieszka Jaworska convincingly argues that "carings are inherently internal" and "cannot be legitimately construed as an alien force, or as a mere occurrence within the agent's psychological makeup that does not belong to him" (Jaworska 2007: 532, 531; see too Frankfurt 2004, 2006; Seidman 2009). For criticism of wholeheartedness and also love or care as sufficient for respect-worthy agency, see Velleman 2006: 330–60. I discuss Montessori's views on love in Chapter 9.

13 The point here is not merely about persistence. It is also important to distinguish the sort of attention that arises from coercion—one might, after all, force a child to repeat an exercise forty-four times—and that which arises from the child's own interest, as with Sofia's self-directed repetition of the cylinder blocks work.

14 See too Montessori 1924, where she explains the importance of moral judgment for distinguishing true agency from mere impulses:

> If the teacher cannot distinguish mere impulse from the spontaneous energy which wells up from a spirit at rest, her actions will bear no fruit. The very foundation of the teacher's efficiency consists in the power of distinguishing between these two kinds of activity, both of which appear to be spontaneous, because the child in both cases acts of its own accord, but which have an entirely opposite significance.
>
> It is only when she has acquired this power of discrimination that a teacher can become an observer and guide. The necessary preparation is similar to that of a doctor of medicine: he must first of all learn to distinguish physiological from pathological facts. If he is not capable of distinguishing between health and disease—if all he can do is to distinguish a live man from a dead man—he will not be able to arrive at the fine and ever finer distinctions between pathological phenomena; it will be impossible for him to diagnose disease correctly.
>
> This power of distinguishing between the good and the bad is the lantern we must carry in hand to lighten us upon the obscure road of the discipline that leads to perfection.

(1924: 185)

15 As we will see in Chapter 4, this fact about agency has important implication for respect.

16 Two points are worth briefly adding in this context. First, while attentive work is Montessori's paradigm of agency, she does allow that habitual responses or sudden responses to new situations can express agency, particularly when those habits—or a capacity for rapid choice in general—are products of the cultivation of will that takes place through attentive work. As people become more adept at choosing their

own path in conditions conducive to agency, they are able to respond to sudden situations without deliberation but also without mere reactivity. Second, for those with well-formed wills adept at making choices for themselves throughout everyday life without reflective deliberation, emergency situations can actually be occasions for deliberation rather than contexts for bracketing deliberation. In cases where something unexpected happens that breaks down one's normal and unreflective decision-making process, one might fall back on mere reactive instinct, or one might be forced into deliberation about what to do, and in both cases, one might in retrospect find that one does not identify with the choice made in the circumstances. (For more on failure to identify with deliberation, see Chapter 6).

17 Note that Schapiro's view is nuanced in that "cultivating our inclinations is a way of cultivating your active self" because "cultivation of our inclinations involves a kind of learning and growth that we can attribute to ourselves as a matter of character" (2021: 54).

18 My addition. My point in the succeeding discussion is that these considerations can be seen as effects of agency if agency is more broadly defined.

19 I discuss related points in more detail in Chapter 6.

20 Though Wallace shares an emphasis on "rational" agency and "reflective verdicts" and a commitment to "reflexivity" in a strong sense (Wallace 2006: 83, 191), he also rightly points out that much of the relevant reflection remains focused on normative details of one's situation rather than directly reflecting on one's desires themselves. That is, one considers whether such and such (proposed by desire) is a good thing to do, rather than whether such and such a desire is a good one to act on. As with most theorists, he focuses on the issue of whether one will follow through on a course of action proposed by a desire rather than *how* to follow through on that desire, and in that sense his approach does not map well onto the child who is attracted to cylinder blocks and focuses on how to do them well (or to the adult who comes up with an objection to a paper they are reading and is focused on how best to explain and defend it). Particularly once we acknowledge that even the sorts of reflections that Wallace takes as paradigmatic ultimately rest in proposals (such as that we should do what's entertaining) that are merely taken (for the time) as given, we can rightly see the child's agency expressed in her concern with norms internal to an activity chosen on the basis of her attraction to it as something she desires to do well, rather than requiring that she *also* reflect on whether the activity itself is something that is worth doing.

21 At least, no part of the "will" traditionally conceived. Montessori develops an embodied conception of volition such that our bodily capacities are partly constitutive of rather than mere instruments of our volition; in *that* sense, working against tendencies of the muscles involves a conflict of will (see, e.g., 1: 121–6, 201–3; 9: 137–41; 15: 174).

22 Note that there can be a highly self-conscious version of such "paying attention," one that requires taking oneself as an object and attending to oneself, but there is also—as in Sofia's work on her cylinder blocks—a close attention to error that focuses on the task at hand and how to do it better.

23 There are differences. MacIntyre's concept of a "practice" requires that it be "cooperative," and his conception of how "human powers to achieve excellence ... are systematically extended" is social rather than individual, excluding practices like tracing sandpaper letters, putting cylinders in holes, or scrubbing chairs that merely allow individuals to extend their powers.

24 Cf. Wallace 2006: 190–211, which argues that this problem arises due to Frankfurt's crude hierarchical model. My point here is that it also arises for deliberation.

25   He doesn't see reflectiveness as essential for "agency," however (see Bratman 2018: 210).
26   For example, beyond obvious differences in each's particular activities, Bratman's takes longer than Sofia's, focuses less on repetition, and can involve reflectively seeing himself as a temporally extended agent.
27   As I note below, Montessori's critique ultimately applies to even more modest time-horizons such as Bratman's or Sayre-McCord and Smith's. Her point is that the temporal *extension* of one's commitment, as long as it has some such extension, is less important than its agential *intensity*. Jaworska (1999) develops similar points in her broadly Kantian accounts of Alzheimer's patients' agency.
28   Importantly, even when she talks about character, Montessori focuses on the character that is present in children in respectful environments. Not only minimal agency, then, but even character itself, can be present without developed capacities for reflective deliberation. Such capacities further contribute to the development of agency, but not in ways that are essential for individuals to meet its basic constitutive standards. Reflective deliberation is akin to the home office addition to a house, which makes it suitable for new purposes and even—in a sense—better as a house, but not better in a way that implies that houses without home offices are deficient as the sorts of houses that they are. Moreover, as noted in §1, the basic elements of character are already present from infancy, rather than acquisitions through self-cultivation.
29   "Independence" is independent *adaptation* to the world, not a *radical* independence by which one seeks complete self-sufficiency. Human beings live in a constructed world that facilitates agency and in a social world where expressions of agency depend upon properly interacting with others. Thus, for example, adolescent "independence" requires "earn[ing] a livelihood through work" (10: 105; cf. 12: 61), where one is "independent" in that through one's own effort—albeit in the context of a constructed environment and mechanisms of exchange—one satisfies one's needs. Likewise, Admiral Byrd depended upon wealthy philanthropists and the support of his crew and teammates for his polar expedition, but he raised support in the spirit of asking others to "help me to do it by myself" (22: 175).
30   While pursuing a degree in philosophy at the University of Rome, Montessori studied the philosophy of education with Luigi Credaro, a translator of and expert in the philosophy of J. F. Herbart. While I have not found direct evidence that Montessori read Herbart's works, her involvement with Credaro ensures that she was exposed to his ideas.
31   To some extent, Montessori sees conduciveness to perfection as connected with attentive work for purely empirical reasons; the activities she found to attract children were those that promoted their perfection. Within her metaphysics, moreover, the tendency—even unconscious—toward perfection is also a general feature of life.
32   For discussion of Nietzsche's influence on Montessori, see Simons 1988.
33   This does, to some degree, constrain possible good lives—Montessori rejects the notion that human beings are "here only to enjoy" (17: 91)—but it does not specify any *particular* work upon which an individual must direct his concentration.
34   Montessori also periodically points out that there are cultural differences that affect the paths individuals take. The notion of progress varies from person to person and also from culture to culture. Admiral Byrd went to the South Pole because this kind of striving for perfection was comprehensible as a form of progress given his historical-

cultural context. Character-driven writers, dancers, explorers, or scientists all work within histories of exemplars and seek to add to that repertoire of excellence, starting with the effort to do excellently what has already been and rising to the desire to do something new and recognizably more perfect from within existing norms of their "circle of perfection." This open-endedness contributes to legitimate moral pluralism even in the context of the "absolute" value of character as such (cf. Chapter 2, §2).

35 Nietzsche hints at this understanding when he suggests that each of us has a "fundamental law of our true self" (Nietzsche 1997: 129) or that our "conscience" says "You should become who you are" (Nietzsche [1882] 2001: 152; cf. Franco 2018).

36 Elsewhere Montessori deepens the justification for applying this approach to adult civilization, noting that the shift in focus from criminal punishment to social welfare is justified whether one draws from "the Catholic dogma of the communion of sinners" or the point "in sociology [that] we are all guilty of the social causes of [moral] degeneration [and so] we all have a duty to contribute to improving the environment that brings about [moral] degenerates" (Montessori 1903: 330).

37 As I will explain in more detail in Chapter 6, deliberation itself should be an activity in which each of us engages as something that expresses and enhances our agency, an activity that has internal norm and that we should seek to do well.

Chapter 4

1   But cf. Swanton 2011.
2   Compare, in this context, Rawls 1971: 325 with Conant 2010.
3   I put "private" in quotation marks here partly to indicate that these realms might not be private in the strict sense. Playing soccer is "private" in the relevant sense (in that I may not want to defend my choice to play soccer in a public realm, and I may not even want to deliberate about it), but it's a private activity that I can only do with others.
4   Montessori points out that even adults who freely interrupt children generally perceive the wrongness of this activity but repress that recognition: "How often at the bottom of our hearts we have felt that we have been unjust, but have stifled this impression" (9: 223).
5   For philosophers like Kant, who see human nature as radically evil (see Formosa 2018; Wood 1999), and for those with strong doctrines of original sin, this empirical claim about effects of character might seem "romantic," mere wishful thinking, or even heresy. For discussion of the doctrine of original sin in Montessori, see De Giorgi 2019. For empirical evidence in support of Montessori's claims, see Lillard 2007.
6   Nietzsche's "republic of genius" (Nietzsche 1997: 111) arguably involves a similar sort of mutual respect, albeit with a narrower scope of application.
7   Recall Chapter 3, §9.
8   Because Kant's moral theory includes the importance of promoting others' happiness, some of Montessori's objections to his way of understanding happiness apply to utilitarianism as well.
9   There are Kantian and utilitarian ways of arriving at the same conclusion that Montessori arrives at in this case. We might note, as Montessori does, that the child experienced less joy as a result of being lifted up and so—with utilitarians—make a

case for allowing him to expend effort for the sake of maximizing overall happiness. We might also—with Kantians—claim that the teacher failed to respect the child's capacity to set his own ends by misunderstanding his end as "seeing the spectacle" rather than accomplishing the task for himself. Both explanations miss Montessori's fundamental point. Against utilitarians, her point is that the relevant "joy" is not mere happiness but a specific affective appreciation of the fact that humans are not made for happiness but for the expression of agency in effortful activity. Against Kantians, the point is that it is not the mere capacity to choose one thing rather than another that expresses agency, but the choice to *engage in work*, so that even if the child were to see his end as "to see the spectacle," respecting *that* end would often fail to respect his *agency*.

10 For an important application of this general principle of discounting reflectively endorsed policies for the sake of direct expressions of agency, see Jaworska 1999, which discusses the case of Alzheimer's patients.

11 See, e.g., Korsgaard 1996b: 123 for defense of this view. Dean 2006: 35–42 argues that only the good will warrants recognition respect. For my discussion of Dean, see Frierson 2007.

12 In the context of this essay, which is a discussion of Lombroso, Montessori concedes that there may be essential biological differences between human beings. Her point is neither to defend nor to deny such differences, but to shift focus from diagnosis of essential difference toward education as the means for development of all people, whether "normal" or "deficient" (Montessori 1903: 331).

13 Relatedly, children offer help when another does not know the proper way to do something, a sort of help often condemned under contemporary, exam-oriented pedagogical regimes: "When in an examination the children, seated side by side, have there and then to give a sample of what they have learnt ... if then one child helps another, he is [seen as] not merely naughty, but wicked, for he has not only displayed activity, but activity for the benefit of another" (9: 227).

Chapter 5

1 In this way, children come to respect and respond to one another not only directly out of recognition of the value of one another but also to "express and constitute [their] first-person plural commitment to the import of the community" (Helm 2017: 225). Helm lays out a rich account of communities of respect that helps show how commitment to "communities of respect" (Helm 2017) supports and deepens mere interpersonal respect.

2 At least, part of the fascination of the Silence Game is its social dimension. Montessori does affirm that silence itself is fascinating (7: 51).

3 As psychologists Ryan and Deci note, "autonomy refers not to being independent, detached, or selfish but rather to the feeling of volition that can accompany any act, whether dependent or independent, collectivist or individualist" (Ryan and Deci 2000: 74).

4 For psychological research supporting this "self-expansion" theory of social relationships, see, e.g., Aron and Aron 1986.

5 In a different way, Sellars (1974) is another singularist, in that "we-intentions" are always intentions *of* individuals.

6 This discussion of solidarity leaves many metaphysical issues about group agency unaddressed. For discussion of some of these issues, see Gilbert 2013; Huebner 2014; List and Pettit 2011. Montessori's metaphysics, within which lower-order forces are organized into complex wholes that come to have new properties (governed by new forces), provides the general framework for her ultimate metaphysical account of solidarity (see Frierson 2018).
7 Here I bracket the possible role of obedience in getting people who lack character to concentrate and thereby develop character.
8 See too Linda Zagzebski's discussion of intellectual autonomy: "autonomy is not epistemic self-reliance" (Zagzebski 2012: 236).

Chapter 6

1 Except when I specifically discuss obedience, I hereafter use "solidarity" to include both typical social solidarity among peers and the sort of solidarity that takes place when one obeys another.
2 Young children also have capacities that adults lack, so there are aspects of ethical life that are richer in childhood than in adulthood. Most notably, children's activities have a much greater influence on their lasting tendencies and dispositions than adults' activities. When children express their characters, they thereby form those characters. When adults express their characters, they largely play out a script written by their childhood selves. Montessori highlights this difference with her frequent invocation of Wordsworth's line, "the child is ... the father of the man" (22: 26). For discussion of the different tasks of adults and children, see Frierson 2016b: 343–7.
3 Montessori occasionally claims that "this power [of abstraction] is within the child when he is born" (24: 190), and all children have at least the rudiments of abstraction in their capacities to isolate features of objects for attention, but she sees later childhood (starting around age 7) as the period within which abstraction matures.
4 Monetary acquisition and use, contracts, mutual promises, and friendships provide cases where respect for preferences is required in order to respect active work.
5 Montessori here is specifically discussing the Boy Scouts, but her observations apply to any society with determinate rules of behavior for its members.
6 There are two further features often associated with deliberation on which I do not focus in this section. First, deliberation is often described in terms of responsiveness to "reasons" (e.g., Arpaly and Schroeder 2014: 19). I do not focus on this feature of deliberation here because it is not unique to reflective deliberation. Children engaged in norm-governed activities regularly respond to reasons; such reasons-responsiveness is part of what it means to be normatively self-governed. Second, many philosophers see deliberation as essentially responsive to Reason, that is, to considerations that have an abstract, universal, or principled form. I might feel like watching television but choose to prepare for the class I must teach tomorrow because of a generalized commitment to fulfill my responsibilities to others, or a desire to feel more expert and confident, or a specific sense of my practical identity as a teacher, or in order to conform to a particular moral (or prudential) rule. In discussions of deliberation, it is not always clear how explicit these abstractions must be; Schapiro, for instance, allows guiding conceptions to be "inchoate and unarticulated" (Schapiro 2021: 22). But Schapiro, Korsgaard, and others often

see deliberation as structured by concerns of a general kind, rooted in Reason, in contrast to the responsiveness that Sofia has to the norms literally built into the apparatus with which she is engaged. This Reason-responsiveness, especially insofar as it is more explicit, does distinguish some deliberative adult expressions of agency from the agency of very young children, but it does so in ways already discussed in §1.2, so I do not specifically focus on it in this section.

7   Schapiro makes explicit her view that infants cannot experience the moment of drama and that in children it is at most only developing (2021: 10fn).

8   That said, there is also a *loss* of internality, in that reflection sets me apart from my first-order desire. This is the sense in which adults in flow feel more in control of themselves when they have less second-order reflection. There are costs and benefits to reflective deliberation; in this subsection, I focus on the benefits. Chapter 3, and subsection 2.1.3 below, focus on the costs.

9   Because all character-driven activities aim not only at completion of a particular task but also at self-perfection, no such activity is ever fully completed. For that reason, Sofia continues removing and replacing cylinders more than forty-four times, and violinists practicing a particularly challenging piece will repeat key sections over and over. The relevant "completion" here refers to the fact that one has finished engaging in the task as much as is necessary and/or possible at the time.

10 As we will see in Chapter 8, there is a sense in which Sofia does share solidarity with friends and light candles for the sake of friendship or Catholicism, insofar as these commitments are partly constituted by unreflective desires and bodily comportments, but she does not self-consciously act for the sake of such abstract commitments.

11 As I will argue in §2.1.4, if deliberative agency is an expression of healthy character, we will come to feel like acting on values when we endorse our commitment to those values in deliberation. My point here is that we need not antecedently have an occurrent, felt commitment to a value in order to come to endorse it through reflection.

12 In young children, extrinsic motivation undermines agency because it involves manipulating the child's behavior by an external force with which they cannot identify. Older children and adults, however, can recognize an influence as external and nonetheless, by virtue of reflection, integrate it into an overall plan or project to which they commit themselves. Cf. Ryan and Deci 2000, 2017 on integrated autonomy.

13 Thus Bratman, for example, observes that for both individual and group agents,

> a planning agent will have a web of plans that settle ... on certain projects, as well as on certain consideration that are to matter in the pursuit of those projects. These plans will normally cross-refer to each other: one's plan for today will typically involve a reference to one's earlier and later plans; and vice versa. These issue-settling cross-referring plans will frame much of one's practical thought and action over time. They will pose problems about how to fill in so-far partials plans with sub-plans about means and the like sub-plans that mesh with each other. And they will filter options that are potential solutions to those problems.
>
> (Bratman 2018: 212)

While I argued in Chapters 3 and 5 that these sorts of reflective higher-order plans are not necessary for agency or social solidarity as such, Bratman's description captures several of the ways in which deliberative planning facilitates forms of agency that are not possible without it.

14   One might make comparable claims about responsibility, that deliberation is neither necessary nor sufficient for responsibility. I highlighted these points briefly in Chapter 3 (§10). Here I note only that my considerations about the necessary non-deliberative components of deliberation suggest ways we must hold people responsible for non-deliberative attitudes, and also ways deliberation might be insufficient for responsibility. For example, if someone literally fails to consider implications of a particular decision for my welfare, I might hold them responsible for that failure, even though they did not deliberately decide not to consider these implications. If that same person does consider implications that I think warrant less consideration, I might blame them even more. But if it turns out that the deliberator's whole train of deliberation was a thoughtless rehearsal of arguments to which they have been subjected by overbearing caregivers or authorities, I would blame them less.

15   At the same time, reflection can generate higher-order pleasures in activities, such that one enjoys not merely spending time with another person but also the ways that spending time with them contributes to the development of oneself, the other, and the relationship. One can even enjoy an activity *more* by virtue of having chosen to participate in that activity through careful deliberation. The point of this section is not that deliberation contributes nothing to ethical life, but rather that non-deliberative agency is necessary.

16   This emphasis on pre-deliberative agency in response to situations calling for rapid responses has some affinity with recent discussions of Type-1 and Type-2 processes within contemporary dual-systems models of reasoning, though Montessori's pre-deliberative agency cannot be precisely mapped onto most accounts of Type-1 processes. See Frankish 2010 for an overview of recent dual-process and dual-systems theories.

17   Note that Montessori's example (rightly) does not focus on merely habitual activities. When one acts merely from habit, one does not deliberate, but one also does not—insofar as one's action is *merely* habitual—choose. A life of purely habitual behavior can even prime one for (fruitless) reflective deliberation. Csikszentmihalyi highlights this phenomenon as an inhibition to the genuine agency that comes from flow:

> Because many jobs, for instance, consist of repetitive actions that require little concentration, the attention of a worker is likely to begin to wander. In this state of split attention the worker begins to wish for more satisfying things to do, or begins to ruminate on unpleasant subjects. In either case the situation in which he is involved is devalued, and the person experiences boredom or frustration. In comparison with this all-too-frequent condition, the total involvement of flow is experienced as rewarding.
>
> (Csikszentmihalyi 1993: 190)

Montessori's "mother of a family" is constantly at work making decisions that require only first-order deliberation, consideration of what to do and not of whether her inclinations are worth acting on. Her agency remains engaged, in contrast to the factory worker whose actions are so habitual that they call for no exercise of will.

18   In some cases, we see no reason to call them into question, and in other cases, the relevant reason just has no standing relative to our desire. The discomfort in Sofia's third finger as she manipulated the cylinders did not give her a reason to stop; moving through this discomfort was part of what made the task challenging for her. Marathon runners often must talk themselves into continuing, but these reflective conversations occur far past the point at which they have inclinations to stop; prior to that point, contrary inclinations are inhibited without deliberation or reflection.

19 This is not to deny that such reflection might sometimes be called for. I might actually not be able to spend so much time in conversation at this time, or I might come to suspect that the conversation is actually harming our friendship for some reason, or that the friendship is dysfunctional, or some other such consideration. My point is not that reflection can't ever be agency-enhancing, but that it is not *always* agency-enhancing.

Note too that even in cases when one might seem to deliberate, often "reflection" occurs only *after* one decides without reflection, and sometimes such reflections are really post hoc confabulations, just-so stories about what one's motives for X or Y must have been. Montessori emphasizes, with respect to young children, that they often do not actually know the reasons that they are engaged in work of one kind or another (see 7: 4–5). There is good evidence that adults, too, make choices with which they identify and only later develop rationalizations for those decisions (see Haidt 2001), a point already emphasized by J. F. Herbart, with whose psychology Montessori was familiar:

> The ordinary and natural phenomenon—that men invent the maxims for their inclinations afterwards, in order to enjoy the convenience of an inward prescriptive right to do as they like—must direct education to devote its chief attention to the [pre-reflective] part of character, which forms and raises itself slowly enough under its observation and influence. If this first is in order, results may then be hoped for from the regulating power of good moral teaching.
> (Herbart 1908: 202)

20 Gavin Victor helpfully pointed me to a related point made by Alan Watts: "A person who thinks all the time has nothing to think about except thoughts" (Watts 2018).
21 One might make an analogy here between provisional property rights and property rights established by a rightful authority (see Kant 1996: 409–10).
22 Granted, some cases of deliberation might be the consequences of other deliberative processes, so I might decide after deliberation that I should spend time deliberating before making this or that further choice. Deliberation cannot *in general* begin with deliberate choice, however, on pain of an infinite regress.
23 My addition. My point in the succeeding discussion is that these considerations can be seen as effects of agency if agency is more broadly defined.
24 Those who have seen the sitcom *The Good Place* (2016–2020) will be familiar with this mania of doubt in the person of Chidi, the Kantian moral philosopher who can never conclude deliberation. The classic example of Buridan's ass illustrates a similar problem.
25 Again, consider Chidi (*The Good Place* 2016–2020).
26 The specific example she gives in this text, which she calls "perhaps the most essential, is the rule that that we should never stop reflecting until we have reached a satisfactory answer, one that admits of no further questioning" (Korsgaard 1996a: 258). Since there is always further possible questioning, this cannot be a constitutive rule of reflection, or if it is such a rule, it shows why we cannot be excellent agents unless we cut short the work of reflection in order to do more important work.
27 Properly speaking, it is unlikely that any child would put aside an immediate inclination toward cylinder blocks in order to research horses because by the time a child would be researching horses, she would be too old for strong inclinations toward cylinder blocks in particular. The broader point, though, is that whatever work happens to most immediately attract an eight-year-old Sofia at a given time could be set aside for the sake of work in which she is more interested overall.

28 Korsgaard (1996a and 2009) does an excellent job of explaining the importance of this sort of respect for morally mature human beings.
29 See Tsai 2014.
30 For the same reason, if she does not solicit advice, giving advice can actually be disrespectful, since she needs to carry out this activity for herself, learning—in part through error—how to be a good, self-sufficient, consumer. Cf. Tsai 2014.
31 This prima facie clause makes room for the second consideration.
32 Cf. List and Pettit 2011: 191–3, who note that organized unities can and should give rise to a we-consciousness but don't attend to how such a possibility builds on early childhood experiences of solidarity.

Chapter 7

1 It is worth pointing out, and Montessori does point out, that the apparent asymmetry between the daughter and the wife is particularly stark *today* because we no longer approve of paternalism toward women, but there was a time when a husband was perfectly within his "rights" to force his wife to wear whatever he chose for her. As an ardent feminist, Montessori regularly notes parallels in rhetoric used to oppress children and that used to oppress women:

> Some time ago a very important question arose—that of the role of women in society. The same kinds of things were said at that time about women as are now being said about children and their role in society. In those days, too, it seemed absurd to speak of women as forgotten human beings. "We've neglected women, you say? How can that be, when we do everything possible for them, when we love them so much, when we protect them and are ready to die for them, when we work all our lives for them?" Nonetheless there was still such a thing as the question of woman's place in society. And there is such a thing as the question of the child's place in society.
>
> (10: 45)

Montessori also regularly compares the struggle for children's rights with struggles for the rights of workers (e.g., 7: 81; 22: 187–8).
  Similarly, after a poignant story highlighting the double-standard applied to adults and children, bell hooks rightly points out how even where "most call themselves good liberals, supportive of civil rights and feminism ... when it came to the rights of children, they had a different standard" (hooks 2000: 21).

2 It might turn out that interference is more justified for children (or for adults) for contingent reasons related to how well individuals reason (e.g., about means to their ends), but this would not imply a principled difference in the prima facie legitimacy of paternalism.

3 To these three arguments Mill adds a fourth: given humans' imperfect knowledge about what is conducive to well-being, "it is useful that ... there should be different experiments of living ... and that the worth of different modes of life should be proved practically" ([1859] 1989: 57). I do not discuss this fourth argument here.

4 Strikingly, and quite relevant to the present chapter, Mill immediately adds,

> For the same reason, we may leave out of consideration those backward states of society in which the race itself may be considered as in its nonage. The early

difficulties in the way of spontaneous progress are so great, that there is seldom any choice of means for overcoming them; and a ruler full of the spirit of improvement is warranted in the use of any expedients that will attain an end, perhaps otherwise unattainable. Despotism is a legitimate mode of government in dealing with barbarians, provided the end be their improvement, and the means justified by actually effecting that end.

([1859] 1989: 13-14)

We now (mostly) look back on these once common-sense racist defenses of colonialism as utterly unjustifiable. In the future, we may see affirmations of paternalistic treatment of children in the same way.

5   Note that this unconscious appreciation of the value of our activities applies even to reflection and the "love of freedom" itself. We value reflectively endorsed choices, deliberation, and liberty from interference, but we generally value these goods not as a consequence of careful reflection upon the value of deliberation, but from an unconscious and nonetheless veridical sense of its value.

6   Another reason the constitutive value of liberty does not unconditionally prohibit paternalism is that even if liberty is *one* constitutive part of well-being, it might not be the *only* constitutive part, so one might justify paternalism on the grounds that one sacrifices a little of one part of well-being (liberty) for the sake of other constitutive elements. In that case, the father might sacrifice the daughter's liberty for the sake of her well-rested-ness, or her overall health. Again, however, this allowance for paternalism would not introduce a distinction between adults and children; if a certain facilitation of health outweighs a certain restriction on liberty, there is no reason in principle that this should apply to the daughter and not also to the wife.

7   Including Schapiro 1999, 2003; Korsgaard 1996a, 2009; and Wood 1999; though contrast Dean 2006.

8   At least, one may not infringe on others' choices as long as those choices do not infringe on the authority of others to make choices. The details of Kant's account of the legitimate uses of coercion in his *Metaphysics of Morals*, while directly relevant to Kantian accounts of paternalism, are beyond the scope of the present chapter. See Ripstein 2009 for discussion.

9   See Chapter 6.

10 In footnote 14, I return to the words elided by ellipses here: "who shapes all of mankind."

11 These arguments are typically focused on duties to animals. My point here is that whatever we want to say about animals, Montessori's claims about children are different than Korsgaard's claims about animals. (In fact, I think that the account of respect here could have important implications for thinking about animal rights, but that's a topic for a different book.)

12 And perhaps animals; see previous note.

13 I have reproduced the Montessori-Pierson translation of this passage. The present sentence, in the Italian original, reads, "E dopo tutto questo ci contentiamo d'insegnargli che «volere è potere»." The expression *volere è potere* literally means "willing is power" but roughly corresponds to the English saying, "where there's a will, there's a way." The translators chose to parenthetically include the Italian expression and translate it as "to will is to do."

14 A further Montessorian argument against paternalism could be seen as an extension of the developmental argument. For Montessori, children not only work to build up the adult that they will become; they are also the means by which humanity as a whole rises to higher levels. Consistent with the basic respect for children explicit in Montessori's

moral sense epistemology, she insists that respecting the inner dignity of the child is the means for psychological, social, and moral progress in humanity as a whole:

> Rights of the child! Rights in one sense is a bad word. It appears that the rights of the child might be considered as something that is for the child's good. But it is something far greater than that, it is as it were the rights of the soul of humanity, the rights of the greatness and possibility of man to live, a cry that the spirit of man shall be given the possibility to develop to heights such as have already been reached on the material side.
>
> (7: 100; see too 22: 187–8)

Thus, "his rights as a human being *who shapes all of mankind* must become sacred" (10: 34, emphasis added). Not only does the child's agency form his own character, but it allows for human progress as a whole.

15 A commonplace strategy in defenses of paternalism involves showing that any arguments against paternalism would also preclude these sorts of non-paternalistic interference (see, e.g., Conly 2012; Hanna 2018), but paternalists from Kant and Mill to the present develop arguments for why interference with agency for the sake of, say, preventing harm to third parties is permissible and, in some cases, even required. For the purposes of this chapter, I take for granted that some such argument works.

16 Even in these cases, as I discuss in §4, Montessori endorses methods for preventing such interference that do not compromise children's agency.

17 I deliberately refrain from saying that it *justifies* such intervention. In fact, many of the cases I will discuss are ones where Montessori emphasizes that parents tend to overindulge themselves at the expense of their children. Thus what I refer to as the parents' exertion of property rights is described, by Montessori, as parents' tendency to let their own "instinct of defense" and even "of avarice" overtake their children's rights to free exercise of agency (22: 18). Montessori sometimes goes too far in her condemnation of parents, but her insights into the real bases of parental control are both accurate and convicting for many particular cases.

18 There are at least two different ways in which choices can be "part of" attentive work. First, in order to constitute agency, attentive work must be *chosen* work. A child forced to work on the cylinder blocks does not express her agency in that work (unless or until the "force" ceases to be a reason for her to work on the blocks). Second, attentive work *consists in* making and executing choices. The child must choose which block to pick up, where to place it, and so on. Both sorts of choices are, for Montessori, expressions of agency. (They are also necessarily connected, in that the choice of work is only agential insofar as it is a choice of an activity that involves norm-governed choices, and those norm-governed choices are only agential insofar as they are part of a work that one has chosen.)

19 Note that even when children are choosing in ways that do not express agency, intervention can and should aim toward facilitating rather than displacing agency. In an important defense of intervention with the non-agential choices of children, Montessori writes,

> A child who wants to grasp everything senselessly, without aim, becomes an active danger. Therefore, the adult represses the child. We must understand that in stopping this kind of senseless action, the adult does well for the child. After all, why should the child prolong in this fashion what can only be called a mistaken life? Unfortunately, what happens is that the disorderly movement

of the child is [replaced] by the will of the adult, and the movement of the child obeys the will of the adult. Meanwhile, what happens to the child's mind?
(24: 113)

On the one hand, when children "want ... senselessly," they are not expressing agency, and thus can and should be "stop[ped]." Often in such cases, however, adults stop the children in ways that preserve the status of the child as passive, as someone who will either passively submit to this or that whim or passively submit to the direction of the adult. Instead, Montessori suggests, we can and should invite the children to activities in which they express agency. In a related passage elsewhere, she notes that even when children fall short of perfect agency by insufficiently directing their attention to the normative demands of their work, "correction can and must be given, but never during the activity. First the teacher must respect the cycle of activity and observe the child at work. Afterwards, the errors observed must be made the center of a new lesson. Therefore, to eliminate an error a lesson is given, not at the moment of activity, but later" (24: 199). Rather than interrupting the budding agency of the child, adults should allow the child to be as agential as possible and then offer further opportunities, later, for fuller expressions of agency.

20 Sometimes, a child may choose pajamas because they provide an opportunity for attentive work. The obstinate daughter, for instance, might select the short-sleeved pajamas because these are the only ones that she can (yet) put on by herself. In that case, her agency is genuinely at stake, and parents should respect that expression of agency. In such cases, children are also particularly receptive to the right kinds of direction toward better options. If the father waits until his daughter has worked on and succeeded at wearing the inappropriate pajamas and then invites her to put the longer ones on top of them, or challenges her with trying to put on the longer ones instead, a child normalized by the free exercise of attentive work will almost universally welcome such encouragements.

21 As Jaworska 1999 has shown, Odysseus-style cases cannot be straightforwardly generalized.

22 In modern consumer culture, adults' abilities to act on arbitrary preferences are part of their overall "work," such that undermining these choices would be akin to, say, knocking down a tower that one's child just attentively built.

23 Montessori was not the first to emphasize the role of choice architecture in pedagogy. It is also a major theme in Rousseau's *Emile*, and is present at least as far back as Plato's *Republic*.

24 A young child's insistence that she be allowed to wear pajamas that are insufficiently warm is a result, at least in part, of parents' provision of pajamas inappropriate for her given the season. (Even the desire to sleep without pajamas altogether can be due, in part, to providing a sleeping situation that makes it at least minimally comfortable to do so.)

25 Other responsibilities include protecting children from interruption or interference in the pursuit of their attentive work, giving lessons on particular materials (which is an essential part of the attractiveness of those materials and also facilitates the child's normative engagement with them), inviting children into group activities that exercise attentive self-control, and modeling the grace and courtesy that children aspire to imitate.

26 I am not saying that all of these are examples of permissible paternalism. Montessori points out, for instance, that forcing children to go to bed is often motivated by parents' "fear of the small disturber of his comfort," and many a parent covets for selfish reasons the time after children go to bed, despite justifying early bedtimes because of "the need to make the child rest a lot for the good of his health" (22: 60).

27 Some forms of libertarianism allow even for selling oneself into slavery (see, e.g., Nozick 1974: 58, 331; Philmore 1982). To the best of my knowledge, such theorists have not carefully thought about the implications of such views for children, and as feminists like Susan Okin (1989: 84) have pointed out, most assume that all relevant humans are adults (and men, and, seemingly, born ex nihilo as adult men).

28 Note that such justifications need not be "proficiency arguments" of Schapiro's sort. Rather, they can appeal to the partly constitutive nature of instrumental reasoning for agency itself. If I interfere with behavior of yours that is oriented toward suicide but that you engage in only under the description that you are hopping outside the window for a quick flutter on the breeze, I don't really interfere with your choice, since you are not actually about to do what you intend to do.

29 See Chapter 3, §6.

30 Some of these justifications for paternalism also come close to showing that apparently paternalistic behavior is not really paternalistic. Someone who chases a ball into a street may well be choosing to get the ball, but they are not choosing to put their life in danger in order to get the ball.

31 A related principle that I do not discuss here is that paternalistic intervention in the choices of another has a higher burden of proof than "paternalistically" withholding cooperation with their choices. Thus, for example, a policeman or social worker who forcibly takes from a person the drugs that they abuse has a higher burden of proof than the doctor who refuses to prescribe those drugs or the pharmacist who refuses to honor the prescription. With respect to both adults and children, avoiding paternalism does not require giving someone everything they want.

32 In this case, however, factors (1)–(3) are not present, and thus the burden of proof for true paternalism is likely not met. The daughter should be allowed to wear her lightweight pajamas. (Doing so might even be just what she needs in order to overcome ignorance and choose to wear better pajamas in the future.)

33 As I discuss in §6, these responsibilities should not require paternalistic intervention. In principle, adults should promote children's agency through the alternatives to paternalism discussed in §§3–4. Having failed to do so, however, adults' best *present* option might require some degree of paternalistic interference.

34 One of the most important features of children's development in adolescence is precisely this ability to bind themselves to long-term, socially enforced forms of self-constraint. Montessori often uses the Boy Scouts as an example (see 12: 8–9).

35 This effort is really only an acting-on-behalf-of children; it need not be strictly paternalistic.

36 The argument I'm presenting here focuses on intervention in the context of paternalism, but Montessori makes the same points regarding the use of coercion and interruption to protect rights or prevent harms interpersonally. In a well-constructed environment, coercion in general would be unnecessary.

Chapter 8

1 While much research remains to be done about the universality of disgust reactions, most theories of disgust give a prominent role to the place of disgust as a "pathogen avoidance mechanism," and snot is often specifically mentioned along with "feces ..., semen, and other animal bodily secretions" that "are found contaminating" through

the emotional response of disgust (Curtis and Biran 2001; Kelly and Wilson 2011: 51; Nussbaum 2006: 89; cf. Rozin and Fallon 1987; Tybur et al. 2013).
2. The revitalization of emotions construed as bodily plays an important role in some feminist critiques of patriarchal ethical systems in part because of how Western philosophy's "association between women and embodiment" (Schott 1988: 19) situates the devaluation of emotion as part of an overall assertion of patriarchal power. For an account of embodied emotions from a different perspective, see Prinz 2004.
3. In the next chapter (9), I discuss in detail the central emotion in Montessori's moral philosophy, love, from which springs the whole of ethical life. Here I offer more general remarks about emotion in Montessori's moral philosophy.
4. Identifying emotion, in contrast to reason, with the body is somewhat artificial. While there are complex historical reasons for linking "body" with "emotion" rather than with reason, both reason and emotion are essentially embodied in the sense that both are realized in various bodily states. Beyond emotions-as-embodied, other senses of "embodiment" important in contemporary philosophy are also largely ignored in this chapter. Some contemporary thinkers use notions of embodiment to refer to human vulnerability or to socially recognized features of bodies such as gender, race, or disability (cf. Alcoff 2006; Bergoffen and Weiss 2011, 2012; Butler 2004, 2015; Gooding-Williams 2005), but these are beyond the scope of my discussion here.
5. Theorists such as Andy Clark insist that the mind is not only not localized to the brain, but even extends beyond the body into the broader environment, such that, for instance, one's cell phone could be part of one's mind. This notion of the mind as extended beyond the body also has applications to moral theory (see, e.g., Heath and Anderson 2010), and Montessori's concepts of "prepared environment," "materialized abstraction," and "supernature" (the human-made environment in general) provide resources for developing a Montessorian account of extended will. For the purposes of this book, however, I limit my focus to embodiment.
6. Even those who expand attention to include feeling, desire, and emotion often treat these as states that can be articulated independent of agents' literal bodies.
7. Note that the pronoun "its" here refers to the will, which Montessori thereby describes as having a physical/material structure, namely the muscles. (The Italian reads, "Un parallelo perfetto esiste tra la formazione della volontà e la coordinazione di movimento dei suoi ordegni materiali, i muscoli striati" (Montessori, Maria. *Opere* (Italian Edition) (p. 542). Garzanti. Kindle Edition).
8. A full discussion of the relationship between Montessori's embodied ethics and Bourdieu's notions of habitus and hexis is beyond the scope of this book. One problem with an overly hasty application of Bourdieu to Montessori is that the former develops the notion of hexis as a way of de-centering individual agency, while Montessori emphasizes the cultivation of bodily competence as part of a conquest of independence whereby one develops, expresses, and extends agency.
9. As noted in Chapter 7, both principles preclude paternalistic interference with others. In Kant's case, while the duty of non-interference is clearest in his political theory (from which this quotation is taken), non-interference is implied and required by his moral philosophy, especially the "Humanity" formulation of the categorical imperative (Kant 1996: 79–80; see Schapiro 2003).
10. Montessori describes the challenge that she had in helping experienced teachers develop sufficient self-control to sit and watch children work without interfering, and I have both seen in others and personally experienced for myself the fidgeting

and jumpiness and other evident bodily discomfort that can arise from watching a child work on a challenging task for themselves, knowing that one could "help," but holding oneself back. It takes practice to bring oneself to the point where the sight of a child hard at work generates a restful bodily orientation of observation rather than an anxious and alert bodily orientation toward intervention.

11 Translation modified. The Italian reads, "*la vita sociale infantile*" and the Montessori-Pierson edition translates this as "infantile social life."
12 Buss discusses various objections to this emphasis on politeness as an expression of respect, and I discuss some others—particularly with respect to the cultural variability of good manners—in Frierson 2019b, but a full treatment of all the complexities of politeness as a form of respect is beyond the scope of the present chapter.
13 Sherman (following Seneca) emphasizes the equally important inverse point, namely that "manifesting certain looks and appearances are ways of acting appropriately even when the corresponding inner states are absent. Sometimes that is all we can muster. Of course, it is better, if outer conduct matches inner virtue. But when that cannot be achieved, the appropriate outer expression itself is ethically important" (Sherman 2005: 285).
14 Granted, in this case, Montessori says that "we are careful" to have the proper bodily movements, but in the context of her broader account of the way the will manifests itself in virtuous action, the relevant care here need not be (and indeed should not be) effortful care, and may not even be conscious.
15 See chapter two, note 4 (p. 219).
16 For a relevant discussion of the agential role of habit in Bergson, Montessori's contemporary, see Grosz 2013.
17 Translation of "suo volto commosso" modified from Montessori-Pierson edition. "Commosso," translated in the Montessori-Pierson edition as "mobile," here means "moved" in the sense of emotionally moved.
18 Even in Gilbert's account of one person "drawing ahead" of the other (Gilbert 1990: 3), she focuses on the other's verbal response and the implied "rights" and "obligations" of the parties to the walk, rather than on the embodied practice of actually coordinating steps.
19 Similarly, playing a team sport well requires specifically bodily skills, say of passing and receiving, that are required in order to create and sustain the *shared* activity of the team as a whole, and the style of each individual on the team shifts to accommodate the way the team as a whole plays together.
20 For a good short introduction to contact improvisation, see https://youtu.be/jcrbIdY3HZc. For a more detailed discussion, see Novack 1990.

Chapter 9

1 Montessori specifically applies this definition to love of humanity, but it applies to love more generally.
2 Standing refers to Stoppani as the uncle of Montessori's mother Renilde (Standing 1984: 21), but research into the family tree, both by outside researchers and the Montessori family, has not been able to establish this claim (according to Joke Verheul, private communication).

3   In this context, she also rejects overly cognitive conceptions of moral philosophy.

> We cannot become moral by committing codes and their applications to memory, for memory might fail us a thousand times, and the slightest passion might overcome us; criminals, in fact, even when they are most astute and wary students of codes, often violate them; while normal persons, although entirely ignorant of the laws, never transgress them, owing to "an internal sense which guides them"
>
> (9: 242).

4   Elsewhere she reiterates the connection between sensitive periods and love, describing the motivation of "sensitive periods" to "ardent love, a violent attraction to something, in the young one," where "this enthusiasm, this vivacity, this love that nature has put in the soul of the child, is necessary for life" (24: 13).

5   For an excellent example of such a scientist, see Jackson 2010.

6   Montessori also describes "religion" as another special love (17: 95). Because religion involves not only solidarity with other persons but also "worship" directed toward God or other transcendent realities, I bracket discussion of it here.

7   Quite likely, the reference to The Child here is at least partly Christological, that is, a reference to the Christ Child, Jesus. Montessori often blends Christological imagery into her emphasis on the child (see too, e.g., 2: 36, 48). A full discussion of the role of religion, in general and Christianity in particular in the philosophy of Montessori is worth elucidation but beyond the scope of this book.

Bibliography

References to Montessori's works are typically made by volume and page number to versions published in *The Montessori Series* (twenty-four volumes, The Montessori-Pierson Publishing). Works not present in *The Montessori Series* use the author-date system of references. Works that I have cited in this book are listed here by volume number: 1: *The Absorbent Mind* (trans. C. Claremont); 2: *The Discovery of the Child* (ed. Fred Kelpin); 3: *The Formation of Man* (ed. A. M. Joosten); 5: *Education for a New World*; 6: *To Educate the Human Potential*; 7: *The Child, Society, and the World* (trans. C. Juler and H. Yesson); 8: *The Child in the Family* (trans. N. Cirillo); 9: *The Advanced Montessori Method*, volume 1, formerly entitled *Spontaneous Activity in Education* (trans. F. Simmonds and L. Hutchinson); 10: *Education and Peace* (trans. H. Lane); 12: *From Childhood to Adolescence*; 13: *The Advanced Montessori Method*, volume 2 (trans. A. Livingston); 14: *Citizen of the World: Key Montessori Readings* (ed. G. Sackett); 15: *The California Lectures of Maria Montessori, 1915* (ed. R. Buckenmeyer); 17: *The 1946 London Lectures* (ed. A. Haines); 18: *The 1913 Rome Lectures* (ed. S. Feez); 19: *The Mass Explained to Children*; 21: *Montessori Speaks to Parents: A Selection of Articles*; 22: *The Secret of Childhood*; 24: *Creative Development in the Child: The Montessori Approach* (ed. R. Ramachandran). Quotes of Maria Montessori © Copyright 2022 by Montessori-Pierson Publishing Company.

Adams, M. R. (2006) "The Concept of Work in Maria Montessori and Karl Marx," *Proceedings of the American Catholic Philosophical Association* 79: 247–60.
Ahmed, S. (2004) *The Cultural Politics of Emotion*. Edinburgh: University of Edinburgh Press.
Alcoff, L. M. (2006) *Visible Identities: Race, Gender, and the Self*. New York: Oxford University Press.
Anscombe, E. (1957) *Intention*. Cambridge: Harvard University Press.
Anscombe, E. (1958) "Modern Moral Philosophy," *Philosophy* 33: 1–19.
Aristotle (2002) *Nicomachean Ethics*, S. Broadie and C. Rowe (eds). Oxford: Oxford University Press.
Aron, A. and E. N. Aron (1986) *Love and the Expansion of Self: Understanding Attraction and Satisfaction*. New York, NY: Hemisphere Publishing Corp/Harper & Row Publishers.
Arpaly, N. (2002) *Unprincipled Virtue: An Inquiry into Moral Agency*. Oxford: Oxford University Press.
Arpaly, N. and T. Schroeder (2014) *In Praise of Desire*. Oxford: Oxford University Press.
Audi, R. (1998) "Moderate Intuitionism and the Epistemology of Moral Judgment," *Ethical Theory and Moral Practice* 1(1): 14–34.
Audi, R. (2004) *The Good in the Right: A Theory of Intuition and Intrinsic Value*. Princeton: Princeton University Press.
Audi, R. (2013) *Moral Perception*. Princeton: Princeton University Press.
Babini, V. and L. Lama (2000) *Una "donna nuova": Il femminismo scientifico di Maria Montessori*. Milano: Franco Angeli.

Babini, V. (2000) "Science, Feminism, and Education: The Early Work of Maria Montessori," translated by S. Morgan and D. Pick, *History Workshop Journal* 49: 44–67.

Babini, V. (2013) "Scienze umane e pratica di democrazia. Da Maria Montessori a Franco Basaglia," *Rivista Sperimentale di Freniatria* 137: 9–32.

Barnes, E. (2016) *The Minority Body: A Theory of Disability*. Oxford: Oxford University Press.

Bergoffen, D. and G. Weiss eds. (2011) *Ethics of Embodiment*, special issue of *Hypatia* 26(3).

Bergoffen, D. and G. Weiss eds. (2012) "Cluster: Contesting the Norms of Embodiment," special issue of *Hypatia* 27(2): 241–275.

Bettmann, J. (2003) "Grace and Courtesy: The Basis of a Normalized Community Nurturing the Respectful Community through Practical Life," lecture, "The Child as Builder of Humanity" Conference ~ 26–28 September 2003, Sydney, Australia.

Biss, J. (2020) *Unquiet*. Newark: Audible Inc.

Bornstein, M. H. (1989) "Sensitive Periods in Development: Structural Characteristics and Causal Interpretations," *Psychological Bulletin* 105: 179–97.

Bourdieu, P. ([1972] 1977) *Outline of a Theory of Practice*, R. Nice (trans.). Cambridge: Cambridge University Press.

Bourdieu, P. ([1987] 1994) *In Other Words: Essays towards a Reflexive Sociology*, M. Adamson (trans.). Cambridge: Polity.

Bratman, M. (1987) *Intention, Plans, and Practical Reason*. Cambridge, MA: Harvard University Press.

Bratman, M. (1993) "Shared Intention," *Ethics* 104: 97–113.

Bratman, M. (2007) *Structures of Agency: Essays*. New York: Oxford University Press.

Bratman, M. (2009) "Shared Agency," in C. Mantzavinos (ed.), *Philosophy of the Social Sciences: Philosophical Theory and Scientific Practice*. Cambridge: Cambridge University Press, pp. 41–59.

Bratman, M. (2013) *Shared Agency: A Planning Theory of Acting Together*. Oxford: Oxford University Press.

Bratman, M. (2018) *Planning, Time, and Self-Governance: Essays in Practical Rationality*. Oxford: Oxford University Press.

Brighouse, H. (2002) "What Rights (If Any) Do Children Have?" in D. Archard and C. M. MacLeod (eds), *The Moral and Political Status of Children*, Oxford: Oxford University Press.

Brighouse, H. (2003) "How Should Children Be Heard?" *Arizona Law Review* 45: 691–711.

Buss, Sarah (1999) "Appearing Respectful: The Moral Significance of Manners," *Ethics* 109(4): 795–826.

Butler, J. (1726) *Fifteen Sermons Preached at the Rolls Chapel*. London: J. and J. Knapton.

Butler, J. (1990) *Gender Trouble: Feminism and the Subversion of Identity*. New York: Routledge.

Butler, J. (2004) *Undoing Gender*. New York: Routledge.

Butler, J. (2015) *Senses of the Subject*. New York: Fordham University Press.

Butler, J. and S. Taylor (2010) "Examined Life: Judith Butler and Sunaura Taylor," available at https://www.youtube.com/watch?v=k0HZaPkF6qE, accessed April 27, 2010.

Clark, A. (2011) *Supersizing the Mind: Embodiment, Action, and Extension*. Oxford: Oxford University Press.

Clark, R. (2010) "Skilled Activity and the Causal Theory of Action," *Philosophy and Phenomenological Research* 80(3): 523–50.

Cimino, Guido and Renato Foschi (2012) "Italy," in D. B. Baker (ed.), *The Oxford Handbook of the History of Psychology: Global Perspectives*. Oxford: Oxford University Press, pp. 307–46.

Colgan, A. (2016) "The Epistemology behind the Educational Philosophy of Montessori: Senses, Concepts, and Choice," *Philosophical Inquiry in Education* 23(2): 125–40.

Conant, J. (2010) "Nietzsche's Perfectionism: A Reading of Schopenhauer as Educator," in R. Schacht (ed.), *Nietzsche's Postmoralism: Essays on Nietzsche's Prelude to Philosophy's Future*. Cambridge, UK: Cambridge University Press, pp. 181–257.

Conly, S. (2012) *Against Autonomy: Justifying Coercive Paternalism*. Cambridge: Cambridge University Press.

Csikszentmihalyi, M. (1990) *Flow: The Psychology of Optimal Experiences*. New York: HarperCollins.

Csikszentmihalyi, M. (1993) *The Evolving Self: A Psychology for the Third Millennium*. New York: HarperCollins.

Csikszentmihalyi, M. (1996) *Creativity: Flow and the Psychology of Discovery and Invention*. New York: HarperCollins.

Cuneo, T. (2011) "Reid's Ethics," *The Stanford Encyclopedia of Philosophy* (Spring 2011 Edition), Edward N. Zalta (ed.). https://plato.stanford.edu/archives/win2016/entries/reid-ethics/.

Curtis, V. and A. Biran (2001) "Dirt, Disgust, and Disease: Is Hygiene in Our Genes?" *Perspectives in Biology and Medicine* 44(1), pp. 17–31.

Dancy, J. (2004) *Ethics without Principles*. Oxford: Clarendon Press.

Darwall, S. (1977) "Two Kinds of Respect," *Ethics* 88: 36–49.

Davidson, D. (1963) "Actions, Reasons, and Causes," *The Journal of Philosophy* 60: 685–700.

Dean, R. (2006) *The Value of Humanity in Kant's Moral Theory*. Oxford: Oxford University Press.

Deci, E. L. and R. M. Ryan (1985) *Intrinsic Motivation and Self-determination in Human Behavior*. New York: Plenum.

De Giorgi, F. (2019) *Il Peccato Originale*. Brescia: Editrice Morcelliana.

DeSousa, R. (1987) *The Rationality of Emotion*. Cambridge, MA: MIT Press.

Deutsch, Diana, Trevor Henthorn, and Mark Dolson (2004) "Absolute Pitch, Speech, and Tone Language: Some Experiments and a Proposed Framework," *Music Perception* 21: 339–56.

Döring, S. (2007) "Seeing What to Do: Affective Perception and Rational Motivation," *dialectica* 61(3): 363–94.

Dorsey, D. (2010) "Three Arguments for Perfectionism," *Noûs* 44: 59–79.

Dweck, C. (2006) *Mindset: The New Psychology of Success*. New York: Ballantine Books.

Dworkin, G. (1972) "Paternalism," *The Monist* 56: 64–84.

Dworkin, G. (2020) "Paternalism," in E. N. Zalta (ed.), *The Stanford Encyclopedia of Philosophy*, Fall 2020 edn. https://plato.stanford.edu/archives/fall2020/entries/paternalism/.

Foot, P. (1978) *Virtues and Vices: And Other Essays in Moral Philosophy*. Berkeley: University of California Press.

Foot, P. (2001) *Natural Goodness*. Oxford: Oxford University Press.

Formosa, P. (2018) "Evil, Virtue, and Education in Kant," *Educational Philosophy and Theory*. https://doi.org/10.1080/00131857.2018.1487284.

Foschi, R. (2012) *Maria Montessori*. Rome: Ediesse.

Foschi, R. and E. Cicciola (2006) "Politics and Naturalism in the 20th Century Psychology of Alfred Binet," *History of Psychology* 9: 267–89.

Franco, P. (2018) "Becoming Who You Are: Nietzsche on Self-Creation," *The Journal of Nietzsche Studies* 49(1): 52–77.

Frankfurt, H. (1971) "Freedom of the Will and the Concept of a Person," *The Journal of Philosophy* 68: 5–20.

Frankfurt, H. (1988) *The Importance of What We Care about and Other Essays*. Cambridge: Cambridge University Press.

Frankfurt, H. (1999) *Necessity, Volition, and Love*. Cambridge: Cambridge University Press.

Frankfurt, H. (2004) *The Reasons of Love*. Princeton: Princeton University Press.

Frankfurt, H. (2006) *Taking Ourselves Seriously and Getting It Right*. Palo Alto: Stanford University Press.

Frankish, K. (2010) "Dual-Process and Dual-System Theories of Reasoning," *Philosophy Compass* 5(10): 914–26.

Frierson, P. (2007) "Review of Richard Dean: *The Value of Humanity in Kant's Moral Theory*," *Notre Dame Philosophical Reviews*.

Frierson, P. (2010) "Kantian Moral Pessimism," in S. Anderson-Gold and P. Muchnik (eds), *Kant's Anatomy of Evil*. Cambridge: Cambridge University Press, pp. 33–56.

Frierson, P. (2013) "The Double Problem of Liberal Education in Kant, Rousseau, and Montessori," presented at the 2013 Conference of the International Society for Intellectual History: "The Importance of Learning: Liberal Education and Scholarship in Historical Perspective," Princeton University, June 5–7, 2013.

Frierson, P. (2014a) *Kant's Empirical Psychology*. Cambridge: Cambridge University Press.

Frierson, P. (2014b) "Maria Montessori's Epistemology," *British Journal of the History of Philosophy* 22: 767–91.

Frierson, P. (2015) "Maria Montessori's Philosophy of Empirical Psychology," *HOPOS: The Journal of the International Society for the History of the Philosophy of Science* 5(2): 240–68.

Frierson, P. (2016a) "The Virtue Epistemology of Maria Montessori," *Australasian Journal of Philosophy* 94: 79–98.

Frierson, P. (2016b) "Making Room for Children: Maria Montessori's Argument That Children's Incapacity for Autonomy Is an External Failing," *Journal of the Philosophy of Education* 50: 332–50.

Frierson, P. (2018) "Maria Montessori's Metaphysics of Life," *European Journal of Philosophy* 26: 991–1011.

Frierson, P. (2019a) "Character in Kant's Moral Psychology: Responding to the Situationist Challenge," *Archiv für Geschichte der Philosophie* 101: 508–34.

Frierson, P. (2019b) "Universal Virtues and Local Norms: A Montessori Perspective," presented at a conference on *Virtues: Local or Universal?* at Oriel College, Oxford University, January 3–5, 2019.

Frierson, P. (2020) *Intellectual Agency and Virtue Epistemology: A Montessori Perspective*. London: Bloomsbury Academic.

Frierson, P. (2021) "Kant and Montessori on Discipline and Autonomy," *Journal of the Philosophy of Education* 55(6): 1097–111.

Galison, P. (1997) *Image and Logic*. Chicago: University of Chicago Press.

Galison, P. (2003) "The Collective Author," in P. Galison and M. Biagioli (eds), *Scientific Authorship: Credit and Intellectual Property in Science*. New York: Routledge, pp. 325–53.

Gewirth, A. (1974) "The Is-Ought Problem Resolved," *Proceedings and Addresses of the American Philosophical Association* 47: 34–61.

Gibson, J. (2015/1979) *The Ecological Approach to Visual Perception*. New York: Psychology Press (Classic Edition), originally published in 1979.

Gilbert, M. (1990) "Walking Together: A Paradigmatic Social Phenomenon," *Midwest Studies in Philosophy* 15: 1–14.

Gilbert, M. (2006) *A Theory of Political Obligation: Membership, Commitment, and the Bonds of Society*. Oxford: Oxford University Press.

Gilbert, M. (2013) *Joint Commitment: How We Make the Social World*. Oxford: Oxford University Press.

Goldie, P. (2007) "Seeing What Is the Kind Thing to Do: Perception and Emotion in Morality," *dialectica* 61(3): 347–61.

The Good Place (2016–2020) Created by M. Schur. USA: NBC Studios.

Gooding-Williams, R. (2005) *Look, a Negro: Philosophical Essays on Race, Culture and Politics*. New York: Routledge.

Gopnik, A. (2009) *The Philosophical Baby: What Children's Minds Teach Us about Truth, Love, and the Meaning of Life*. New York: Farrar, Straus, and Giroux.

Grenberg, J. (2018) "Autonomous Moral Education Is Socratic Moral Education: The Import of Repeated Activity in Moral Education out of Evil and into Virtue," *Educational Philosophy and Theory*. https://doi.org/10.1080/00131857.2018.1487285.

Grosz, E. (2013) "Habit Today: Ravaisson, Bergson, Deleuze and Us," *Body and Society* 19: 217–39.

Haidt, J. (2001) "The Emotional *Dog* and Its *Rational Tail*: A Social Intuitionist Approach to Moral Judgment," *Psychological Review* 108(4): 814–34.

Hanna, J. (2018) *In Our Best Interest: A Defense of Paternalism*. Oxford: Oxford University Press.

Hausman, D. and B. Welch (2010) "Debate: To Nudge or Not to Nudge," *Journal of Political Philosophy* 18(1): 123–36.

Haugeland, J. (1998) "Mind Embodied and Embedded," in Y. H. Houng and J. Ho (eds), *Mind and Cognition: 1993 International Symposium*. Sinica: Academica, pp. 233–67.

Heath, J. and J. Anderson (2010) "Procrastination and the Extended Will," in C. Andreou and M. White (eds), *The Thief of Time: Philosophical Essays in Proscrastination*. Oxford: Oxford University Press, pp. 233–252.

Hegel, G. W. F. ([1820] 1991) *Elements of the Philosophy of Right*, A. Wood (ed.) Cambridge: Cambridge University Press.

Hellbrügge, T. (1982) *Die Entdeckung der Montessori-Pädagogik für das behinderte Kind*. Reinbech: Kinder Verlag, selection translated as "The Discovery of the Relevance of Montessori's Education to Handicapped Children," in *Basic Ideas of Montessori's Educational Theory* (ed. P. Oswald and G. Schulz-Benesch). Oxford: Clio (1997).

Helm, B. (2001) *Emotional Reason: Deliberation, Motivation and the Nature of Value*. Cambridge: Cambridge University Press.

Helm, B. (2017) *Communities of Respect: Grounding Responsibility, Authority, and Dignity*. Oxford: Oxford University Press.

Herbart, J. F. (1908) *The Science of Education*, H. and E. Felkin (trans.). Boston: D. C. Heath and Co.

Herman, B. (1993) *The Practice of Moral Judgment*. Cambridge: Harvard University Press.

Herman, B. (2007) *Moral Literacy*. Cambridge, MA: Harvard University Press.

Hersey, J. (1956) *A Single Pebble*. New York: Random House.

Hooker, B. and M. Little eds. (2000) *Moral Particularism*. Oxford: Oxford University Press.

hooks, bell (2000) *All about Love: New Visions*. New York: William Morrow and Co.

Huebner, B. (2014) *Macrocognition: A Theory of Distributed Minds and Collective Intentionality*. Oxford: Oxford University Press.
Hume, D. ([1751] 1975) *An Enquiry Concerning the Principles of Morals*, in L. A. Selby-Bigge (ed.), *Enquiries Concerning Human Understanding and Concerning the Principles of Morals*, 3rd edn. revised by P. H. Nidditch. Oxford: Clarendon Press, pp. 169–323.
Hume, D. ([1940] 1975) *A Treatise of Human Nature*, L. A. Selby-Bigge (ed.), 2nd edn. revised by P. H. Nidditch. Oxford: Clarendon Press.
Hursthouse, R. (1999) *On Virtue Ethics*. Oxford: Oxford University Press.
Huseyinzadegan, D., J. McAuliffe, J. Shorter-Bourhanou, B. Kimoto, E. Islekel, M. Draz, and E. Brown (2020) "Continental Feminism," in E. Zalta (ed.), *The Stanford Encyclopedia of Philosophy*, Winter 2020 edn. https://plato.stanford.edu/archives/win2020/entries/femapproach-continental/.
Hutcheson, F. ([1726] 2004) *An Inquiry into the Original of Our Ideas of Beauty and Virtue*, W. Leidhold (ed.). Indianapolis: Liberty Fund.
Hutcheson, F. ([1728] 2002) *An Essay on the Nature and Conduct of the Passions, with Illustrations on the Moral Sense*, A. Garrett (ed.). Indianapolis: Liberty Fund.
Jackson, K. (2010) *Mean and Lowly Things: Snakes, Science, and Survival in the Congo*. Cambridge: Harvard University Press.
James, W. (1896) *The Will to Believe, and Other Essays in Popular Philosophy*. London: Longmans, Green, and Co.
James, W. (1906) "G. Papini and the Pragmatist Movement in Italy," *The Journal of Philosophy, Psychology and Scientific Methods* 3(13): 337–41.
Jaworska, A. (1999) "Respecting the Margins of Agency: Alzheimer's Patients and the Capacity to Value," *Philosophy and Public Affairs* 28: 105–38.
Jaworska, A. (2007) "Caring and Internality," *Philosophy and Phenomenological Research* 54: 529–68.
Kahneman, D. (2011) *Thinking Fast and Slow*. New York: Farrar, Straus and Giroux.
Kant, I. (1996) *Practical Philosophy*, M. Gregor (ed.). Cambridge: Cambridge University Press.
Kauppinen, A. (2014) "Moral Sentimentalism," in Edward N. Zalta (ed.), *The Stanford Encyclopedia of Philosophy*. https://plato.stanford.edu/archives/spr2014/entries/moral-sentimentalism/.
Kelly, D. and R. A. Wilson (2011) *Yuck! The Nature and Moral Significance of Disgust*. Boston: MIT Press.
Kerstein, S. (2012) *How to Treat Persons*. Oxford: Oxford University Press.
Korsgaard, C. (1996a) *The Sources of Normativity*. Cambridge: Cambridge University Press.
Korsgaard, C. (1996b) *Creating the Kingdom of Ends*. Cambridge: Cambridge University Press.
Korsgaard, C. (2009) *Self-Constitution: Agency, Identity, and Integrity*. Oxford: Oxford University Press.
Korsgaard, C. (2018) *Fellow Creatures: Our Obligations to the Other Animals*. Oxford: Oxford University Press.
Kramer, R. (1976) *Montessori: A Biography*. New York: Hachette.
Krogh, S. (1981) "Moral Beginnings: The Just Community in Montessori Preschools," *Journal of Moral Education* 11(1): 41–6.
Lakoff, G. and M. Johnson (1999) *Philosophy in the Flesh: The Embodied Mind and Its Challenge to Western Thought*. New York: Basic Books.
LaLoy, L. (1902) *L'Evolution de la vie*. Paris: Reinwald.

Lewis, D. (1969) *Convention: A Philosophical Study*. Cambridge, MA: Harvard University Press.
Lewis, D. (1989) "Dispositional Theories of Value," *Proceedings of the Aristotelian Society* 63(Supplement): 113–37.
Lillard, A. (2007) *Montessori: The Science behind the Genius*. Oxford: Oxford University Press.
List, C. and P. Pettit (2006) "Group Agency and Supervenience," *Southern Journal of Philosophy* 44(S1): 85–105.
List, C. and P. Pettit (2011) *Group Agency*. Oxford: Oxford University Press.
Ludwig, K. (2016) *From Individual to Plural Agency: Collective Action I*. Oxford: Oxford University Press.
MacIntyre, A. (1981) *After Virtue*. South Bend, IN: University of Notre Dame Press.
Mackie, J. L. (1977) *Ethics: Inventing Right and Wrong*. Harmondsworth: Penguin.
Matellicani, A. (2007) *La "Sapienza" di Maria Montessori: Dagli studi universitari alla docenza 1890–1919*. Rome: Arachne editrice.
Mayo Clinic Staff (2021) "Yips," available at https://www.mayoclinic.org/diseases-conditions/yips/symptoms-causes/syc-20379021, accessed February 24, 2021.
McDowell, J. (1998) *Mind, Value, and Reality*. Cambridge: Harvard University Press.
McKenna, M. (2012) *Conversation and Responsibility*. New York: Oxford University Press.
Mele, A. R. (2003) *Motivation and Agency*. Oxford: Oxford University Press.
Mele, A. R. and P. K. Moser (1994) "Intentional Action," *Noûs* 28(1): 39–68.
Merleau-Ponty, Maurice (1962) *Phenomenology of Perception*, C. Smith (trans.). London: Routledge.
Mill, J. S. (1863) *Utilitarianism*. London: Parker, Son, and Bourn.
Mill, J. S. ([1859] 1989) *On Liberty*, S. Collini (ed.). Cambridge: Cambridge University Press.
Miller, C. (2013) *Moral Character: An Empirical Theory*. Oxford: Oxford University Press.
Montessori, M. (1902) "Norme per una classificazione dei deficienti in rapporto ai metodi speciali di educazione," in *Atti del Comitato Ordinatore del II Congresso Pedagogico Italiano 1899–1901*. Naples: Trani, pp. 144–67.
Montessori, M. (1903) "La teoria Lombrosiana e l'educazione morale," *Rivista d'Italia* 6(2): 326–31.
Montessori, M. ([1909] 1912) *The Montessori Method*, A. E. George (trans.). New York: Frederick A. Stokes Company.
Montessori, M. ([1910] 1913) *Pedagogical Anthropology*. New York: Frederick Stokes and Co.
Montessori, M. (1924) *The Call of Education* 1(2–3), available at http://www.montessorischools.org/blog/on-discipline-reflections-and-advice/, accessed March 18, 2021.
Montessori, M. (1949) *The Absorbent Mind*. Adyar: The Theosophical Publishing House.
Montessori, M. (1984) "Moral and Social Education," *Communications* 4: 15–19. Amsterdam: Association Montessori Internationale.
Montessori, M. (1997) *Basic Ideas of Montessori's Educational Theory: Extracts from Montessori's Writings and Teachings*, G. Shulz-Benesch (ed.). Santa Barbara: Clio Press.
Montessori, M. ([1929] 2000) *The Child in the Church*, E. M. Standing (ed.). Chantilly: The Madonna and Child Atrium.
Montessori, M. (2007) *The Montessori Series*. 24 vols. Amsterdam: Montessori-Pierson Publishing Company. Throughout, texts are cited by volume and page number.

Montessori, M. ([1936] 2008) "Cosmic Education: 4th Lecture," *Communications* 2008(2): 52–8.
Montessori, M. ([1936] 2009) "Cosmic Education," *Communications* 2009: 33–43.
Montessori, M. (2012) "Moral and Social Education," From the 1938 Edinburgh Montessori Congress Lectures, reprinted in *The NAMTA Journal* 37(2): 81–8.
Montessori, M. ([1931] 2019) "I reattivi psichici," in F. De Giorgi (ed.), *Il Peccato Originale*. Brescia: Scuole, pp. 87–95.
Moore, G. E. (1903) *Principia Ethica*. Cambridge: Cambridge University Press.
Moretti, E. (2013) "Teaching Peace in a Time of War: Maria Montessori's 1917 Lectures," *AMI Communications* 2013(1–2): 8–22.
Moretti, E. (2021) *The Best Weapon for Peace: Maria Montessori, Education, and Children's Rights*. Madison, WI: University of Wisconsin Press.
Murdoch, I. (1970) *The Sovereignty of the Good*. London: Routledge.
Nagel, T. (1970) *The Possibility of Altruism*. Princeton: Princeton University Press.
Nietzsche, F. (1966) *Beyond Good and Evil*, W. Kaufmann (ed.). New York: Random House.
Nietzsche, F. (1967) *On the Genealogy of Morals and Ecce Homo*, W. Kaufmann (ed.). New York: Random House.
Nietzsche, F. (1997) *Untimely Meditations*, D. Brazeale (ed.). Cambridge, UK: Cambridge University Press.
Nietzsche, F. ([1882] 2001) *The Gay Science*, B. Williams (ed.), Cambridge: Cambridge University Press.
Noë, A. (2004) *Action in Perception*. Cambridge, MA: MIT Press.
Noë, A. (2009) *Out of Our Heads: Why You Are Not Your Brain, and Other Lessons from the Biology of Consciousness*. New York: Farrar, Straus, and Giroux.
Novack, C. (1990) *Sharing the Dance: Contact Improvisation and American Culture*. Madison: University of Wisconsin Press.
Nozick, R. (1974) *Anarchy, State, and Utopia*. New York: Basic Books.
Nussbaum, M. (2000) *Women and Human Development: The Capabilities Approach*. Cambridge: Cambridge University Press.
Nussbaum, M. (2001) *Upheavals of Thought: The Intelligence of Emotions*. Cambridge: Cambridge University Press.
Nussbaum, M. (2006) *Hiding from Humanity: Disgust, Shame, and the Law*. Princeton: Princeton University Press.
Nussbaum, M. (2016) *Anger and Forgiveness: Resentment, Generosity, Justice*. Oxford: Oxford University Press.
Okin, S. (1989) *Justice, Gender, and the Family*. New York: Basic Books.
O'Neill, O. (1988) "Children's Rights and Children's Lives," *Ethics* 98: 445–63.
Paxton, S. et al. (1979) "Definition," *Contact Quarterly* 5(1): 35.
Petit, P. (2012) "The Reality of Group Agents," in C. Mantzavinos (ed.), *Philosophy of the Social Sciences: Philosophical Theory and Scientific Practice*. Cambridge: Cambridge University Press, pp. 67–91.
Philmore, J. (1982) "The Libertarian Case for Slavery," *Philosophical Forum* 14(1): 43–58.
Prinz, J. (2004) "Embodied Emotions," in R. Solomon (ed.), *Thinking about Feeling: Contemporary Philosophers on Emotion*. Oxford: Oxford University Press, pp. 44–60.
Prinz, J. (2007) *The Emotional Construction of Morals*. Oxford: Oxford University Press.
Rathunde, K. and M. Csikszentmihalyi (2005a) "Middle School Students" Motivation and Quality of Experience: A Comparison of Montessori and Traditional School Environments," *American Journal of Education* 111: 341–71.

Rathunde, K. and M. Csikszentmihalyi (2005b) "The Social Context of Middle School: Teachers, Friends, and Activities in Montessori and Traditional School Environments," *Elementary School Journal* 106: 59–79.
Rawls, J. (1971) *A Theory of Justice*. Cambridge: Belknap Press.
Reath, A. (2006) *Agency and Autonomy in Kant's Moral Philosophy*. Oxford: Oxford University Press.
Reichold, A. (2007) "Embodiment and the Ethical Concept of a Person," in H. Fielding, G. Hiltmann, D. Olkowski, and A. Reichold (ed.), *The Other: Feminist Reflections in Ethics*. London: Palgrave, pp. 169–85.
Reid, T. ([1788] 2010) *Essay on the Active Powers of Man*, K. Haakonssen and S. Harris (eds). Edinburgh: Edinburgh University Press.
Ripstein, A. (2009) *Force and Freedom: Kant's Legal and Political Philosophy*. Cambridge, MA: Harvard University Press.
Roberts, R. and R. J. Wood (2007) *Intellectual Virtues: An Essay in Regulative Epistemology*. Oxford: Oxford University Press.
Roeser, S. (2010) *Reid on Ethics*. London: Palgrave Macmillan.
Rogers, F. (1997) "What Do You Do with the Mad That You Feel," available at https://misterrogers.org/videos/what-to-you-do-with-the-mad-that-you-feel/.
Rosati, C. S. (2016) "Moral Motivation," in E. N. Zalta (ed.), *The Stanford Encyclopedia of Philosophy*, Winter 2016 edn. https://plato.stanford.edu/archives/win2016/entries/moral-motivation/.
Rousseau, J.-J. (1762) *Du contrat social, ou Principe du Droit Politique*. Amsterdam: Marc Michel Rey.
Rousseau, J.-J. (1979) *Emile, or on Education*, A. Bloom (ed.). New York: Basic Books.
Rozin, P. and A. E. Fallon (1987). "A Perspective on Disgust," *Psychological Review* 94(1): 23–41. https://doi.org/10.1037/0033-295X.94.1.23.
Rutherford, D. (2018a) "Nietzsche as Perfectionist," *Inquiry* 61: 42–61.
Rutherford, D. (2018b) "Nietzsche and the Self," in P. Katsafanis (ed.), *The Nietzschean Mind*. Abingdon: Routledge, pp. 201–17.
Ryan, R. and E. Deci (2000) "Self-Determination Theory and the Facilitation of Intrinsic Motivation, Social Development, and Well-Being," *American Psychologist* 55: 68–78.
Ryan, R. and E. Deci (2017) *Self-determination Theory: Basic Psychological Needs in Motivation, Development, and Wellness*. New York: Guilford.
Sackett, G. (2003) "Grace and Courtesy Lessons and the Birth of Social Life," *AMI Communications* 2003(1): 7–18.
Saito, Y. (2016) "Body Aesthetics and the Cultivation of Moral Virtues," in S. Irvin (ed.), *Body Aesthetics*. Oxford: Oxford University Press, pp. 225–42.
Santucci, A. (1963) *Il pragmatismo in Italia*. Bologna: Il Mulino.
Sartre, J.-P. (1993) *Existentialism and the Human Emotions*. New York: Carol Publishing Group.
Sayre-mccord, G. and M. Smith (2014) "Desires … and Beliefs … of One's Own," in M. Vargas and G. Yaffe (eds), *Rational and Social Agency: Essays on the Philosophy of Michael Bratman*. Oxford: Oxford University Press, pp. 129–51.
Scanlon, T. M. (1998) *What We Owe to Each Other*. Cambridge, MA: Harvard University Press.
Schapiro, T. (1999) "What Is a Child?" *Ethics* 109: 715–38.
Schapiro, T. (2003) "Childhood and Personhood," *Arizona Law Review* 45: 575–94.
Schapiro, T. (2012) "On the Relation between Wanting and Willing," *Philosophical Issues* 22: 334–50.

Schapiro, T. (2014) "What Are Theories of Desire Theories of?" *Analytic Philosophy* 55(2): 131–50.
Schapiro, T. (2021) *Feeling Like It*. Oxford: Oxford University Press.
Schlosser, M. (2019) "Agency," in E. Zalta (ed.), *The Stanford Encyclopedia of Philosophy*, Winter 2019 edn. https://plato.stanford.edu/archives/win2019/entries/agency/.
Schott, R. M. (1988) *Cognition and Eros: A Critique of the Kantian Paradigm*. University Park: Pennsylvania State University Press.
Schueler, G. F. (1995) *Desire: Its Role in Practical Reason and the Explanation of Action*. Cambridge: The MIT Press.
Searle, J. (1990) "Collective Intentions and Actions," in P. Cohen, J. Morgan, and M. Pollack (eds), *Intentions in Communication*. Cambridge: MIT Press, pp. 401–15.
Sellars, W. (1974) *Essays in Philosophy and Its History*. Dordrecht: Reidl.
Sei Shōnagon (1982) *The Pillow Book of Sei Shōnagon*, I. Morris (trans.). Harmondsworth: Penguin Books.
Seidman, J. (2009) "Valuing and Caring," *Theoria* 75: 272–303.
Shapiro, L. (2016) "Revisiting the Early Modern Philosophical Canon," *Journal of the American Philosophical Association* 2: 365–83.
Sherman, N. (1999) "Taking Responsibility for Our Emotions," *Social Philosophy and Policy* 16(2): 294–323.
Sherman, N. (2005) "Of Manners and Morals," *British Journal of Educational Studies* 53(3): 272–89.
Shernoff, D. J. and M. Csikszentmihalyi (2009) "Flow in Schools: Cultivating Engaged Learners and Optimal Learning Environments," in R. Gilman, E. S. Huebner, and M. Furlong (eds), *Handbook of Positive Psychology in Schools*. New York: Routledge, pp. 131–45.
Shoemaker, D. (2003) "Caring, Identification, and Agency," *Ethics* 114: 88–118.
Shotwell, A. (2016) *Against Purity: Living Ethically in Compromised Times*. Minneapolis: University of Minnesota Press.
Simons, M. (1988) "Montessori, Superman, and Catwoman," *Educational Theory* 38: 341–9.
Singer, P. (1971) "Famine, Affluence, and Morality," *Philosophy and Public Affairs* 1(3): 229–43.
Singer, P. (2015) *The Most Good You Can Do: How Effective Altruism Is Changing Ideas about Living Ethically*. New Haven: Yale University Press.
Smith, A. ([1759] 1982) *The Theory of Moral Sentiments*. Indianapolis: Liberty Fund.
Smith, Angela M. (2005) "Responsibility for Attitudes: Activity and Passivity in Mental Life," *Ethics* 115(2): 236–71.
Standing, E. M. (1984) *Maria Montessori: Her Life and Work*. New York: Penguin (Plume).
Strawson, P. F. (1962) "Freedom and Resentment," *Proceedings of the British Academy* 48: 1–25.
Sumner, L. W. (1987) *The Moral Foundation of Rights*. Oxford: Oxford University Press.
Sunstein, C. and R. Thaler (2003) "Libertarian Paternalism Is Not an Oxymoron," *The University of Chicago Law Review* 70(4): 1159–202.
Swanton, C. (2011) "Nietzsche and the Virtues of Mature Egoism," in S. May (ed.), *Nietzsche's on the Genealogy of Morality: A Critical Guide*. Cambridge: Cambridge University Press, pp. 285–308.
Talbert, M. (2019) "Moral Responsibility," in E. Zalta (ed.), *The Stanford Encyclopedia of Philosophy*, Winter 2019 edn. https://plato.stanford.edu/archives/win2019/entries/moral-responsibility/.

Tappolet, C. (2011) "Values and Emotions: Neo-Sentimentalism's Prospects," in C. Bagnoli (ed.), *Morality and the Emotions*. Oxford: Oxford University Press, pp. 117–34.

Taylor, C. (1992) *The Ethics of Authenticity*. Cambridge, MA: Harvard University Press.

Thaler, R. and C. Sunstein (2003) "Libertarian Paternalism," *The American Economic Review* 93: 175–9.

Thaler, R. and C. Sunstein (2008) *Nudge: Improving Decisions about Health, Wealth, and Happiness*. New Haven, CT: Yale University Press.

Thelen, E. (2000) "Grounded in the World: Developmental Origins of the Embodied Mind," *Infancy* 1(1): 3–28.

Thompson, E. (2007) *Mind in Life*. Cambridge, MA: Harvard University Press.

Thompson, M. (2008) *Life and Action: Elementary Structures of Practice and Practical Thought*. Cambridge, MA: Harvard University Press.

Trabalzini, P. (2003) *Maria Montessori. Da «Il metodo» a «La scoperta del bambino»*. Rome: Aracne.

Trabalzini, P. (2011) "Maria Montessori through the Seasons of the Method," *The NAMTA Journal* 36: 1–218.

Tsai, G. (2014) "Rational Persuasion as Paternalism," *Philosophy and Public Affairs* 42(1): 78–112.

Tuomela, R. (2005) "We-Intentions Revisited," *Philosophical Studies* 125: 327–69.

Tuomela, R. (2007) *The Philosophy of Sociality: The Shared Point of View*. New York: Oxford University Press.

Tuomela, R. (2017) "Non-Reductive Views of Shared Intention," in M. Jankovic and K. Ludwig (eds), *The Routledge Handbook of Collective Intentionality*. London: Routledge, pp. 25–33.

Tybur, J., D. Lieberman, R. Kurzban, and P. DeScioli (2013) "Disgust: Evolved Function and Structure," *Psychological Review* 120: 65–84.

Valentini, L. (2012) "Ideal vs. Non-Ideal Theory: A Conceptual Map," *Philosophy Compass* 7(9): 654–64.

Vargas, M. (2013) *Building Better Beings: A Theory of Moral Responsibility*. New York: Oxford University Press.

Varela, F., E. Thompson, and E. Rosch (1991) *The Embodied Mind*. Boston: MIT Press.

Velleman, D. (1997) "How to Share an Intention," *Philosophy and Phenomenological Research* 57(1): 29–50.

Velleman, D. (2000) *The Possibility of Practical Reason*. Oxford: Oxford University Press.

Velleman, D. (2001) "Identification and Identity," in S. Buss and L. Overton (eds), *The Contours of Agency: Essays on Themes from Harry Frankfurt*. Cambridge, MA: MIT Press, pp. 91–123.

Velleman, D. (2006) *Self to Self: Selected Essays*. Cambridge: Cambridge University Press.

Wallace, R. J. (1996) *Responsibility and the Moral Sentiments*. Cambridge, MA: Harvard University Press.

Wallace, R. J. (2006) *Normativity and the Will*. Oxford: Oxford University Press.

Wallace, R. J. (2019) *The Moral Nexus*, Princeton: Princeton University Press.

Warnick, B. (2015) "As Long as You Live under My Roof...," *Phi Delta Kappan* 96: 36–40.

Watson, G. (1988) "Responsibility and the Limits of Evil: Variations on a Strawsonian Theme," in F. Schoeman (ed.), *Responsibility, Character, and the Emotions*. Cambridge: Cambridge University Press, pp. 256–86.

Watts, A. (2018) "A Person Who Thinks All the Time Has Nothing to Think about Except Thoughts," available at https://alanwilsonwatts.tumblr.com/post/170688230711/, accessed July 7, 2021.

Williams, B. (1981) "Persons, Character, and Morality," in *Moral Luck*. Cambridge: Cambridge University Press, pp. 1–19.
Williams, B. (1985) *Ethics and the Limits of Philosophy*. New York: Fontana Press (reprinted 2006 by Routledge).
Wood, A. (1999) *Kant's Ethical Thought*. Cambridge, UK: Cambridge University Press.
Wood, A. (2014) *The Free Development of Each: Studies of Freedom, Right, and Ethics in Classical German Philosophy*. Oxford: Oxford University Press.
Woolf, V. (1929) *A Room of One's Own*. London: Hogarth Press.
Wordsworth, W. (1802) "My Heart Leaps Up," in *Poems, in Two Volumes*. London: Longman, Hurst, Rees, and Orms, p. 44.
Zagzebski, L. (2003) "Emotion and Moral Judgment," *Philosophy and Phenomenological Research* 66(1): 104–24.
Zagzebski, L. (2012) *Epistemic Authority: A Theory of Trust, Authority, and Autonomy in Belief*, Oxford: Oxford University Press.

Index of Names

Ahmed, S. 178
Alfieri, V. 40-1
Anscombe, E. 3, 8
Aquinas, T. 60
Arendt, H. 5
Aristotle 5, 9, 27, 60-1, 120
Arpaly, N. 9-10, 35, 39, 47, 135

Barnes, E. 183, 197
Barzelloti, G. 4
Beethoven, L. 96, *See* also Biss
Bergoffen and Weiss 197
Bergson, H. 5
Bettmann, J. 76, 188
Biss, J. 117, 134
Bourdieu, P. 183, 192, 196
Bratman, M. 37-8, 138, 225, 229
    planning theory of agency 52-7
    shared agency 101-3, 124, 140
Buss, S. 84, 184-5, 189-90
Butler, Joseph 134
Butler, Judith 184, 196, 198
Byrd, R. E. 61-3, 79, 117, 119, 184, 207

Cavendish, M. 5
Cicero 190
Clark, A. 180, 237
Conant, J. 61, 63
Confucius 71
Conly, S. 147, 234
Credaro, L. 4-5, 225
Csiksentmihalyi, M. 38-9, 41, 50, 118, 125-6, 131, 133, 222, 230

Dante 211
Darwall, S. 83-4, 190, 210
Darwin, C. 27
Descartes, R. 5
Dweck, C. 75
Dworkin, G. 146, 156, 158-60, 162, 166-7, 171
    Odysseus example 158-60, 167

Foot, P. 15, 27-8, 192-3
Foucault, M. 196
Francis of Assisi 211
Frankfurt, H. 9, 38, 40-7, 51-2, 54-5, 66, 126, 128, 137, 206
Freud, S. 5, 9
Frierson, P., *Intellectual Agency and Virtue Epistemology* 7, 16, 18, 182-3, 197, 206, 219

Galileo 118
Galison, P. 141
Gewirth, A. 74
Gibson, J. 182, 187-8
Gilbert, M. 100-2, 194, 238
Green, T. H. 60

Hanna, J. 147, 149, 158
Haugeland, J. 180
Hausman and Welch 163
Hegel, G. W. F. 5, 10, 11, 80
Heidegger, M. 5
Hellbrügge, T. 197
Helm, B. 96
Herbart, J. F. 5, 59
Herman, B. 38, 187
Hershey, J. 193
Hitler, A. 111-12
Hobbes, T. 71, 142
Honnold, A. 117
hooks, b. 232
Hume, D. 15, 17, 56
Huseyinzadegan, D. 178
Hutcheson, F. 15, 17, 21, 25-6

James, W. 5, 135
Jaworska, A. 40, 206, 223, 225, 227, 235
Jung, C. 9

Kahneman, D. 149
Kant, I. 4-5, 8, 15, 20, 50, 118
    Evil in human nature 226

Good will 59, 84, 192, 227
  on Love 179
  Respect 79–84, 151–2, 154, 237
  see also Paternalism, Kant and
Kauppinen, A. 21, 25–6
Korsgaard, C. 15, 74, 126–8
  Constitutive standards 9, 35, 58, 136–8, 231
  Duties to animals 152–3, 233
  Provisional life-long application of plans 55–6, 117–18
  Reflection central to agency 37, 48, 128, 134, 231
Krogh, S. 70

Labriola, A. 5
Lakoff and Johnson 180–1, 197
Lewis, D. 100
List and Pettit 100–1, 141–2
Locke, J. 53, 142
Ludwig, K. 95–6, 99

MacIntyre, A. 50, 59
Maradona, D. 183
Marx, K. 5, 60
Mayo Clinic 131
McKenna, M. 66
Mill, J. S. 15, 118
  On Liberty 148–51, 155–6, 158, 166, 184–5, 232
Murdoch, I. 209
Mussolini, B. 111–12

Nagel, T. 45
Nietzsche, F. 5, 9, 11, 74, 79, 111, 213, 226
  Concept of life 27, 205
  Egotism 71–2
  Individuality 60–61, 63–4, 226
  Moral relativism 24
  Self-overcoming 59–60, 71
  Übermensch 71, 74
Noë, A. 180
Nussbaum, M. 8, 66, 83, 169, 178

Ohno, K. 183
Onorado 2–3, 7, 45, 193, 204, 212–13

Papin, D. 117
Paxton, S. 195–6

Pettit, P. 141
Plato 71

Rawls, J. 15, 142
  Reflective equilibrium 29–30
Reichold, A. 180–1
Roberts and Wood 109
Rogers, F. 132–3
Rousseau, J.-J. 15, 169
Rutherford, D. 61, 63–4
Ryan and Deci 121

Sackett, G. 189
Saito, Y. 190
Sartre, J.-P. 128
Sayre-McCord and Smith 56, 225
Scanlon, T. 15, 45, 74
Schapiro, T. 171–3
  Children and moral responsibility 64–5
  Feeling Like It (Schapiro 2021) 45, 47, 126–8, 131–4, 221
  Obstinate daughter example 145–6, 156–60, 164, 168, 235
  Paternalism towards children 36–9, 77, 145–52, 157–60, 166, 171–3
  Plan of life necessary for agency 52–6, 119, 130, 139, 169
  Reflection necessary for agency 9, 37–41, 44–9, 139
Schiller, F. 80
Schopenhauer, A. 4–5
Schott, R. M. 178
Schueler, J. F. 45
Searle, J. 103
Séguin, E. 5
Sei Shōnagon, *The Pillow Book* 190
Seidman, J. 206
Sergi, G. 202
Sherman, N. 46, 178–9, 189–90
Shoemaker, D. 41
Shotwell, A. 198
Singer, P. 15, 184, 186
Smith, Adam 17, 21
Smith, Angela 135, 179
Socrates 71
Sofia 1–2, 7, 35–8, 47–9, 67, 101–2, 117–20, 125–9, 138–9, 197
  Active 44–5
  Love 204, 206, 212, 216

Persistent in work 54–6
  Wholehearted 43, 54
Spencer, H. 4
Stoppani, A. 203, 211, 238
Strawson, P. F. 65–6
Sunstein and Thaler 147, 161–3

Talbert, M. 65–6
Taylor, S. 63
Thelen, E. 180
Thompson, M. 27–8
Thrasymachus 71
Trollope, A. 52
Tsai, G. 137
Tuomela, R. 100–1

Vargas, M. 67
Velleman, D. J. 9, 40, 100, 209

Wallace, R. J. 11, 15, 37, 48, 65–6, 224
Warnick, B. 157
Washburne, C. 103
Watson, G. 66
Williams, B. 10–11
  "one thought too many" 192
Wood, A. 151
Woolf, V. 73
Wordsworth, W. "the child is father of the man" 62, 228

Zarathustra 63, 213

Subject Index

Abstraction 115–24, 228
 and Agency 83, 115–21
 and Character 117–21
 Construction of institutions 106, 123–4, 142
 and deliberation 125, 128
 and Identity 120, 128
 and love 123, 211–13
 Materialized 116, 237
 and perfection 119–20
 and persistence 119
 and respect 122–3
 and solidarity 123–4
 Universality 117–18
Activity vs. passivity 44–8
Affordances 182
 Moral 187–8
Agency, *See also* Character
 and character 57–8
 Definition of 8
 Embodiment of 175–8, 180–4
 Group 99–105
 Intellectual 8, 182
 and responsibility 64–8
 Requirements of 35–57
 Types of 7–10
 and Work 38–40 (*see also* Work)
Argentinian ambassador 96–7, 103
Attention 2, 36, 49
Authenticity, ethics of 63–4

Blowing one's nose 175–6, 188

Catholicism, *See* Religion
Character 34–6, 57–64, 97–100, 117–22, 206–8
 Definition of 34–5, 68, 117
 Develops through exercise 154
 Embodied 180–4
 of a Group 99–100, 211
 Respect for 69–76, 81–3, 122

Choice architecture 147, 161–2, 235
Conquest of Independence, *See* Independence (conquest of)
Control of error, *See* Error, control of
Cosmic task 60, 207
Cultural relativism 21–6
Cylinder blocks, *See* Montessori materials

Dance 131, 183
 Butoh 183
 Contact Improvisation 195–6
Deliberation
 Enhances agency 127–31
 Group 141
 Infinite regress problem 52, 136, 138, 179, 231
 Inhibits engagement 133–4, 229
 Limits and insufficiency of 131–6
 and paternalism 152–3
 Requires non-deliberative agency 134–6, 138
 and respect 139–40, 168–9
 and second-order desires 41, 126, 137
 Unnecessary for agency 10, 46–7, 50–2, 101, 121, 225
 as work 136–9
Desire
 Identification with 41–8, 51, 129, 137
 Second-order 41–2, 53, 126–9, 137
Disability 196–9
Discipline
 Negative 29
 positive 161, 164–5
 self-discipline 2, 20, 74, 98

Effortful work, *See* Work
Emotion 33, *See also* Love
 and agency 46–7, 179–80
 and character
 and ethical life 178–80
 Muscular 180

Mutual sympathy 95, 179
Responsibility for 46–7
of solidarity 103, 124
Environment
Love of 208–9, 216
Prepared 29, 90, 162–5, 170–1, 201, 237
Social 6, 18–20, 74, 164–5
Error
Control of 50, 76, 116, 118
Love of 50, 67–8
of moral sense 21
Necessary for development 154
Ethical life, definition of 10–12
Exemplars of ethical life, *See* Byrd, R. E.; Onorodo; Sofia
Extended cognition 237

Flow 38–9, 41, 50, 83, 150, 222
Interruption of 161, 168–9
Necessary for well-being 131–2
Non-deliberative 125–6, 133–4, 137, 230
of thought 118
"Follow the child" 6
Framing effects 149, 162, 165

Generosity, *See* Love
Government 112, 147
Grace and courtesy 76, 176–7, 184–5, 188–91, 193, 219
Group character, *See* Character (of a group)
Guiding instincts 27, 39, 43, 47–8, 71, 126–30,
and paternalism 147

Habitus 183, 237
Help
embodied 186–8
"help me do it by myself" 68, 89, 225
as form of respect 87–90
vs. service 88
and solidarity 94

Imposition 85–7, 156
Independence, conquest of 34, 59, 219, 225, 237
Indirect Preparation 89, 164, 199
Individuality 62–4, 182–3
Instinct, *See* Guiding instincts

Intelligent do-ing 45
Internality 37–44, 87, 206, 223
abstraction and 120
obedience and 108
reflective deliberation and 128, 137, 228–9
Interruption
contrary to respect 38, 73, 85–7, 161, 185, 190
and deliberation 47–8, 139
as paternalism 161, 185

Justice 71, 77, 117, 157
in adults vs. children 67, 123–4
sentiment of 17, 152, 179, 208

Life 11, 26–8, 31 205
Live options 135
Love 201–17
Abstract 212–13
as a child's need 217
Generosity 213

Mania of doubt 52, 136, 231
Moment of drama 47, 128, 132–3, 229
Montessori materials
Color tablets 22
Cylinder blocks 1–2, 48–50, 67, 118, 125, 231
Geometrical cards 95
Materialized abstractions (*see* Abstraction (materialized))
Puzzles 59, 87, 89, 167–8
Scarcity of 70, 73
Smelling bottles 22
Walking the line 76
Moral epistemology, *See* Moral sense
Moral sense 15–31, 51, 219–21
Calibration challenge for 21, 25–6
Love and 204–5
Respect and 70, 73–4, 86, 88
Motivation, intrinsic 121
Music
Piano 59, 130, 177, 183
violin 45, 56, 194

Normalization 4, 34, 74, 196, 220
Normative self-governance 48–50, 55, 59, 109, 129

Obedience 107–13
Obstinate daughter, *See* Schapiro, T. (obstinate daughter example)

Paternalism
  Arguments against 147–55
  Definition 146–7
  as false love 214–15
  in Kant 151–2, 155–6, 172
  Legitimate criteria for 167–8
  Libertarian 147, 161–4
  in *On Liberty* 148–50, 155–6
  Soft vs. hard 147–8
Patience 53, 76
  Embodied 177
  see also Persistence
Patriotism 94, 105, 123, 140, 210, 212
Perfection 58–64, 67–8, 71–2, 74–5
  Abstract idea of 119–20
  Appraisal respect for 84
  of groups 96–9
  of movement 177–8, 182–3, 199
  Open-ended 60–4, 182–3, 207, 225–6
Persistence, *See also* Patience
  Abstraction and 119–21
  Deliberation and 130, 136, 138
  Intensive vs. extensive stability 56–7, 225
  Necessary for agency 52–7, 87, 102, 222
Politeness, *See* Grace and Courtesy
Possessiveness 75, 208
Prepared Environment, *See* Environment (prepared)

Reason 25, 37–8, 50–1, 116, 172, 228–9
Reflection, *See* Deliberation; Reason
Relativism, moral 21–6
Religion
  Commitment 129–30, 140
  Ritual 140
Respect 69–92
  Appraisal vs. recognition 83–5
  and deliberation 139–40
  Embodiment of 184–94
  for mere choices 81–3, 139–40, 159–61
Responsibility, moral 64–8
Rules of moral salience 187

Self-overcoming, *See* Nietzsche
Silence Game 141–2
  and collective agency 97–99, 102, 105–6
  and obedience 107, 109
Smoking 41–3
  and deliberation 135, 137
  Paternalistic laws against 147
Solidarity 93–113
  and character 97–100
  Embodied 194–6
  Growing from respect 94–7
  Joint commitment 100–2
  Metaphysics of group agency 100–5
  Shared plans 140–1
  Social organization 106–7, 123–4, 141–2
Sports
  Marathon running 230
  Rock-climbing 56, 117
  Soccer 226
  Tennis 45, 52, 56, 96, 132, 193
  the yips 131
Stability, intensive and extensive, *See* Persistence
Sympathy 17, 70, 94–5, 103, 204–5, 210

Übermensch, *See* Nietzsche, F.
Unconscious interests 58, 150, 202, 225, 233
  solidarity 142
Utilitarianism 8, 148, 226

Wholeheartedness 41–3, 54
  vs. dutifulness 80, 206
Will
  Weakness 137, 158–60, 169
  vs. wish 44, 181
Women
  gender roles in dance 196
  degraded by being served 88
  paternalism towards 145–6, 158, 169
  rights of 214, 232
Work 10, 11, 49, 58–9
  Deliberation as 136–9
  Proper focus of respect 81, 87, 227
  Proper locus of self-expression 64, 67
Worker's rights 90, 232

www.ingramcontent.com/pod-product-compliance
Lightning Source LLC
Chambersburg PA
CBHW062127300426
44115CB00012BA/1839